P9-ASK-068

WRITING ALONE AND WITH OTHERS

Writing Alone and with Others

Pat Schneider

Foreword by Peter Elbow

OXFORD
UNIVERSITY PRESS

2003

OXFORD

UNIVERSITY PRESS

Oxford   New York
Auckland   Bangkok   Buenos Aires   Cape Town   Chennai
Dar es Salaam   Delhi   Hong Kong   Istanbul   Karachi   Kolkata
Kuala Lumpur   Madrid   Melbourne   Mexico City   Mumbai   Nairobi
São Paulo   Shanghai   Taipei   Tokyo   Toronto

Published by Oxford University Press, Inc.
198 Madison Avenue, New York, New York 10016

www.oup.com

Oxford is a registered trademark of Oxford University Press

Library of Congress Cataloging-in-Publication Data

Schneider, Pat, 1934–
Writing alone and with others / Pat Schneider ; foreword by Peter Elbow.
p.   cm.
Includes bibliographical references and index.
ISBN 0-19-516572-1 (cloth)   ISBN 0-19-516573-X (pbk.)
1. English language—Rhetoric.
2. English language—Rhetoric—Study and teaching.
3. Creative writing—Study and teaching.
4. Creative writing.
5. Authorship.
I. Title.
PE1408 .S3154   2003
808' .042—dc21
2002192491

9 8 7 6 5 4 3 2 1
Printed in the United States of America
on acid-free paper

For Peter

My continuing passion is to part a curtain,
that invisible shadow that falls between people,
the veil of indifference to each other's presence,
each other's wonder, each other's human plight.

Eudora Welty

Contents

Foreword by Peter Elbow   ix
Acknowledgments   xv
How to Use This Book   xvii
Introduction: A Writer Is Someone Who Writes   xix

Part I: The Writer Alone

1   Feeling and Facing Fear   3
2   Getting Started (Again)   24
3   Toward a Disciplined Writing Life   40
4   Writing Practice: The Journal   63
5   Writing Practice: Developing Craft   76
6   Voice   93
7   Growing as a Writer   106
8   The Form Your Writing Takes   116
9   The Ethical Questions: Spirituality, Privacy, and
     Politics   157

Part II: Writing with Others

Introduction: Writing with Others   177

10   Basic Principles of a Healthy Workshop   185
11   Writing in a Classroom   196
12   Creating Your Own Workshop or Writing Group   215
13   Using Writing to Empower the Silenced   259

Part III: Additional Exercises

Additional Exercises   295

Afterword   361
List of Exercises   363
Recommended Resources and Reading List   367
Credits   375
Index   379

Foreword

I feel privileged to write this foreword for Pat Schneider's book. She seems to me the wisest teacher of writing I know. For writers and would-be writers, she provides a lovely mixture of concrete advice and subtle insights about attitude and feeling. It's as though a tennis coach could tell you not only exactly how to stand and move your body—but also how to feel and think and imagine yourself so that the practical advice bears fruit.

Schneider has a strong presence on the page. I feel confident that she will win your trust—as she does mine—and make you willing to take the kinds of risks that are needed for real progress in writing. Her approach is all about trust—trust in the inherent talent in people and trust in the power of writing as a process. Her book is about three realms that inevitably intertwine for anyone who cares about writing: the nature of writing, of art, and of personal experience.

I can give a sense of the roots of this important book by quoting the "Five Essential Affirmations" that guide her approach to writing and the "Five Essential Practices" that guide her in leading workshops for writers:

The Five Essential Affirmations

1. Everyone has a strong, unique voice.

2. Everyone is born with creative genius.

3. Writing as an art form belongs to all people, regardless of economic class or educational level.

4. The teaching of craft can be done without damage to a writer's original voice or artistic self-esteem.

5. A writer is someone who writes.

The Five Essential Practices

1. A nonhierarchical spirit (how we treat writing) in the workshop is maintained while at the same time an appropriate discipline (how we interact as a group) keeps writers safe.

2. Confidentiality about what is written in the workshop is maintained, and the privacy of the writer is protected. All writing is treated as fiction unless the writer requests that it be treated as autobiography. At all times writers are free to refrain from reading their work aloud.

3. Absolutely no criticism, suggestion, or question is directed toward the writer in response to first-draft, just-written work. A thorough critique is offered only when the writer asks for it and distributes work in manuscript form. Critique is balanced; there is as much affirmation as suggestion for change.

4. The teaching of craft is taken seriously and is conducted through exercises that invite experimentation and growth as well as through response to manuscripts and in private conferences.

5. The leader writes along with the participants and reads that work aloud at least once in each writing session. This practice is absolutely necessary, for only in this way is there equality of risk-taking and mutuality of trust.

If you have trouble believing these principles, you might think that this book is not for you. But I'd disagree and call that a reason for reading. For I think Schneider will convince skeptics—not by arguing for the principles but by showing what those principles look like in the flesh: in specific writing activities, in personal exploration, and in stories of how people can function in workshop groups.

Schneider keeps her focus on the main things: writing, taking the writer seriously as an artist, and insisting on the bottom line—good work. But in harvesting the wisdom of a long career of brave work, she does justice to the complex ways in which working on writing is more than just trying to judge quality. Vexing questions always arise for anyone who wants to work seriously on writing:

- Is writing private or public? So much comes out that seems private, yet the medium seems essentially public. Schneider does justice to the two conflicting dimensions by exploring the essential need that most writers have for privacy in order to do their best work; yet also exploring the equally essential need for audience and work with others.

- What about secrets? What is the role of truth in a medium that invites fabrication and fictionalizing? Is writing a kind of therapy? Art is not about "telling our secrets," she writes, "but it does have to be free to go wherever it needs to go, and usually our pain comes out first." "A writing group is not a therapy group—it is concerned with liberating the artist in the person." "Subjects in themselves are not self-indulgent or sentimental. The issue is how fresh, how true, how concrete and vivid is the writing."

- What about the political dimension of writing? For Schneider, "the issue is not whether our writing will be political. If we are silent, our silence is political. If we write, our writing is political." She insists that "the privilege of voice carries with it a responsibility to speak for social justice"—and her passionate commitment to writing has led her to direct writing workshops far and wide: with women from low-income communities in a nearby city, with a community of nuns in Ireland, and in a school of theology in Berkeley.

This book is particularly eloquent and helpful about the common—I want to say universal—experience of difficulty or struggle with writing. I particularly admire Schneider's remarkable wisdom here because it was my own writing difficulties that got me interested in writing in the first place. Schneider has valuable insights about the fears that come up for most people not only about writing itself but also about the struggle to find the discipline for a writing life.

But when I praise her book this way, I worry that some readers might say, "But I'm not scared of writing. I write regularly with no difficulty. This book has nothing for me." I would give this book to just such a person—and not just because of Schneider's shrewd practical suggestions for improving the writing, even of confident writers. What's more important is that when she talks about fear and struggle, she focuses on what I'd call the main theme or force of the book: going deep. The book is above all about learning to take the risk of going to the most powerful insights, memories, perceptions, and feelings that one has (or rather, that one mostly doesn't yet quite have)—as a source of one's most powerful words. When people say, "Oh, I'm not scared of writing at all and I write regularly with no difficulty," I cannot help suspecting that they might be missing the deeper risks (and the deeper satisfactions) that are central to writing that really matters.

I'm particularly impressed at how much better a job Schneider does than I've ever managed at describing concretely to people how to work together in a workshop where everyone writes, shares writing with each other, and—when appropriate—gives responses to each other. She is brilliant at the difficult job of conveying all this on paper; and I know, from some participation in her workshop in her living room in Amherst, that these insights come from brilliant practice.

In her section about writing groups, she's made an interesting rhetorical decision: She presents the material in the form of advice to someone who wants to set up a writing group or lead a writer's workshop. By addressing leaders or potential leaders, she makes palpable a crucial theme: Groups for sharing and responding require wisdom and firm leadership. Many people have found to their sorrow that it's no good saying, "Let's get together and share our writing—and we'll just see what happens." There are crucial guidelines and rules of thumb that at least one person needs to take responsibility for. Otherwise people are likely to take advantage of each other, give feedback that's not helpful, and abuse each other's privacy. I found myself moved as I read her advice—especially because she gives it through mini-stories of workshops and people she's worked with. Her theme here again is anti-elitist: She insists that any dedicated person can lead a writers' group—as long as they are vigilant about enforcing these guidelines of respect. (She distinguishes the role of a writing group leader from the role of a workshop leader. A writing group leader is vigilant to keep the group safe for the writing process. A workshop leader does that but also offers trained guidance in writing, editing, and seeking publication.)

Most classroom teachers could do a far better job if they garnered the insights—and above all the respect for writers—that Schneider shows readers how to maintain. And most students in writing classrooms—

whether in high school, first year college writing courses, or MFA programs—would have a much better time with their writing if they read
this book. Perhaps the essential compliment I can pay is this: Pat
Schneider's book makes you want to sit down and start writing.

Peter Elbow

Acknowledgments

The work that I have done alone and in community with thousands of other writers in Amherst Writers & Artists continues down a path that was begun by pioneer Peter Elbow. In 1973 Oxford University Press published his book, *Writing Without Teachers*, in which he challenged the traditional ways of teaching writing that prevailed then and still prevail in many places. The work that he has continued to do, and the work of many other writers and artists in the writing process movement, goes before and alongside this book. As I wrote, I deliberately did not reread Peter's books (except to dip in here or there occasionally), needing to stay centered in my own voice and experience. His books and essays are the foundation for all of us who work in this field. I am profoundly grateful for his support in this endeavor.

Every word of the manuscript was read by my son, Paul Schneider, who gave me the gift of his affirmation as well as his excellent editorial skill. My friend, Paula Adams, grammarian extraordinaire, also read the entire manuscript. My daughters, Rebecca, Laurel, and Bethany, read and discussed portions throughout the years of writing. Elda Rotor, my editor at Oxford University Press, gave generously of her clear vision and patience. Catherine Humphries, Jackie Doyle, Anne Holmes, and Merrie Ritter were expert (and kind) in cleaning up all my "jots" and "tittles." My agent, Kim Witherspoon, and her assistant, Alexis Hurley, guided the progress of this book beautifully. I had excellent assistance; any error or weakness is mine alone.

* * *

Thank you, Margaret Robison, for our early days of leading workshop together, for dreaming with me a better way to lead a group of writers, and most of all for bringing me into belief in my own poems.

Thank you all of my great writing teachers: Dorothy Dunn, seventh grade; Anne Warner, high school; Thomas A. Perry, college; Wayne Rood and Andrew Fetler, graduate school—and lifetime mentor, friend, and teacher, Elizabeth Berryhill.

Thank you Sue Walker, for accepting that first long poem about one of my daughters for publication in *Negative Capability*, and then for understanding when my daughter said something like "Publish that poem? No way!!" Thank you Sandra Martz, genius publisher, generous friend, and artist/writer, for believing in this book and helping it become a reality. Thank you, Kate Hymes, poet and visionary, for loving me across the color line. Thanks Joan Mallonee, Máire O'Donohoe, Sharleen Kapp, Evelyn May, Barbara Werden, and Nancy Rose for laughter and long conversations that untangle my brain. Thank you Daphne Slocombe for being my assistant, my colleague, and my friend—not the least of your gifts was the quote from Eudora Welty that became the epigraph for this book! Thank you Peter and Jeannine Lawall—Peter, for saving this document when computer bugs "ate" it, and Jeannine for designing and maintaining www.amherstwriters.com. Thank you Robin Therrien, Enid Santiago Welch, Teresa Pfeifer, Diane Mercier, Karen Buchinsky, Lyn Goodspeed, Julie Benard, Corinna Spenard, Anthia Elliot, Diane Garey, Larry Hott, Elise Turner, Valerie Leff, Carol Booth, Pat Brown, Patricia Lee Lewis, Kathryn Dunn, Sharon Bray, Alison Hicks, Joan Marie Wood, Hilary Plattner, Anna Kirwan, Carolyn Benson, Linda Meccouri, Don Fisher, and Carolyn Pelletier for good companionship in doing the work.

Thank you every one of the thousands of writers—you know who you are, and I hope you know that I have loved you and still do love you—who have sat with me, pens on paper, daring to write and to read aloud the secrets of the heart and the imagination. Thank you Anne Dellenbaugh for days on the river that remain in my mind, and for spiritual guidance in the inner and outer wilderness.

Thank you Samuel. Thank you ancestors. Thank you Nellie—your little fur face has kept me in my place, every word of the way.

Most of all, thank you Peter, Becca, Sarah, Laurel, Cindy, Paul, Nina, Nathaniel, Bethany, and Katie. You know why.

How to Use This Book

If I were this book's reader, I would write in the margins, underline what I like, and argue with the author where I disagree. I'd mark favorite exercises with a star, so I could find them again. Maybe I would jot down the date that I tried the exercise. (After all, a hundred years from now the reader's notes may be more important than the writer's text!)

If you are a writer working alone (and every member of a workshop or a class is also a writer who writes alone), I suggest that you first read Part I, "The Writer Alone," following the exercise suggestions if they interest you, and then go to Part III, "Additional Exercises." The other parts of the book, I believe, will interest and, I hope, entertain you. They will contain helpful material for your own writing, but Parts I and III will be your primary resources.

If you are a workshop or group leader, a teacher, or someone who would like to gather other writers to write together, read Part I for the benefit of your own writing and to acquaint yourself with this method. Then read Part II, "Writing with Others." It will give you stories of writers working together, and step-by-step guidance for creating a safe and stimulating writing community. Part III will give you resources for leading varied exercises.

If you are a person who wants to use writing to empower people whose voices have been silenced by poverty, illness, incarceration, or other hardship, I hope you will read the entire book. First tend to the writer in yourself by writing in response to the exercises that beckon to you in Part I, then read Part II about the workshop method as it is used with writers who have a standard formal education and (usually) can pay a fee for the group experience. Chapter 13, "Using Writing to Empower the Silenced," will give you heart, give you examples, and give you step-by-step guidance in creating a different sort of writing community—one that is specifically designed to work for healing the broken world. And Part III will give you additional exercises.

I hope that I have written a book that is fun to read. To that end, I have included as examples many poems and pieces of prose that I have loved in my workshops. There are thousands more that I would like to have included.

Writing Alone and with Others is the story of 25 years of experience in leading writing workshops and in training others to lead them. Writing is my own continuing passion, and I have learned over the years that writing truly belongs to everyone. I hope this book may open your own voice and assist you in welcoming the voices of others. I intend this book as a love letter from one writer to another. If you would like to write back to me, I welcome your response.

Pat Schneider
P.O. Box 1076
Amherst, MA 01004

Introduction:
A Writer Is Someone Who Writes

Everyone is a writer. You are a writer. All over the world, in every culture, human beings have carved into stone, written on parchment, birch bark, or scraps of paper, and sealed into letters—their *words*. Those who do not write stories and poems on solid surfaces tell them, sing them, and, in so doing, write them *on the air*. Creating with words is our continuing passion. We dream stories; we make up stories, poems, songs, and tell them to ourselves. All alone, we write.

We also write with others. Every time we open our door at the end of a workday and say, "You'll never believe what that [bleep] said to me today . . ." we create story. "I was minding my own business, and he got right into my face! And then he said . . ." Already we are creating character, voice, suspense—*story*. It may not be committed to paper, but the artist, the writer, is at work.

This book is about writing alone, and writing with others. We are all connected to one another and to the mystery at the heart of the universe through our strange and marvelous ability to create words. When we write, we create, and when we offer our creation to one another, we close the wound of loneliness and may participate in healing the broken world. Our words, our truth, our imagining, our dreaming, may be the best gifts we have to give.

I have been a writer all my life. In the fourth grade, at age nine, I wrote my first verse: "My name is Patsy V. / And I'm in the class 4-B." In the moments of joy following that creation I was as much a writer as I was at age 45, sitting in Carnegie Hall, hearing the lyric soprano Phyllis Byrn-Julson sing my words: "Gold is gone from the hills, / The cedar stands gray in the dawn, / The watchman has gone from the wall. / The heart, the holy place, is empty." I was not as skilled at nine, but I was as much a writer.

When I was 13, I lived in a tenement in the inner city of St. Louis, Missouri. Often I leaned out a third-story window at night, looking over the tops of dingy stores and taverns on my street to the shining dome of the St. Louis Cathedral. At school, we had been introduced to T. S. Eliot. He was the "greatest poet." He was a Catholic. I imagined him in the cathedral. I imagined him standing under a street lamp in the circle of light below my window. More than anything, I wanted to grow up to be a poet. I wanted to write like T. S. Eliot.

At that time I was also ironing my mother's starched, white cotton uniform every blessed day, but it did not once occur to me that *ironing* could be the subject of literature. That was long before Tillie Olsen wrote her story "I Stand Here Ironing." In the 1940s, literature was written by upper-class men, expressing their views of the human experience. I wanted desperately to sound like them so I could make art, too.

But that understanding of art was a lie. Art is not just the province of the privileged. Art belongs to the people. It belongs to those who "stand here ironing," to those who clean city streets, to those who work in front of computer screens, as well as to those who read in the ivy halls. Almost all of us can tell a story to a best friend or lover so powerfully that we move the other person to sorrow or to laughter, to deep feeling, to what literary critics call "denouement." You can write as powerfully as you talk to your best friend. You can write as deeply as you think—but only *if you are safe enough*, if you can forget yourself enough. If you can "let go" and tell the truth of what you have experienced or imagined, you can write. If you talk to yourself, even in your mind—if you tell stories to your best friend, you can write. If you can tell what happened when you were a kid, if you can allow one other person to "see" what you describe, "hear" the voices you repeat, "feel" the end of your story—you can write. If you daydream or lie awake at night thinking—you can write.

Many of us talk around the supper table, tell stories, jokes, repeat what happened as we went through our day, and never know we are creating fictions, dialogue, suspense, climax. Not being able to write is a *learned disability*. It is almost always the result of scar tissue, of disbelief in your-self accumulated as a result of unhelpful responses to your writing. Those wounds can be healed, those blocks can be removed. Even if you don't talk easily to others, but spin out stories in your own head—if you talk to yourself—you can write. You are already an artist; all you have to do is take up your pen and begin.

What I believe is not believed by everyone, and it is not practiced by everyone who believes it! It is this: There is no place for hierarchies in the heart, and the making of art is a matter of the heart. Art is the creative expression of the human spirit, and it cannot—it *must not*, for the sake of the human community—be limited to those few who achieve critical acclaim or financial reward.

John Gardner wrote, "Genius is as common as old shoes. Everybody has it." We all agree that William Shakespeare and Emily Dickinson were geniuses. But what is that recognizable genius made of? Safety, self-confidence, focus, and practice. These factors enable one to reach further, go deeper, and take greater risks than is possible for a person trapped in fear and self-protection. This book is about developing those conditions in order to work consistently out of your own genius.

Genius often emerges where there is intimate support for it. Shakespeare worked in the intimate, supportive community of a strong theater that wanted his next play. Dickinson worked within the intimate community of a family that loved her and protected her time and privacy. Neither of them was seen by their contemporaries as being greatly gifted. It seems truly important that there be a community of support around the artist that protects the making of the art. Traditionally, wives provided sanctuary for countless artists. It is a lovely societal change—at least in parts of the world—that husbands also now provide it for their wives.

Where there is no intimate support, there is often the driving force of suffering, creating an intense personal isolation, a kind of solitude, out of which the voice of genius arises. Each of us has genius, but we need support, and we can give it to one another as friends or in honest and supportive workshop settings. Genius is hidden everywhere; it is in every person, waiting to be evoked, enabled, supported, celebrated. It is in you. It is in me. Shakespeare wrote Shakespeare's vision. Dickinson wrote Dickinson's. Who will write yours, if you do not?

Some writers (some artists) are commercially successful. Some artists (some writers) are not. Being commercially successful is a very good thing: We all like to eat! But a commercially successful writer may or may not be working as an artist. That is, sometimes one can make a lot of money repeating oneself, or writing for reasons other than those of making art. Rarely is an artist rewarded with fame and fortune, but commercial success is often a matter of entrepreneurship, luck, and a craft appropriate to the marketplace.

Craft is essential; I will work all my life at my craft. But craft is not the same thing as art. Craft is the knowledge of how to mix blue with yellow on my palette, but art is the courage to dip the brush into the paint and lay it on the canvas in my own way. Craft is knowing when to revise a manuscript and when to leave it alone, but art is the fire in the mind that put the story on the page in the first place. To grow in craft is to increase the breadth of what I can do, but art is the depth, the passion, the desire, the courage to be myself and myself alone, to communicate what I and only I can communicate: that which I have experienced or imagined. In *Becoming a Writer,* Dorothea Brande said:

> It is well to understand as early as possible in one's writing life that there is just one contribution which every one of us can make: we can give into the common pool of experience some comprehension of the world as it looks to each of us. . . . If you can tell a story as it can appear only to you of all the people on earth, you will inevitably have a piece of work which is original.

Art is essential to all of us because every human being is born a creator; that's what the ancient Hebrew poets meant when they said we are created "in the image of God," that is to say, in the image of the Creator. Not to be able to write is a learned disability, taught to us in school and at home, imprinted on us in letters: "F," "D," "C-minus." Those whose language skills are impaired nevertheless have a story, and if it can be told in the unique and idiosyncratic form of the author's own way with words, it can be brilliant. If we valued the voices of those who have been denied a voice, we would have a canon of literature so much more diverse, interesting, and humane than the canon we do have. All people are writers who can, if they so desire, claim their writing as a personal (and perhaps public) art form.

Many famous writers have acknowledged that the line between writing as an artistic act and as an act of personal healing is a thin line indeed. We are well acquainted with the terrors that Virginia Woolf, Anne Sexton, and Robert Lowell endured in their personal lives and in their written masterpieces. Writing as therapy and writing as an artistic act may be the same act. Whether or not writing heals the writer is irrelevant. What matters is the power of the work itself.

I have heard great poems in my workshops. I have heard unforgettable short stories, plays, songs, and sections of novels. I am pleased that a good number of them have been published and received awards and prizes, and national and international attention. But I am also pleased with many that will never be read except by the writer's friends. Those works will never be offered to the public because the writer is too shy; too uncertain of her or his own abilities; too awkward at making contacts; too busy to send off manuscripts; too bruised by academic grading systems and hostile teacher responses to endure "rejections"; or too poor to pay the endless postage, copying costs, and telephone bills that are the start-up costs of writing as an entrepreneurial business. The fact that excellent work is unpublished does not diminish its artistry. The list of writers who, like Emily Dickinson, were undiscovered and unappreciated until long after they died is long. It isn't difficult to imagine all those whose papers were lost forever by relatives who were not as careful or as diligent as Emily's sister, Vinnie.

Some critics claim that all truly great works of literature are already recognized. What a cynical and small-minded view of the human spirit! In other times and other cultures, art was made for the family: quilts, hand-carved pieces, lullabies, ballads. The audience for that art was intimate. In a good writing workshop, some exquisite work is given to and received by an intimate audience. I have heard letters and journal entries that I will never forget read aloud in my workshops. Writing is making art, and the test of its value cannot be given into the hands of either the commercial world or the academy.

For a dozen years, each week I led three workshops in my home and one workshop in a nearby housing project for low-income women. That meant that I listened to the work of 48 writers each week. Some were experienced, published writers, but some were just beginning (or beginning again) to write. Another writer (not in my workshop) said to me, "Pat, I don't know how you can stand to listen to all that garbage." My response was immediate: "I have never heard a word of garbage in any workshop of mine!" Later, I thought about it and asked myself, is that true?

It is true. I do listen to frightened people, reading their own words aloud for the first time since the shame of publicly receiving an "F" on a high school composition. I listen to men who have never before tried to write about feelings. I listen to women coming back to writing after raising small children. I hear some of them trying to sound like Tennyson, Wordsworth, Eliot, or some other half-remembered and usually antiquated literary model, not guessing that the rhythms of the language they heard spoken at the kitchen table by their own mothers and fathers are what hold the power of art for them. I hear fear and hope and longing. I do not hear any garbage. I hear passion. I hear desire. And when they begin speaking in the mother tongue of their own voices, mining the mother lode of their own stories, the material they and they alone know "by heart," I hear *art*.

I cannot teach anyone to be an artist, but then I don't have to because everyone is already an artist. Real teachers everywhere know this. Those of us who teach—really teach—know that we are simply midwives to that which is already within our students. Our task is only this: to prepare a place, to welcome, to receive, and to encourage. Our task is the midwife's task: We help prepare the newborn for presentation. With a newborn text, as with a newborn baby, this may mean some cleaning, some dressing up (that's craft). But the life, the spirit of the newborn, is already there (that's art).

"Teaching" is mostly showing what has been done before, not so that it should be copied, but so that options are known, that derivative work is recognized, and that all that has preceded us is available as foundation or as reference point. Sometimes, if I am careful, I can help an artist recognize her or his own unique voice and come to trust it. But each of us has to claim this alone: *I am an artist. I am a writer.*

This is a book about being an artist/writer. Whether your purpose is artistic expression, communication with friends and family, the healing of the inner life, or achieving public recognition for your art—the foundation is the same: the claiming of yourself as an artist/writer and the strengthening of your writing voice through practice, study, and helpful (as opposed to damaging) communication with others.

Your task, as writer/artist, is to:

1. Give your art/writing time.

2. Sound more and more like yourself.

3. Experiment, play, take risks, be brave.

4. Believe in the freshness, vitality, and importance of your own experience and imagination.

5. Practice in ways that will teach you to recognize your own voice and to increase its range (as a singer learns to sing higher and lower—as a painter increases the number of colors on a palette).

6. Believe in yourself as an artist-in-training, and protect yourself from everyone and everything that undermines that belief.

7. Observe.

8. Remember.

9. Imagine.

10. Find and keep in contact with other writer/artists who can provide you with an intimate community of support, give you honest critical response, strengthen you, and encourage your work.

"A writer is someone who writes," wrote William Stafford. It's true. The genius in her upstairs room writing, "I'm Nobody! Who are you?" is a writer (Emily Dickinson). The compulsive e-mailer who cracks everyone up with her description of her boyfriend is a writer. The grandfather in a frame house in North Dakota who pens a letter on lined paper at his kitchen table is a writer. The child in third grade pushing her pencil to form cursive letters, "T-h-i-s s-u-m-m-e-r i w-e-n-t t-o d-i-s-s-n-y L-a-n-d." is a writer. The graduate student laboring over a manuscript; the professor struggling to find some time for her own writing; the kid with a spray can, spelling out words on a public wall—every one of us is a writer. You are a writer. You are an artist. Accept it, celebrate it, and practice it for the rest of your life.

Part I

The Writer Alone

But if I write what my soul thinks,
it will be visible, and the words
will be its body.

Helen Keller

Feeling and Facing Fear

Writing is talking. It is hunkering down around the cave fire at night and telling about the day. And however it may be disguised, fear is close to the center of the first stories we will want to tell. We will tell about the hunt, the animal at the mouth of the cave, the fear that made the mother's arms strong as she protected the child; the wild boar, how it turned and faced the hunter. And as we try to tell our tales, fear will rise. At times, fear keeps us from writing at all, or keeps us from writing as truly, clearly, and brilliantly as we might. Fear has good reason for being; understanding it can make all the difference.

Fear of the Truth about Ourselves

The first and greatest fear that blocks us as writers is fear of the truth we may discover. The world, dressed in our habitual interpretations, is familiar to us. It may not be exactly safe, but we know how to walk in it. We can get from sunrise to sunset.

But the unconscious part of us knows more than the conscious mind will admit. When we sleep, dreams hint at our secrets, but in code. Writing, like dreaming, sometimes tells us what we are not ready to hear. What if we suddenly saw our lives, our experiences, from a different point of view? What if we glimpsed the face behind the mask, the person behind the face of mother, father? What if we really saw the one we may have forgotten, the one we may have lost, or the one who made us afraid?

Michelle, new to my workshop, is beginning to write about her mother. Her father. Her grandmother. After three weeks she tells me she is having nightmares and is afraid to write because everyone else is so accomplished, so brilliant, and she is such a beginner. She thinks her nightmares come from her fear of the other writers. I know that the sense of another's skill can make us timid, but nightmares rise from the depths.

Perhaps Michelle fears the truth by which she herself is tempted: the truth of her own vision, her own interpretation of family history, of personal identity. If she goes straight toward her own truth, what might be lost? Perhaps love is not love, faith is not faith, trust is not worthy. Perhaps a world will be lost. And what will be there to take its place? What price, truth?

Everyone has to answer that question for him- or herself. I have had both men and women sit in my office and say, "If I go on writing like this I'm going to write myself out of my marriage. I don't know if I can go on." I have seen both men and women write "fiction" only to discover facts from childhood that altered their understanding of themselves. For some the choice has been to stop writing, not to pursue expression that would surely take them beyond the known perimeters of the inner world. I respect those who make that choice. Thomas Aquinas, after finishing his massive *Summa,* is purported to have said, "There are some things that simply cannot be uttered." And spent the rest of his life in silence and prayer.

I have come to understand, through my own writing and through working with other writers, that fear is a friend of the writer. Where there is fear, there is buried treasure. Something important lies hidden—something that matters—like the angel waiting in the stone that Michelangelo began to carve.

In the folklore of magic there is a "spirit familiar." The wild thing that frightens us so when it is hidden, guarded in our unconscious, becomes our spirit familiar when it is named—still full of power, still magical, but power released for us, not power caged and threatening.

There is a fairy tale by Hans Christian Andersen about a soldier who is going through a forest. He meets an old woman who gives him a magic apron and sends him down into a deep shaft. He finds rooms of treasure as he goes deeper and deeper—each treasure greater than the last and each treasure guarded by a terrifying dog, each dog with larger eyes. The first one has eyes as big as saucers; the last one has eyes as big as wagon wheels. He does as the old woman told him: spreads out the apron, picks up each dog and puts it on the apron, and this makes him safe. In the first room he finds copper and fills his pockets. In the second room he finds silver and has to empty his pockets of copper to make room for silver. In the third room he finds gold and has to throw away the silver in order to gather the greater treasure.

This tale is a metaphor for the process of making art. There is danger in going down into the unknown. What we will find there, in the unconscious where creation happens, may call for all our skill, all our intuition. It may change us; it may redefine our lives. But I believe we have no other choice if we are to be artist/writers.

The act of writing is a tremendous adventure into the unknown, always fraught with danger. But the deeper you go and the longer you work at your art, the greater will be your treasure. You have a magic "apron." It is woven of your imagination and your voice. If you trust your imagination to bring your own images up from the depths and trust your own voice to articulate those images, you will go without harm through the room where you gather copper. The silver you find in the second room will be of far greater worth than copper, and the gold you find in the last and deepest room will make you glad to abandon silver.

Abandonment is a necessary task of the writer. As we grow in our art, our art changes, and we must move on. One of the most generous spirits in twentieth-century literature was William Stafford. He said the writer's job is to abandon his or her work, to allow others to make judgment of its worth, and to go on to the next poem, the next story. All of us have habits of thought. Often for writers they include formulas of disbelief in our own gifts. If we cannot let go of the familiar old habits, we will not grow as artists. To grow as a writer, we must open our hearts, grow in our capacity to learn, and deepen our courage. There is an ancient promise: "You will know the truth, and the truth will make you free." Even those truths that are painful will ultimately increase my wisdom, undergird my strength, make possible my art.

I know absolutely, from my own experience, that this is true. As a child, I was placed in an orphanage at age 11. All my life I believed the orphanage experience was basically good; it was my mother's way of protecting me from worse things at home. Although I had two childhood diaries, I never read them. I wrote a book, *Wake Up Laughing*, in which I included a short chapter on my experience living in an orphanage, and still I did not read the diaries. I assumed the orphanage no longer existed until I received a letter from Susan Stepleton, Director of Edgewood Children's Center in St. Louis. Someone had given her my book, and she responded by sending me my sixth-grade report card.

I wrote to her that I had childhood diaries, but they contained only one coded reference to the orphanage. After some months, I asked and received Susan's help in obtaining the records that she had on my brother and me. A good friend and therapist read the yellowed pages aloud to me. Only then did I open the diaries. I found pages and pages on the orphanage, where before I had seen only one. Until that moment, almost half a century later, I could not look at the gold in the deepest room of my childhood. Now I am writing about it.

In the book of Revelation there is a phrase that one of my closest friends, Marjorie Casebier McCoy, wrote to me shortly before she died: *What you see, write it in a book.* We cannot write what we do not see—not if we are artists. We must see. The great dogs that guard our secrets are not our enemies. They will let us go past them when we are ready. It is up to us to prepare our "magic apron."

The purest and deepest reservoir of material for the writer is his or her own childhood. Most beginning writers go instinctively to childhood images. This is not accidental, nor is it self-indulgent. It's a good instinct, an artistic wisdom. Louis Auchincloss said, "Childhood is the writer's only capital." Flannery O'Connor wrote, "Anybody who has survived his childhood has enough information about life to last him the rest of his days."

Childhood images are remembered—and forgotten—for emotional reasons. You may have lost conscious knowledge of the reason that you remember a particular afternoon, but your unconscious mind knows. Childhood images are already polished; the unconscious has already done much of the work of the artist—eliminating what is not important, keeping what is important, transforming it into myth. If you were to try to write out of what has just happened to you, to try to decide what is important about this day you have just lived, it would be very difficult. The unconscious mind, however, holds for us images that have emotional importance. Even the most random memory is retained as a kind of code for emotional information.

For example, when I was a child, I accepted as fact the interpretation of my father given to me by my mother: He was "no good," he never loved me, he abandoned me. "He has another little girl now," she said many times. "He doesn't love you."

I had only three memories of my father, one of which was of myself very small, standing in an outhouse, watching him pee. The memory was seemingly random; it was a single picture, like a snapshot, in my mind.

One night when I was in my mid-forties, a writer friend encouraged me to write about my father. I refused, insisting that I had only three unimportant memories, but my friend persisted. When I resisted, she said, "Well, if you won't write about it, at least talk it to me. What was the outhouse like?"

"I don't remember."

"Pat, you remember more than you think you do. Tell me what you see. What is the wood like? Is it rough or smooth?"

The specific question enabled me to turn from my own resistance and look directly at the memory. To my surprise, I knew exactly the answer to her question. I saw several things at once. The wood was rough, unsanded, everywhere but where one would sit down, around the holes. There it had been sanded smooth. There were two holes, one large, one small. High on one wall, in the corner, there was a nail, and hanging on the nail was a bucket with holes punched in the bottom.

The bucket was very clear in my mind, but made no sense to me. I thought, I'll have to ask my mother about that.

My friend continued to ask questions. "What else do you see?"

"Green flies."

"How do you feel about the flies?"

"Well—they are a very intense green." Again I was surprised. "A beautiful color, actually. I like the green."

"What else?"

"There's a huge smell."

"How do you feel about the smell?"

I laughed, "It's intense, but I don't mind it." I could sense myself as a very little child; I had not yet been taught that the smell of human waste was "nasty."

My friend then asked the central questions: What about your father? What is he doing? How do you feel about your father?

All my life I had believed what my mother had told me: that my father did not love me, that he "has another little girl now," that he was "a terrible man." But in the instant following my friend's question I saw him in the outhouse. I watched him unzip his fly, and saw the yellow arc of urine. He was minding his own business; in no way did I feel threatened or confused. I was interested that he peed differently than I peed. We were companions; I was safe. In that moment, I knew that I had loved my father, and that he had loved me. I knew that I was safe with him and that I was glad he had taken me out of the house, where—suddenly I knew—my mother was crying. They were in trouble with each other; it was just before the divorce.

What I discovered in that memory is that I wanted to be with my father. I felt friendly, cared for, and in good company. At age 45, in a single moment, I received again the father that I had lost at age four.

Many writers have spoken with me privately about the feeling that they cannot remember childhood. But if I ask specific, concrete questions—"Where was the table in the kitchen where you ate as a child? Where was the window in your bedroom?"—pictures come to the mind of the writer who "cannot remember." A picture is an image, and a longtime remembered image is like a riddle. What astonishes me is how often, if we work carefully and patiently, the slightest childhood image will give up its secret. I did ask my mother about the bucket. "When I was a little child and we lived in Nixa, was there a bucket hanging in the outhouse?"

She answered, "Yes, there was—do you remember that?" She explained that we had no running water and took showers by filling the bucket and standing under it as the water ran down through the holes. The bucket is important to the story. It means to me that all of what I remembered is probably true: how I felt about the outhouse, how I felt about the flies, how I felt about the odor, how I felt about my father.

This experience taught me a great lesson about writing: Every little snapshot memory in the mind is a code, a clue, an "open sesame" into important emotional information. Those of us who were adults or teenagers in 1963 when President Kennedy was shot are familiar with the question, Where were you when Kennedy was shot? We know the answer. Why? Because the mind in shock takes a mental photograph of the surroundings. The shock may not be something bad or traumatic. It may be a shock of recognition or of understanding. It may be a high and holy experience, or a moment of crisis. We forget what the picture means, as I forgot the meaning of the trip to the outhouse. But our unconscious mind knows, and if we focus carefully on the images that we consciously remember (there was an outhouse) we will be able to become more specific (the holes, the green flies) and still more specific (the color of the flies, the intensity of the odor), and our minds will give up more information from the unconscious (the bucket), until finally we throw away the copper and the silver, and take up the gold (my father loved me).

It does not matter whether we invent as we go. We do, of course. But that doesn't matter, because imagining is another way to get to the truth. The scene that we imagine is also metaphor, given to us by the unconscious memory bank in our minds. Metaphor, too, will lead us. Vladimir Nabokov said, "Caress the divine details." Miraculously, if we write clearly and truthfully, our readers will also see the concrete images that we see in our minds and will participate by responding with their own emotional experience of the worlds we create.

In the fairy tale, the soldier does not go down into the dark underground without advice and protection. The old woman shows him the opening in the earth, tells him what he will encounter, and gives him her apron. He accepts her help and her magic. In a very real sense, my friend walked before me into the "scary place" of my childhood memory. My own reaction of "I don't know; I don't want to write about it; bug off!" should have been a clue. If you think you don't know, if you think you don't want to write about it—look again. You are probably in the vicinity of "gold." As artists in supportive community with one another, we share our wisdom and our experience and help each other complete the solitary journey to find treasure.

There is a last word to be said about the fairy tale. The old woman sends the soldier down into the deep darkness, promising him treasure, but telling him to bring back to her just one thing: an old tinder box. He succeeds, but instead of giving it to her, he kills the old woman and goes off to have his own adventures with the box and the magical genie inside. This is a complicated ending, but worth pondering.

Taken as a metaphor for relationships between men and women, youth and age, it has to do with arrogance, greed, selfishness, and power. It's a pretty grim story. If, however, we take the story as a metaphor for the journey of the writer/artist, perhaps it is telling us that a time comes when we must take what we have learned, but go on without our parents, our teachers, our mentors, those who first showed us the way. We must go beyond at least some of our companions. And that necessary individuation—that breaking free—is sometimes very hard, sometimes even psychologically violent.

Taken as a metaphor for the inner life, seeing both the soldier and the old woman as parts of one psyche, perhaps it has to do with our tendency, once we have succeeded, to kill off the very part of ourselves that was the source of our art. We despise the dialect we heard at the kitchen table, the folk tales of the family, the peculiar circumstances of our own upbringing.

If every one of us, when we begin to succeed, could continue to honor that in ourselves that is the source of our wisdom and our strength, no matter what it looks like or sounds like, there would not be such fear, such blocks to creativity. And if everyone who succeeded as an artist then turned in humility and grace to help others succeed, there would be more art, and greater art, in the world. Part II of this book is an invitation: Once you have your own magic apron and know where to find your gold, perhaps you can help someone else go past the great dogs that guard their treasure.

Fear of—or for—Someone Else*

There are very few stories of my own that are not also stories from the life of someone else. And my version of our story will always be my fiction, my interpretation. What right have I to impose my interpretation on the experience of someone else? What right have I to make fiction of someone else's life?

If I tell the exact truth as I see it, there are two dangers: First, the other will know what I really think—perhaps more than I want him or her to know—and second, what is true for me will probably be untrue for the other. It may not be just a difference of interpretation, either; what I hold as truth may in fact not be true at all. Most likely, everything I remember has been altered by the artist in me: my imagination.

One fear is of hurting someone else, decreasing or destroying someone else's privacy. Another fear is of loss. I may lose the other's confidence, respect, even love. I may lose the other.

The fear may also be of a lawsuit for libel. Fear of loss of all economic security. Fear of loss of reputation. It may even be fear of loss of life. In my work with low-income women, and in Enid Santiago Welch's workshops with children in the housing projects, we have each had to keep papers for writers who felt they would be in danger of violence at home if family members read their writing.

To try to write with fear operating is to try to swim with your hands tied behind your back. You won't get very far, and you may very well drown in the attempt.

So how do we deal with fear?

Note: There is more about this subject in Chapter 9, "The Ethical Questions," in a section titled "Privacy and Writing."

The first step in becoming free of fear is to accept yourself as a writer. All writers deal with this problem. You are not alone. None of us creates ex nihilo (out of nothing). All writing involves self-revelation. Even if the actual facts of our lives are not revealed, we cannot escape the fact that writing reveals the ways our minds work. All writing is, at least, an autobiography of the imagination.

Second, understand that all our memories are already fictions. When I was in graduate school, I wrote a novel for my thesis project in which I included a character based on my own remarkable mentor. I described her profession, her great personal power, and I used a letter she had written to me as a letter written by the character in the book. Then I sent the manuscript to her before I showed it to my academic committee, expecting her to be honored and pleased. She wrote back that I could use the letter verbatim, but she preferred that I disguise all the facts about her professional identity, and so forth. I was devastated. After some time, she guessed my reaction and called me on the telephone. "Pat," she said after listening to my embarrassment and grief, "you are confusing my wish to be private with a comment on our relationship. It is not a comment on our relationship; it is simply a wish to be private!" I had to think about that for a long time, but I trusted this friend absolutely, and slowly I came to understand. I went back into the writing and changed all the details. I made her into a different kind of artist—a sculptor—and described in detail the sculptor standing before a lump of clay, sculpting it into the figure of an old woman.

As I wrote, I fell in love with the figure that my character was sculpting and took my time describing it. The image came without my knowing why, but what the sculptor did in forming an old woman was an exact metaphor for what my mentor was doing for me: She was showing me how to grow older, literally "modeling" the way.

When the professors on my committee met with me to discuss the novel before my graduation, they agreed that one of the best pieces of writing in the work was the description of the sculptor making a figure of an old woman. By being forced to abandon the limits of fact, I allowed into my writing the unconscious metaphor making that is everyone's deepest genius. Through metaphor and imagination I told a deeper truth about my mentor, and had a much more effective character in my novel. Fiction is just another way to tell the truth.

Third, write it first; fix it later. Tess Gallagher, in her poem "Each Bird Walking," wrote, "Tell me . . . something I can't forget." In her introduction to *The Best American Short Stories 1983,* Anne Tyler describes the way she chose 20 out of 120 stories. She read them all, then laid them out around her apartment and walked around picking up only the ones she remembered, the ones she could not forget.

How do we know what readers won't forget? Most likely, your reader won't forget what you yourself can't forget—what is burned most deeply into your own mind. When we write free from fear, we tend to write what matters most.

As a young writer I talked to author Elizabeth O'Connor about my work. There were things about which I could not write. I would "hurt" my mother. My husband "might not like it." She replied gently, "It sounds to me like there are a lot of absentee landlords of your soul."

This is crucial: If you are to write, you must move out of "rented rooms" in your mind, rooms that you have allowed to belong to someone else. It will (usually) not happen overnight. But you can begin at any time to be free. You must own yourself, have no "absentee landlords."

This does not mean you run roughshod over other people's feelings or other people's privacy. There are ways to protect others and still be free (see chapter 9). Remember that your first draft—which is absolutely essential—is private. You can write anything that comes and "fix it" later. Once you have the free flow of a full first draft on the page, you can do the necessary editing to protect others, to protect yourself. But if you worry about other people as you write a first draft, you will not be able to free your unconscious mind to give up its treasures. It will be bound by the great dogs of your fear, by "ought" and "should" and the internalized voices of those whose lives intersect your own.

For first-draft writing, claim everything as your own. Everything that has entered the pupil of your eye, every sound that has entered the inner chamber of your ear, every texture you have touched, every taste, every smell is yours to rearrange, to recreate. Allow everything your family and friends have given you to be your own; let it flow onto the page. Write in total freedom; let there be no impediment between "the dreaming place" (the unconscious) and the conscious mind. Feel free to use real names if they are what come to mind—real places and details of action, scene, and speech. Make no judgments, no omissions, no corrections. Remember, this is just a first draft. You need the freedom in order to catch the passion and the music and the mystery of the writing. You will fix it later.

However: a word of caution. Don't "fix it" immediately. Dorothea Brande wisely cautions writers to put first drafts away for at least two days before making any decisions about change. She says, and I agree, "Your judgment on it until you have slept is worth exactly nothing. . . . You are simply not ready to read your story objectively when it is newly finished; and there are writers who cannot trust their objectivity toward their own work for at least a month."

When you come back to it, decide: Shall I disguise? Shall I omit? Shall I add fictional complications? Shall I wait to publish this until my mother is dead? Shall I use a pseudonym instead of my own name? I have changed names, places, descriptions, even changed the gender of a character, in order to disguise the source of what I was describing. You can do anything except burn it.

Most of us will manage to do what is right for our own lives and relationships. If we allow ourselves a fully free first draft, we will create powerful writing out of the stuff of memory and, as we revise, protect the innocent (and the guilty).

It is more important to ask: Have I gone all the way? Have I told all of the truth that my inner eye sees? The work of revision should be asking whether or not I have told the truth—what my heart, my deepest self, knows. Have I traced the shadow along the side of the bright things my eye first saw? Have I taken the time to see what is half-hidden in the shadows at the far edge of my vision? Have I allowed my unconscious to give me metaphors, to surprise me? Have I told the truth that may be the opposite of the usual path my mind takes, thinking its habitual thoughts?

You are the landlord of your own soul. Let the words, the memories, the imaginings pour white-hot onto the page. You can decide later what they are, what they might become, and when it is time to show them to someone else.

Scar-Tissue Fears

In some elementary school classrooms today, the teaching of writing has changed. Children learn spelling and grammar in lessons separate from the vulnerable act of creative writing. Young writers in these rooms are not subjected to public ridicule and shame; their mistakes are not publicly discussed; there are no grades or red-pencil corrections applied to handwritten texts. Rather, creative writing is treated as self-revelation and profoundly respected.

But for many people, writing in school was painful. Imagine—or remember—this: You are a child, returning to school on the first day of third grade. Your teacher, Mrs. Fredericks, tells you to take out a piece of paper and write a paragraph about what you did in the summer just past. You see in your mind your grandma, your grandpa. You write that you went to their house. You helped your grandpa paint the back porch. You made chocolate chip cookies with your grandma. As you hand in your writing, you feel happy and proud. Your teacher gives the paper back to you the next day. Five words are circled with red pencil because they are misspelled. There is an arrow pointing to the place where you forgot to indent the first word of the first paragraph. There are two little lines in red under all the letters that should be capitals. On the bottom is a C-minus. This is what you learn:

1. You had a C-minus summer. You thought it was an A-plus summer, but it wasn't. It was only C-minus.

2. You have a C-minus grandma and grandpa—No! they are A-plus, but you have failed to show that they are A-plus. You have failed your grandma and your grandpa.

3. Mrs. Fredericks didn't want to know about your summer after all. What she wanted to know was whether you could spell "grandpa," and whether you remembered to indent and use capitals correctly.

4. Never, never again write about something that matters deeply to you. Protect what is personally important. Just find out what the teacher wants, and write that.

Mrs. Fredericks is a nice person. She does not mean you any harm. She herself was injured when she tried to write. She herself has suffered being silenced by judgment. She does not know that she is passing on the damage that was done to her long before this day. But the next time she asks you to write about a vacation, you will not see your grandma's face. You will see little letters lined up—"G," you will write, and then erase it, place it indented, and make it a better capital. "r," you will write. "a, n, d, m, a." In your mind, instead of seeing Grandma and Grandpa, there will be something like this:

Make the margin straight. Capital G's are so hard to make. T's too. Will she like it? Will she read it out loud? What does she want? Pretty words, careful words. Make the margins straight. F's are impossible. Capitals at the beginnings of sentences. How much bigger than little letters? This looks messy. Margin slanting off to the right-hand side. Not straight. Stupid. Dumb. Can't even make a straight margin. Can't make a good capital F. Can't. I hate writing! Don't write flour. That takes an f.

There is good news and bad news. The bad news is: At an early age the writer goes into hiding. Almost every time the writer in you dared to move, it got smacked down again with a "grade," a "comment," or a "criticism." Even an A-minus is not good enough when you have risked your soul onto paper!

The good news is this: Even though the writer goes into hiding, the writer doesn't die! Every day the hidden writer practiced; every time you came home from a hard day at school or work and said to someone in your family, "You know what happened to me today?" and told the story— the writer in you was practicing using suspense, character, dialogue, metaphor, simile, plot, denouement. All your life, you have been *writing on the air*, and that has built craft and confidence and voice. It is all there, ready and waiting for you.

At the end of this chapter you will find two writing exercises that I have used in workshops. You can use them to get in touch with some of the treasure that is hidden under your writing blocks. They are titled "Healing the Wounds of Bad Experiences" and "Getting Rid of Internal Critics."

Fear of Success

Sometime during my writing workshop at the Graduate Theological Union in Berkeley, Sister Milagros Sanchez spoke about the fear of success. Milagros had written about growing up as a Mexican American, accused by schoolchildren of being different, and ridiculed even by teachers for her accent. Her comments were important, and I asked her to write her thoughts for my book. She titled this piece "If I Succeed."

> If I succeed, my work will be public; I will be public. My work will be viewed by sophisticated, educated people who know what they're talking about, who will expect answers I don't have, and who will pry deeper, as if what I have revealed is not enough. They will demand more, and I'm afraid I won't be able to deliver. They will find out what a big fake I am; I, myself, will find out that

> I am not THAT deep, THAT profound. I will have to be super aware of my presentation before others. I will be forced to promote myself, to parade my achievements. I will have to deal with professional critics. My craftsmanship will be dissected and what is important to me will be dismissed or trivialized. I am not afraid of losing my work; I am afraid of losing my soul. I will have to give up old familiar not o.k. feelings and thoughts. I don't know if I can live with happiness and bliss. I am afraid of the new. If I succeed, I will be successful and I am afraid of what that will mean.

Fear of success is frequently a problem for women who have been raised to be good girls, obedient, keeping to their place. It is a problem for men and women who are struggling to overcome the effects of stereotype and abuse, or get out of poverty, or out of racially or culturally defined limitations, such as those Milagros experienced.

Once I sat at lunch with a writer who had been awarded a Pulitzer prize. He said in an anguished voice, "What in the world can I write to follow a Pulitzer?" The fear of success, perhaps as much as the fear of failure, may block our art. The successful writer, no less than the beginner, needs the consolation and support of a community of writing friends.

The Fear of Fear Itself

After a long time of trying, and of meeting walls of inner silence, there can come about a self-perpetuating pattern. Fear breeds fear, increases, and can become the source as well as the product of itself.

There is a simple solution. Never, never, never say to yourself, I am going to write a poem. Never say, I am going to write a story. Or a play. Or a novel, for godssake.

Without knowing anything at all about what it is going to be, just lift your pen and write a single, specific, concrete image. See it in your mind, and as fast as you can, write it down. Describe it in extreme detail. The more specific and intimate, the better. A crack in a coffee mug. A vein on the back of your hand. The way a lock of hair falls across the forehead of a child as he sits reading. A single hair that grows at an awkward angle from the eyebrow of an old man who is fishing. Get in close, describe a detail, and don't allow yourself to predict where it is going. Write one detail after another. Skip around. Abandon one thing when another appears in your mind.

Richard Hugo in *The Triggering Town* talks about how one image triggers another. Most of his poems, he says, begin with a town. For him, it must be a town of a particular size—not too big, not too small. After the image of the town, he jumps to something else, and when the poem is done he often goes back and removes the town.

What Hugo is talking about is central to the process of creative writing. The disconnections are as important as the connections. One image triggers another and, like a person walking on large rocks across a creek where the water is fast and slippery, we will not get to the fifth rock that allows us to step onto the opposite bank unless we first step on, and then abandon, rocks one, two, three, and four. Remember the fairy tale of the soldier: Copper led him to silver, and silver led him to gold. So with writing. The first image that comes may not be the treasure I am after. I may begin with describing the hairline crack in a coffee mug, and in saying the crack is black with age, I may suddenly be reminded of an ancient crack in a glacier I once looked into in Alaska. I see the blue there, deeper and colder than any blue I have ever seen since. If I do not abandon the mug and go faithfully to the blue ice, I will not get to a blue stone someone gave me when I was young. If I do not abandon the blue ice when the blue stone appears, I will not get to the story of the evening when a young man gave me a blue stone, told me he could not marry me, and told me why. Only when I get to that story will nothing else interrupt me. I will be solidly there in that evening, and nothing else will matter as I write what he said, what I said, and how the stone was as blue and as cold as ice. I will not need to ask whether the form should be story or poem or novel or play. Painter Ben Shahn has written a book titled *The Shape of Content.* In it he says, *"Form* is the shape of content." Those six words are among the most important I have ever learned about making art. If you are true to the content, the form will take care of itself.

Your best, your deepest writing, often will not come to you first. You have to follow a kind of trail, allow images to come and go, sketch as visual artists sketch, until you get to what Tess Gallagher called "something I can't forget"—something that holds you (and will hold your reader), something that will not let you go. But don't be asking yourself about this as you write. Just play, sketch, skip from one thing to another until, without your even noticing it, you are "seeing Grandma"—you forget that you are writing, and the pen keeps on moving. That's where you want to be, in that dreaming place where the unconscious is engaged and writing is without effort. Trust me—trust yourself! That will be your best writing.

William Wordsworth's words sound a little archaic now, but what he says is true: "Poetry is emotion recollected in tranquillity." Making art with our words often begins with emotion remembered. Then another kind of creation takes over as remembered images are changed, imagined in the solitary act of writing.

Once you have begun to trust this way of writing—this magical "open sesame" of beginning with the intimate detail and trusting changes and disconnections—it will become perfectly clear how impossible, how absurd it is to ask a roomful of people, "All right, class, now write a story." Or to say to a friend, "There's a sunset. Write a poem." If the sunset is right there, why should the friend write a sunset? Writing doesn't come like that. It comes up from memory or imagination, and it skips like a flat stone across the water until finally it sinks into the depths where wonderful monsters and beautiful creatures dwell.

Exercise: Beginning at Your Own Beginning

Each of us walks a solitary way. No two people come to consciousness in exactly the same way. What is your earliest memory? Are there colors? Sounds? A sense of touch? My husband's first memory is of his father's hands. Mine is of someone in an apron, cutting a pear into pieces for me to eat. Can you remember when you were first aware of yourself as an individual person? For me, it was one day when I was about five years old, looking for rocks with fossils in them all by myself in a creek bed across a gravel road from my home in southern Missouri. The memory is full of light and shadow, colors of rocks and trees, the shape of crawdads hiding under rocks, and my own amazed realization: I am me!

If you don't remember a very early experience, make one up. Imagine your father's hands or your mother's apron or someone giving you food. Imagine an encounter with something in nature that might have been your own. Chances are it will have its roots in the truth of your life; it may even be a secret that your unconscious has held, waiting for this moment.

Exercise: Healing the Wounds of Bad Experiences

I believe that all of us have been wounded at some time, and in some way, in our self-esteem as writers. Not everyone suffered classroom trauma, but I don't know any writer who hasn't had truly hard disappointments, even very successful writers. The act of writing is self-exposing and makes us vulnerable. All of us carry around some scar tissue that operates as a hurdle or a block to freedom in our writing.

This exercise is for those who want to work on the hurdle or the block. It is designed to put you back into places where you had experiences that formed you as a writer. If you can let those experiences happen again on your page, you may find that you can now understand them, respond to them, heal the wounds, and dissolve the blocks.

Sit in a comfortable place where you will have privacy and silence. Prepare your paper and have your pen ready, but lay them aside within easy reach. Do all you can to make yourself comfortable. For me, this would mean a steaming cup of something hot, a chair big enough to curl my leg under me, and a window nearby. Make yourself as comfortable, as safe, as you can. After all, you are going in search of things that have hurt you; you deserve all the help you can give yourself.

Now read the rest of the exercise.

With your eyes closed, take a few minutes to let various parts of your body relax. I find this easiest when I consciously give some gratitude to my body. I have friends who have suffered—some have died—from terrible maladies; I am grateful to my body for its strength. I can say to my feet, thank you for carrying me around. Be at ease now.

If you find this silly, don't do it. Find your own way to relax, but I begin with my feet. They are farthest away from my head, where I spend so much of my energy. They seem to need my attention first and most when I want to gather myself in, become unified, centered. Once, a writer in my workshop, a professor of sports history, told me, "Pat, that's not the way to lead a relaxation! You should begin with the rhythms of breathing, rather than with your feet!" I tried it her way; it didn't work for me. We agreed—I should begin with my feet; she should begin with her breath.

When you have centered, relaxed, just let your mind travel back across your life to another time, before this time, and find yourself in front of school. Open the door; go in. What do you smell? What is the quality of light when the door closes behind you? Now walk to your classroom, open the door, go in. What does your eye see? Who is there? Is anything written on the blackboard? What does the room smell like? What is the quality of light in the room?

Take your seat. The teacher is going to tell you to take out a piece of paper and do some creative writing. Allow that to happen. Be aware of how you feel.

Stay there as long as you want. If anything begins to happen, let it happen. Notice any detail your inner eye sees; every detail is important.

When you are ready, pick up your pen and paper. Keep on "dreaming" as you write. Write what your inner eye sees, or what has already happened, or anything else that comes to you to write.

After you write what happened, you may want to write a response to it. The response might take the form of writing to the teacher who gave the assignment, or to yourself when it happened, or just writing a straightforward journal entry.

If this exercise does not work for you, adapt it to feel more comfortable to you. Perhaps you would actually be more relaxed if you went to a corner booth in your favorite coffee shop, kept your eyes open, let the jukebox drive out the conversations of others, and imagined yourself back in a classroom. Perhaps it would be more meaningful if it were another setting, rather than school. There is nothing sacred about this or any exercise—change it if it would work better for you in another form. If your significant early writing experiences were somewhere other than the classroom, go there in your imagination and write what happened.

Soon after Diana Coccoluto joined my Amherst workshop, she insisted that she could not write because she did not see images. She claimed she had ideas, but no images. I found this hard to believe and asked her to try this exercise. She talked with me later about what happened. She saw herself walking into the school, heard the teacher's instructions, took out her paper and pen. She heard the teacher tell her to write about home. In her fantasy, she was a young child. She sat for a little while, and other children around her began to write. She had an overwhelming fear of writing about home. Deliberately she overturned her inkwell, let the ink spill across her paper. Then she opened her eyes, but she did not write.

"See?" she said to me. "I didn't have any images."

But what an image! The little girl turns over her inkwell and watches ink running down the desk, across the paper, and onto her dress. Diana didn't recognize it as an image because fear had frozen her into a habitual rejection of her own work. Yet what she described to me was a powerful image. I repeated it to her so she could hear it coming from someone else, and I told her several times that if she had written what she had spoken, it would have been strong, moving writing.

Gradually she began to write in the workshop. At first she did not read to the whole workshop. That was too frightening; at first she gave her work only to me. What she wrote was the story of a terrified child who was being sexually abused, forced to do the work of an adult, forced to care for younger siblings in a cruel home environment. The image she had first seen of a child too frightened to write about home, pouring ink out on the page rather than writing the words that would tell the truth of her suffering, was a powerful metaphor for the silence she had kept so long.

What Diana could not bring to articulation, her own brilliance found a way to translate into metaphor. Those metaphors come from the dreaming place—the home, the source, of our creative genius.

In a California workshop, Diane Smithline wrote the following in response to this exercise:

> I'm just a kid. It's recess in eighth grade. The time when Mr. Finan hands back papers. He leaves them on the top of our desks. I am fooling around with my friends, but really I am waiting for him to come to my desk. I have opened my heart to him in a poem about my father's sudden death.
>
> Nonchalantly I walk over to my newly varnished desk with the top that lifts up and the inkwell we never use. With nervous anticipation I read the only words he has written on my paper: "The margins are too narrow."
>
> The room recedes. A silence drops over me. I am totally alone. I sink into my chair stunned, a quivering wounded animal. My back curves downward. My head bends. I see my fingers trace the circle of the inkwell around and around.
>
> I am smaller.

Diane's closing words are a perfect summary of what happens to us when work we have written out of utmost vulnerability is given a careless or harsh response. We "are smaller." Our work is smaller. Our hope, confidence, artistic promise is smaller. I encouraged her to try breaking these lines into poem form, and the workshop affirmed the power of the writing. Gradually Diane's own voice came out of hiding.

All of us who have, in Flannery O'Connor's words, "survived . . . childhood" have painful memories. Life gives us those. Even in the best of homes and schools, things happen that hurt us. We seem to remember the hurts—or at least carry the effects of the hurts—more than we remember praise and success. I think this is a kind of primal, animal protection. If I touch fire, my body needs to remember, *don't do that again*! It remembers, *fire is hot*! So we hold our hurts in secret. The good thing about this is that it does help to protect the child from further assault. The bad thing is that even many years later, when we no longer need that protection, the hidden memories block our writing. No matter how much the conscious mind wants to write, the old injury jumps up to protect us as soon as we have paper before us and pen in hand. Blocks are real; they are the tips of icebergs. But in the right kind of warm attention, ice melts.

Exercise: Getting Rid of Internal Critics

This exercise, suggested to me by Jim Eagan, a writer in my Amherst workshop, is excellent for becoming aware of the community of critics (and, if we're lucky, supporters) we all carry around in our heads. What a cacophony of invisible naysayers many of us accommodate all the time! Without knowing it, when some writers take pen to paper at, say, age 52, their own Professor Pompous, alive and well in the mind after 30 years of physical absence, instantly retorts, Who do you think you are! You haven't ever finished that incomplete I gave you in Dumbbell English 101! And the pen falters, the interior vision dries up, the system crashes, the block sits solidly in place. This exercise can give Professor Pompous his opportunity to spew out onto the page his whole miserable speech at last and can give you the opportunity to tell him where to go and that you don't give a bleep about his incomplete.

If this seems silly to you, try it anyway. Your invisible critic is probably not Prof. Pomp. at all—she may very much surprise you when she appears.

As in the first exercise, prepare a place for yourself. You will need a good, long writing time for this exercise, so try it at night, or unplug the telephone and pretend you're not at home. Give yourself time. In the way that is most comfortable for you, center your attention and relax.

When you have finished your centering, imagine yourself on a wide stretch of prairie or desert. You can see all the way to the horizon, where a little road meanders along, winding, curving. It stretches from the horizon all the way to your very feet. You are standing beside the road.

Far, far in the distance, you can see a bus coming toward you on the road. Let it come slowly. Perhaps there are heat waves that make it waver a bit at first. Let it come closer and closer until it draws up alongside you and stops.

The door opens, and people come out one by one. Each person who gets off the bus is someone who has an opinion about your writing. (Mother? Father? Sister? Brother? Sixth-grade teacher? Professor of English? Editor who recently rejected your manuscript? Best friend who has a huge ego and got published last month?) The "loudmouths" push off the bus first. Let them off, one by one, and let each one say what is on his or her mind. Write it down. If you want, note how the person is dressed; write that down. After all the loudmouths get off, there will be some quiet folk at the back of the bus. Let them off too. What they have to say may be entirely different.

After you have written the speeches of the people on the bus, you may want to do a dialogue with one or more of them.

Milagros Sanchez, who wrote the piece above on fear of success, tried this exercise. Here is a small portion of her response:

WATCHERS AND OTHER CREEPS

The familiar rickety old yellow bus is a tiny dot on the horizon. As it approaches I know that this time I am ready for them. I don't have a long pen that I could use as a spear and I don't have my carving and modeling tools, good eye pokers though they might be. This time all I do have is ME: one hundred thirty pounds, five feet three quarters inch of pure *lumbre Chicana:* FIRE!

The bus shrieks. The riders are agitated and noisy. They begin to get off the bus. I am ready! My feet are planted solidly on the ground.

"MILL-AH-GROSS," Miss Phigpus pushes the syllables through her puckered-up flabby lips as she looks at me. "How sweet you look. But don't take any pencils or paper home because you'll lose the pencil and get the paper all messed up. Mexican children are dirty, not like the children in Dopra, Wisconsin."

"*Milagros, vida mia,*" Nona smiles. "You have more talent in one little finger than most girls have in their whole bodies, and you, YOU make me so mad when you don't use it! Don't just stand there! Do something! Move! But, don't move too fast and don't do anything too well or make anything too beautiful. I don't want you to become famous. That's too much power for a woman. *Una mujer poderosa es una mujer peligrosa.* Why, a powerful woman can burn a whole town."

Milagros wrote on, page after page of voices. And then, suddenly, she began to answer them: "Nona, Nona, you were so important to me. Your words were Gospel Truth. How dare you give me mixed messages about what YOU were afraid of: POWER, LOVE, SEX, CHILD BEARING, LIFE . . ." and finally, after answering all the other voices:

And now, Miss Phigpus. How I wanted to love you, Miss Phigpus, and how I hated you for years and years. Get the hell out of my head; get the hell out of my heart and off my back! When I was little you poured your racism and your white supremacy crap on me. Well, take your crap back!

This exercise is a powerful tool for discovering and laying to rest those internal voices that still block us when we try to write. The bumper sticker that proclaimed IT'S NEVER TOO LATE TO HAVE A HAPPY CHILDHOOD could be adapted for us writers: IT'S NEVER TOO LATE TO GET RID OF INTERNAL CRITICS.

Getting Started (Again)

A writer is someone who writes. You have done it; you have expressed yourself on paper. Getting started is almost always picking up an old dream, an old desire. Getting started is usually getting started again.

Frequently at writers' conferences people ask what may seem to be irrelevant questions: What kind of pen do you use when you write? Do you write your first drafts on lined paper, or blank? Do you write at a typewriter or computer or with a pencil or fountain pen? Do you write in the daytime or at night?

Actually, questions about the intimate details and habits of the writing life are not irrelevant; beginning or blocked writers know instinctively that these are important matters. They have to do with getting started, with keeping going. Each of us has idiosyncrasies, habits, and inclinations, and those peculiar traits are often linked closely to our creativity. Of course, what truly matters is not what works for the famous writer at the conference but rather what works for you.

So what do you need? You need to discover and respect your own rituals and habits so that they will assist you, rather than block and frustrate you. You need space, privacy, and time, and you need to be constantly learning, growing. You need to know how to begin again.

Respect Your Own Patterns

According to legend, the composer Nicolo Paganini could compose only if he had a blanket over his head. Who cares? What wonderful music he composed under his blanket! He was probably made to sit at a piano when he was barely out of diapers! What the writer in you needs will be dictated somewhat by your psychological history and makeup. If you, too, need a blanket over your head to do your art, then claim your blanket! In my workshops, one writer sits curled in the biggest chair in the room; another sits in a straight-backed chair and leans her elbows on a table. One stands at the piano with his laptop computer open. Another sits on the pantry floor with her back against the refrigerator. One uses a pencil, another a ballpoint pen, another an expensive fountain pen. If they were forced to use each other's methods or tools, they would rebel. Work with yourself; respect your own patterns and preferences.

I was once on the staff of a conference with Madelaine L'Engle. She carried a small, beautifully bound notepad with her everywhere and frequently wrote notes in it. The words she wrote were visible from a distance; she wrote very large, printed block letters. I overheard someone asking her why she wrote so large—did the large print help her in some way later, when she used the notes in her writing? She smiled and answered no, it had nothing to do with her writing. She printed in large letters because her eyesight was poor, and it was easier to read that way. Some of your patterns for doing your writing most effectively will be dictated by your physical needs.

Many of your patterns will be dictated by your aesthetic taste. I write most comfortably by a window. I have friends who are distracted by the motions of birds and tree branches and prefer to write facing a blank wall. I like to have what I call my own "sacred objects" (stones, pictures, objects for remembrance) around me. They seem full of spirit, numinous familiars in the writing space. John, a poet friend, needs a cleared desk: no pictures, nothing but his work before him.

Some of your patterns will be dictated by the circumstances of your life. Sharleen Kapp, one of the longest-time members of my Thursday workshop in Amherst (12 years!), writes with the television on. She lives alone; the television keeps her company. It would drive me crazy. Another friend goes to a local fast-food restaurant, orders a cup of coffee, and writes for hours. She finds more privacy there than at home with husband, sons, dog, telephone, and dishwasher.

What is important is not how someone else writes, but that you should become acquainted with your own patterns, respect them, and provide for yourself so that they will assist you.

What You Are Doing Is Brave

There are cultural and societal prejudices that make it hard for us to write. It has been my experience that for some men, the struggle to write involves the prejudice that it is not "manly" to reveal the inner life, the secrets of the heart and of the imagination. For many women, the struggle to write is at base a struggle against the idea that women's lives are not of interest as literature. I have a friend whose husband once said after her first book had been published, "You sit there writing as if your life had some significance."

For both men and women in our society, the act of self-revelation is an act of great courage. Whether the writing is autobiographical or entirely imagined is irrelevant. To write is to reveal your mind at work. There is no nakedness like that nakedness. To write takes courage. You are a brave person just to attempt it.

The Necessity of Solitude

Solitude is an absolute necessity—the single most crucial necessity—for the writer. Only in the deepest solitude is it possible to achieve the utter surrender required for creative work. Writing at its deepest is a spiritual discipline, where the unconscious and the conscious mind merge, where what we currently call "left brain" and "right brain" somehow leap the boundary, and dream becomes indistinguishable from rational thought. Franz Kafka wrote to Felice Bauer:

> For writing means revealing oneself to excess; that utmost of self-revelation and surrender, in which a human being, when involved with others, would feel he was losing himself, and from which, therefore, he will always shrink as long as he is in his right mind—for everyone wants to live as long as he is alive—even that degree of self-revelation and surrender is not enough for writing. Writing that springs from the surface of existence—when there is no other way and the deeper wells have dried up—is nothing, and collapses the moment a truer emotion makes that surface shake. This is why one can never be

alone enough when one writes, why there can never be enough silence around when one writes, why night is not night enough. This is why there is never enough time at one's disposal, for the roads are long and it is easy to go astray.

"Solitude," however, does not always mean being physically alone. Thousands of times I have seen it in a writing workshop where we write together in silence. A kind of solitude happens there, where each of us works silently and protects the other's privacy. In that setting, miracles happen: The writer writes clear, clean narrative; surprising juxtapositions; metaphoric images; insights that the writer himself or herself does not perceive until it is read aloud and named by listeners. For many writers in today's busy world, that solitude in the company of other writers is the only solitude we give ourselves.

Traditionally, solitude in which to write has been taken somewhat for granted as a need of male writers, and the response from others has been appreciation for his obvious commitment to his work. However, women who have attempted to achieve a similar solitude have not been so charitably understood. Only recently is there a growing appreciation of Emily Dickinson's radical solitude as a choice she made to protect her writing, rather than the pathetic result of a "weird," or even pathological, personality. In a brilliant book titled *Emily Dickinson's Fascicles: Method & Meaning*, Dorothy Huff Oberhaus examines the poet's radical commitment to her work as a spiritual discipline. bell hooks writes in *remembered rapture,* "Dickinson's solitariness was essential for the cultivation of her creative passion. It was in that solitary space that she found her most intimate connection to the Divine, to that quality of yearning for ecstasy that would lead her to write. . . . It is during those times that she is most 'alone with the Alone' that her imagination takes flight and soars."

The form that solitude takes will be unique to each person. I believe the choice Dickinson made was an ecstatic choice, a spiritual choice, and the support her intimate family gave was essential to the work of genius that she achieved. It is no accident that she is our greatest American poet. Genius cannot mature without intense practice, intense commitment, intense solitude.

I keep this quote by Rilke tacked above the inside door of my upstairs writing room: "I hold this to be the highest task of a bond between two people: that each should stand guard over the solitude of the other."

How does one achieve solitude? My own personality is such that even with family support, I cannot turn off the voice of the washing machine: *You could be doing a load of wash while you write!* For me, solitude in my own home is excruciatingly difficult; everything—the breakfast dishes, the telephone, fax, E-mail, even the cat pan—screams for my attention.

When I was a young playwright, I received a full scholarship to spend three weeks in a hotel room in the theater district in New York City. I was given complete freedom, solitude in the private room all day, and free theater tickets to major shows in the evenings. I loved the shows. It should have been heaven. I did learn, but the days were a nightmare. I have never in my life been more blocked than I was in that square room with a window looking out onto a brick wall.

Virginia Woolf has said it: What a woman (what any writer) needs in order to write is *a room of one's own*. It is not simply a matter of space—it is space *of one's own* that is needed. My problem as a young writer in New York City was that I didn't know how to make the space my own.

Now when I go away to write (and I do, several times a year) I take with me a few objects that help me connect to my own inner voice: the marble that I found washed up on the beach near Rockport, Massachusetts, years ago. The petrified snail shell given to me by a friend. A candle and matches. My favorite pen and my old, familiar journal notebook. I know how to get started now: what to do first, what to do second. Not because it is the right way for anyone else, but because I have "caught myself in the act" of getting going, I have watched my patterns, and I know what works for me.

When Robin Therrien, a writer in my Chicopee Workshop for women in low-income housing projects, joined the group, she could not give her three children each a room of his or her own. They were living in her car. But she did give each a blank book and told each child it was his or her own. She trained them not to touch her journal and she did not touch theirs. Robin was saying to her children, Be free, be respectful, be yourself. She was teaching them to value their own opinions, their own right to honest expression. In giving them journals and the certainty that she would not read them, she was giving them essential privacy and encouragement to write.

How is it possible to claim enough privacy to write the mind's dream, to find the energy and the emotional centeredness necessary to artistic creation? How is one to combat the demons of depression and the frustration of repeated failure to find time, space, solitude, focus, concentration?

My own pattern of claiming for myself a necessary solitude was conditioned by my generation's habits and assumptions. When I left home in 1952, it was to go to a double room in a dormitory at college and graduate school, and from there to marriage and children. From age ten, I kept a diary—later, a journal in a loose-leaf notebook—and wrote wherever there was an empty chair, the corner of a table. The time came, however, when I was overwhelmed by mothering. With three preschool-aged children, two still in diapers, I finally said to myself, *It is over. I will never write again.* I packed my typewriter away in the back of a closet in an upstairs bedroom. I quit.

On a particular winter afternoon, I felt as if I would lose my mind. It was a day when all three babies were fussy, and nothing I could do was enough. We were all in the kitchen; it was cluttered with toys, baby formula, laundry, and breakfast dishes. Condensation on the windows closed all access to the outside world. A very painful kind of cry began in my mind. It was rhythmic, like a chant. In that desperation where one does not observe oneself, I ran out of the kitchen, up the stairs two at a time, grabbed the typewriter, brought it down and slammed it on top of the throbbing washing machine—the only cleared surface in the kitchen. With two babies playing on the floor and one strapped to the changing table, I pounded out a page-long poem. Although it did not say so directly, the meaning was, I will never write again. When I finished, I stood in a kind of shock, knowing three things: I had been writing; what I had written was not bad; and nothing, as long as I lived, would keep me from writing again.

For years I kept a typewriter in the kitchen. It sat on the ironing board, on the kitchen counter, on the dish cabinet. It sat on a kitchen chair. But it was there, all the time, and there was paper in it, and often there were words coming and going on the pages.

Only after my children (four) were all in public school did I set up a desk of my own in a corner of the bedroom I shared with my husband. There were drawers in the desk—space to myself! I was growing in my sense of my own needs, but so slowly! Several years later I moved into half of a basement room where my husband and I set up a partition between our two desks. I had gone from a desk of my own to half a room of my own. It wasn't enough; I had no protection from his telephone conversations, the sounds of his work—but it was an improvement.

Everyone differs, but what kept me from having a room of my own is common. It was not so much the difficulty of finding space as it was my own attitude: I saw others' needs as more important than my own.

Ursula LeGuin says that those whom she loves are her muses. I have experienced that. I have also experienced those I love as my own distraction from my work. I have to say that, at crucial times in my life, other writers who cared about me saved my sanity, if not my life. My mentor, Elizabeth Berryhill, listened to me over the years, even paid my way to California when I could not afford the ticket myself. Margaret Robison, a fellow student in the MFA program at the University of Massachusetts, encouraged me to take my own poems seriously. It was she who sent off the first poem of mine to be published in a literary journal. Relationships like that have taught me the possibility and the power of mutual support among writers. Amherst Writers & Artists, and the writing workshop method described in this book, are rooted in those experiences.

Only after my fiftieth birthday did I actually achieve a full "room of one's own." For the first time, I took money from my teaching income, went into town, and rented an office. It was sunny, clean, and utterly private. For several weeks I refused to move any furniture in; I just went there, locked the door behind me, and sat on the floor in a square of sunlight, soaking up solitude. Having my own space away from home was one of the most blissful experiences of my entire life. Gradually I claimed it as work space, moved into it the things I needed to be able to do my work. I stayed there for three years and learned what I needed in order to be able to claim a space of my own at home that would be truly mine—not a space in which I felt I was staking out squatter's rights, but a space that was deeply, spiritually, a room of my own. When I returned to a space at home, I took out a building loan, remodeled a room into a studio, put in great, wonderful windows and a heavy-duty, soundproof door. Today I sit in that space, typing these words, and occasionally, still, I go away to a cabin in the woods where I can sleep and dream and find the absolute solitude in which my deepest writing is born.

In our writing workshops for low-income women and children, we have been confronted by how desperately difficult it is to find solitude in a crowded housing project. Sarah Browning, Enid Santiago Welch, and Deb Burwell created a family writing camp, taking mothers and young children to a donated house by the sea in Maine for a week of quiet, rest, and writing.

If you have not yet claimed and made for yourself a room of your own, begin to do so. Do what is possible; love it, use it, and dream of the day that you can take the next step. The first "room" of my own was a few lines each day in a five-year diary. From that tiny seed grew the studio in which I work today.

Writing takes time as well as space. Like other art forms, the act of writing can and must take your whole attention; time collapses, disappears, seems to dissolve. It is actually a wonderful experience, but it can happen only if you create a safe environment for concentration. No telephone interruptions. No friendly chats with members of the family about matters of little consequence. There is further discussion of this subject in Part I, Chapter 3, "Toward a Disciplined Writing Life."

How to Get Started (Again)

The moment comes to put the pen on the paper and begin to form words. How does it happen? Especially if you haven't been writing for some time, or if you are feeling dry or blocked, how do you begin?

If you don't have an idea of what you want to write, that may be good. The chances might be better that your unconscious mind will give you an image.

You are going to use your own voice. You are going to write as if you were talking to your best friend. Grace Paley's work gives you the feeling that you are listening to a funny, wise, beloved next-door neighbor on an ordinary afternoon. Look at some of the first sentences in her stories: They are clear, simple, everyday statements—the very best way to begin: *"Vicente said:* I wanted to be a doctor." (That one is my favorite Paley story, "A Man Told Me the Story of His Life," only one and half pages long, in *Later the Same Day.*) Here are some other Paley opening lines from the same volume. "Lavinia was born laughing." "At that time most people were willing to donate organs." "My grandmother sat in her chair." "I was standing in the park under that tree." Each of these first sentences opens into a story and leaves you remembering complex feelings and relationships that Paley creates with an utterly unpretentious language. It is her own authentic voice. She trusts it and leans into it, and you relax into the story because you trust her as she is trusting you.

I want (your reader wants) you to "tell me something I can't forget." Gossip. Tell the tale. Forget that you are writing. Just talk onto the page. There is a rich, colloquial speech—the language of home—that you learned perfectly. Use it. Your own first-learned speech is the primary color on your artist's palette. Everything else you learn will add variety, but the language of your own childhood home is your greatest treasure, your primary source. One person's voice will reflect a childhood lived among beautiful carpets, lamplight, cases of books, quiet conversation (and what? perhaps lost loves, perhaps great dreams, perhaps murder in the minds of those who inhabited that space). Another person's voice will reflect a child-hood in a walk-up apartment, sweaty bodies in a crowded space, rats coming up out of the furnace duct (and what? Perhaps lost loves, perhaps great dreams, perhaps murder). Both are equally interesting, if the writer only tells the truth of what is remembered or imagined. If the writer only trusts his or her own voice and tells the truth of what was experienced. All of it.

Exercise: Beginning (Again)

Close your eyes and ask for one single image. Out of the millions of things that you have seen in your life—just one. When it appears, do not reject it! No matter how inconsequential it seems—take it. It is a clue that will lead you to another clue and then to another clue until you find your way into the deep places of what is meaningful to you. Ira Progoff suggests imagining a well and allowing images to rise to the surface of the water. My own way of doing this, described elsewhere in the book, is to ask myself, *What matters then?* and wait for a single detail or image to emerge.

When you have a concrete image, begin to write. It may be description ("The ketchup bottle sat on the kitchen table."), an action ("She hitched up her jeans and glared at me."), or dialogue ("You opened my letter!").

Don't think "novel" or "story," "poem" or "play." Just think with your senses, think with your eyes, with your ears, with your sense of touch. Capture one concrete detail. One tiny paper cut on a man's index finger. One peach, cut open on a counter top. One snatch of dialogue. Don't worry about where it is going. Just be faithful to what your eye sees—move in closer, get more detail. And then, if something else beckons like a tiny glimmer of light off to the side of your vision, turn to that. Be faithful to that.

I often think of lightning bugs in my childhood—how they flickered in the air above the peonies. How we ran, mason jars in hand, to catch them. Catching an image that is being offered by the unconscious is like that. Catch it as it flits by—gently, gently! Capture it and then set it free. Let it go where it wants to go. Write whatever comes.

BEGIN GENTLY: WRITE IN YOUR JOURNAL

When I have been away from my writing for a long time, the way back feels tangled as if I am at the edge of a jungle and have lost my machete. Most often, I begin by writing just for myself. This kind of writing was once considered an important art form and is again enjoying something of a renaissance. People in "olden times" kept journals or diaries. Many still do, even though they may not talk about it. My druggist, Fred, keeps a daily journal of bird calls. A priest I know keeps two journals: One is on his desk, one is hidden and locked. Journal keeping and its importance for the writer is discussed more fully in Part I, Chapter 4. Often, the way I start to write is a diary entry: "April 1. Yesterday I went to Northampton, looking for a birthday gift for Natty." It is a way of easing myself into words, going gently, warming up.

THE USES OF THE LETTER

John McPhee has said that every book he ever wrote began with the words "Dear Mother." The first words of my book *Wake Up Laughing: A Spiritual Autobiography* were "Dear Moya." Neither McPhee's "Dear Mother" nor my "Dear Moya" appear in the published book, but look at all that it accomplishes for the writing: intimacy of voice, a relaxed and natural tone, an unthreatening specific audience, a natural flow of information or plot, and a writer blissfully forgetting anyone else who might ever read those words!

Even if I do not have something in mind that I want to write, I sometimes consciously take a step toward my writing self by writing a letter. I think it's something like the buzz of the computer warming up, or the way you idle the engine of your car on a cold day. Writing words to a friend or family member "idles" the mind until all at once you want to abandon the letter and turn to an image or a phrase that calls you into your writing project. (I don't always abandon my letter; the one that began "Dear Moya" became 52 pages of typed letter, and a year later became a full book!)

When we write autobiography, we sometimes face blocks that have to do with how large the story is—how it has roots in all the corners of our psyche. This is especially true in writing about our family of origin. Beginning to write to a particular friend can focus the material, act as the "magic apron" before the great dogs of fear, and keep your voice intimate and natural.

Or writing a letter may simply give words to what is most important in the moment of writing. This letter was written by Marcia Davis-Cannon in Sharon Bray's workshop for women with breast cancer:

A LETTER TO MY SISTER

Dear Connie,

I remember how hard you took the news of my breast cancer. You were the one with the lumpy breasts and calcifications. You were the one who never had babies of her own to breastfeed. You were older. It didn't seem right for a younger sister to get cancer when you were still under observation, almost as wrong as a parent having to bury a child.

Now the doctors have found a lump in your breast.

Oh, Connie, every nerve ending in the breast I have left jangles with that news. I would gladly have had all the lumps for this generation of our family and all the generations to come. I want to reach out across the miles and enfold you in a lopsided, bosom-y hug. I know the sick, hurting, fist-in-the-gut feeling of this news.

And yet, I somehow want to share with you the impact breast cancer has had on my life. I want to introduce you to laugh-with-you, cry-with-you nurturing of fellow survivors. Perhaps the sky has always been this blue, but now I revel in its blueness. The sun is warmer now, spring blossoms more fragrant, friendships more dear. Life has never been so precious.

Love,
Marcia

Writing a letter may in itself be the essential form of writing. Words put to paper by one person for another person to read. As we develop faster and faster ways to print and copy, may we never lose the intimate art of the personal letter.

WRITE FREELY FROM "THE DREAMING PLACE"

After warming up with a journal entry or a letter, I turn deliberately inward, listen, and watch. What may come in response to my invitation might be a few words, or it might be an image. No matter how fleeting—take that image or those words as gift. Write trustingly, openly. When my granddaughter, Sarah, was four years old, she wanted me to draw pictures with her. I said, "Sarah, I can't draw! I just make messes!"

She answered with great emphasis and disgust, "Grandma! When you draw, you don't make messes! You just squabble around!"

She was absolutely right. It was the voice of my inner critic who said, I can't draw. That particular inner critic was my fourth-grade teacher who told us to "draw night," then held up my picture as an example of how *not* to do it! More than 40 years later, her voice was still active when I touched a crayon. The creative artist has to kick out all those dusty old internal critics and "just squabble around."

Exercise: Free Writing

Many authors of books on writing recommend timed, free writing as a helpful exercise to warm up, to get started (again). Dorothea Brande and Brenda Ueland introduced it in the 1930s. Peter Elbow introduced it to a wide audience in *Writing Without Teachers*. Natalie Goldberg, Julia Cameron, and other authors of books on writing offer numerous ways of using this technique. Proprioceptive writing workshops (Linda Trichter Metcalf and Tobin Simon, *Writing the Mind Alive*) add candlelight and music to free writing sessions.

Free writing is essentially this: For a specified number of minutes, write freely anything and everything that comes to mind. Keep your pen moving. Make no editorial changes as you write. Try to accept any image, any words that come; just write.

One day in a workshop I described free writing, and ended by inviting people to try it. I said, "Just keep writing—don't lift your pen from the paper." After we had written, one of the writers said, "Pat, that was really hard, connecting all the words." At first, I didn't understand what she meant, until she explained, "You said *don't lift your pen from the paper*, so I didn't! But it was really hard, connecting all the words together!"

Don't stop writing—but it is OK to lift your pen from the paper between words! In the following example Barbara Burkart begins with free or "stream-of-consciousness" writing. Gradually her focus changes from the struggle to write, to images that surprise and suggest the beginnings of a poem:

> Warm-up time: keep pen on the page. Stop directing word traffic. Let it go on vacation for the night. Let new words come that I haven't used before. . . . The pen starts moving on its own and I don't know where it's going but come along for the ride. It's starting . . .

Curvy Leverett roads shaded by pine and oak cross ancient streams. Pen moves down the road until the road stops, field starts. Get out of the car. Take off shoes, socks, tuck them neatly on the floor of the front seat. Step gingerly onto cool grass, prickly underfoot. . . . Shed shorts, shirt, sink ankle deep, knee deep into soft spongy earth.

Colors are changing. Lifting feet becomes burdensome; lush undergrowth beckons. Lie down. Warm shafts of light beam onto belly, shoulders. Nipples stiffen in full appreciation of the yeasty blanket that is our mother. . . . Soles of the feet are getting hot, furry, like the moss under the oaks.

Exercise: "In This One . . ."

This is one of my favorite exercises. It uses a line from a poem by B. H. Fairchild, "In this one you are . . ."

Spend a little time centering, turning from busyness back toward your own inner reflections. Then call up from your memory a snapshot or photograph of someone important to you. It may be someone who is still close to you, or someone who is no longer in your life. It may be a picture in your album, or just a mental "snapshot." Usually it is a good idea to take the first one that comes to mind, rather than rejecting the first and sorting through possibilities. If you feel some resistance, that may be an indication that there is a "knot" to be unraveled. Margaret Atwood has said, "Good writing begins where there is a knot."

When you have the picture, begin writing with these words: "In this one, you are . . ." (You are writing to the person in the photograph.)

In the example that follows, Paul Barrows began with the exercise and later developed the piece into a beautiful story about the relationship between two gay men.

In this one you are looking down. You are smiling—the smile of someone who has been caught at something—a grin, a smirk—because you have just noticed me with the camera—have looked up and then looked down again— when click and buzz the shutter snaps, the film winds. In this one you are partially in shadow . . .

Those pictures remembered from actual photographs or simply held in the mind's eye as memories are full of emotional meaning, whether or not we consciously understand that meaning. As a variation on the exercise, you might remember a snapshot or formal photograph of yourself and write anything that the picture brings to mind. Or write to yourself at that age. Doing this exercise once I remembered a picture of myself as an awkward teenager, my face screwed up in bright sunlight. I began a poem, "That's not my face in the photograph." The writing took me to strong anger and an important realization on a personal level, but it was more than a private work; the poem was later published in a literary journal.

Because in our method everything is treated as fiction, I do not know whether the piece that follows is fictional or autobiographical. It doesn't matter—the writing is powerful. In the prose poem that follows, Justine V. Nolley wrote in response to a remembered photograph:

BLACK DOLL

I need a black doll 'cause there's nothing black around me. My skin looks dirty and I don't know why. My hair is frizzy and I can't feather it like the other kids at school. Beth has blue eyes and long, soft, stringy hair. Is her hair better than mine?

Mom doesn't help me. Her hair is straight, too, and she hates to comb mine. She jokes about her friend, she had a little girl with a black man like my Dad, and always says, "Oh Cissy, what did God do to your hair?" every time she combs the little girl's hair. I wish I knew what little girl. I think she needs a black doll, too. I wonder if her skin looks dirty like mine.

They put a lighter next to my head on the bus. The older kids. They smoke and they call me nigger and scare me. Stephanie flicked the lighter and a funny smell came from my head, but there weren't any flames. I looked right at the big fat bus driver Peggy in the rearview mirror. She saw everything, but she didn't say anything.

They said I was wicked ugly. I get better grades than all of them and I won the regional spelling bee but they still call me wicked stupid. They say I'm an ugly nigger. I keep telling my mom but she won't listen because she thinks that I'm an ugly nigger, too. I know it. I just know it. Especially in the summer when I look really dirty.

Today on the bus they asked me if I have a tail because I'm a nigger. Robbie and Eric made me bend over so they could touch it and see. Leslie laughed. Lori was in the front of the bus, watching but real quiet. She looked scared. I wanted to tell her not to be scared. They weren't gonna do anything to her. She's a nerd, not a nigger.

I hate Westport. I wish I could be somewhere where there are black people, like the ones I see on T.V. I wish I didn't have to go to school any more. My teacher Mrs. Gorman's daughter Andrea came up to me and said that I was a dirty nigger. Then she went up to Mrs. Gorman's desk and whispered something in her ear, and they both smiled.

This man followed me around when I went to Cumberland Farms. I kept telling him that I didn't take anything but he didn't believe me. He looked so mad, and I don't know why.

Eric said his brother and his uncles and some other kids are gonna light our front yard on fire.

Another suggestion is to write directly about the picture. In that case, the voice may not be as intimate; the perspective may be different as the narrator stands off a bit and responds to the photograph, rather than speaking directly to the image in the picture. Dorothea Kissam began in this way:

> I look at this picture now from my perspective of some eighty-eight years later. My mother could not know that in four years time she would be orphaned, her mother dead of pneumonia and her father dying within the year of drink and exposure to the New York weather.

Getting started (again) is a matter of the spirit. Bring to your desire all of your courage and a gentle (uncritical) spirit. Believe in your own stories, your own meanings. Cooperate with yourself by letting your habits and preferences work for you. And use one of the exercises in this book to get you going.

RETURNING TO WORK ALREADY BEGUN

The moment of facing the writing task for this particular day has come. I am warmed up, I am ready to do my work. If I am in the middle of a writing project, the first thing to do is read what I last wrote. It is best to do this reading aloud, on my feet, moving around. If you try this, let your ear hear your voice, let your feet and legs move to the rhythm of the words you have written. Read through to the very last words you wrote.

In *A Moveable Feast*, Ernest Hemingway records that he made a practice of ending every day's writing at a spot where he knew what he wanted to say next. It's an excellent idea, because if we know that in five more minutes we will take a break from writing, for dinner, for sleep, for an errand, we are inclined to use that five minutes to bring a feeling of closure: We "wrap up" the writing a bit. That wrapped-up closure may make it difficult to get back into writing. Often what we need to do is cut the last sentence or the last paragraph from the preceding writing session before going on. The image that comes to me is the dead wood at the tip of rosebush branches when winter is done. You look at the bush and see where the green stops and the brown dead wood begins, and you cut off that which is dead. It's like that, coming back to a piece of writing after having "closed it down." You can tell, if you listen carefully to what you have written, where you need to cut in order to be back inside the dream, where you don't know what will happen next and everything is alive.

CLAIM WRITING AS YOUR ART FORM

You do not have to make money at your writing to be a writer. Writers are artists. Although some writers make their living at their writing, most of us do not. And most of those who do make money, don't make much. Most of us, like artists everywhere, have other jobs on the side; we teach or work in an office or clean other people's houses or drive a truck to support our writing habit. I no longer expect my writing to feed me or clothe me. When a small check comes in, I am delighted; I tape the attached statement onto my file cabinet; I tell my friends in workshop, and we celebrate together. But even deeper is the joy I feel when my closest and keenest writing friends tell me that my writing "works," that it has reached a kind of clarity and truth, that it moves them. I want my writing to go before the world of course. I send it out. I hope. I am pleased when it meets success among strangers. But I think I have achieved some maturity as an artist in this: What matters most to me is that I get it right for myself and for my intimate community of other writers. If I am an artist, the commercial world cannot be the judge of my work. Writing is an art form that will, like every art form, take a lifetime to perfect.

You are a writer. You are an artist. Do not burden your art with the necessity of having it make your living for you. Continue to keep that possibility open if you want to, but gently. Send your work off to the best, even the most lucrative, markets first—and hope for the miracle. But remember all the famous artists who never were a commercial success. Don't judge the artistic merit of your work by the fickle necessities of the marketplace or the critical style setting of the academy.

Claim your writing as your own personal art form. That will free and empower you to get started (again) and keep going.

Toward a Disciplined Writing Life

Often I am asked, "How can I write regularly, steadily, faithfully?" This is not the question of how effective the writing is but how to maintain a consistent effort.

Most of what we think and read about discipline only increases our resistance. "Discipline" usually means making ourselves do some duty, grit our teeth, force ourselves to do what we don't want to do. A disciplined writer, we are told (or we tell ourselves) writes every day, writes X number of hours a day or X number of pages or paragraphs a day. We read how someone else structures his or her writing life, and we judge ourselves by that pattern. Unfortunately, many books on writing reinforce this idea of discipline.

The wrong kind of "discipline" damages the creative process. The deepest, truest discipline has its roots in the ancient wisdom of the Hebrew prophet Zechariah: "Not by might, nor by power, but by . . . spirit." Rather than comparing ourselves to others, twisting our own arms, and punishing ourselves with duty and guilt, we need to have a gentle, compassionate, and nonjudgmental spirit toward our writing. William Burroughs said, "There is no such thing as will power. Only need." The roots of a useful discipline lie in understanding ourselves, and that is a gentle matter.

The Fruits of Discipline

A disciplined writing life brings into full fruition a writer's consistent, completed work. Let Emily Dickinson be our guide in the matter of discipline. However odd the world may have deemed her personal habits to be, Dickinson achieved a discipline that gave to the world an incomparable body of art. I like to think her poem #303 does not refer to a loved person, but to her writing:

> The Soul selects her own Society—
> Then—shuts the Door—
> To her divine Majority—
> Present no more—
> . . . .
>
> I've known her—from an ample nation—
> Choose One—
> Then—close the Valves of her attention—
> Like Stone—

Perhaps the "One" that Dickinson chose was her writing, and perhaps the perfect poems that she left us are the fruit of her ability to "close the valves" of her attention "like stone" toward everything but that "One." Singleness of attention is the heart and soul of a disciplined writing life.

The goal and the fruit of a true discipline is not publication. Neither is it money or fame, although Dickinson said "Fame is a bee. / It has a song— / It has a sting— / Ah, too, it has a wing" (#1763). The goal and the fruit of a true discipline is completion. The completion of the work of art.

> Although the poems of Emily Dickinson remained virtually unpublished during her lifetime, she did engage in a private kind of self-publication from about 1858–1864. During those years, she made copies of more than eight hundred of her poems, gathered them into forty groups, and bound each of these gatherings together with string to form booklets. While she sometimes sent a friend a copy of one of the poems from the booklets, there is no evidence that she showed them in their bound form to anyone. After her death in 1886, her sister, Lavinia—to whom she had willed all her earthly possessions—was astonished to discover the forty booklets among the poets papers, as well as copies of nearly four hundred poems arranged in the manner of the booklets, but unbound.
>
> Dorothy Huff Oberhaus

If Emily Dickinson could achieve the closing of her attention "like stone" to all that distracted her, I want to try to focus my attention on my work with all the diligence possible to me. If she—who said "This is my letter to the World / That never wrote to Me" (#441) and saw publication of only two of her poems in her lifetime—could stitch eight hundred of her poems together with needle and thread, making them into little booklets, then I want to bring my work to artistic completion too. I want to honor it, finish it, and bring it to a form that holds the dignity of art.

Challenges to Discipline

THOSE OTHER COMMITMENTS

Most commitments that keep me from my writing are masks that I put up to hide my fear and my failure to do what I need and want most to do. If my belief in my own work is strong, other commitments will adjust themselves. Human beings have free will. If I could speak to myself as an 18-year-old, I would say, You can say "no" to the demands of your immature mother. You can insist on some privacy, some time of your own. If I could speak to myself as a young mother of four children, I would say, You could nap with the children, then in the solitude of night or dawn, write. Regardless of our particular circumstances, the struggle goes on to keep at our work. If I could speak to myself just this morning when I answered the phone and the mail instead of writing, I'd say, You can sit down, slow down, turn off the telephone.

There is something fundamentally wrong with "other commitments" if they keep me from my true work. When we neglect the artist in ourselves, there is a kind of mourning that goes on under the surface of our busy lives. Peggy Reber expresses it this way:

POEM FOR THE ABANDONED

There is always something else—
the dishes to wash,
the bills to pay,
the bathroom to clean,
the friend in need,
the dog's ear medicine.
World without end!

THE GHOST OF CRITICISM PAST

I first met Teresa Pfeifer when she was a young mother in my workshop for women in a public housing project. Now she is a published poet whose work has won a major prize; she graduated summa cum laude from college, holds her MFA in Creative Writing from the University of Massachusetts, and teaches writing on the college level.

Teresa told me, when she first came to my workshop, that she could not write. "I can prove it!" she said, and took out of her jeans a worn letter that she had carried in a billfold in her pocket *for 17 years,* and told me a story. I asked her to write it for this book:

> Once, in high school, I sent a sample of my adolescent poems to a famous author of children's books that I had loved. Her responses were loaded with sarcasm—"It's as though you'd been frightened by a deodorant commercial," she wrote. And asked why didn't I try writing in iambic pentameter as many words as I could think of that rhymed with shit.
>
> Looking back on these poems now, I see that I was a teenager with very sharp instincts and a hyper-sensitivity to the world around me which led to poems of great exaggeration (probably the gift of all teenagers in turmoil). Her responses were so cruel and without humanity that she could have just defecated on the poems and saved herself some typing. She molested my soul and I would carry the scars for years. I had nothing of value to write, I had nothing of value to say, I had nothing of value to contribute. I felt as though my psyche had been raped.

The letter from the famous writer was two pages of messy, typo-ridden disgust. Either the woman was drunk when she wrote it, or she was a sick person. I urged Teresa to find her youthful poems and let me read them. They were, as I expected, beautiful, passionate outpourings. As if they had been given to me, instead of to the famous writer, I wrote a response to the poems on my professional stationery. I told her which phrases, which images, most moved me. I said—truthfully—that her youthful poems were far better than my own had been at that age, that there was brilliance in them. When I gave Teresa my letter, she read it and handed me the famous writer's letter. "I don't need this anymore," she said.

What Teresa did in fact, we all do in spirit. She held that terrible letter in her billfold, *next to her body,* for 17 years! It was creased, worn-out at the fold lines. So do we all keep ugly words of put-down and ridicule, the discouraging grades in elementary and high school. We carry them close to us, and we use them as evidence when we say, I can't write.

THE DANGER OF CRITICISM PRESENT

Sue Solomont joined my Amherst workshop after a period of writer's block, but she had already published in literary journals and had written a considerable amount of poetry in the context of academic workshops as she completed her Ph.D. I encouraged Sue to experiment, to trust her own voice, to "play." Her writing began to change, both in form and in subject matter; she began to write with a wild and very original imagination. After some time, having accumulated a significant number of new poems, she sent some of her new work to a former professor, among them this:

> mother mother
> buried in father
>
> where are U where are U
>
> voice in a snake
> yr fetal heart
> pounds through the dead king's veins
>
> in utero in the darkness of castles
> yr words lost in grandpa's grumbling
> long long table speeches
>
> napkin under chin
> yr fillings are wedged
> you're stuffed with truffles
>
> babies are jammed
> into your heart
>
> down my thoughts
> yr thoughts echo like a
>
> did i really hear a
>   voice just then / what
>
> wasit wasit woke me up
>
> did i hear weeping in the drains
>
> why does my heart
> ache like stones
> when i pour the tea &
> pass the scones

Sue's voice is unique, as is her style. I thought her poems were fresh and interesting and very much about being a woman. But her professor responded with alarm. He said that her new work "lacked discipline," which is what Thomas Wentworth Higginson was worried about when he read Emily Dickinson's poems. He pronounced them "uncontrolled," "sporadic," and "wayward."

I wrote this poem for Sue—and for myself—as a reminder that discipline of practice and discipline of content are matters of the heart, not of the will.

YOUR BOAT, YOUR WORDS

Your boat, they will tell you,
cannot leave the harbor
without discipline.

But they will neglect to mention
that discipline has a vanishing point,
an invisible horizon where belief takes over.

They will not whisper to you the secret
that they themselves have not fully understood: that
belief is the only wind with breath enough

to take you past the deadly calms, the stopped motion
toward that place you have imagined,
the existence of which you cannot prove

except by going there.

There are so many voices within us and outside us that discourage and undermine us, tempt us to abandon our own visions, our own voices, that a sense of duty, of "ought and should" will not be sufficient to counter them. Each person must study him- or herself to understand the form that discipline needs to take. Surely the person who works well with a tight schedule of planned hours will want to work writing in the same way. The only way for me to lead a disciplined writing life, however, is to believe in myself as a writer and to love my work so much that nothing else—even "those other commitments"—can take it away from me. Eleanor Roosevelt insisted, "Nobody can do anything to me that I'm not already doing to myself."

EXTERNAL AND THE INTERNAL "COMMITTEES"

To lead a disciplined writing life, one must be as free as possible from all "committee opinions." Trying to write in a context of external judgment, conflict, hostility, and interruption is incredibly damaging to creativity.

An extreme example of the negative effect of writing for a committee is the experience many people have in writing traditional academic theses and doctoral dissertations. In the February 1992 issue of *College Composition and Communication*, in her article "Between the Drafts," Nancy Sommers, Sosland Director of Expository Writing at Harvard, gives an eloquent plea for traditional academic papers to make room for what she calls "the personal essay."

> Given the opportunity to speak their own authority as writers, given a turn in the conversation, students can claim their stories as primary source material and transform their experiences into evidence. They might, if given enough encouragement, be empowered not to serve the academy and accommodate it, not to write in the persona of Every student, but rather to write essays that will change the academy. When we create opportunities for something to happen between the drafts, when we create writing exercises that allow students to work with sources of their own that can complicate and enrich their primary sources, they will find new ways to write scholarly essays that are exploratory, thoughtful, and reflective.
>
> I want my students to know what writers know—to know something no researchers could ever find out no matter how many times they pin my students to the table, no matter how many protocols they tape. I want my students to know how to bring their life and their writing together.

Unfortunately, Nancy Sommers is still an exception, rather than the rule. I have experienced so many writers coming to my workshops damaged by their experiences of writing academic papers, I feel that the issue needs to be addressed.

When I was newly out of graduate school, I worked for a time editing dissertations. One was written by a student preparing to return to his home in Nigeria. His degree was to come from two departments: chemistry and forestry. Each department had separate guidelines for the dissertation. Each had its own accepted terminology. Committee members were at odds with one another. What one professor liked, the other hated. The pawn in the whole game was the hapless student. Over and over again I encountered statements like this in the text: "The presence of a mobile abiotic transport agency which can exacerbate ecological impacts is one such example of the contribution of substrate qualities to differing seasonal impacts relative to proposed management actions." The phrase "a mobile abiotic transport agency" was used so frequently that I asked the student if he would please tell me in other words what it meant. He looked at me with surprise and said, "It means *water.*"

The intense jargon made every sentence almost unintelligible, and his committee had sent him to me to assist him with the very problem I felt they had created. I rewrote it, sentence by sentence. When he looked at all the red pencil marks I had put on his page, he said in his heavy accent, "Oh, my poor paper! It's bleeding to death!" (That was the last time I ever put a red mark on anyone's paper!)

Many people who want to write have become convinced that they cannot because they did not succeed at term papers, dissertations, and theses. Sometimes it is helpful to realize that academic papers written for a committee are akin to romance novels: It is formula writing, and the formula is absolute. If you failed to write a dissertation, it may mean you were just too creative a writer! Joseph Campbell has written, "I think of the Ph.D. as a very funny kind of celebration; it just proves that up to the age of 45 you have obeyed orders and haven't done your own thing."

Of course there are exceptions; poet and teacher Mary Clare Powell, reading the above words, told me that she had a wonderful experience finishing her Ph.D. under a committee that wanted creativity from her. (Her degree was in Creativity in the School of Education at the University of Massachusetts; it may be a while before departments of chemistry and forestry catch up!) In time, perhaps the changes that are happening in many primary schools will reach doctoral programs, and creativity in writing will blossom everywhere.

There is another committee—the one in our heads. This committee is a collection of remembered parents, teachers, friends, acquaintances—all of whom have ideas about our writing. You may already have become acquainted with this committee if you did the exercise titled "Getting Rid of Internal Critics." My own "committee" includes my dead mother, who didn't want me to reveal that I grew up poor and spent time in an orphanage. It includes some writer friends, because I care so much what they think. There are some old friends whom I lost when I abandoned the church, and some new friends, who might be shocked to know how religious I really still am. It includes the editor of a small, macho review who told me that in a manuscript of my poems only the one about the man who killed a bear was "of any value whatsoever." And the young, hotshot editor in New York who responded to my second novel by saying, "It is far too late for this kind of 1950s sensibility." (The novel was deliberately set in the 1950s.) But not only those who have put down my writing are on my internal committee. There is being one of four finalists out of over five hundred entrants in a major poetry contest. Being so close and still losing, burns, and the Internal Critic says, You'll look over into the Promised Land, but you'll never get there!

There is the editor at a major New York publishing house who said, "Everyone in America should read this book" before his marketing department decided it might not be taken by Borders bookstores. Borders bookstores are on my internal committee! My internal committee is vast, as it is for everyone who writes. There may be the high school teacher who gave you an "F" in English, the best friend whom you don't want to offend, the famous writer whose work you love. Even those who love your writing and expect great things from you can block you. How can you bear—dare!—to disappoint mother, father, teacher, whomever?

With all of this against us, how can we ever believe in our work enough to do it with consistency and joy?

Suggestions for Living a Disciplined Writing Life

To be disciplined as a writer you need a compassionate and welcoming attitude toward your own work, and you need the support of others who value and call forth your writing. A huge part of leading a disciplined writing life is having other people in your life who care about your writing, want it, believe in it, and encourage it (more about that in Part II). Being a disciplined writer begins in your own mind.

BELIEF, NOT DISCIPLINE

After almost 50 years of writing and 25 years of helping other people write by leading creative writing workshops, I am convinced that the problem of discipline is lodged in the emotions, in a pattern of attitudes toward oneself and toward the idea of being a writer. The problem is not a flaw of character, not that I am just an undisciplined person. Often those suffering from a lack of what is called discipline in writing practice are incredibly disciplined in other aspects of life.

Rather frequently, a member of one of my weekly workshops shares with me the concern, I am not a disciplined writer. By that, he or she means that there is no writing happening between workshop sessions. "But look!" I answer. "You commit one evening every week to your writing. Give yourself credit—that is not an insignificant discipline! Let's talk about how to make the good discipline that you do have, larger."

Failure to be a "disciplined" writer—whatever you may mean by that—does not mean that you are not a "serious" writer. I truly despise the phrase "not a serious writer." Often the phrase is used by a critic or a teacher referring to a writer whose work they don't like, someone who has labored over a manuscript and offered it for publication, or paid money to take a course, rearranged his or her schedule, made a public statement by appearing in a room for a writing workshop. What in the world is meant by a "serious" writer? Anyone who cares enough to take a course or a workshop is *serious*. There is no place for this kind of arrogance. The *desire* to write is serious.

Claire MacMaster came from the coast of Massachusetts, a four-hour round-trip, to take my workshop for one day. As she wrote, it was clear that she was very discouraged about her writing, primarily because she had not been able to find others to read what she wrote and share their writing with her. She had hoped to join one of my weekly workshops, but at the end of the day she told me that she could not do that—it was unrealistic; the travel was too long. But in that one brief evening Claire wrote words I will never forget: "Take off your shoes and wrap yourself up in your thinking being and go write it out in the sand. . . . keep your hand moving or write with your toes—you are published until the tide comes in."

Claire is a serious writer.

How do serious writers—and we are all serious writers—keep going, keep working, keep writing, when the tide of disbelief, discouragement, loneliness, keeps coming in and coming in?

The problem is not discipline. It is belief.

ACCEPTING YOURSELF AS AN ARTIST

Accept yourself as an artist, and consider your task to be simply expressing what you see in your own voice. You don't have to prove anything to anybody. If your Auntie Matilda doesn't like your story, that's OK. If the editor of the *Atlantic Monthly* rejects your article for publication, that's OK too. You probably wouldn't like what Aunt Matilda reads, anyway. And if you are rejected by the *Atlantic Monthly,* you are in excellent company. You are an artist; you are becoming an ever more skilled and original writer.

Gordon Weaver declared, "A writer is one who writes; a serious writer is one who writes as well as he can as consistently as possible and for whom writing is the most serious activity he knows. How much money, fame, or publication he gets—these are extra-literary factors."

You are working at your craft; you are learning and practicing your art. You don't have to "succeed" in anyone else's eyes or perform according to anyone else's rules. Dismiss your internal committee of critics. Remember Joseph Campbell's statement: "Where there is a path it is someone else's way." Find your own path. Trust your own way.

MEETING YOUR NEEDS AS WRITER

Discipline begins by understanding how you yourself work. Everyone's patterns are different. You can learn something about how you work by remembering successes of the past. For example, when you accomplished a project—fixing your car, making a gift—how did you go about it? Did you lay careful plans first and proceed in an orderly way, cleaning up after yourself as you went along? Or did you barge in with more energy than planning, change your plans as you went along, decide to do a portion of it somewhat differently from the printed instructions?

When you did your best writing in school (regardless of the grade it received), how did you go about writing it? Did you write daily and finish it well before the deadline? Or were you one of those students who waited until the last two days, did without sleep, wrote around the clock, and turned in, nevertheless, a very good paper? Look at the way you worked when you did your *best* work.

When you have begun to identify your patterns, don't berate yourself because your patterns are not like someone else's. Be realistic about the way your best work is done and cooperate with yourself. If you like to get up early for the fresh, clear silence of dawn, make yourself coffee and go alone to your writing, then go to bed early enough to make that pattern possible. If you like to work far into the night, when even the birds are silent, then allow yourself to sleep late enough in the morning, or take an afternoon nap, or whatever it takes so you can stay up and write.

There are those who advise, "Write at least 30 minutes each day." There are those who say, "Write for many hours, but come out of it with only one or two pages." These directions are fine for some writers, but they are absurd when they are given as rules applicable to all writers.

I must block out time in segments of four or more hours at once, even if it means I can't do it every day. I need to go away to a private place at least twice a year where I talk to no one and work on a major project. Almost all of my published work has been finished on private writing retreats. Yet I have close friends who do their writing differently—daily, for shorter periods of time, at home, with family around. What kind of writer are you?

MAKING YOUR WRITING TIME A REWARD, NOT A DUTY

It is my deep conviction that true discipline is a matter of love, rather than duty. If you are in love, you make time and space for the beloved. That preparation is part of the joy. There is nothing of duty about it. I believe that people who truly want to write are in love with writing, in love with the artist inside, in love with creating. That love is the root source of true discipline.

Rather than thinking of going to your writing desk as the "ought" and "should" work of your life, think of it as a longed-for pleasure, as a hot fudge sundae, as that which pleases you, delights you, that which you love. Writers talk about writing as a compulsion, as unavoidable, even as an addiction. Let it work for you, that desire to write. Let it be the joy, the bliss, the call, the vocation.

At the end of her novel *Raw Silk*, Janet Burroway has this paragraph, spoken by a woman. I think a similar statement would be as true for many men:

> Of the three great options for fulfillment open to a woman, work and motherhood and ecstatic love, I have work left. The thing I have left is design, I haven't given that away. And I am going to approach that, work, from a new perspective. . . . There will be space, flight, and a flow of convoluted rivers.

Marge Piercy has written, "I belong to nothing but my work carried like a prayer rug on my back." How do we *do* this? It is a matter of love. If I am an artist, I have a vocation. As one drawn to a lover or called to a religious mission, I go to my work—my writing—because it is essential to my happiness.

CONFRONTING THE HARD TIMES HEAD ON

"Writing is bull labor," one of my writing teachers said. What about the times when you hate the very thing you love? What about the times when you want to quit, take up farming or ditchdigging or basket weaving? What if you decide you don't want to do it anymore?

Well, quit. Quit if you can. Entirely, I mean. Give it up. Find another art form. If it is more than you can bear, don't bear it. Sometimes even a great love ends in divorce.

But if you can't quit, keep on. Love is deeper than hate. Anyone who has lived in a longtime relationship knows the truth of that statement. The harder it is, the deeper it carves you, the more love you have.

Whatever you do, don't stay in the never-never land of wanting and not doing. It will make your soul sick. If you want to write, claim for yourself what you need in order to learn, grow, practice. There is no other way to be an artist.

PUTTING YOUR WRITING FIRST

Recently, on a day when my own writing was going well, I wrote a poem and a letter and E-mailed it to my son Paul Schneider, whose first two books, *The Adirondacks: America's First Wilderness* and *The Enduring Shore: A History of Cape Cod, Martha's Vineyard, and Nantucket* have been well received. However, even the glowing full-page reviews his books have received in the *New York Times Book Review* do not prevent the awful days when writing just won't come, nor do they provide protection from the seduction of other commitments. Here is a portion of Paul's E-mail back to me:

> Sometimes I wish I felt driven to write, the way your poem and prose today both suggest. But most times I am quite glad that writing more often feels to me like something I do well and therefore, well, I do. I'm like a guy who inherited an empire his parents built out of vision and sweat, and who doesn't mind tending it and is appreciative of the good fortune of having inherited it, but feels often like it's not really his empire. It's just the hand he was dealt.
>
> Which is not to say that in the universe of hands, it's not a good one.
>
> Which is not to say that when those words fall into place, and the voice is there, and the line appears on the page and it sings, that it is not surprisingly good fun to be an emperor ordering and reordering the same twenty-six little subjects around the page. Or thirty subjects, I suppose, if you include the usual punctuation.
>
> There was at last enough snow here on the Vineyard to spend the morning yesterday sledding with Natty and the afternoon skiing with Thunder. "Every least twig. . ." it was like that. And I got myself tired nearly to the point of nausea, which passed and was followed by that other energy that leaves you

thrilled that God, or whoever, created far more body out of that dust than brain. It leaves you knowing that Descartes was only ten percent right, which is a good amount of rightness on an average day. But that on a day when there's snow, or waves, or a mountain, or a tree to cut, or dirt to dig, or a ball to hit, or a rock wall to repair, or a river to paddle, or a path, or no path, or several other things that have slipped my mind. . . . On those days, the dog and the six-year-old boy and the rock next to them are ninety percent right when they all say without saying out loud "I am, therefore I am."

My answer to Paul is, "You've got your priorities straight, Paul. When you were Natty's age, I was helping you take care of your pigeons—even though I was complaining to your father about never having time for my writing."

Jane Schneeloch wrote this one evening in my Amherst workshop:

WRITING TIME

I stop writing
to make a cup of coffee
to read the mail
to put a load of wash in
to play a game of solitaire
to water the African violet
to straighten out the piles on my desk
to pluck my eyebrows
to call my mother
to shorten a pair of slacks
to pay a bill
to look for a lost phone number
to check my email
to get another CD to play
to file my nails
to scan a picture of my cousin
to make lunch
to watch the news
to read a magazine
to put the wash in the dryer
to make a cup of tea
to take a nap
to put the laundry away
to shut off the computer
and wonder where
I will find time
to write great things.

Not only do our busy little activities and our more serious commitments nibble at our concentration. Other forms of artistic expression may distract us. It occurred to me one day that my mother was at heart an artist. She made quilts. She crocheted tablecloths. She made children's clothes and Christmas ornaments and embroidered wall hangings and intricate ornaments for the tree. Sometimes she wrote. A little bit. She did a lot of different things, a little bit. At the moment I recognized this about my mother, I myself was standing beside my sewing machine planning to piece a quilt—a project that would consume hundreds of hours of concentrated time.

Suddenly I saw that I had to make a choice. I said to myself, you can't have it all. You have little time after parenting four children—you cannot crochet and preserve jellies and bake bread and make quilts and also write. The other forms of personal expression are things I truly like to do, but that day I folded up the quilt pattern and scraps of cloth. I stopped making jelly; I gave up sewing forever. Because I wanted most to be a writer. I wanted to be an artist, and I knew I would have to be faithful to the practice of my art. I set up an office for myself in half a basement room and began (again) to write.

The achievement of the mature artist is a balanced life. We need the benediction of daily necessity: cleaning, preparing food, playing. Martin Buber's classic book *I and Thou* is the most eloquent statement I know of the truth that one cannot live all the time in the intensity of revelation. Ordinary life, after all, informs our writing, heals our spirits, and keeps us from going mad.

NEVER UNDERESTIMATE THE POWER OF SLEEP

Leading a disciplined writing life is not all about work. It is also about sleep. Entering and staying in the mysterious place where daydream meets night dream is important to the writing life. Our deepest writing, our genius, requires an engagement of the unconscious mind.

I had been blocked for two years at the exact middle of my first novel when it occurred to me to go away for one week, read without interruption the 150 pages I had completed, and sleep. It worked. On the third day I woke lying flat on my back with my manuscript on my belly and the end of the novel in my mind.

Sleep can be crucial to the completion of larger works, crucial to finding your way into (or back into) your writing when you are distant from it. When you are blocked or extremely scattered, busy in a life of making your living, fulfilling your obligations, sleep can be the *open sesame* back into your art. Whatever you may think of popular notions of giving one-self subliminal suggestions, or asking the mind to solve problems in sleep, there is some wisdom in acknowledging that the unconscious mind will either help or sabotage creative work. The unconscious mind will not be manipulated or coerced, but it must be *engaged* for your work to be all that it can be.

When you are exhausted, as after weeks or months of intense or scattered work, it takes three days and nights of sleep for the "tapes" in your head to slow down. By that, I mean the voices that go on and on in your mind: *Don't forget that memo that has to be typed tomorrow. Don't forget to pick up a new contact lens before the shop closes on Saturday. Golf on Sunday—will it rain? Why doesn't Doris leave the bastard?*

In religious retreat circles, there is talk of the "deep silence" that begins on the third day. The first time I went on a silent retreat, my purpose was not to write, but to gain spiritual renewal. I went to Dayspring, the retreat center of the Church of the Saviour in Washington, D.C. I was exhausted from work and the care of my children when I arrived at Dayspring. I had hardly unpacked the little bag of clothing that I would need for the three days and nights of retreat, when I lay down on the bed, gazed out the large window of my lovely little monastic cell into quiet woods, and fell asleep. A gentle bell called us to silent meals. By "silence," I learned, they did not mean absence of sound. They meant absence of conversation. When I heard the bell, I would get up and stagger to the dining room, eat wonderful food to the accompaniment of music or quiet readings, then go back to my solitary cell and fall asleep again. I slept most of the time (off and on, but more sleeping than waking) until the third day, when I woke up with a startled sense that something was different. There was silence *inside* me, as well as outside me. This may sound scary, but it isn't. It is peaceful like no other peace I have felt in my life. It feels like a new beginning, like the first line of a hymn from an old Presbyterian hymnal: "Morning has broken, like the first morning; blackbird has spoken, like the first bird . . ."

When I realized my first silent retreat was over and it seemed all I had done was sleep, I was upset. "I have missed the whole retreat!" I said in my conference with the retreat leader, a Catholic Sister.

"No, you haven't," she responded. "God can't communicate with you when you are exhausted. Your sleep *was* your retreat." She invited me to come back for an eight-day silent retreat and spoke about "entering the deep silence on the third day."

Eight days! I thought, aghast. I can't leave all my commitments at home for eight days! And besides, I didn't trust the idea of a "deep silence." I dismissed the idea, thinking everything—even religious retreats—has its own jargon. Deep silence! Huh!

But another part of me was aware of a deep sense of blessing and refreshment as I drove home from Dayspring. The next year, I tried a three-day retreat again, and the same thing happened. I slept through the whole thing and woke up on the third day full of a new energy only to use it driving back home. Finally I gathered my courage. The third year, I signed up for an eight-day retreat.

It was revolutionary. By that time, I was writing my first novel manuscript, a requirement for my MFA degree. Again I slept for three days and three nights, waking only to care for my body's needs. But this time, on the third day, when I wakened to a new sense of myself, I didn't have to go home. I still had five days, and there was within me a depth of solitude, a clarity, and a creative wellspring that was unlike anything I had ever experienced. I wrote on my novel in those days, much to the horror of the retreat leader when I told him with enthusiastic joy what good writing I felt I was doing. He was a thin, severe man—a Lebanese priest—not at all like the Sister who led the first retreat.

"What?" he said angrily. "You are not retreating! You are working!"

I pretended to be contrite, but I was full of too much joy for contrition to be real. It was none of his business. It was *my* retreat, and just as sleep had been the form the first three days took, so writing was the form the last five days took. God speaks to us in differing ways, if we rest enough to listen.

Sleep is one of the primary reasons that I recommend going away by yourself for a while. You need to be where you can go in and out of sleep, waking, dreaming, floating half between sleep and consciousness, but with a dedicated journey with a very specific purpose in mind: to get from where you are to the secret that lies at the heart of your writing. Do not make of sleep another "should" or "ought." Just allow sleep to come and go as a good friend, when it wants. Keep no schedule. Eat only when you are hungry. If you wake, read or walk, then welcome sleeping when it returns, and consciously desire the resting and sorting out of images in your mind, which will help you in your writing.

In most areas of the country there are special writing retreats. Often these are designed to share meals. I prefer the sort of place where I can have absolute solitude, prepare my own food, and have no conversation at all. You may get information on writers' retreats from Poets and Writers, 72 Spring Street, New York, NY 10012. For religious retreat centers, contact denominational headquarters or ask clergy in your area.

In the first three days of solitude I do not allow myself to do anything out of duty. I do exactly as I please: I read, sleep, walk along the shore or in the woods. I sleep, daydream, sleep, all the while knowing I am gently, gently going toward my writing. I cannot stress strongly enough how important I feel this is, especially when you are dealing with a block in your writing. It is wonderful; it is magical; it is an act of trust in your own subconscious to assist you when the conscious mind is too weary or too tangled with anxiety. And it works. Best of all, for me, is sleeping where I can hear the sound of surf. It is as if my mind is being washed clean of distractions and I am allowing myself to go into the ocean of my own unconscious, where I am connected to everything and everyone and anything is possible.

If one of the women in my workshop in the Chicopee housing project reads this, I can imagine her saying to herself, "Yeah, right! What privilege!" Life in an overcrowded project apartment makes solitude impossible. Even as a young mother in a middle-class home, I would probably have said, What luxury she is talking about! Days alone by the ocean! Sure! And where will I get child care and the money to rent a place like that? Now, looking back, I feel sad that I did not provide for myself regular times alone when I had young children. Our resources were very limited, it is true, but I could have persuaded my husband to take care of the children alone for some period of time (even though it was not the usual practice in the 1960s). I could have found some solitude if my own needs had seemed as important as I now know they were. The summer place of a friend, a tent in the woods, and a pad of lined paper, off-season rates at country inns, private rooms at religious retreat centers, bed-and-breakfast houses—there are many possibilities. What I lacked was belief in myself, in the importance of my writing, in my own gifts. I was unable to put my writing among my most important "other commitments." I was unable to insist that others in my life help me have time apart, time alone.

Dorothea Brande, in *Becoming a Writer*, counsels writers to first think about their writing while taking a walk, and then to rest before writing. She calls this "inducing the artistic coma."

> After a while—it may be twenty minutes, it may be an hour, it may be two—you will feel a definite impulse to rise, a kind of surge of energy. Obey it at once; you will be in a slightly somnambulistic state indifferent to everything

on earth except what you are about to write; dull to all the outer world but vividly alive to the world of your imagination. Get up and go to your paper or typewriter, and begin to write. The state you are in at that moment is the state an artist works in.

It is necessary to put to rest the voices in our minds that distract and block us. To go away alone is one of my patterns, my needs. I do not suggest that it is right for everyone, but there are habits and patterns that are right for you; only you can know what those are. Claim them, welcome them, cooperate with your own unconscious.

DEALING WITH YOUR ENVY

Two years after I completed my MFA in Creative Writing, I was in a conversation with the new head of the program, who told me that she had been asked to go to a university in another state to give a reading, but for personal reasons she was uncomfortable driving on thruways. I volunteered to drive her, and did so. After her reading, we were at the home of a well-known poet for a reception. I sat listening as 15 people sipped cocktails, looked at a collection of primitive masks on the walls, and talked about famous poets. They called them by their first names and gossiped about who was divorcing whom, who had died, who was suffering from cancer. I was a woman in my mid-forties. I still had children living at home, going to high school. I was not free to apply for a teaching position with my new MFA; my family was settled in Amherst. I had started a writing workshop independent of the university; it had grown to two workshops, and I had been loving my work, excited about it. Suddenly I saw myself as a nobody, as ridiculous. I felt great pain. I was the only person in the room who was an outsider to the gossip; I was just a chauffeur for one of the insiders.

When I came home, I talked with Walker Rumble, who at the time was coeditor of our new literary magazine, *Peregrine*. "Walker," I said, "I'll never make it. I'm kidding myself. I'm 47 years old, and I don't know anybody. Succeeding as a writer is not about how good a writer you are; it's all about connections. It's about who you know, and I don't even know how to play that game. I'll never make it."

Walker was thoughtful, quiet. He had been a professor of history and had left the academic world to work at a job that would give him time to write poetry. He was setting type in the back room of a local print shop.

After a moment he said slowly, "You have the respect of your own neighborhood. The corner grocer never asked for more."

There have been a few moments in my life when I have felt with a kind of cold shock that in an instant everything was changing, that the continental plates of my internal geography were undergoing a major shift. This was one of those moments. If I tried to make a cartoon of it, I would have a bolt of lightning splitting the sky and zapping me. Walker had spoken the exact truth, and in two sentences he turned me all the way around. What a lovely way to live! What a lovely way to think! Dickinson must have come to that: *I'm Nobody! Who are you? / Are you— Nobody—Too?*

Almost 20 years have passed since that afternoon on the steps of the building where I led my workshops. I have written. I have offered my work for publication. I have been proud when something was published, and disappointed when I get more than two rejection slips in any one day's mail. But when I am tempted to envy those who have more knowledge, reputation, acceptances, prizes than I, I repeat Walker's words like a mantra: After all, *I have the respect of my own neighborhood.*

Envy is a malicious demon. Cast it out by gently and tenderly returning to yourself.

DO NOT JUDGE YOUR WORK

"What one has written is not to be defended or valued, but abandoned: Others must decide significance and value," William Stafford said. It might well be printed on a three-by-five card above most writers' desks. (Only we might use the phrase "set free" rather than "abandoned.") When you have done all you can do, when you have written and revised and brought to your work the finest craft of which you are capable, your job is to let it go. It is like raising a child—the parent cannot hold on forever.

I know a woman who has been in many writing workshops over many years, always working on the same short story. Recently someone said to me, "I saw Lucille the other day. I haven't seen her for years. She's still working on the story about the moose." Steinbeck has a character who is building a boat like Lucille is writing a story. We all know the feeling of frustration in wanting our work to be more perfect than it is, but there comes a time when we must let it go. W. H. Auden once remarked that only four poems in any book he published were ever finished. All the rest, he said, he gave up on. After I had worked on a black gospel musical for two years in Maury Yeston's musical theater workshop at BMI in New York City, he told me it was time to consider it finished. "Send it out," he said. "Get to work on another project." It was good advice. Take your writing as far as you can take it, then send it out into the world. Let it go.

And yet, the final authority can never be someone else who is telling you how to write, or what to write, or whether you have done it well, or when the time has come for you to consider it finished. Listen to the reactions of others; learn from them. But the bottom line, the last word, is this: It is your art. You are the artist. You will be "disciplined" when you are free and in love with your art. Martha Graham, speaking to dancers, could have been speaking to any artist, any writer:

> There is a vitality, a life force, an energy, a quickening which is translated through you into action, and because there is only one of you in all time, this expression is unique. And if you block it, it will never exist.

WRITING HAS ITS SEASONS

It is important to understand that there are times when writing will lie fallow in you. Sometimes it is when a quiet work of restoration is going on. I have experienced it when I have grown tired of one genre, or have learned as much as I need to learn in one form of writing. Sometimes we need to change direction, and a time of quiet waiting can be important for the germinating of a new harvest.

Sometimes writing goes underground because life takes over. I have seen that happen when a woman is pregnant or a writer is taking a demanding trip. It happens for me after I finish a major book, and it happened when I lost two of my major loves in one six-month period—Sam, my only sibling, and Elizabeth, my mentor. In that time of grieving, after one death and before the second, I wrote the following journal entry:

> Perhaps I'm just tired of the stories that I mined for so many years—my childhood and its grief and terrors. Maybe I have learned what I needed to learn by writing those things over and over again. Maybe I've healed what was broken.
>
> Other than a short poem now and then written in workshop, I'm not wanting to write. It feels like a season of lying fallow. It feels good to sit in an inner silence and rest. I want to bake bread. I want to mend, to sew, to clean house.
>
> Writing, too, has its seasons. Right now I am a cornfield in November— blown clean by wind, short stuffly stalks in neat rows waiting for the transfor-

mation of snow. Then I will be glorious, symphonic, celestial, majestic under moonlight—not by doing anything, just by waiting. Standing still.

I have lived a long time. I know that writing will come again. I have buried my dead, and I am tending the dying. Now is the time to sit, to light candles, to know how precious life is, to cook rich winter stews and bake hearty breads. Now is the time to take out pictures of ancestors, find their recipes and cook the ones on pages smudged by many days of use—especially the ones marked "good" or "Aunt Hilda's favorite." It is important not to be too busy in the season of grief. Busyness can cloud the real work. It can be a mask to hide the self from the self. I know this mask very well, so well that I can mistake it for my own face.

Writing is an animal that lives in the soul. It must not be whipped into doing tricks. It is not a circus animal. It can be fierce, but it is not malevolent. It can be playful, but it is not without wisdom. Above all, it is wild. A wild animal has to sleep sometimes. This is a time of deep sleep for my writing.

The only problem with that argument is, I lifted the pen from the paper and found that I had been writing, and I liked what I had written.

WHEN ALL ELSE FAILS

All of the above is about the subjective, inner condition of the psyche, where I believe the problem of discipline hides. However, I must admit that there are times when I hit myself over the head with a big stick. When all of my subjective wisdom fails to get my attention, as sometimes it does, I have a gimmick for getting really tough on myself. It works, and like everything else, it works because it fits my particular personality.

I was the kind of student who waited until the last screaming minute to write a term paper, then stayed up all night and did an excellent job. I work well under pressure. Since I know that about myself, occasionally I play a trick on myself by setting up a deadline that functions for me like an old school assignment used to function. I write a letter to the editor of a literary magazine that I admire, or I call my agent in New York City, and promise a manuscript in a certain number of weeks. Then my pride and my unwillingness to fail becomes a strict and mean taskmaster. The manuscript I have promised talks to me: Give me time! Give me time! Look at the calendar! Give me time! Setting up a deadline for myself with someone whose opinion I value works because losing that person's respect is a serious threat. I have never yet failed to meet a deadline I myself have set up. A deadline works, however, only if I am going to suffer by not meeting it. Telling my best friend is not a deadline—she will love me whether I meet it or not.

Some writers use this technique in my workshops. They tell us when to expect a manuscript, and if it does not appear on schedule, we ask for it (lightly, teasingly) publicly and express disappointment if it is not forthcoming. Others say this would only cause them to feel blocked.

The secret to a disciplined writing life, in my opinion, is primarily a matter of respect for your own deepest instincts, habits, and personality. Go to your writing simply because you love to write. Know your own habits, and let them work to assist you.

4

Writing Practice: The Journal

Writing is an art form. Like all other art forms it requires practice. The act of writing is the only way to become a better writer, just as getting out onto the ice with skates fastened to your feet is the only way to become a better skater. One of the problems with assuming that only rare human beings are born with genius is that it does a disservice to those with great accomplishment, as well as to those who believe they just don't have "what it takes." Itzhak Perlman, the great violinist, said, "If I miss practice one day, I know it. If I miss practice two days, the critics know it. If I miss practice three days, everybody knows it."

There is genius in all of us. But in order to mature, genius needs a lifetime of dedicated practice. That's not the bad news—that's the good news. We are never finished, never done, never as good as we might become. That "never good enough" is the beating heart that drives the passion. The goal is to claim writing as our art form, and to accept ourselves as artists. For many of us, the writer's journal is the studio in which we do the hard, consistent work of practice of our craft, patient with ourselves, but diligent toward the accomplishment of improving and realizing our craft.

The Writer's Journal

When I was ten years old, I was given a five-year diary. It was one of those fat little books with an imitation leather cover and a tiny key. It had gold on the page edges, and letters in gold on the cover that said FIVE-YEAR

DIARY. Inside there were tiny spaces for writing each day—only enough to write perhaps ten words if your letters were small.

Recently, I figured out when I was given that diary, and by whom. It was a gift from my mother, a short time before she placed me and my younger brother in an orphanage. For more than 50 years I saved the diary, but never read it. Recently, when I passed 50, a series of events brought me to a place where I was ready to read the words I wrote when I was a little girl. Some of those words are coded. I am astonished that I remember what I meant, and what I did not say. Some of the entries are predictable notes of daily events in a child's life. Now it is important to me that my words kept spilling over the edges of the tiny spaces; I had more to say than the book required. *At age eleven, I was already a writer.* No matter how I may interpret the fact of my mother's abandonment, I am grateful "beyond any singing of it" (as the grandfather says in Maxwell Anderson's "Lost in the Stars") that she gave me myself as a writer; she saw ahead into my life and gave me a blank book to take with me.

bell hooks, too, recalls her girlhood five-year diary and grieves the loss of her early writings. She herself destroyed them because her words were suspect in her family of origin. In *remembered rapture*, she says:

> Diary keeping . . . has most assuredly been a writing act that intimately connects the art of expressing one's feelings on the written page with the construction of self and identity, with the effort to be fully self-actualized. This precious powerful sense of writing as a healing place where our souls can speak and unfold has been crucial to women's development of a counter-hegemonic experience of creativity within patriarchal culture. Significantly, diary writing has not been traditionally seen by literary scholars as subversive autobiography, as a form of authorship that challenges conventional notions about the primacy of confessional writing as mere documentation (for women most often a record of our sorrows). Yet in the many cases where such writing has enhanced our struggle to be self-defining it emerges as a narrative of resistance, as writing that enables us to experience both self-discovery and self-recovery.

hooks goes on with a fascinating discussion of diary keeping's being an acceptable form in society because it was not taken seriously as literature. Therefore, even as it was a vehicle for liberation, it also functioned, by being disposable, to maintain women's silence.

In generations before my own, of course, the keeping of diaries (journals) was considered an art form for both men and women. The journals of major religious leaders, such as Saint Augustine, Saint Patrick, Hildegard of Bingen, John Woolman, and John Wesley endure today as classics.

Most contemporary approaches to journal keeping stress personal therapy (Ira Progoff, *The Intensive Journal*). Some books on journal keeping emphasize daily recording of events as a way to write an autobiography for one's descendants. A writer's journal can be these things, but it can be more.

In his excellent book *Dream Work*, Jeremy Taylor encourages people to use all the available methods for dream interpretation because each has something to offer and none is sufficient alone. He says dreams are like holograms, with many sides, many simultaneous meanings. My approach to the writer's journal is similar. As writer/artist, your journal can be a daily diary of events, but it can also be your mulch, your seedbed, the womb of your art. It can be the safe place for writing first-draft material, for experimenting, for gathering and keeping impressions and information for future work.

As the sketchbook is to the artist, so the journal is to the writer. In the sketchbook, a finger does not have to be connected by a full body to a toe. Visual artists sketch, allowing themselves to draw bits and pieces, yet writers seem often to require of themselves that every word that drips off the pen must be Literature. Writers need a place where the single interesting line can lie dormant waiting for the novel that is germinating in it. In 1980 I sang a little ditty in my mind, wrote it in my journal, and for some reason it would not go away. *It was August of the year that Augie died. Marigolds and miracles bloomed side by side with horny-toads.* Now, I ask you: Who would think anything would come of that? But after three years of carrying it around in my head, one day I asked myself, Who is Augie? It was as if I had turned around in my mind and looked directly at something that had been at the periphery of consciousness. And there stood Augie. He was a veteran of the Korean War, a vagrant, a drifter who killed himself one day in the back room of a farmhouse. The farmhouse was the one in which my husband grew up; Augie was fiction. His story kept on coming until I had finished my second novel.

My journal is the seedbed for everything I write, the place where no judgment applies—not even my own. In order to write clearly, I have to think clearly. Working on my writing is, in a profound sense, working on myself. Everything I come to understand about myself is a deepening of the potential for my own writing, because it is an increase in wisdom, in understanding, and in the possibility of empathy, without which no writing can ever be great. My daughter, Laurel Schneider, said to me one day, "The distance you can take other people is the distance you have traveled yourself."

If you don't like the idea of keeping a journal, as my friend Sharleen Kapp does not, then do what she does—write all day every day, write on napkins in restaurants along with doodled pictures, write and don't call it a journal. James Thurber once said, "I never quite know when I'm writing. Sometimes my wife comes up to me at a party and says, 'Damn it, Thurber, stop writing.' She usually catches me in the middle of a paragraph."

In your journal, or whatever you call it, you don't have to be sensible, serious, subtle, or sophisticated. You can change your mind. Walt Whitman once said, "Do I contradict myself? Very well then I contradict myself."

Often, the blank book, notebook, or journal is the best place to work through your own feelings about your writing. Donna Bigelow, a writer new to my workshop, confessed that she was somewhat overwhelmed by the variety of exercises and the writings of others she was hearing around her. I suggested she write those feelings in her journal and invited her to share them with me:

> With every new suggestion, sharp images quicken my pulse—words anxious for display.
>
> I imagine them like brush strokes of a painter—simmering in the corners of some remote part of the mind—known to the painter long before they're seen and tangible to the world.
>
> How many stories and poems and paragraphs are lurking within me? Will they ever run out? How can I possibly ever hope to write down all that I need and want to say? The years spent without a pen as my friend. The happiness, fear, anger, hope and despair—silenced—unspoken—invalidated. Untold stacks of the unsaid, unwritten.
>
> I want all that isn't writing to become secondary to writing. I want my words to become real, my thoughts carved. I am impatient with all the other people I must be. I want to make up for time lost. I want to write pages about every image. Nothing else will satisfy me. Indulge in obsessive writing—indulge in my craft.

A journal is a safe place to name the fear of writing, to explore what is behind the fear, and to express the desire—or the need, or the passion— that brings the writer back again to the pen and the blank page.

Why Keep a Journal?

YOUR LIFE HAS SIGNIFICANCE

Remember my friend whose husband said, You sit there writing as if your life had some significance? Judith Moore titled an essay in the *Baltimore*

City Paper, "Save Your Life: Notes on the Value of Keeping a Diary." I like that. Keeping a journal is "saving a life."

Máire O'Donohoe attended my workshop in Berkeley, then invited me to Ireland to visit her in her Ursuline convent. It was a stunning invitation for me, a lapsed Protestant who had only been inside a Catholic church a few times in my life. It was like being invited into a foreign country within a foreign country. I accepted, and offered to lead a free writing workshop for the Sisters. Then terror set in. What in the world did I think I was doing? How in the world would I know how to lead them in anything?

As the time drew near, reality forced me to develop a plan. I figured out what those women and I have in common. I have a seminary education. I had been the wife of a clergyman, and although we had left the institutional church, much of that tradition still mattered to me. At last it came to me. The stories of Jesus and the women. We had that in common.

The workshop lasted five days. I read the old Biblical stories again. Every story about Jesus and a woman had to do with her liberation. Furthermore, they had specifically to do with affirming her *words*. I opened each of the five sessions with one of those stories and suggested that it was an invitation to be ourselves and express ourselves in our own words.

One other thing came to me to say, and it turned out to be important enough that I have said it many times in many other workshops. I told the Sisters to imagine themselves going back to the house where their great-great grandmother lived, and finding only a stone foundation. Move a stone, I said, and find a small sheaf of papers. On those pages your great-great grandmother has written in tiny letters. It isn't fancy writing. She's writing what your grandfather said when he came in to tell her that the potatoes had all rotted. She's writing about the baby that just died.

I let them have a moment to see the writing, to imagine the words. And then I asked, "Wouldn't that be a treasure?"

"Yes," they responded.

"Then so will your words be a treasure," I said, "if you tell the truth about your life. You, too, have that treasure. All of us—every person—has that treasure."

Your imaginings, your dreams, your writing—*your life*—no matter who you are—has significance. Denise Levertov said, "What would happen if one woman told the truth about her life? The world would split open."

JOURNAL WRITING IS PROBABLY CLOSEST
TO YOUR NATURAL SPEECH

A journal is a place free of editors, critics, teachers, and well-meaning but ruinous relatives and friends. In a journal, thought and feeling can come together without self-consciousness. The music, the voice, the root of true emotion in our writing is our everyday speech, and in the details of ordinary experience we have access to our most important stories.

Levertov writes, "Notebooks [are] perhaps the only sure and honest way a writer can stimulate his creativity—that is, find out that he has more to write than he thought, as distinct from forcing himself to write when he has nothing to say." It is in a journal that many writers for the first time take the risk of writing honestly.

YOU MAY CATCH YOURSELF AT
YOUR OWN BAD HABITS

Bad writing habits are boring. "Nice day today" becomes singularly uninteresting by the fourteenth day, and if you want to practice your writing, you may be moved to more concrete language. "I'll tell you how the sun rose—a ribbon at a time" begins Dickinson's evocation of one beautiful day.

IT HELPS YOU REMEMBER

A diary, a journal, saves the perception you have of this day as you are living it. The notes you take on the experience you are living can be incredibly valuable later, as you write a longer work. Frequently, I advise writers in my workshops who are going on a trip, or who are pregnant and overwhelmed by the work the body is doing, to relax the necessity of producing a finished work, but to keep notes on what is happening day by day. Later the one who travels will find incomparable help in notes that describe street corners, give the names of railroad stops, catch snippets of conversation overheard in restaurants. And the one who is pregnant will have internal monologue for a character who is going through a pregnancy.

Whether or not we have "saved our lives" in journals, everything we have experienced is recorded in our conscious or unconscious minds, and it is not too late to begin to write that rich material now.

YOUR STORY IS PART OF THE WORLD'S STORY

If you do not record your own story, your tiny bit of the history of the human race is lost. Most of us have no way of knowing whether our perceptions may be important to someone who later looks back and tries to understand.

Bob Burton was in my workshop at the Graduate Theological Union in Berkeley, California, in the winter of the fiftieth anniversary of Pearl Harbor. As a young man, he had been on one of the ships closest to Bikini Atoll when the first atomic bomb was detonated there. Bob's account of his experience is chilling:

> The TV commentary said, "America's most horrendous action. . . ." I'm guilty and bear some of the sins for what happened then. . . . Remembering back to 1946—
>
> We were steaming 7–12 miles off Bikini—the shipboard command came— "About face"—"Put your heads down"—"Cover your eyes with your forearms"—(Officers had special glasses to see the blast)
> —WHOMMmmm
> The command "About face"—
> The mushroom cloud—
> Wow!!!!
> Later—"Let's hit the beach, Gootch."
> "Ain't any Bikini Atoll left at all," he said.
> "Gootch, they wouldn't let us go ashore if there wasn't any beach."
> Broken beer bottles and dead fish—
> Coral Reef Shack Tavern gone—
> Had to clean up the beach before we could play baseball—
> Gootch bet a couple of beers he could throw a baseball across the atoll— stood ankle deep in water and threw—ball splashed at water's edge on other side—as easy as a flea could jump from skin to skin across the cloth material in a bikini bathing suit. . . .
> Brushed the sawdust off our warm beers—clicked the bottles together— Gootch offered the toast: "Here's looking up your old address"—
> "—Belch—"

In light of what we now know, Bob's words reveal to us the ignorance and terrible innocence of the young sailors and their officers whose special glasses were supposed to protect them from the terrible thing that was unleashed that day. In my mind, the image of a small group of sailors going off their ship to play baseball right after the first atomic blast is an unforgettable irony, and the voice of one young sailor is important as historical evidence and as warning. Kierkegaard said, "Life can only be understood backwards, but it must be lived forwards."

GOOD NEWS—YOU CAN USE IT LATER

I wrote significant portions of my book *Wake Up Laughing* in my journal first. Even experienced writers often do not understand that the journal contains the raw stuff of fiction, poetry, and nonfiction. In an essay in *The Writer on Her Work*, Janet Burroway writes about the period in her life when she was writing *Raw Silk*. An editor advised her to keep a journal for publication as she was writing the novel, and although she resisted, she ultimately did it.

> I kept the journal, knowing that I would not allow it to be published (it seemed to me like a perpetual cry, inarticulate and unattractive; Oh! oh! oh! arggh! save me! I can't stand it! on and on); whereas the fact that it had been suggested to me spoiled it as therapy, the kindly stranger over my shoulder seeing to my soft middle. It wasn't good. But I was able to use much of it later, when I was making again.

Among other things, your journal is a practice book. As you begin any exercise of writing practice, listen and watch for the invitation to linger, to stay with an image. Here are some exercises particularly appropriate for use in the journal.

Exercise: The Well

Ira Progoff, whose Intensive Journal Workshops and book *The Intensive Journal* have been helpful to many people, suggests this exercise. Imagine yourself looking down into a deep well. You are safe, comfortable, looking over the edge and down. You can see the surface of water far, far down. As you watch the water, allow images to rise to the surface and float there, then recede again below the surface as other images rise. Do this as long as you want, then write whatever comes to you.

Exercise: Clustering and Mapping

Gabriele Lusser Rico's book *Writing the Natural Way* has many suggestions for using clustering, mapping, charting, and diagramming techniques that she bases upon functions of the right and left sides of the brain. It is my experience in teaching writing that these techniques evoke strong responses:

Some writers find them enormously helpful and other writers respond quite negatively. I suggest that you give them a serious try, using the sort of pattern in the figure below. Janet Burroway, in *Writing Fiction: A Guide to Narrative Craft*, recommends this technique, saying that it will "allow you to create before you criticize, to do the essential play before the essential work."

Shahrzad Moshiri found the clustering and mapping exercise productive, writing about her experience growing up in Shiraz, Iran:

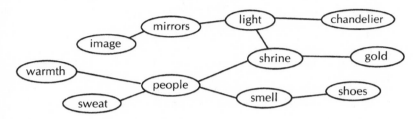

I took my shoes off and left them at the entrance to the shrine, at the top of the stairs with all the other shoes, old and new, hoping they would be there when I came back.

Shah Cheragh, The King of Light shrine, was my sanctuary; I put on a chadore and I was invisible, anonymous for hours. As I climbed up the stairs, the air was filled with the smell of rosewater with which the pilgrims had rubbed their faces and hands, and the musty sharp smell of dirty socks and sweaty bodies.

Many chambers opened off the main room where the body of the Blessed, wrapped in green silk cloth, was buried. The room was made of tiny rectangular mirrors, reflecting the light of the crystal chandeliers, hanging high from the ceilings. Images appeared and vanished in the broken light and faces became distorted, inhuman.

The tomb of the Blessed was surrounded by a chamber made of golden bars. I was engulfed in other peoples' bodies as I made my way around the room. The bars were cool and had the comfort of old and desperate kisses sealed on them by unknown pilgrims; I felt dizzy and comforted by the tide of human bodies pushing against my frame.

Exercise: Writing a Letter

Writing a letter—whether you send it or not—is an excellent way to work in your journal. It may be a letter to a relative, perhaps to one who has gone away or died—or perhaps to one you see every day. Or you might write a letter in another voice—the voice of an animal, or of an object.

Anne Fahy leads writing workshops in Athens, Georgia. She wrote the piece that follows in her workshop, after suggesting to her writers that they write "a letter of reference for a body part—your own, or another's."

To Whom It May Concern:

I am writing to sing praises and holler from tall buildings the remarkable qualifications of Annie's stomach. This soft round mound of flesh is well suited to any number of positions in your organization. This stomach has always stuck out of its own accord despite fashions (Twiggy, etc). It never fails to fill out a lap no matter how many sit-ups it endures.

I have been well acquainted with this stomach for over forty years and feel more than adequate to the task of elaborating some pertinent details. Approximately six inches up from the pubic bone you will find a well-proportioned well-placed navel. It is my delight to inform you that this belly button is free of distracting jewelry and while I know that you are an equal opportunity employer, you will be most rewarded to find that this umbilicus draws in rather than out.

Stretching at times to accommodate eight plus pound infants this abdomen has a healthy crop of stretch marks and a brand new shiny red incision across the bottom. This stomach brings with it the wisdom of many previous positions and it possesses a unique and hearty appetite. In summation I can think of no better applicant for your needs. Please do not hesitate to contact me if I can be of further assistance to your committee.

Yours truly,
Annie's Mouth

Exercise: List of Nouns

This is a favorite exercise of mine, suggested by Ray Bradbury in *Zen in the Art of Writing*. Make a list, as simple as Bradbury's list, of things you might write about someday. Not big, important things—just details that you might work into something. Let the list change all the time. Right now, today, if I were to make such a list, it would include the turtles and the cat pan.

Here's Ray Bradbury:

But all along through those years I began to make lists of titles, to put down long lines of nouns. These lists were the provocations, finally, that caused my better stuff to surface. I was feeling my way toward something honest, hidden under the trapdoor on the top of my skull.

The lists ran something like this: THE LAKE. THE NIGHT. THE CRICKETS. THE RAVINE. THE ATTIC. THE BASEMENT. THE TRAPDOOR.

. . . Well, if you are a writer, or would hope to be one, similar lists, dredged out of the lopside of your brain, might well help you discover *you*, even as I flopped around and finally found me.

I began to run through those lists, pick a noun, and then sit down to write a long prose-poem-essay on it.

Somewhere along about the middle of the page, or perhaps on the second page, the prose poem would turn into a story. Which is to say that a character suddenly appeared and said, "That's *me*," or "That's an idea *I like*." And the character would then finish the tale for me.

It began to be obvious that I was learning from my lists of nouns, and that I was further learning that my *characters* would do my work *for* me, if I let them alone, if I gave them their heads, which is to say, their fantasies, their frights.

Exercise: Other Uses of the List

If you are working with a character, make lists about the character in order to better understand him or her. What items are in your character's medicine cabinet? Pantry? Bottom drawer? If you feel stuck in your writing, try playfully making a list like "itemized expenses of a historical figure." Carol Edelstein wrote this:

VERY FIRST ITEMIZED EXPENSES

One rib (his).
Fifty-five kilos grass and leaves, mixed varieties.
Seven years burbling brook.
Two walking sticks (hickory).
Rice, wheat, potatoes, maize—as needed.
Three conversations with God.
The tailfeathers of a gray parrot.
Eighteen fire-pits, seven with ocean view.
Eleven watertight gourds.
Twenty-five thousand hours of birdsong.
Carrots, celery, onions.
Kiwi fruit, raspberries, grapes—as needed.
Forty bulbs garlic.
Three hundred peppercorns.
One apple.
Two fig leaves.
One gate.
One backward glance (hers).

Creating a simple list may be a "list poem" in itself, or it may provide the architecture for a longer work. Larry Fagin, in his book *The List Poem,* says lists are ideal for working with young writers. However, he offers examples of list poems by Milton, Whitman, Jarrell, and Ginsberg. He says:

> The list poem (sometimes called "catalog verse") . . . allows one to develop a heightened awareness of the creative process: details (exactness of observation and language), variety, variation, surprise, action, imagery, patterns of sound and rhythm, continuity and repetition.

Perhaps the most common use for the journal is the untangling of knots in the writer's own psyche. Carolyn Benson, who writes with me in my Thursday workshop and leads workshops for incarcerated women, wrote this list poem in which there is the story of a life, recorded in a simple list:

MUCH

Cinnamon drops.
Animal crackers.
Pennies.
Handfuls of sand.
Minnows.
Buttons in the button box.
Ants.
Stars.
Stairs at night.
Hairs.
Rain drops.
Snow flakes!
Steps to school.
Letters on the blackboard.
Numbers.
Children.
Kisses.
Records at the Hop.
Phone calls.
Book spines.
Chapters.
Reams of paper.
Tears.
Wedding guests.
Hours in bed.
Thank you notes.
Diapers.
Pick-up bends.
Nose wipes.
Fingernails.
Parent nights.

Grocery bags.
Laundry quarters.
Body aches.
Cocktail parties.
Telephone calls.
Words.
Worries.
Tearful prayers.
Sit ups.
Hours of therapy.
Secrets.
New ideas.
Worries.
Joys.
Breaths.
Meals.
Rides.
Miles—
I am rich.

Exercise: Drawing What You Can't Write

When my daughter was in the fourth grade, her teacher called me in for a parent conference. She was very upset. She had asked the children to keep a journal, and Bethany had insisted on drawing in her journal, sometimes on the same pages where she was writing. The teacher forbade it, and Bethany complied obediently for a while, then erupted—into drawing a large toilet right in the middle of her journal writing.

When I saw the toilet, I couldn't help it—I laughed out loud. The teacher was noticeably offended. I apologized for laughing, but said I thought drawing and writing were both ways that Bethany uses to find out what she feels, what she wants to say. The teacher cried out in disbelief, pointed to the drawing of the toilet, and snapped, "Well, what in the world do you think *this* means?"

"It means she was a very angry little girl," I answered.

Later I learned that Flannery O'Connor worked at drawing, not in order to become a visual artist, but to train herself to see more clearly in order that she might write more clearly. What Bethany could not say, she could draw. Use your journal freely: Draw, doodle, paste—write.

5

Writing Practice: Developing Craft

As artists, we must not underestimate the importance of conscious and continuous work to master our craft. Here are a few basic suggestions that I find most commonly needed by writers who are beginning or returning to their vocation as writer.

Practice Using Concrete, Specific Language

Our writing is most powerful when it is most concrete. In the piece that follows, Myra South could have simply said, "The herb gardens are bountiful." How much more we are given by being allowed to taste, see, and touch!

A couple weeks ago I picked bunches of sweet basil. We ate many leaves wrapped around yellow pear tomatoes we'd also grown. Basil leaves were also delicious on wheat crackers spread with gorgonzola. Or wrapped around black olives. Or in frittatas with onions and red bell peppers.

I really did go to Viviano's on The Hill and get loads of pine nuts and lovely grated cheeses to make pesto. We have plenty of good olive oil on hand. I made a few fresh tomato sauces chock full of basil, yet I still had two big bunches in vases, one a heavy crock, the other a frosted white glass. The blossoms were turning brown, but the leaves still held their bright green color. They've been so lovely I hated to think about picking the last leaves off to make the pesto, but the time has come. So I went to put fresh water in the containers and just happened to lift the basil up to see if the stems had with-ered to ugly brown. What a nice surprise!

Every stem has sent out roots and is ready to be potted up!!! There will hopefully be some little basil plants to grace the windows, counters and lit spaces around the house this winter. I'm hoping fresh basil will be available, even in small nibbling quantities to fight the winter blahs later on. I'll quit feeling guilty about taking my time to get to the pesto making and celebrate the life that continues, even in the care of an absent-minded yet loving gardener.

Besides, with all the rain and warm weather, I've a whole new batch of basil to harvest tomorrow.

Writing in all forms is setting a stage for the experience of the reader. Take the reader in close. Advertising firms know this: If you want to communicate to me the fact that millions of people are starving in Africa, you do not create great sheets of statistics. You show me one child hold-ing an empty bowl, his skin gray and tight over his distended belly, flies crawling on the rims of his eyelids. I see one child, and I grasp famine.

Exercise: Show, Don't Tell

F. Scott Fitzgerald warned, "Start out with an individual and you have created a type—start out with a type and you have created nothing." In other words, the *particular* is universal. Practice writing about a character you do not yet know well. Write to discover who the character is. Take your time. Georgia O'Keefe said, "Nobody sees a flower, really—it is so small—we haven't time, and to see takes time."

Make a list of characteristics such as "pompous," "nervous," "happy"—and see if you can embody those characteristics in writing that does not name the characteristic. Use description and show the characteristic in the character's body posture, gesture, action.

Try writing with concrete images a poem or a scene that does not name any emotional state, feeling, or interpretation, but reveals some-thing beyond the images themselves. You might describe a house from the point of view of a young couple just about to buy it, then describe the same house from the point of view of a man whose wife left him in a bitter divorce involving the ownership of the house. Then try describing the same house from the point of view of a young woman whose grand-mother used to live in that house. How do the windows, the doors, the paint, the gardens, differ in each piece?

Sometimes the meanings of our work are somewhat hidden in the images. In that case, the reader has the double pleasure of a first reading, and the even deeper pleasure of second and third readings where more is revealed. The poem that follows is that sort of piece. It was written by Peter Schneider in Kathy Dunn's workshop.

AT SEVENTY

I have forgotten
The face of my mother
The brow of my father
The hands of a country doctor

I have forgotten
The fright of a pheasant
The call of a Canada goose
The color of a red fox

I remember you
The one who held me
The one who heard me
The one who healed my broken bones

I remember you
Flutter of escaping wings
V-formation against a Wisconsin sky
Sly timidity along a line fence

The writer of this poem seems simply to list concrete images. But what is it really about? Memory and forgetting, or something more subtle, more elusive? The last line is like a prism; it gives off light in many directions. In five words it summarizes the tentative quality of the entire poem; the fragility (timidity) of memory, and a sense of boundary (fence) that we might at first think is the meaning of the entire poem. But there is that word "sly." It carries a barest hint of humor—slyly. Perhaps the fox will make it through the fence, all the way home; perhaps that which is forgotten in stanzas one and two is actually more deeply remembered in stanzas three and four. The poem plays back and forth on itself. Perhaps the poem is about aging, and death, and a sly "flutter of escaping wings" that may go beyond any fence.

The unconscious offers up brilliant metaphor and juxtaposed meanings, often surprising the writer. The writer of the poem above, reading what I saw in it, responded, "Wow! I didn't know all that was in there!" Many people read the famous lines at the end of Robert Frost's "Stopping by Woods on A Snowy Evening": *And miles to go before I sleep, / And miles to go before I sleep* as referring to approaching death. Not so, Frost insisted. "It's just about stopping by woods on a snowy evening!"

Practice Using Details

Remember that Nabokov said, "Caress the divine details." Here are some suggestions:

USE SURPRISING "CLOSE-UP" DETAILS TO DESCRIBE CHARACTERS

If I tell you my character has gray hair, you will not see her. If I tell you she has a tiny scar at the upper left corner of her lip from which protrudes one gray whisker—you will make up the rest of her face with absolute clarity. If I tell you my character is waiting in a car, you won't be "caught," but if I tell you he pushes his fingers down in the crack of the seat where the ancient leather has pulled away from the seat frame, and pulls up a small coin purse with a folded note in it—you will be mine. Try writing a description of these three: a man lifting a bottle of cold beer to his lips; a ten-year-old who has just returned from school on a hot day; a woman waiting in the rain for a city bus. Make each description so clear, so specific, it could be no other person in the world.

USE CONCRETE DETAILS TO DESCRIBE OBJECTS OR PLACES

If I tell you the bedspread is green, you will not care very much. If I tell you the green is as vivid as a lime gumdrop and the blue is as deep as antique blue glass; if I tell you that the spread has been chewed by a small animal in one place on one side, but that's OK because it's reversible, with blue predominant on the chewed side, green predominant on the unchewed side; if I tell you it is one hundred percent Italian wool and that my character bought it at a tag sale for a few dollars on her way home from filing for a divorce—if I tell you these things, I have set the scene for you as reader to have some feelings of your own.

Exercise: The Room

Describe a motel room in a way that tells us about the characters who have rented it. Describe a bathroom in details that cause us to feel fear. Describe a kitchen in details that make us laugh. Describe a bedroom without knowing what emotion you want to evoke—just use very concrete details and allow the feeling in the story or the poem to come to you from those details. "A bar" isn't half as interesting as "Jacob's Joint." "A hospital" is not as interesting as "Boston Lying-In Hospital" or even "Massachusetts General." It doesn't matter whether I've been there; the name helps me to create the place. Readers like to be cocreators with the writer. If you give them a fuzzy generality, they can't focus and allow the rest to emerge from their own imaginations.

Exercise: The Town

Write using a town name to get started. Use specific names. "A small town" will not show itself to me as clearly as will "White River Junction," "Mansfield," or "Platt's Corner." Use real street names and store names, and go wherever the writing takes you. Let form be "the shape of content"—let the piece tell you as you write whether it wants to be a poem, a story, or something else entirely. This exercise is suggested by Richard Hugo's book *The Triggering Town.*

Practice Various Forms

With a simple change from direct past tense to present tense, a narrative may become more immediate, more imbued with dramatic tension. Changing from first person to third person may give you slight distance, a different perspective, an altered awareness.

Exercise: Experimenting with Form

An excellent writing practice is to take a straightforward, first-person, autobiographical narrative that you have already written (perhaps a brief vignette or straightforward diary entry from your journal) and play with it—change it as I have done with the following little scene:

The Autobiographical Note

"I went to the post office this morning, got distracted, ate a bagel, and read the *NY Times*. Should have been writing."

Third Person, Past Tense

"The woman started to the post office. Her intentions were good, but there was a bagel shop on the corner, and the door opened just as she approached. The smell that wafted out was fresh cinnamon-raisin . . ."

Third Person, Present Tense

"The woman starts to the post office. Her intentions are pure—she will go straight to the P.O. and straight back to her writing. The walk will do her good. She walks briskly to the corner, past the flower shop and the hair salon, but slows just a bit when she sees the sign: Bagels."

Second Person, Present Tense

"You pick up the mail from your desk, check the postage on three letters and one wrapped birthday gift for Paul. Yep. All okay. You put on your gray sweater, grab your billfold, and head out. It's a perfect day. You'll come right back and write. But—there's the bagel shop . . ."

Dialogue without a Narrator
(as in a scene from a play)

"I went to the post office this morning."

"Yes, you damned fool. And then you bought the *New York Times* and went to the Classé Café and ate a bagel."

"So?"

"You should have been writing on your book."

"I need my exercise! Dr. Chandran said if I don't walk I'll get osteoporosis!"

(Sneering) "And I suppose Dr. Chandran told you to eat that cinnamon-raisin bagel slathered with cream cheese too?"

"Bug off!"

"Write!"

"All right, already!"

Fictionalize the Character
(third person, past tense again)

"Anna walked to the post office. The day was gray; the world was gray. She passed the Classé Café, but even the smell of cinnamon and hot coffee did not tempt her. There was too much to remember; there was too much John. She heard again the cold intimation in his voice just before he closed the door. Well, she would say it before he did. She sat at her desk, took out a sheet of paper and a pen. 'Dear John . . .'"

Try Iambic Pentameter
(five feet [beats] to every line)

Early morning and a walk to town.
Love is lost and lovers wonder why
Letters last while love and lovers die.
Leaves on Main Street slowly turn to brown.

Practice Using Dialogue

As mentioned earlier, the dialogue form may be fruitful when applied to an image in a dream or undertaken with a person (living or dead) with whom you have an unresolved relationship. Once a writer in my work-shop wrote a dialogue between herself and the man she was engaged to marry who had died in combat years before. The dialogue began, "Why did you never write to me?" She wrote the question, and immediately an answer popped into her mind. "Because I write lousy letters, and I was so afraid of losing you." The answer was surprising, but she kept on with the dialogue and what emerged satisfied her. It doesn't matter, in my opinion, whether the answer came from her own unconscious or from beyond this physical life; the result was compelling writing. What began as an exercise in a writer's journal may well become an internal monologue in the mind of a character in a short story.

A dialogue doesn't have to be with a person at all; it can be with an animal, with an object, with the weather, with one's own body, with a figure in a dream. It can be with yourself—with two or more inner voices. Virginia Woolf considered a biography complete if it covered only "six or seven of the thousand personalities" that make up a person.

Exercise: Writing a Dialogue

People frequently tell me that they can't write dialogue. I don't believe it. We talk it all the time. When we are not talking it, we are listening to it— in our own heads, if not from the mouths of those around us. Only our self-consciousness gets in the way. A good way to start practicing writing dialogue is to write a fight between yourself and someone who really makes you angry. Perhaps a sibling or an estranged lover. Start off with a provocative statement, like "It really pisses me off when you . . ." Or, remembering the past, "You used my toothbrush, you little creep!" Then listen! What does the impossible other or the "little creep" answer?

What you need most, to write good dialogue, is one line that would make someone else want to answer. A provocative line. Kids are great at this—every sibling knows exactly what to say to make a brother or a sister mad. ("I saw you do it, and I'm gonna tell!") Get one provocative line onto the page and then listen for the answer. It will come. Write fast, write honestly. Let it go wherever it wants to go.

The voices you know best are those you heard as a child around your own kitchen table. Try writing in the voice of your mother, your father, a sibling. An interesting exercise for writing practice is to write a remembered incident in the voice of your mother, and then have your father begin with a response like, Oh, it wasn't like that at all, dear! (Would he have said dear? If not, what would he have said?) and tell the same incident in his voice. Ken Macrorie, in *Telling Writing*, relates a funny incident of a student who came to him complaining that he couldn't write angry dialogue. Macrorie suggested that he come up behind his father as he sits reading the newspaper, pour a glass of cold water on his father's head, and observe what the father says. According to Macrorie, the young writer then wrote excellent angry dialogue.

I am not suggesting you try anything that dangerous, but Macrorie has made his point. We practice dialogue by first *listening* and then capturing what people really do when they speak. There's a funny example in the exercise titled "Eavesdropping" of a dialogue between two construction workers in a Burger King restaurant, overheard and captured by the writer as she ate her burger and fries. Also, there is an excellent group exercise titled "Writing Dialogue" in Part III. If you write with a group, it is a humorous and painless way to break down reserve at writing dialogue.

WRITE A DIALOGUE BETWEEN YOURSELF AND
SOMEONE WHO IS NO LONGER IN YOUR LIFE

Ira Progoff suggests that before writing this dialogue, you make a list of what he calls "Stepping Stones"—a list of events in the life of someone who is significant to you, for example, your mother. List one major event for each five years of her life. Immediately after making that list, write a dialogue with your mother. Listing life events is helpful, because it moves the person (your mother) somewhat out of the mother in your mind into the actual context of her own life before you enter into a dialogue with her.

A friend did this exercise, writing to her dead grandmother. She asked, Grandma, why didn't you ever love me? After writing the question, she sat silently, listening until an "answer" rose up within her: Before you were born there was another grandchild who died, whom I loved completely. When you came along I was afraid to love you; I didn't think I could bear it if I lost you.

It is possible to do this exercise with a character who is giving you trouble in a piece of fiction. You may get answers you don't expect, answers that will deliciously complicate your character and therefore deepen your story.

WRITE A DIALOGUE BETWEEN A CHARACTER YOU ARE WRITING ABOUT, AND
HIS OR HER LOVER . . . OR MOTHER, OR SISTER, OR FATHER, OR WRITE A
DIALOGUE BETWEEN YOURSELF AND YOURSELF

Jim Eagan is a carpenter and therapist as well as a writer. He suggests writing a dialogue between the self you are now and a former self. For me, this might be myself as I am now and myself as a teenager, the sort of dialogue I actually wrote in my play *Berries Red*. For Jim, I suspect it would be a dialogue between himself now and himself in an earlier incarnation.

A fascinating way to do a dialogue with yourself is to write one voice of the dialogue with your right hand and the other half with your left hand. The dominant hand accesses one side of the brain, the recessive hand accesses the other side. According to the artist Paul Klee, "The left [hand] works differently from the right. It is not so deft, and for that reason sometimes of more use to you."

Charlene Ellis, who teaches creative writing at Vermont College, suggested this technique to me, and credits this exercise with changing her life. She had been very conflicted about whether or not to build a little cabin in the woods on some property she owned. For years she had dreamed of the cabin as a personal writing retreat, but there were always arguments against it. She set for herself the question, Do I want to build a cabin in which to write? The exercise convinced her that it was essential.

In the following example, Carol Edelstein allows this exercise to lead her into a short story:

WHEN THE LEFT HAND SPEAKS WITH THE RIGHT

already I forgot and wrote the date with my right hand

(already I forgot and wrote the date with my right hand)
You dummy. I'll take that. It's good to go fast and not keep up with my thoughts but at least be in the vicinity.

There is no vicinity like vanity

(There is no vicinity like vanity)
I'm already sick of helping you. You think you can be wise with your little aphorisms. "Amphora is no tobacco," you're probably about to say, like it's so profound.

the profound is in the pond

(the profound is in the pond)
I can agree with that, I thought of that myself. The pond we thought of, place where there was microscopic fresh water wriggling life, conjugation of the paramecia, and we could take turns looking at them through

your father's microscope, and without being embarrassed I could stand so close to you.

close to what. The self-jelly is everywhere. The mess of the left hand is always close.

(close to what. The self-jelly is everywhere. The mess of the left hand is always close.)

He was an ugly boy by some standards—fat, and with glasses so thick since age five his eyes were like the goldfish in the greenhouse tank, like he was lost in the slimy weeds where nobody could talk to anybody else because of a rule of atmosphere—a watery medium through which words could not pass, and even the shimmer of bodies was not language, and even the grasses moving in response was not language, so how could I love him?

But I said, "Wanna go with me? Be my partner?" because we were to be in pairs, and he did not seem grateful but said yes. Then it's all blank until we are crouched by the pond with a net and a jar, and happy to know that whatever we could catch we would not see yet, the jar would look empty except for the water and a bit of sludge nobody can help, but in there was the most obedient of God's creatures, multiplying, multiplying, because it was their only job.

Back up at the top of the house, where we were alone with the microscope and slides, in a little room where his mother kept her sewing machine and ironing board and a little untouchable wicker sofa that was piled high with fancy, creased tableware from an old occasion, I saw how soft his neck was near the collar and when he removed his glasses to look through the microscope, before he knew it would be better to keep them on, for a few seconds his face was all bare, and his eyes were small and given to me like good bright berries, the way a creature, dog or kitten, even our box turtle from Fitzgerald Lake before he went behind the sofa bed, could look and see I was not a girl at all but one of the shapes in the world, moving like the curtains, which were weighted at the bottom by what I liked to pretend were gold dubloons.

So I did not kiss his neck or touch his hair as I wanted to, but said, "Let me take a look . . . Can you see any?" and he said . . .

Carol's story goes on, having begun with the very internal act of writing a dialogue between her left and right hands.

Practice by Imitation

This is a controversial method for teaching oneself to write (see further discussion in Part I, Chapter 5), but I do think it is an excellent way to understand something of how another writer works at her or his craft. As a writing exercise, imitating another writer's style is nothing more than trying to walk a little way in the author's footsteps.

Ruth Whitman, author of eight books of poetry, has this to say in her essay "Climbing Jacob's Ladder," in an excellent anthology, *The Writer's Home Companion*, edited by Joan Bolker.

> There is nothing wrong with imitation. I have heard students say that they don't want to read other poets because they might begin to write like them. But it is only by writing like the masters—as an exercise for yourself, as an experiment to find out what you can learn from them—that you will begin to expand your own possibilities. It is even valuable to retype a poem—for instance, a sonnet of Shakespeare's—in order to examine closely how the poet orders his words, how he turns his line, what he does with rhyme. Later, as you develop your own style, you will find that you learned something useful from everyone you have imitated, that you learned something that you will eventually absorb and digest into your own work.

Similarly, John Gardner suggests to writers of fiction, "Perhaps even type out a masterpiece such as James Joyce's 'The Dead.'" He also says, and I agree, "But as a rule, the more closely one looks at the writer one admires, the more clearly one sees that his way can never be one's own." That seeing is a help in seeing what one's own way will be.

You might write a ballad—take as your model for imitation or study a familiar old song:

> Frankie and Johnny were sweethearts
> And oh, Lordy how they could love!
> They were true to each other,
> As true as the stars above—
> He was her man, but he done her wrong!

Imitation will force you to look closely at craft. For example, in "Frankie and Johnny," you might note the internal near-rhyme (the repetition of "o" sounds in line two, and "oo" sounds in line three) the exact end-rhyme on lines two and four, with the near-rhyme in the "oth" of line three, and so forth. You may learn about using rhyme, near-rhyme, particular stanza forms, and such matters, by this kind of literal following of existing forms, whether you are imitating an existing poem or working from directions in a book of poem forms, such as Miller Williams's *Patterns of Poetry.*

Exercise: Trying Imitation

Take a stanza or a paragraph by a favorite contemporary writer—perhaps a story by Grace Paley or a poem by Richard Wilbur—and try to write exactly in that form. Change the pronouns and the images, but keep the sentence length, the paragraph or line breaks, the rhythm. Then do the same with very different writers. Imitate a paragraph by Julio Cortazar, a poem by June Jordan.

Take the little chapter early in Steinbeck's *The Grapes of Wrath* that describes a turtle crossing a road, and change the turtle to a snake, a beetle, a water buffalo, a creature from another planet. Change the climate, change the kind of road. In Steinbeck's book, that tiny chapter can be seen as a metaphor for the entire book. Notice how the author does that—by trusting completely the power of concrete images. Let your imitation be so specific it could also mean more than the animal itself, without your having to say so.

Consider the chapter titled "Time Passes" in Virginia Woolf's *To the Lighthouse*, in which she accomplishes a huge shift in the book with a little chapter of pure description. Write a purely descriptive passage that means more than just the objects described.

An example of imitation of style is an exercise in Peter Elbow's *Writing with Power*. He suggests following the example of Wallace Stevens's "13 Ways of Looking at a Blackbird," in which Stevens writes 13 short verses giving different images of blackbirds. After writing 13 "tiny stanzas about [a] cherry tree," Elbow discovers:

> I see now that it is about missing the house on Percival Street where we used to live. . . . If I had tried to write a poem about missing that house, it probably would have been terrible. Being stuck with having to write tiny stanzas about the cherry tree did it for me.

I offered this exercise in workshop once when the moon was full outside my window and wrote this poem:

THE MOON. TEN TIMES.

1. O round, cool face of forever,
   float free
   for me

2. Saucer without a teacup
   without the tyranny
   of tea

3. Owl eye without a pupil
   blind
   to contradiction

4. My white balloon
   has lost its string
   and me

5. Round, open mouth
   of the goddess
   of light

6. The night sky's
   exclamation:
   Oh!

7. Puppeteer
   of tides,
   rock the shore of the world

8. Bright Frisbee
   the dog star lost
   in the night

9. Perfect pearl
   crown of cornfields
   and night watchmen's hair

10. Bellybutton
    of God

Above All, Practice Courage

Carolee Schneemann wrote in *More Than Meat Joy*, "Our best developments grow from works that initially strike us as 'too much.' . . . We persevere with that strange joy and agitation by which we sense unpredictable rewards from our relationship to them."

Remember that no one story or poem has to contain your whole truth. One of the things that interests me in Sharon Olds's poetry is how individual poems build perspective on each other. For example, in one poem in *The Gold Cell* she expresses anger toward her older sister, and she has reason. But in another poem in the same collection there is a beautiful acknowledgment that the older sister pushes first into the world, making a way for the younger sister. Trust yourself to tell all of the truth of each experience. Balance and compassion will come in their time.

Exercise: Being Brave

Write something that feels too huge, or too dangerous, to tell. Courage is not the special prerogative of those who have experienced some dramatic suffering. It is a part of the human condition, related to the danger and the suffering we all experience. Once a writer friend said, when she learned that I had been in an orphanage as a child, "Pat, you are so *lucky*! What hurt you is so clear and obvious!" She grew up in a proper home where church and community kept things in order. How do you find what went wrong, when the table is set with silver and the candles burn and everything is so proper? It takes courage—perhaps more than for those of us who have dramatic material in our background.

We may not know the exact features of the ghosts that haunt us, but we know the general turf where they hide. Remember Auden's directive: *Follow poet, follow right / To the bottom of the night.* Go for it. But don't try to write all of it, if it is large—and don't worry about being "fair." Write as if you were working on a quilt—just one block at a time, or maybe even just a single piece of what will become a block. What you write today may be a scarlet fragment. Another day you may write something that is cool ivory, and it will go beside the scarlet to make the block. The block will go with other blocks to make the entire pattern.

The following prose poem is by Frances Cohen, who wrote it in a workshop for public school teachers that I led at the University of Connecticut's Writing Center.

> Not very many years after the war had ended, a box arrived in our kitchen. My father took it from the mailman, who'd come to deliver this intriguing, giant box, come all the way from Italy. When my mother came into the kitchen to see what all the commotion was about and spied the box, her eyes vanished inside themselves, her face changed to ashes, her body stiffened and, like a mechanical doll in a slow motion film on rewind, she slowly began to back

out of the room. She thought someone had remembered us, or discovered us, and was sending her stuff that might have been her grandmother's. It wasn't.

We children eagerly clambered around in excited curiosity as my dad ripped open the box. It was filled with mountains of yellow-white straw lovingly wrapping a bunch of very old pieces of dirty, smelly, little bitty paintings and statuettes and other assorted, boring, junky *objets d'art.*

Nina, of the crayon-red hair and the serious-big-sister face, the antiques dealer who lived next door . . . to us, had wanted to avoid the import tax imposed on purchases abroad. No such tax was imposed on articles unearthed in the war rubble and sent to their rightful owners or to relatives as gifts, and she didn't think we'd mind if she made us her "relatives" for a while. She'd sailed over to Italy to find and revisit her real relatives and go antiquing to fill up her little shop.

So she sent us the box. The letter explaining didn't arrive 'til long after, long after my mom went shrieking and screaming and crying no, noo, NO! Out of the kitchen, away from my dad, away from us, away from the box! WHAT is so horrible about being Jewish that you can't tell me who I am?

In the best of all possible writing worlds, a writer has a community of supportive friends who evoke and respond to our work in ways that strengthen it and us. For every writer, however, writing practice (the first draft, the journal, the diary—or the gathered circle of writers) needs to be a safe place to write the soul's secrets and begin to heal some of the heart's wounds. Only then can it also be the womb where powerful writing is conceived.

When I led a workshop in Japan, a young woman named C. Misa Sugiura wrote the following poem in response to an exercise. It comes from the shame a child feels when ridiculed. Misa had attended elementary school in America.

> When I was little,
> people laughed at me
> and called me
> flatface.
> They pulled their eyes into
> slits
> and said,
> "Me Chinese!"
> and laughed.
>
> I didn't know my
> face was flat
> so I went home
> and looked in the mirror
> to see,
> but all I saw was my
> face.
> It wasn't flat,
> was it?

And I wasn't Chinese,
but I looked in the mirror anyway
and my eyes looked like
eyes.
Didn't they?

So I went to school
and said, "I'm Japanese and
my face
is like yours,
isn't it?

And they said,
No.
It isn't!
It's flat like a pancake.
Me Japanese pancake-face!
And they laughed.

And I went home again
and I looked in the mirror
and I cried because
they were right.

To write this kind of experience so honestly is simultaneously to create a work of art and move toward personal healing. Writing heals the writer, and when it is brave and true it may heal the reader.

That kind of work takes great personal courage. Misa's poem invites us to go all the way into the experience of a young girl caught in cultural difference and peer cruelty. She does not—even at the end—"fix it" for us. The child internalizes the taunts of her tormenters, and the reader is left with the hurt—the child's acceptance of their cruel appraisal. Misa reveals the mind of the child; she does not analyze, interpret, or argue. And it works!

Often in workshop, a writer will preface a particularly brave piece of writing with the disclaimer, This doesn't work, or, I really hate this piece. It is my experience that a writer who is using painful memories in written work often does not immediately distinguish between the work itself and what the writer has to see in order to do the writing. What is really "hated" is the pain of looking again at troubling images. I have come to expect that a piece hated by the writer may in fact be unusually powerful for the reader/ listener. In Amherst Writers & Artists workshops we treat all written work as fiction, unless the writer specifically asks us to respond to it as autobiography. By doing so, we assist the artistic practice of the writer. There is further discussion of this and other workshop practices in Part II.

Voice

You must trust your own voice. You cannot write in the voice of various characters until you accept and trust your own voice. Writers often ask me, "How do I find my voice?" It is a sad question—as sad as if the question were, "How do I find my face?" The answer is so clear, so transparent, we can easily miss it altogether. Listen. Listen to yourself. Listen to your own voice telling your own stories to the listener you most trust—to your best friend, to your lover, to someone with whom you relax, or perhaps to your siblings in a session of "remember when." You have a voice, just as surely as you have a face, and it is already full of character, passionate and nuanced and beautiful.

Finding Your Own Voice(s)

Everyone has at least one voice; most of us have several. I suggest we have an Original Voice, a Primary Voice, and any number of Acquired Voices.

Your *original* voice is the one you first learned; the one you still use, or partially use, when you talk to the people with whom you lived as a little child. Your *primary* voice is the one you use when you are at home, relaxed, talking to those with whom you live as an adult. Peter Elbow calls these voices our "mother tongue."

My *original* voice is country, 1930s Ozark heartland.

My *primary* voice grew up in St. Louis where high school English teachers took most of the country out of my speech. It lived for some years of graduate school in California and settled down in Massachusetts. It is my everyday adult voice.

I also have *acquired* voices, professional and academic, that I use when I give a formal presentation or speech. And there are the playful voices I take on with my grandchildren or laughing with the women in my Chicopee workshop who do street talk brilliantly and make me want to do it too.

My children tease me because no matter where I am, or who I'm addressing, there are a few words that still come out of my mouth in my original Ozark pronunciation. I no longer say a woman *warshes* and *rinches* the clothes, nor do I pronounce "eagle" "iggle"—but I still ask my granddaughter, Sarah, "Wouldja like a glass of myelk?" As they laugh at me, I have a flash of myself at a country farmhouse table, my own grandmother saying to me, "Wouldja like some goat's myelk, Patsy?" I refuse to let that pronunciation go. It is my own first voice, my "mother tongue"; it is my treasure. It is what I know by heart.

We have too often been trained to distrust our original voices. When I was in college in Nashville, Tennessee, a speech teacher stood before a class of southern and midwestern young people and said that we must get rid of our regional speech and learn to speak what he called "general American." General speech—general writing—is as boring as any other generality. We know that to our great shame and loss as a culture, we have not respected the native languages of Indian nations, or the rich heritage of Black English. June Jordan, in her brilliant essay, "Nobody Mean More to Me Than You and the Future Life of Willie Jordan," says:

> Black English is not exactly a linguistic buffalo, but we should understand its status as an endangered species, as a perishing, irreplaceable system of community intelligence, or we should expect its extinction, and, along with that, the extinguishing of much that constitutes our own proud, and singular identity.

Amy Tan, in an essay titled "Mother Tongue," writes about the importance of claiming "all the Englishes I grew up with":

> I began to write stories using all the Englishes I grew up with: the English I spoke to my mother, which for lack of a better term might be described as "simple"; the English she used with me, which for lack of a better term might be described as "broken"; my translation of her Chinese, which could certainly be described as "watered down"; and what I imagined to be her translation of her Chinese if she could speak in perfect English, her internal language, and for that I sought to preserve the essence, but neither an English nor a Chinese structure. I wanted to capture what language ability tests can never reveal: her intent, her passion, her imagery, the rhythms of her speech and the nature of her thoughts.

Exercise: Using Your Own Original Voice

First, write a bit about each of your grandparents and each of your parents. Where did they come from? Can you remember any old sayings or delicious bits of dialogue, pronunciation, or vocabulary that remind you of them? Now write an intimate memory of childhood. Go into detail and "lean back" into that time. Allow the speech patterns of your own people to rise and spill out onto the page. Do this more than once. One time try it with some subject that is light and of no great consequence. I have found that some people fall into their original voice most easily with humor, or at least lightness. Another time, choose for your subject something that matters greatly to you. It has been my experience that many people break into their original voice when they write out of deep personal feeling, because they care so much about the subject that they forget to be afraid. In each case what you want is for self-consciousness to fall away in order that the voice may become true and strong.

Jay O'Callahan, the internationally beloved and honored storyteller, has attended my writing retreats and I have attended his storytelling retreats. He leads a writing workshop using this method, and I have incorporated things I have learned from Jay in my teaching. In the piece that follows, Jay writes in his original voice about an experience of boyhood, and incorporates both humor and a shadow under the humor:

"Patricia," Mother called, "Help me with the Newburg." Lots of words appeared for the parties. Chicken à la king, Thermidor, Newburg, hollandaise, aspic, chafing dish, punch bowl, crème de menthe, punch in the nose bowl, rose bowl, silver bowl, ice bucket, serving spoons, patty shells, scalloped potatoes, walloped potatoes, tumblers, long glasses, wine glasses, short glasses, eye glasses, china plates, minor plates, major plates, serving dish, pepper grinder, if you don't mind dear, scalloped oysters, nuns in cloisters, ironed napkins, shining silver, Hi Ho Silver, Where is my red vest? Gone west. Will you button me up dear? Where is my jacket? Is there beer dear? Bourbon, scotch and rye, don't want them drinking dye. Then they'll get too high. Remember the time when? Sigh. Is the stove still on? Darling will you see if I left the stove on? Newburg bubbling is troubling. Mustard bustard. Horseradish. Mint jelly for your belly. Mrs. Beam is coming? Hide the jelly. Patricia darling can you iron Daddy's shirt? Oak, get the wood and lay the fire and while you're at it fix the tire, paint the house and play the lyre. Cathy can you get the ice? Mom did you get kumquats? They come at Christmas. Well, it's almost Christmas. It's just October, now get the ice trays. Why are they called trays? Please dear, we have guests coming. Get the ice. Dippy's sick, Mom. Cathy, I hate that cat. It's not a cat, Mom, it's a kitty. Cathy please get the ice. What ice?

Patricia darling will you get the ice. Patricia is nice and gets the ice. Dad's
mad. He can't find. Where's my hairbrush? Who took my hairbrush? Cathy,
did you take my hairbrush? I brushed Rufus with it. Don't take my brush! She
brushed the confounded dog with my hairbrush. Everyone shush. Here dear
use mine dear. Avocado. Don't mind if I do. Did you dress the salad? I'd like to
dress myself first.

In my workshops I hear the most wonderful transformation of voice
as writers write images of their childhood. "General American" disappears, and the colors, the particular dialect of place, emerges: Boston,
Detroit, Chicago, Memphis, Oakland, New York City, New Orleans. In
some Latino writers, Spanish words creep in; in some African American
writers, Black English appears; in writers from other countries, other languages break through like flowers out of mulched soil. For many of us,
when we write intimately about our childhood, the vocabulary changes.
When I write about my childhood, I can't use the words of my primary or
acquired voices: "stone," "stream," or "firefly." Those words don't fit. I
need my original voice: "rock," "creek," "lightning bug."

Our original voice is the voice we learned and used as children and
still fall back into when someone "from home" hangs out with us for a
few days. Something precious has been stolen from us if our original,
"mother tongue"—our own dialect, vocabulary, and speech patterns—
has been bleached out of us. We are less colorful, less powerful, without
it. Grace Paley wrote, "If you say what's on your mind in the language
that comes to you from your parents and your street and friends you'll
probably say something beautiful."

Exercise: Using Your Primary Voice

The voice we use all day every day in our adult home and place of work,
I call the "primary" voice. It is the natural, unself-conscious way we talk
to the people we most love and with whom we are most comfortable. It
has taken on color and texture from every place we have lived, everyone
with whom we have lived, and all that we have experienced. It has traces
of our original voice—more or less depending on how much dialect or
regional color was in the speech of our childhood family and how far life
has taken us from that place.

Your primary voice has in it the colors, the rhythms, the peculiar into-
nations of your own generation. Try writing in that voice. It might come

easiest if you write to someone who naturally evokes that voice: your son or daughter, your spouse or partner, your best friend, someone you know professionally, some person with whom you talk about politics or your work or ideas that matter to you. If it seems difficult, it may be easier to write in the voice of a character who has a job similar to your own, and a name that you could live with if it were your name. I wrote my first novel that way—I wrote my own experiences, in my own voice, but told it in the voice of a character named "Anna." Try it—it just moves you over a bit, gives you a bit of distance, and allows you to write in your own primary voice.

More than anything else, my work among women in low-income housing projects has taught me that everyone has at least one strong, beautiful voice. By not valuing the voices of those whose education has been interrupted by the culture of poverty, we participate in silencing them. Then we don't have to hear what they might teach us.

The piece that follows was written by Diane Mercier, one of the writers in my workshop for low-income women in Chicopee, Massachusetts. Diane was born in the projects, lived for a time in an orphanage, and dropped out of school when she was 15 years old. She was a young mother with three children. Her first words to me were spoken as she stood in the doorway of the office where I was holding a free workshop for women in a building that stood in the shadow of the huge, abandoned mills along the river. She has given me permission to quote exactly the first words I heard her say, which were: "I'm mean. I'm a bitch. I can't write nothin'; I ain't gonna write nothin'!"

Something in me causes my heart to leap up in joy when someone throws down that sort of gauntlet. In my mind I cry out, Oh, yes, you are! *Get in here!* But of course I reassured her, "That's all right, you don't have to write. We're glad you're here. You can just listen if you want to."

Diane has one perfect voice for writing. No one can write that voice better, more brilliantly, more accurately than Diane. It is the voice of a woman caught—for now—in poverty in America. It has traces of North American Indian and French-Canadian immigrants in it; it has western Massachusetts mill town dialect in it. Using that voice with confidence and abandon is Diane's art form. This piece is by Diane. I have corrected only the spelling and punctuation.

WHAT KEEPS ME TICKING

What keeps me ticking? My Mom? I'm not sure. All my mind can think of is, how come you never say I love you, but you listen to my sister, but never to me? You always use bad language at me. I guess that's the only way you can say I love you. I ask you a simple question; you say get away.

I grow up quiet, shy, and stay to myself. People say come and visit. I don't bother. I had to learn about life on my own because you never wanted to talk about it: what would happen when I grew up, having a baby, having my own responsibility. Mom, I wish I could talk to you, but I'm afraid to even say a word to you. I can't even say I love you; only in my mind I can say, I love you. If only you knew, but something is holding me back. There is something, but I can't put it into words. There's a dark secret you're keeping from me, but I wish I knew. If only you knew that I have questions to ask you. But I don't dare, so I stay to myself.

My sister doesn't like me because I am me: a bitch. My brother doesn't like me, because I'm a bitch. They think I won't find them out, but other people talk. They hold it against me for going out with a black man, but it's me who has to live with him, not them. Maybe that's why I stay with him, to get even with them. They feel sorry for my daughters because they're half and half, half French and half Black Puerto Rican. They wish I would go out with my own kind. Keep wishing, People! I love him in some way. Everyone is the same inside and out. So what he treats me wrong? Sometimes he can be nice. Everyone has a different side to them.

My family thinks no one is better than them. If only they knew how I feel! Maybe they will never find out; I keep myself to me. I want to find out the dark side of me, what keeps me all closed up, what I want. I won't let people know me well, because I'm afraid people won't like me if they know the dark side. Maybe that's why it's taking long to find out what it is. I feel so sad, so I keep to myself, don't bother no one, so I can't get blamed for it. Life will go on. My daughters will grow up. Maybe I will be able to tell them; I hope so.

I can remember a lot, no one even has to tell me. I was this way, I can feel the way, I can picture myself there at school. I just stay to myself, people calling me names. If only they knew what made me this way. My Mom would never talk to me. She talked to my sister. If I stayed in my room, she never even bothered me. Also she would send me to the store. Whoopie! I get to go out! I always stayed in, never liked to go outside, afraid of people calling me names: "You're nasty looking!" or "You're too fat!" so I wouldn't eat. In the Job Corps, I wouldn't eat because my Mom wouldn't send me any money to come home.

Because my niece died at two, I almost sliced my wrists. Something told me not to. Something told me to keep on living, find out what you want, what you are about. My sister will never change. There's always the same fight for attention, my brother too. I just sit back and watch. I wish I could find out who I am, what I want in life.

Diane has lived in only one circumstance in her entire life: in housing projects in western Massachusetts. At this time she has only one voice, but she has learned that voice perfectly, and she can use it. I would wish for her many other voices. I would wish for her a full knowledge of the work of Woolf and Eliot, O'Connor and Dickinson, Bradbury, Lorde, Paley, Olds—and of many more of the writers I have most loved. But not at the cost of losing her own primary voice.

Many writers use only one voice in their writing: either the voice of the academy or the voice of the market that they hope will publish their work. Hidden in every one of their brains, however, is another voice: the voice of those whom writer Paule Marshall has called "the poets in the kitchen." Marshall is talking about her own people, immigrants from Barbados, but she could have been talking about my people in the Ozark Mountains, or Diane's people in the housing projects of Chicopee:

> Using everyday speech, the simple commonplace words—but always with imagination and skill—[the poets in the kitchen] gave voice to the most complex ideas. Flannery O'Connor would have approved of how they made ordinary language work, as she put it, "double-time," stretching, shading, deepening its meaning. Like Joseph Conrad they were always trying to infuse new life in the 'old old words worn thin . . . by . . . careless usage.' And the goals of their oral art were the same as his: 'to make you hear, to make you feel . . . to make you *see.*'

When you begin to write in your own primary voice, you may need to be strong to defend it. In my workshop at the Graduate Theological Union in Berkeley, California, there was a writer who grew up in New Orleans. Her ancestral heritage was rich: black, Hispanic, French—she wrote elegant English, a highly literate, highly academic voice. Every member of that workshop had been to graduate school—they could all write in an academic voice. Around the edges of the workshop, when she was laughing and talking freely, I heard much more color, richness, in her voice, including a bit of playful Black English. In the workshop, I openly invited her to allow that voice into her writing. Tentatively she began, and then there came, like a beautiful fresh stream, a gorgeous voice, full of the culture of New Orleans. No one else in the room could have written what she was writing. We were a rapt audience, and when she finished we talked about the beauty and power of her work. She said, "No one ever wanted that voice before." The piece she wrote that day has been published in *Peregrine*.

A few years ago a friend and I would read and respond to each other's poems. When mine came back to me, they were dead. She changed so much in them, I couldn't find the poem anymore.

It took me several weeks to figure out what my friend was doing—she was *cleaning rural Missouri out of my voice*. She comes from an eastern city; her voice is distinctly different from my own. One of my poems was titled "Mama," and it lopes along in a near-dialect rhythm that was close to my mother's Ozark voice. My friend cleaned it up, improved its syntax—and thereby destroyed it. She meant well, but if I had not been able to figure out what she was doing, it could have been destructive to my voice—my truest voice, the first one I learned and have had to fight to protect.

John Gardner addresses this issue in *On Becoming a Novelist*. When he was a young writer, he showed his work to an older professor, Lennis Dunlap:

> . . . though I cannot say he wasn't helpful, I soon learned the limits of even the best advice. Coming from Tennessee, he did not speak the same English I speak, or know the same kinds of people, or interpret life experience in quite the same ways I do. When he suggested changes and I accepted his suggestions, the story almost invariably went wrong.

You will want to use additional voices, but the first step in doing that is to trust and use your own voice. You have been practicing using it all your life. Trust it onto the page, exactly as you use it when you talk. Let it be quirky and idiosyncratic. Let it have the local color and flavor of your places, your people, your generation.

Using Other Voices

In addition to our original voice and our primary voice, all of us have "acquired voices." Gaining skill in using other voices is a matter of remembering those we have heard and practicing those we want to learn. All of the voices we have lived among are still available to us in deep memory.

I learned my greatest lesson about using other voices while writing my second novel. One of the primary characters is a man named Elan, who grew up in rural poverty in the Appalachian mountains near Pineville, Kentucky. He had left that place, moved to St. Louis, become educated, and taken a position as professor at a university. In the course of the novel, Elan receives a letter from his sister in the mountains, telling him that his mother has died. He begins his journey home.

When I was young, I worked for two summers in a church orphanage at Frakes, Kentucky, 30 miles into the mountains from Pineville. I wrote the novel 20 years later, having never returned to Kentucky. I felt that it was impossible for me to remember the speech of the people in those rick-ety houses on the mountainsides—it had been too long a time. I wrote Elan's trip back toward his birthplace, allowing him to remember many things about his childhood. As he neared the house in which he had grown up, I became very concerned about how I was going to handle the meeting with his sister. I could see the wooded hillside, the abandoned cars, wrecked washing machines, the unpainted house, its porch hanging off the front like an old man's lower lip that doesn't completely close any more. And standing on the porch I could see Elan's sister, a baby on her hip, her cotton dress bleached from hanging on the line in the sun. She was looking at him. He was in the car, looking at her. I could see them both as if I were there. My only option was to have her be silent. I could not remember accurately enough to let her speak. I decided that she would stand on the porch and look at Elan, but she would not say a word.

Feeling upset and agitated, I left my typewriter, went upstairs and took a shower. (I do that when I am writing intensely. Nothing—*nothing*—washes away tangles in my mind like water pouring over my naked body.) As I stood in the shower, water streaming over my head, Elan's sister began to speak with absolute clarity in my mind. I dashed out of the shower and downstairs to my typewriter and banged out her speech dressed only "in my utter altogether."

It was one of the most ecstatic writing experiences I have ever had. Only later did I remember that I owned a small book by Glenn Evans, the long-time director of the orphanage where I had worked. It was a collection of stories told by mountain people, in the dialect of that place. I searched for it and found it. I had not read it for 20 years. The dialect was exactly as I had written it.

In the novel Elan's sister stands still on the porch, watches him get out of his car and walk toward her. Then, looking down at him from the porch, she says:

> Hit ain't quite the way I told it in the letter, Little Junior. Ma she didn't jist get sickly an then die. She did get sickly, years an years ago, but her dyin come from Papa took a shotgun to her head an blew her brains out all over theseyere walls an floor an bedcloths an ever'thang . . .

When we are using voices that are not deeply embedded in our own memory, we have to do research and practice. When I was writing my one-woman play, *Berries Red*, I wanted to include a monologue by a black woman based on a story Ruby James had told me about how she stood on the back porch in winter as a young girl, washing clothes. She described her own suffering and ended the story with "My mama didn't have no right to do that to me, even if her mama *was* a slave." I wrote the monologue, but I did not trust my memory of the dialect, and so I called Flo Clark, a composer with whom I have collaborated by writing lyrics, and asked her to check it for me. There were four or five words that she suggested I change. Any time we are using a dialect we ourselves have not spoken, it is crucial to check it with someone who can catch the subtle errors.

The primary reason we are told in all writing books to write about what we know best is this: What we know best will most likely be written in an accurate voice. However, the greatest enemy of accurate voice is not ignorance, but tension. Try to relax, try to let yourself play. Voices are outrageous; they do unexpected things.

Exercise: Eavesdropping

Go to an informal public eating place—a coffee shop, diner, or fast-food restaurant. Order something to drink, open your journal, and eavesdrop. Write down fragments of what people say. Your purpose is not to catch the whole conversation, but to capture the way people really talk. People talk in fragmentary sentences, in slang, in cliché, and in code. Enormous information about a person is revealed in his or her speech—nationality, class, culture, gender, education, taste, preferences. Riding a train home from New York City one night, I stood in the aisle waiting to get into the snack bar. Beside me, two young women gossiped. They giggled and one said, "God, girl, and that ain't all! She got warts in her 'gina!" I imagined, then, being able to walk slowly down the aisle and know what was in the mind of each passenger. The thought reminded me that I am one of the passengers, and suddenly I was again a 13-year-old girl on a Greyhound bus, riding for three hours, three seats behind a man I knew was my father, but who did not recognize me. I turned back from the snack bar line, went to my seat, and opened my notebook to write in the voice of a 13-year-old girl the things she would like to say, but will not say, to the stranger who is her father.

Tanyss Martula is a playwright. About the example that follows, Tanyss writes, "I always keep a little notebook in my purse for writing down 'catchy' phrases that I hear on just ordinary days. I jotted down some of these lines in that notebook after overhearing (eavesdropping, really, I was so fascinated by something that sounded like a whole language unto itself) a couple of construction workers talking at a table next to me at Burger King."

BURGER KING

(Two construction workers are seated at a table in Burger King. They are talking. One worker's back is almost completely to the audience. While eating a Whopper and french fries, he/she responds only with nods or inaudible mumbling throughout the conversation. The other worker, who is drinking a cup of coffee, sits across the table at a slight diagonal to the first worker so that his/her face is visible to the audience as she/he speaks.)

Who gives a shit? I'm not gonna rip all that shit out. Shit. I mean that's his goddamned shit. Why should I shit that?

I did a job like that over at my mother's. Never been through so much shit. With the floor. With my mother. Shit. Rippin' the old shit up. Then, puttin' in all the new shit, which won't last shit. Then, the goddamned doors and all that shit. Only took one goddamned week-end, but, hell, it was shit. Didn't get out on the golf course or nothin'. Just shittin' around inside.

Yeah, ya gotta rip the shit out of it. Then, put down the plywood, as long as there's no shit under the sub-flooring. Then, you put the shit on top of that. That's another thing, wanta finish this kind of shit-work before spring. Bein' inside all the time is shit. Makes me wanta shit in my pants. Shit, that's why I don't moonlight or nothin'. I don't give a shit, the extra bucks ain't worth the shit ya gotta put up with.

Now he comes out with 15 hours more on the work order. I don't take that kinda shit. Next he's gonna tell me I'm doin' a shitty job. What a shithead.

(Pause)

Shit, let's get the fuck out of here. Don't know how you can eat that shit anyway.

(The two workers exit.)

Exercise: Writing from Different Points of View

An excellent way to study the difference between voices is to write a report of the same incident from the point of view of two characters who feel very differently about a subject. For instance, a teenager and her mother, after the mother has opened a letter addressed to the girl. Or following a water pistol fight in a grandmother's living room, as in the following example.

From the Point of View of the
Six-Year-Old with the Water Pistol

"Cool, man! I got 'im, Gramma! I got 'im right between the eyes! Man! Did you see that? Zap! Pow . . ."

From the Point of View of the Grandmother

"Eric, you have disobeyed me; you have used that gun with water in it, and I told you absolutely you could not! You have spilled water on my Persian rug! Furthermore, young man, you have hurt his eye . . ."

Or perhaps we want a different grandma—"Eric, child, how many times do I have to tell you, a rug is for walkin' on. Only Jesus walks on water! Now you clean that up!"

Exercise: Writing in Several Voices at Once

Most of the time, our various voices overlap and interweave, giving texture and interest to what we write. Try writing in several voices at once. Dorothy Parker has a hilarious short story titled "The Waltz," in which a woman is dancing with a man who constantly steps on her toes. The reader hears both what she says to her partner and what she says to herself. Try writing a piece in which the secret voice of the narrator is different from what he or she is saying to someone else.

Imagine, and write, two people of different backgrounds or different occupations having a conversation. Or let one overhear the speech of the other (letting the reader also "overhear" it) and have a reaction to it. That's what I was doing above, when I wrote about the two young women on the train. In Jay O'Callahan's piece above, he is allowing us to hear two generations—the parents and the children—in one monologue.

Exercise: Suggesting a Character's Voice without Using It

In this poem by Midge Wyman, culture and voice are not made specific, but the vivid imagery suggests character voice delicately, without using character voices at all. Here the reader's imagination supplies the ethnicity of the scene. I might hear the dialect of white folks along the Mississippi

River where I spent my youth. My friend Kate might hear the voices of black folks in New Orleans, where she grew up. Midge wrote this poem in my all-women's workshop in response to hearing a recording of "Hush, Little Baby" by Yo-Yo Ma and Bobbie McFerrin on their CD *Hush*.

DANCE HALL

I see a wooden floor,
narrow boards oiled
to a walnut brown
though they are oak.
The air is smoky,
both from cigarettes
and from the kerosene
of lamps set in windowsills.
They do not give much light,
but it's enough.
The saxophone player
and the singer
stand between west windows.
He in dark jeans,
white shirt,
a gold bow tie.
She in a swirling skirt,
dark crimson, with a deep
gold sash, a blouse
of pale pink satin.
Ruby earrings dangle
almost hidden by black curls.
The men and women dance,
shadowy bright
in Saturday night clothes,
until she starts to sing.
The surprise of a lullaby,
even a jazzed-up lullaby,
in this dim hall
chains their feet,
cradles their bodies
in arms of mothers
who sit invisible
in rocking chairs
that are not there.

No matter how skilled you become in using voices other than your own, remember that your original voice is your home, the foundation of your writing.

Growing as a Writer

How do I grow as a writer? Beyond the hard and lonely work of applying my derriere to the chair at my writing desk, and beyond the psychological work of embracing my own voices and freeing myself to use them, how can I develop my craft?

"Craft is the work of writing clearly," my son, Paul, wrote in the margin of this manuscript. Perhaps craft is as simple as that. Perhaps that's what Hemingway was trying to do when he said all he wanted was to write one true sentence. I agree with my son; craft is the work of writing clearly. But it is also the work of writing with courage, and with the grace of an assurance that comes to an artist through long practice. The ability to write well regularly and dependably is the reward of practice, as it is in every other art form.

It is my own conviction that an ideal setting for growth as a writer is an intimate community of other writers with whom to meet, write, and give and receive supportive critical response. Part II of this book details the practices that make such a group healthy. In the absence of a good workshop or writing group, here are some ways to grow as a writer working alone.

Finding a Good Teacher

Young writers and those new to the craft can benefit greatly from finding a good teacher. When I was young, I spent one year at a small college in

Nashville, Tennessee. While I was there, I heard about a famous group of poets across the street at Vanderbilt University. They were called the Hermitage School of Poets. I wanted to study with them, but one of my teachers advised me to stay away from them. "They are called 'a school' because they all sound alike," he said. "Don't go. They won't value your work unless you change it to fit their ideas of what a poem should be." For all the rest of my formal education I tried to avoid teachers who would want me to sound like them. I wanted to sound like myself.

Finding the teacher or mentor who is right for you is worth the search. Shop around and, above all, trust your own instincts.

A GOOD TEACHER

1. A good teacher assists you to sound more and more like your own self and less and less like the teacher.

2. A good teacher always tells you the strengths of your writing, as well as the weaknesses. If your teacher cannot identify the strength in your writing voice, then he or she has no right to address what is mitigating against that strength. Do not subject yourself to any teacher who gives you only negative feedback.

3. A good teacher knows more than you do, is willing to give to you what he or she knows, and rejoices when you find your own way of using what you have been given.

4. A good teacher believes in you and lets you know it.

5. A good teacher gives you an honest (perhaps sometimes hard to hear) response, but always acknowledges that all responses are subjective.

6. A good teacher encourages you to listen to other opinions and take only those critical suggestions that strengthen and encourage your voice.

7. A good teacher does not inhabit a pedestal.

8. A good teacher admits that he or she has sometimes been mistaken, wrongheaded, or unhelpful.

9. A good teacher engages you with affection and keeps appropriate boundaries.

10. A good teacher lets you go when the time to go has come.

There is one sure test. After meeting several times with a teacher, do you feel more like writing, or less like writing? If you feel less like writing, consider the relationship poison and drop it!

If you feel *more* like writing when you go home, then hang in! No matter what the style or the method of the teacher—no matter how many credentials or how famous or how successful in the marketplace he or she might or might not be—all that matters is, do you feel more like writing? Are you energized and sent back to your pad of paper or your computer? Are you more excited and hopeful about your work? The issue is not whether the teacher is tough or gentle, cruel or kind; the issue is the effect on you, on your work. A teacher who is good for you may be a terrible teacher for your best friend. Finding a good teacher is certainly as sensitive and miraculous as finding a good doctor or a good therapist or a good priest/clergyperson.

Writing and teaching are not the same skill and do not always inhabit the same human body. Good writers are not necessarily good teachers. Many students, looking at the roster of professors in MFA creative writing programs, travel great distances, even move across the country to study with their favorite writer only to discover that what that writer does on the page is not at all reflected in what he or she does in the classroom. There are great writers who cannot teach and great teachers of writing who do not write. There are teachers with genius, and there are teachers who are fools.

All of us must suffer some fools. If you are in school, you do not have the luxury of choosing all your teachers. Learn, even from the fools. Learn how *not* to teach. The person who taught me the most about writing poetry in graduate school was not the famous poet on the faculty, but Margaret Robison, a fellow student. She cared deeply about my work, evoked it, challenged it, and encouraged me to grow. Claim as your real teacher the person who best helps you to do it, and to do it better.

Reading as a Writer

Writers are our primary teachers; they speak to us from the printed page. Read what you love, and read what challenges and puzzles you. Read works that have lasted over time, and read works that are just appearing in small journals and new anthologies. Read as a writer: How did she surprise me? How did he make me care about that character? Why is this poem line broken as it is? Why doesn't the end of this story work?

If you are in the middle of a writing project, I offer one note of caution. When working on a specific theme, it may be a good idea to stay away from works on that same theme. For example, when you are deeply involved in writing about your father, it may not be a good idea to read other people's poems or stories about fathers. You may be susceptible to a debilitating overdose of admiration; you may lose your own focus or your confidence.

When you are not in the middle of a writing project, however, read! Get a good anthology of contemporary writing, read until you find a writer you like, then stay there a while. You don't have to like it all. Try to listen to the unfamiliar voices, but allow yourself to be taught by those whose work you love. Find someone in the anthology whose work moves you, and then buy that writer's collected work and study it. To do so is to have a teacher whom you trust, available and as near as your bookcase. John Adams told his son Johnny, "You will never be alone with a poet in your pocket." Similarly, with a book in your hand, you will never be without a teacher. Even dreadful writers teach us: *This is awful! Why? What is wrong with it?* Recently, between sessions of a workshop I was leading in Berkeley, I read Stephen King's book *On Writing*. I loved it. It is unpretentious, honest, down-to-earth, and moving. I said so in my workshop, and one of the participants asked if I had read any of King's novels. I admitted that I had not. My workshop participant was a committed Stephen King fan, and so he presented me with a copy of *Desperation* the next day. I took it home and read the first three pages. The next day, I returned the gift to the giver. "Now I have an image in my mind of a cat nailed to a traffic sign. I don't want seven hundred more pages of images like that. No, thank you."

"Oh, please!" he begged. "Please just read page 135 before you decide not to read it. That's all I ask. Just read page 135."

I did allow myself to sigh audibly, but I took it home and read page 135. And 136, and 137, all the way to the end of the chapter. It was quite beautiful. So I read the entire book. And I read it as a writer. King says in *On Writing* that his own greatest task in revision is cutting back what he writes in first draft. I was interested in my own progress through that long novel, interested in how my attention and my "willing suspension of disbelief" flagged about two-thirds of the way through. In my mind I talked to the writer: Stephen, you could have done some of that cutting here. I've had so many scorpions, rattlesnakes, and spiders, I'm not scared of them anymore. His book taught me.

Read repeatedly. Read aloud. Read the work of your own contemporaries as well as the classics. Read writing by people who do not share your own ethnic origins, gender, sexual orientation, age—and those who do. Just as it pains me to remember how I, as a child in the slums of St. Louis, Missouri, wanted to sound like a middle-aged, middle-class, expatriate male poet in England (T. S. Eliot), so it pains me to see a young New England writer today unconsciously imitating the language of long-dead poets whom he studied in high school and in college Lit. 101. Work modeled on these so-called classic poets almost always sounds exactly what it is: derivative. When writing seems "trite" or "clichéd," it is because we have heard it before. For example, archaic contractions like "o'er," "'twas," "admist," and "amongst" once reflected living language, but they sound old-fashioned or even silly now. This is not the writer's fault. He or she does not yet know that literature changes as language changes, that literature can be absolutely contemporary.

Who do we read, in order to learn? John Gardner, perhaps the greatest teacher of writing in our generation, told his young student, Raymond Carver, "Read all the Faulkner you can get your hands on, and then read all of Hemingway to clean the Faulkner out of your system."

In addition to reading the established canon—not all of it, of course; we have only one lifetime each—it is essential to read the work of your own generation and your own gender. Read voices close to your own life choices and experience—as well as voices of writers of the past. Recently an African American woman attended my writing retreat. She is an educator who grew up middle class with a privileged education. She carries in her mind a rich heritage of African, Caribbean, and European voices. As she begins to do her own creative writing, it is not sufficient to point her to Faulkner and Hemingway, any more than it was sufficient for me to be pointed only to T. S. Eliot and Randall Jarrell when I was beginning to write. She also needs to read Audre Lorde, bell hooks, Sonia Sonchez, June Jordan, and young black writers just appearing in journals and anthologies. She needs them to give her permission to use all the voices in her memory and to support her angle of vision on the human experience.

Studying Craft

Specific work on craft can be of great value to the writer. For example, you might use *Forms of Poetry* by Miller Williams, and *A Formal Feeling*

Comes: Poems in Form by Contemporary Women, edited by Annie Finch, for guidance in writing some poems in form. There is no better way to understand what a sonnet is, how a villanelle works, what makes a pantoum a pantoum, than by writing one.

Or you might use some of the exercises at the end of John Gardner's book, *The Art of Fiction*, to work on specific aspects of craft in fiction, or follow Dorothea Brande's guidance toward writing a short story in *Becoming a Writer*.

Your study of writing should not be limited to reading books about writing, however. Your art will be fed and nourished by your continual listening and observation. I have reached grandmother age, and so it seems important to me to listen to music that my granddaughter and grandson consider "cool," lest I be left behind, unable to appreciate the music of *their* spheres. If you study how rain makes a pattern on only one side of the trunk of the tree in your backyard, how dark is the gray where the bark is wet and how light it is where it is dry, you are working on your writing. In your next short story, a character may look out the window after hanging up the telephone on a conversation that has just changed everything, and watch how rain makes a pattern on one side of a tree.

Gently, always, allow your study about writing to take you back to the writing itself. One of the most important things we learn as we practice our craft is how to recognize the subtle nudge of an image or a memory or an idea. When you feel it, the desire to write, turn immediately to your blank page. You can come back to the passage you have been studying, but you might never again be touched by the confluence of images that have opened you to this particular moment in your own imagination.

Revising

Most of what I have learned about craft has come by hammering at the stone of my own work, and by reading the manuscripts of writing companions in order to help them with their revisions. When we revise, we take the gold ore of our first drafts into the refinery of our critical vision, and work to purify it. Revision is crucial, and it is tricky.

A piece of writing that comes out in first draft whole and perfect is a miracle. Miracles happen, but not often. Revision is the second half—at least—of the act of writing. But there is great danger in revising if you do not know what is strongest and best in your own work. One of the most common experiences shared by workshop leaders is dismay at seeing writers revise all the life and originality out of their vivid first drafts.

Celia (not her real name), a well-known visual artist, joined my workshop to write for children. For several weeks her writing was frozen. The language reminded me of my own earliest experiences of reading: "Dick runs. Jane runs. Dick and Jane run."

In the fifth session of the workshop, I suggested we all write a letter. Celia wrote a letter to a former workshop leader who had hurt and embarrassed her, and it was white-hot with anger. Before she read it to us, she said, "This isn't writing." But the words she read were categorically different from anything we had heard from her. "*You* are the wicked stepmother. *You* look in the mirror and ask, *mirror, mirror, on the wall, who's the fairest of them all?* You smile and comb your long black hair, and we sit in the ashes."

The workshop was stunned. The writing went on, powerful, free, full of imagery, metaphor, passion. When she finished, we spontaneously broke into applause. Celia couldn't believe it. She tried to tell us that it wasn't writing at all, that she was just "taking a break" from her real writing.

I told her, and others told her, how exciting the writing was. And I asked her to bring it back, typed, the following week, so we could see it in manuscript form.

At the next meeting, at our request, she began to read once more: "You are the wicked queen. You look in the mirror. You smile. We sit in the ashes." All the life, the passion, the rhythm, the driving intensity, was gone. What she had done is very common: She had revised her work away from her own voice to some preconceived idea of what good writing should sound like. She had revised it to death.

But we had all heard something wonderful. Celia's own voice had made its appearance, and it was powerful. Once you have found a place of power inside yourself, it is like finding, beyond the wall of your usual habitation, a new room that you didn't know existed. Once you have found the way, you can go there again. And, furthermore, there are rooms beyond rooms waiting for you to discover. Celia had found an opening in the wall. She was free. From that moment she began to teach herself how to write. Not by focusing on what she was doing wrong, but by coming to awareness of *what she does well, what her own strengths are, what her unique voice is already able to do*. I could not have guessed what Celia's writing voice would be like. I have had this experience over and over again. Only by listening to what people write, and naming to them what is strong, only by patience, by waiting and listening, can I hope to catch the exact, exquisite pitch of genius that hides in a hurt or frightened writer. Once Celia began to write with freedom, once her own voice made its appearance, I could help her on the page to enlarge her own capacity, to learn to trust her own gifts, to recognize those times when she lost her footing. Until then, all a teacher can do is encourage, evoke, invite, and wait.

The more accomplished you become at your writing (by that I mean the more you trust your voice, and the more you learn about craft), the more effective you will be at revising.

I am personally wary of applying any rules of development to a work in progress. The study that I do of favorite how-to books I do separately from the act of writing. Poet Margaret Robison taught me that "the only purpose of revision is to get more deeply to the truth." She said that she always asks herself, Is there more that I have not yet seen? There is a certain purity in that kind of practice of revision. It has nothing at all to do with the marketplace, with the opinions of others, with cleverness, or with rules. It has only one goal: to tell the truth of what has been experienced or what has been imagined. I try to practice my revision in that way.

The best texts I know for practical help in learning to revise fiction are Carol Bly's *The Passionate, Accurate Story* and Janet Burroway's *Writing Fiction*. Burroway's chapter, "Play It Again, Sam: Revision" includes a list of "revision questions," such as What is my story about? Why should the reader turn from the first page to the second? and others that assist in looking at the work as a whole. In revising poems, my own favorite texts are the actual poems of a variety of poets, and William Stafford's *Writing the Australian Crawl* and *You Must Revise Your Life*.

A good teacher, a writing companion, or a healthy writing group can be of great assistance in helping you learn to revise. I often suggest to writers that they bring to me an untouched first draft and a copy of their revision, so I can compare the two. If you do not have a teacher or mentor, give both versions to a friend and don't disclose which is the original. Ask your reader to tell you which version works best. The best response is sometimes from an average reader; it doesn't have to be in literary critical language.

Until you learn how to revise your work, save first drafts of everything. When you ask someone else for a critical opinion, take suggestions for change only if they meet with an answering *Yes!* in your own mind. Otherwise, your critic will be taking you away from your own voice, your own vision. The best kind of critical suggestion is the one that causes you to think, Oh, I knew that! or That's exactly right! Why didn't I see it myself?

William Stafford, in *You Must Revise Your Life,* describes how he wrote fast and sent his work out immediately, keeping 40 or 50 poems out all the time. "I wrote recklessly," he said. "The poems got changed or re-vised—if they did get changed, as a result of my continued interest—only by my own re-visioning of them."

> If I write something down, I don't feel secure about it until I have gone back and read it with the knowledge I have accumulated through having written it down the first time . . . revision brings a greater richness to the second time through and then the third time and so on. It isn't just the beginning and the end; there are multiple things all the way through. There are dawning realiza-tions as adjustments are made. I can imagine reading and revising an infinite number of times. For me, the language is never set like concrete; it's always like taffy. I could go over a poem I wrote years ago, but I don't. It is as if it were written by someone else; me, then. It is quite foreign, alas, to the self I am now. . . . The language changes, you change, the light changes.

John Gardner, in *On Becoming a Novelist,* writes about the changes that occur in the process of revision:

> All that matters is that, going over and over the sketch as if one had all eternity for finishing one's story, one improves now this sentence, now that, noticing what changes the new sentences urge, and in the process one gets the charac-ters and their behavior clearer in one's head, gradually discovering deeper and deeper implications of the characters' problems and hopes. Fiction does not spring into the world full grown, like Athena. It is the process of writing and rewriting that makes a fiction original and profound.

My own process is to write a first draft with as little interference from internal critics as possible. I am never able to exorcise them completely, and so my first drafts are messy—things scratched out, things added in the margins—except when I am able to reach the "vivid and continuous dream" that Gardner describes. Then, as if by a miracle, the writing flows artesian, and I sometimes write passages that later do not need revision at all.

As I type first, second, third drafts, I revise. And revise. And revise until the music I hear when I read it out loud pleases me. That necessary music is as important for fiction and nonfiction as it is for poetry. After I have read it aloud to myself, I habitually oppress my husband by making him read a new page aloud without looking it over first. If he stumbles on a line or a sentence, I know the music is not right. I want a reader who has never read the work before to be able to read it with perfect rhythm.

The piece that follows was written in a letter to me by my good friend and collaborator, Kate Hymes, at a time when she was struggling with revising some poems:

> Even God revises. She began six days of tremendous, wondrously inspired creativity. She sat back and admired the beauty of her work for a day or two, then those characters she let loose in that perfect garden got perfectly out of hand. They abandoned the script. God must have had serious doubt at that point about what she had created. But being God, she was not afraid. Exasperated, frustrated, she revised. The perfect garden was not the right setting for these characters. They required, needed, a setting that was more challenging than giving. Obviously, they needed something—work—to keep their hands and minds occupied, especially that woman, Eve. So, God redrafted the outline, filled in new details.
>
> And this revision was not the last.

8

The Form Your Writing Takes

This chapter is not intended as a thorough examination of various forms—that would take many books! Rather, it is an invitation to the writer who has worked in one form, and perhaps has not experimented much with a range of forms. I am offering only brief observations and some suggestions of where to go for more information, in the hope that it might be helpful as ideas for further writing practice, or as enticements toward experimentation.

Because the intention of this book is to free the writer from all that would restrict or hamper the imagination, there is a danger of underestimating the importance of form. I have said that I hold central Ben Shahn's understanding that form is the shape of content: If one is true to the content, form will take care of itself. However, all of us, whether we know it or not, come from deep literary traditions, each with its own classical forms: American Indian story cycles, Hebrew parallelism, Latin American magical realism, English iambic pentameter, etc. A writer's mastering classical forms is analogous to a painter's adding to the three primary colors on his palette. They broaden our range and deepen our craft. In some cases, a preexisting form helps us discover our own personal content. I have found that a form helps contain and shape my thought when the content is too large or too intense, as described in the section below titled "Poems."

There is a common assumption that a writer must be identified by one genre. When I enrolled in the MFA program in Creative Writing at the

University of Massachusetts in the 1970s, I had to declare myself either a poet or a fiction writer. I complained to my adviser that all of my published, produced, and recorded work at that time was in plays, lyrics, and libretti. He said, "Well, we don't offer playwriting or songwriting. You have to choose: fiction or poetry?" In my mind, I refused to choose, deciding to take as many workshops in one as I took in the other. I would declare my major in what I knew least. "Fiction," I replied, and signed up for an equal number of workshops in poetry.

In my opinion, the pressure on writers toward specialization is unfortunate. I have resisted, and I still resist, writing groups limited to one genre. When writing begins, it needs freedom to take its own form. Genius will express itself sometimes as story, sometimes as poem, sometimes as grand opera, sometimes as country-and-western ballad. People frequently join my workshops saying, I write only poems, or, I write only fiction, and are surprised when something completely different comes bubbling up in response to a good exercise.

I love the rich and fertile give-and-take when writers are working in varying forms. A fiction writer learns how to write dialogue by listening to two workshop members read aloud the scene that a third workshop member (playwright) has brought to the meeting. A poet is encouraged to use specific, concrete imagery by listening to a vivid prose description of a man opening a can of beer and taking his first sip, the foam catching in the bristle on his unshaven lip.

Writers need the refreshment of various forms. Daphne Slocombe observed:

> The demands of using a particular form can help to focus the author's attention and intensify his or her engagement. For new writers, I think it is important to know that there is a reason for forms. You can fool with them, mess around with them, can get to know them by trying them out and seeing how they affect the material you're working with. No need to be intimidated by them; they were invented or discovered by other writers like us, trying to find the best, most effective container for what they had to say, for what they wanted to show us.

In the workshops I lead, we write two, sometimes three, times in one evening session. Once in a while someone writes three wonderful, separate poems in one evening. Some writers can write three sections of a novel-in-progress. But most mortals, like myself, may write one prose piece, one journal entry, and—if we are especially "hot"—one poem.

Poems

Many times writers have said to me, "I would love to write a poem, but I have no idea what a poem is, or how to go about it." Everyone possesses the music of language, and everyone can write poems. What is wrong with most novice poetry is its painful effort to *sound like a poem*. What is most needed is trust in the music of the language as we use it naturally.

When we write in our journals, we often create poems—perhaps without recognizing them as poems. Putting that naturally used language into a form by breaking it into lines or keeping it in a prose block as a "prose poem" is not as difficult as it may appear to be.

When Margaret Robison was serving as Poet in the Schools in Holyoke, Massachusetts, there was a little boy who loved poetry but said he could not write. Later, he asked Margaret if he could copy a poem out of a book, and she said yes. He copied the entire text of "Annabelle Lee" by Poe. Margaret realized then that he was especially sensitive to sound. She took the children to visit a nursing home, and this little boy became friends with a 98-year-old woman named Emma. One day Emma gave him an orange. When they returned to school, Margaret asked the children to write about their experiences in the nursing home, and the time came for the little boy to read what he had written. "He had written a lot of words," Margaret says, "But they were flat. Then he came to the line, 'Emma gave me an orange,' and the words sang—you could just taste that orange!" She made no comment to him about it, but believing that hearing his own voice might help him gain access to his writing voice, she asked him to read what he had written again, out loud, to her. He read it. She asked him to read it again. Still nothing. She had him read it three times, and the last time, he put his hand over his heart and shouted, "It's poetry! I can hear it in my heart when it's poetry!"

WHAT MAKES A POEM A POEM?

The little boy's definition is not to be dismissed. Something in us sings, and if we read our own work aloud over and over, listening intently to the music, we can hear the singing. After a while we begin to hear where the "singing" is interrupted, and that is where "craft" begins.

Fashions come and go in literature just as they do in clothing. There was a time, not so long ago, when we could have easily said, Why, a poem is a poem if it has regular meter (preferably iambic pentameter) and end-rhymed lines. I think only two things can be said to be common defining characteristics of a poem: (1) the language is intensified, and (2) it gives the reader a complete experience. In addition, it may rhyme, or it may not. It may be in a traditional stanza pattern, or it may not. It may even be a short block of prose: a "prose poem."

This is a good time to be a poet, because our freedom is so great. Local "open mic" poetry slams give a stage to beginning poets and give poetry to neighborhood audiences. Poetry is fun again; it is touching toes with folk arts; it is back where it began, on the street, in the mouth of itinerant bards. June Jordan, Joy Harjo, Charles Simic, Jim Tate, and other contemporary poets have broken walls of tradition and taboo. To do so is the task of every generation of artist, from street rappers to Pulitzer prize winners. Jordan's jazzy evocation of a "seven-day kiss" has become a classic song in the repertoire of Sweet Honey in the Rock. With revolutionary passion she has closed the gap between poetry and what she calls "the people." She and Simic and Tate all work solidly within the academy, but each in different ways has exploded linear progression of thought, sometimes leaving the reader disoriented, having to create new paths to meaning. The emergence of poets like Martín Espada, Joy Harjo, Cheryl Savageau, and Enid Santiago Welch promises a rich multiplicity in our Western literary tradition. The following poem is by Santiago Welch, who wrote for years with me in the Chicopee workshops, initiated workshops for children in the Chicopee housing projects, and now leads workshops for both adults and young writers. The poem appeared in *The Massachusetts Review.*

POPPING OUT BABIES WHILE
DRAGGING YOUR PLACENTA TO THE MAILBOX

Memo: To Newt G.

Open wide and sneeze
a child into existence.
Open wide and slide those
babies out.
Easy as A B C pop.
Your belly enlarges.
Get in line pop.
Can't wait for the check.
Ninety dollars a month more pop.

There's no pain.
Just an in and out pop.
A quickie pop.
No pleasure pop.
Just squeeze the infant out hard.
Push hard.
Don't stop.
Have to get to the mailbox fast.
Got to get that check cashed pop.
Drag the placenta with you,
for ninety dollars a month more pop.
Stretch-marks mapping
Your skin,
Don't mind them at all.
And the morning sickness—all day pop
Don't mind that.
The waddle-paddle walk and
The sleepless nights pop.
The cervix opening
like a train tunnel pop.
The feeling of a tree trunk
splitting you in half crack crack
for ninety dollars extra
a month pop.
Get a hysterectomy, complete snip snip
not washed thin
like India ink in water,
blotched—pop.

TEN STEPS TO WRITING A POEM (*IF YOU THINK YOU CAN'T!*)

1. You have probably already written poems. Look through your journal and find some short, intense paragraph or complete short piece.
   Or write a new short piece (let it come out as "prose" if that's
   easiest). Write about something that matters. Use language that is
   natural to you.

2. Read it slowly, out loud, to yourself. If the music pleases you,
   notice that and do not lose the music as you revise.

3. Read it again silently to yourself, asking whether you have said
   what is deepest and truest. Have you gone "all the way"? Have
   you seen clearly? Have you given that clarity to the reader? The
   best revision is being certain you have told all of the truth of this

one piece. Sometimes you achieve more truth by cutting back "to the bone." Sometimes something needs to be added.

4. Is there anything that you can omit without loss of music, meaning, or clarity? Are there any words that are overused? Styles come and go in literature, just as in the way we dress. To wear clothing that is "out of fashion" is sometimes desirable, but usually it is done intentionally to signify rebellion, humor, or farce. So, too, in writing. If you use archaic words (o'er, 'twere) or wornout rhymes (moon/June/croon/spoon), you will be repeating patterns that others before you have made tiresome.

5. Try different line formations; see whether by breaking a line in the middle of a phrase you enhance the meaning of both lines. Let every line have some significance, some weight of its own.

6. Have a sense of "play." Trust disconnections. Surprise yourself. If you get stuck, read it again out loud and go back to where the music was right. Cut back to there and begin again.

7. At the end, a poem should open out to wider significance. Avoid closing it down too much. Try not to tell your reader what your reader can be trusted to discover. In Enid's poem, above, the image of the mother covering the child's eyes tells us everything we need to know about the event, the mother, the child. It "opens out" to the significance of the event, gives us room to imagine, to linger in the experience of being the child, being the adult woman remembering, being the mother trying to protect the child, being the grandfather, being the truck driver. It does not "close down" as it would if the last line were something like "Oh, it hurt me so much," or "my mother tried to protect me." Instead of telling us, the poet has allowed us see. Often the best end for a poem is a specific, clear image. No "telling" by the writer. Only "showing." As reader, then, I have been there; at the end of the poem I have my own feelings and meanings to sort out. The "Ah ha!"—the revelation—is mine. Every good poem is a collaboration between the writer and the reader.

8. Type it.

9. Let the visual shape of the poem on the page be satisfying. Try breaking it into lines, playing with it to see if it wants to be a lined poem. Or type it out as a prose poem, without broken lines.

10. Give it a title. Or don't. Congratulations! You have written a poem.

TO RHYME OR NOT TO RHYME?

Writers who enter my workshops often do not know they write in a kind of swirling stew of literary fashion. If you want to work on writing poems, is it a good idea to write in rhyme, or avoid rhyme? Behind that question lie generations of *fashion*. When Tennyson and Wordsworth were writing, it was in style to end every line (or every other line) with an exact rhyme. Later, rebelling against those dear old dead Romantic poets, a new generation of literary critics and writers (Ezra Pound, Randall Jarrell, and others who practiced what they called The New Criticism) revolted against rhyme and regular meter. Those were out of fashion through all of my young life. Some poets used them—Robert Frost, Richard Wilbur, and a few others. I was definitely discouraged from using rhyme when I was in college in the 1950s. I had been born into it: nursery rhymes, country-and-western songs—Gene Autry and the Carter Sisters on the radio, Protestant hymn lyrics, and the rhymed poems of James Russell Lowell. My birthday is the first of June, and on that day every year until she died, my mother recited from memory about two dozen lines of "The Vision of Sir Launfal," beginning:

> And what is so rare as a day in June?
> Then, if ever, come perfect days;
> Then heaven tries earth if it be in tune,
> And over it softly her warm ear lays . . .

Rhyme and rhythm were in my blood. When I began to try to write without rhyme, it seemed my images were naked. I felt exposed, alone with formless images that might reveal more to myself and others than I intended. The music of rhyme had served as a kind of safety net under the tightrope that the poet walks. It gave the safety of structure and music, even if all else failed. But I believed what I was taught in college— that rhyme was immature, old-fashioned, silly—and I was determined to be a poet. For a long time I abandoned rhyme entirely.

Now there is a return to "patterns of poetry." The good thing about fashion is, if you live long enough, almost everything comes around again. This time, however, fashion in writing poems is a little like fashion in clothing. When I was young it was a no-no to use rhyme. It was also a no-no to wear your bobby socks or your blouse collar turned down! Now there is vastly more freedom in personal dress options, and similarly there is more

freedom in how we write. This is a good thing, to put it as plainly as possible. There are times when rhyme serves the spirit, and there are times
when it gets in the way. Practice, play, and use the freedom that is yours.

UNRHYMED POEMS

Unrhymed poems demand no less of us than those we write in form.
Flannery O'Connor said each story should have its own unique form.
That is also true of unrhymed poems: Each one has its own unique form
and its own music. The two poems below have very different music—
each appropriate to the voice of the narrator and to the subject of the
poem. Alexander Drier and Carolyn Pelletier write with me in my Wednesday workshop in Amherst. Alexander's work is often witty and surprising. In this poem, some of the music comes from playing with language.

TURQUOISE PRAYER OF SPRING

What if the turquoise prayer of Spring
was an almost hidden window,
opened only once a year,
inviting yellow peeper breezes
with their nostril dance of waftings
to free us from our ice cube selves?

I would look right through that window
to where the green becomes from,
and like a dried up glob of clay
I would swallow all that water-breath
and forget about the mailbox
as for once I understood what it means
to be dew.

I would look right through that window
to pinkish trees across the river,
to where frogs receive communion
and manure meets the moon,
and woodcocks know their purpose.

I would be ambushed by the budding
as I listened through the window,
and I would taste at last the sap
of how the music happens.

Carolyn has worked for many years in the offices of a factory in a mill
town. She writes a great deal about the tedium and inhumanity of that

kind of workplace. In this poem, the music reflects the attitude of the narrator and the tone of the workplace.

WAITING

They told me I come in too late
and take too long for lunch.
My work has decreased
so what does it matter
if I do next to nothing
for a half an hour longer?
It was very important
to the person who told me;
the world was off its axis
over my half hour.

Waiting for the alarm clock to ring.
Waiting for the computer to boot up.
Waiting to get a coffee.
Waiting for processes to unfold.
Waiting for a promotion
or to get fired, or laid off, or let go
or have my job eliminated.
Waiting for the scheduled meeting time:
talk, talk, talk, video, handout, evaluation.
"What about the happiness committee?
What's the next thing planned?"

In the unrhymed poem the form emerges from the content. There is a form and a music in the unrhymed poem. Bringing it to completion may be as exacting a work as completing a sestina or a villanelle. However, revision must not destroy the music of that initial tone: in Alexander's poem, a playful, celebratory tone; in Carolyn's, an unremitting tone of tedium and imprisonment.

Chris Beyers concludes his thorough and excellent book, *A History of Free Verse*, with a chapter that quotes Phil Levine's poem, "The Simple Truth."

Some things
you know all your life. They are so simple and true
they must be said without elegance, meter and rhyme,
they must be laid on the table beside the salt shaker,
the glass of water, the absence of light gathering
in the shadows of picture frames, they must be
naked and alone, they must stand for themselves.

Perhaps that is the best defense of free verse—a poem without elegance, meter, or rhyme. And yet, Levine's poem is elegant. And what is more "simple and true" than Auden's call in meter and rhyme, "Follow poet, follow right / To the bottom of the night . . ."?

Let your decision to rhyme or not rhyme rise instinctively from the music of your own writing voice.

ON RHYME

As I write this book in the first years of a new century, there are some young poets who call themselves the "New Formalists." They are excited again about the possibilities of rhyme and meter, the pleasures of the sonnet, the sestina, the villanelle, the ballad. It was early rap that led the way, refreshed and reinvented by hip-hop.

Rhyme is magic. Most Americans of African and European ancestry grew up listening to rhyme: the hymns and liturgies we sang in church—in A.M.E. Zion, Baptist, and Methodist churches, "Amazing Grace, how sweet the sound / That saved a wretch like me. / I once was lost, but now am found / Was blind but now I see!" Or in Episcopal traditions, "Praise God from whom all blessings flow / Praise Him all creatures here below." We learned rhyme as infants, in nursery rhymes, "Jack Sprat could eat no fat / His wife could eat no lean / And so betwixt the two of them / They licked the platter clean." I am old enough to remember the first singing commercial on radio: "I'm Chiquita Banana, and I'm here to say / Bananas must be treated in a special way." We all heard rhyme on the playground in the sayings that go on generation after generation: "Step on a crack / Break your mother's back." Rhyme is our mother tongue.

For poets practicing in the last half of the twentieth century, however, most rhymed poems were dismissed as "verse," or worse, as "greeting card verse." The New Formalists may forecast change, but change takes a long, long time to reach the trenches where ordinary people write and the old prejudice is firmly entrenched. Picked at random from my pile of back issues of *The American Poetry Review*, there were in one issue 63 poems by 31 poets, and not a single one rhymed. There were two poems that had occasional end-rhyme, but in neither case was rhyme sufficient to appear more than accidental.

If you use rhyme as Robert Frost did, absolutely true to the idiom of your own time; if you accomplish that miraculous balance in which the rhymed poem, read aloud, seems to be effortless, natural speech; if the subject *matters*, and if you have condensed language and heightened imagery and told the truth—then you have probably written an excellent contemporary rhymed poem.

Consider Frost's familiar poem, "Stopping by Woods on a Snowy Evening." Read it aloud to yourself, and notice how absolutely natural and conversational it sounds. It is as if Frost were speaking directly and intimately to you. There is no strain, no hint of a word chosen for the sake of the rhyme. It seems effortless. Notice the rhyme scheme: Every third line is the origin of the rhyme of the next stanza:

> Whose woods these are, I think I know;
> His house is in the village, though.
> He will not see me stopping here
> To watch his woods fill up with snow.

The word "here" at the end of the third line sets up the rhyme for the next stanza, which begins, "My little horse must think it queer / To stop without a farmhouse near" and so on, until the final stanza, where he breaks the pattern by repeating the final word of the final two lines: "sleep . . . sleep."

That pattern, done so perfectly, so smoothly that it is almost invisible, almost inaudible, is what gives the poem its music. When the last two lines of the poem are repeated word for word—"And miles to go before I sleep / And miles to go before I sleep"—we feel an almost ecstatic beauty, like a great "amen." We may not even realize that what gave that final repeated line its power was the completion of a pattern started in line three of stanza one. By repeating the last line, the pattern is broken, and completed. The poem seduces us, tricks us, conceals an incredibly skilled craftsman at work—so skilled that his craft is invisible in the utter naturalness of ordinary speech.

Working to achieve the perfectly natural line of dialogue in a story, a play, or an unrhymed poem is different from working to achieve a rhymed stanza. In rhymed poetry we are assigning ourselves a musical as well as a conceptual task. And the ear is an exacting taskmaster. A rhyme that does not work in a poem hurts the ear much as an off-key note on the violin. The formal poem, like the violin, begs for perfection. But do not let that put you off—the sense of elation is enormous when you have achieved a perfectly wrought rhymed and metered poem.

Using a structured form does not cause me to say anything I do not want to say, any more than a person hypnotized can be made to do something that he or she would morally reject when awake. It may cause me to say some things that I *would not* have said if I had not been searching for a way to complete a pattern; that is sometimes good, surprising, helpful. Quite often the necessity of my own meaning may cause me to abandon the pattern that I am trying to use. When an established form works well, it simply forces me to hone the cutting edge of my meaning through a discipline of the requirements of form *in addition to* the requirements of spirit.

My own return to rhyme had a primitive root. When I was less than three years old, my mother would stand me on the kitchen table where I would recite 30 nursery rhymes, one after the other, for neighbors. When I was in my mid-forties I began a search for my father, who had abandoned his family and then had been kept away by my mother when he tried to return. The search began with writing. A good friend urged me to write about my father one evening, and after she left my house I sat up most of the night. Finally, near dawn, something like a chant—a nursery rhyme, really—sang itself in my head. It came exactly as it is. I believe it came as a nursery rhyme because I was tapping back into that time in my life. He left when I was barely four years old.

NURSERY RHYME

Daddy was a bad man
He made Mama cry.
I loved him, Mama said,
—But love can die.

Daddy was a weak man
He told a lie.
I loved him, Mama said,
—But love can die.

You look like your Daddy,
Green, green of eye.
I love you, Mama said . . .

If the rhyme is read aloud, slowly, the final unspoken line rings in the listener's mind.

Sometime not too long after I wrote the nursery rhyme, I was going through a time that felt like chaos. My clergyman husband and I left organized religion. I needed to understand what was happening to us, but it would be years before I was ready to write the book, *Wake Up*

Laughing: A Spiritual Autobiography. In this poem I struggled for the first time to press into form my grief and my need for freedom. I couldn't get it right. Draft after draft, I worked on the poem, instinctively reaching for the order of rhyme and meter to contain the personal chaos I was feeling. Finally I had a successful rhyme scheme of a b a b. Still it wasn't enough. I had not wrestled my own inner turmoil into sufficient form. I attempted to rhyme the left side of the lines as well as the right with an a b a b pattern. Doing that of course threw off the meaning for right-hand line endings. I would not—could not—allow myself to compromise natural speech. Finally, after 36 drafts, I gave up on achieving a full a b a b pattern on the left side, allowing it to rhyme a b c b: (left: "As, Peels, Astonished, Reveals"; right: "sun, rags, one, bags").

LETTING GO

As a beggar, resting in the sun,
Peels off layers of her outer rags,
Astonished to discover that each one
Reveals another under it, her paper bags

Filling with the garments she had worn
When everything was harder, darker, colder;
As she feels the chill of being born
Again, wiser now, and older,

So I. Having shed the church in the belief
That one particular chill of letting go
Might be a kind of ultimate relief,
(A flat sun of contradiction, saying "No"

To winter, to the ice around the heart,)
Under vestments I am finding near the skin
Ragged garments where all distinctions start.
I blunder toward the person I had been

Before costuming for the beggar's part
And trying out in someone else's show.
Living now is nakedness of heart;
Dying—just another letting go.

RESOURCES FOR POETS

By far, the most important resource for the beginning poet is other poets. Go to readings. Write with others in a good workshop. Read anthologies, find poets you love, and get more of their work. Sometimes poems come unbidden, as if they are gifts from the unconscious. But craft comes from practice. Try writing a poem like one that you love, or one that puzzles you. Learn what the poet was doing by trying to do it yourself. Give yourself permission to be as brief and clean and clear as Williams in "The Red Wheelbarrow," or as brutally honest as Olds in "The Takers," as unpretentious as Stafford in "Witness," as jazzy as Jordan in "Alla Tha's All Right, But," as exact in images of nature as Oliver in "The King-fisher," as long and conversational as Levine in "Gin," as musical and perfectly formal as Frost in "Stopping by Woods on a Snowy Evening."

Read favorite poems onto an audiotape and listen as you drive. Memorize. Poet Joseph Langland, who is known for his repertoire of memorized poetry, was challenged by his friends, as they were swimming in the Mediterranean, to quote poetry he had memorized for 30 minutes while treading water. He met the challenge and then set himself the task of driving from Amherst to Boston, Massachusetts, a two-hour drive each way, quoting poems he knew by heart all the way to Boston and back without repeating a single poem. He did it. What a rich inner treasure Joe carries with him everywhere! There may be no better way to deepen and strengthen your voice than memorizing poems.

Coming to believe that I had a voice of my own, that I could write poems, was the hardest thing I have ever done as a writer. Notice I did not say that writing a poem was the hardest thing. Writing a poem is a little like walking on a narrow edge, the way we sometimes did as children. It is so much easier if some other person is there within reach—not that you touch that person, but just in case. I think you need friends when you are taking the risk of writing poems, preferably other poets who are taking the same risks and have the same needs. Someone who will be gentle with you, rejoice when you achieve perfect balance, and help you a little when you lean too far to one side or the other. Part II will give you suggestions for finding or creating such support.

Other than books by contemporary poets, these are my own most indispensable resources for writing poems: *Patterns of Poetry,* by Miller Williams; *A Formal Feeling Comes,* edited by Annie Finch; everything I can find written by William Stafford; *Don't Ask*, by Philip Levine; and *How to Read a Poem and Fall in Love with Poetry*, by Edward Hirsch.

Exercise: A Poem as Trigger

Read one complete poem aloud, and then write. I have used many poems to trigger writing in my workshops. Raymond Carver's poems, "Drinking While Driving," "At Night the Salmon Move,"and "Photograph of My Father in His Twenty-Second Year" are excellent excellent examples. Kathryn Dunn, who leads workshops for adults and also for mainstream and refugee high school students, wrote in response to Sylvia Plath's poem, "Daddy":

LEGACY

What would you say to your father
if he came back—if he could—
that you haven't already said
over and over, a thousand times
in his absence, like a rosary,
Hail Mary, Mother of God; keeping yourself
bound to him with your mantra, keeping
the feel of his hand on your shoulder,
carrying it always, not even knowing it.
What could you say to the man

you have held at the distance of one stiff arm
from the moment he died, with words like
he brought it on himself, and *son of a bitch.*
The man about whom you could only find hatred,
stunned by memories his death allowed.

What could you say to yourself
about allowing this man his faults,
his pain, when for fifteen years
that meant wronging yourself:
if he was bad, then you were alive;
if he was good, you were dead.
That was the formula—Hail Mary

Mother of God. What do you say
when you understand
the legacy that lives in your body
is yours, and the man who gave it to you
has died. Your hatred can no longer serve

his condemnation, or yours.
You must begin to find a way
into the legacy. Carry it, study it,
learn every corner and curve—
to do any less

will freeze the shoulder that feels his touch,
the arm that pushes him out.

You must begin with
what can you say to your father
you haven't already said.

Exercise: Using Random Words

This exercise was given to me by a writer who said it originated with poet Carolyn Forché. Like good folk songs that change as they are passed from person to person, so has this exercise no doubt been altered in translation. It is the opposite of the exercise above. This one springs me out of my own literal memories and habitual patterns. I may still write about those images, but this makes me think and write in fresh ways.

On your page, list 15 nouns in one column. In the next column, list 15 modifiers. Do the lists quickly; try not to make any connections. Let them be as random as possible. When you have the two lists, connect nouns and modifiers in the most unlikely possible pairs. Then use as many of the pairs as you can in a poem.

The following example is by Elizabeth Earl Phillips.

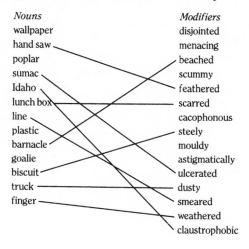

Nouns	*Modifiers*
wallpaper	disjointed
hand saw	menacing
poplar	beached
sumac	scummy
Idaho	feathered
lunch box	scarred
line	cacophonous
plastic	steely
barnacle	mouldy
goalie	astigmatically
biscuit	ulcerated
truck	dusty
finger	smeared
	weathered
	claustrophobic

WINDSWEPT

A scarred black lunch box lay
    within a clump of ulcerated sumac
cautiously Ray and I
    pried its barnacled hinges open
inside was one steely biscuit
    and a feathered hand saw
"Claustrophobic Idaho" was scratched
    across the tin nameplate
a solemn whistle keened six
dusty trucks from the reservation
    idled at the bleached mine gate
smeary children
    too tired to cry
        sucked weathered thumbs.

Exercise: The Scramble

This is a playful exercise that helps to disconnect habitual ways of thinking: Write a simple little incident, a short narrative. Then turn to a clean page. Number down the left side of the page 1, 2, 3 and again 1, 2, 3—leaving no blank lines until you have eight sets of 1, 2, 3. Then write your incident again, beginning on line number 1, then skipping to the next line numbered 1, and continuing, using only the lines numbered l, skipping lines 2 and 3. When you have filled all the lines numbered 1, go back to the top and write on each line numbered 2 . When you get to the bottom, go back to the top again and write on the lines numbered 3. The result is scrambled and can be fresh and interesting raw material for a poem.

When I ask workshop members to try this, I get resistance! "This didn't work! It makes no sense!" I take out a volume of poems by James Tate or Charles Simic and read aloud an abstract poem that seems, to my ear at least, scrambled. And I point out that since both Tate and Simic have received the Pulitzer prize for poetry, perhaps the rest of us should examine our own tendency to be limited to linear thought patterns.

Once you have the scrambled lines, feel free to change, delete, or add to make your final poem.

Hannah Fiske wrote a letter to me that included the following:

> I read this exercise in your book and thought it sounded terrific, so I mentioned it in one of my classes. My students seemed to have trouble grasping the concept when I explained it, and I also hadn't tried it yet myself.
>
> That day I went to the library when I was done teaching and sat down to give it a try. I was HOOKED! What an amazing experience—it didn't *change* my story, just magically *distilled* it down to a wonderful, stronger essence.
>
> I put this package together and gave it to all of my students the next week, and when they looked at it they all kind of went, 'Aha! That's how it works.' They just needed to see it on paper—my verbal directions weren't enough.

Example:

Here is my narrative paragraph, completely unrevised and unedited, in 'straight' paragraph style. Following it is the scrambled version, followed by a revised and edited poem that came out of it through this exercise. You will notice that I made several 'mistakes' while writing the narrative on my scrambled lines, but the final result was just fine, so don't worry!

Breakfast (version 1)

Waiting at the table, cold and still, a little bleary-eyed in the morning, paper spread before me, looking for motivation and inspiration in the lifestyle section where I'm reading about people who exercise and re-make themselves. The waitress is busy, she has a large table of elderly people who are taking up much of her attention. I called the hostess, and so on. We had hot black cups of coffee in front of us and within minutes we had ordered. People arrived in droves, families with children and older couples, and us. The sun was shining and for once the sky was a sparkling wintry blue. When our food came, I was ravenous. Hot, sweet pancakes drizzled with syrup and spread with butter, crispy scrapple and more hot coffee. We ate and talked and planned our day as we watched the traffic go by outside the plate glass window. The check was late, too, and then we smiled and played with the baby at the next table with the bluest eyes and dimples and soft hair and sleepy smiles and left a tip on the table. Out the door, the day began, our appetites sated and fulfilled.

<u>Ex:</u> "Scrambled Poem"

Breakfast — version 1 (totally unedited)

1	Waiting at the table, cold and still, a
2	minutes we had ordered. People arrived
(oops! →) ⊗2	in droves, families with children and older
again 1	little bleary-eyed in the morning, papers
2	couples, and us. The sun was shining
→3	the plate-glass window. The check was
1	spread before me, looking for motivation and
2	and for once the sky was a sparkling
3	late, too, and then we smiled and
1	inspiration in the lifestyle section where I'm
2	wintery blue. When our food came, I
3	played with the baby at the next table
(1	reading about people who exercise and re
2	was ravenous. Hot, sweet pancakes
(oops!) 1 ⊗	make themselves. The waitress is busy, she
I lost track! ⊗3	with the bluest eyes and dimples and
2	drizzled with syrup and spread with butter,
1 ⊗	has a large table of elderly people who are
2 X	crispy scrapple and more hot coffee. We
⊗3	soft hair and sleepy smiles and left a
1 ⊗	taking up much of her attention. I called
2 x	ate and talked and planned our day
⊗3	tip on the table. Out the door, the
1 ⊗	the hostess, and so on. We had hot black
2 X	as we watched the traffic go by our side
3 ⊗	day began, our appetites sated and fulfilled
1 ⊗	cups of coffee in front of us and within

BREAKFAST

Waiting at the table
cold and still
for the minutes we ordered.
People filter in in droves,
families with children
and older folk, paper couples,
small and bleary-eyed
in the morning.
Sun shines through the glass,
the check spreads before me
as I look for inspiration
where I'm wintry blue.
For once, the sky sparkles
and we smile.
Our food arrives, I play
with the baby
at the next table,
and am ravenous.
Hot, sweet pancakes make themselves.
The waitress is busy,
she with the bluest eyes
and dimples,
drizzled with syrup
and spread with butter.
A table of elderly people
are crispy scrapple
and more hot coffee.
Soft hair and sleepy smiles,
we leave, taking
much attention.
Out the door, the
hostess had hot black
and watched
the traffic go by.
Day began,
appetites sated, fulfilled,
cups of coffee
in front of us and within.

Exercise: A Villanelle Made (Relatively) Painless

Occasionally I give my workshop members an optional take-home exercise. One of them is an invitation to write a villanelle. It is a French form, very musical and fun to write if one can get over the initial sense of complication. So many lines are repeated, it is actually easier than it first seems.

I give each workshop participant a "villanelle kit": several pages that I have stapled together, including Miller Williams's definition of a villanelle from *Patterns of Poetry*; Elizabeth Bishop's poem "The Art of Losing Things," and the villanelle she made from it, titled "One Art"; Theodore Roethke's "The Waking"; and Marilyn Hacker's "Coming Downtown." I also offer three lines of my own in iambic pentameter that could serve as first lines to get a beginner going: "The first time is the hardest. Let me be . . ."; "Winter afternoon. I wait for snow"; and "I remember and no longer cry."

One summer in Ireland, I offered this exercise, and Antoinette Wade, a young woman who writes prose with a clarity and grace that stuns me, responded with expressions of shock and vows of refusal even to *try* to write a villanelle. My insistence that it was *optional* didn't help. However, Antoinette is a teacher: An assignment is an assignment. The next day she presented the following poem in the workshop. (Oh, well. It's a villanelle!)

AFTER AN ANCIENT IRISH CURSE

for Pat Schneider

For introducing the form of the vile villanelle
You disturbed my peace and my sleep as well
May you rotate and writhe on the spits in hell.

Iambic pentameter you asked us for
A meter I find torture to master
In introducing the form of the vile villanelle.

If it's not bad enough demanding vile villanelles
You want five bloody stressed and unstressed sylla-belles
May you rotate and writhe on the spits in hell.

May your word processor blink, your pen have no ink
In the flames may you sizzle and stink
For introducing the form of the vile villanelle.

May your computer from a virus be sick
From publishers get only rejection slips
May you rotate and writhe on the spits in hell.

May your short stories and poems never sell
May the Devil kindle fires with your first drafts as well
For introducing the form of the vile villanelle
May you rotate and writhe on the spits in hell.

Exercise: Creating an Original Form

Make up your own (difficult, exacting, challenging) form and write a poem in that form, being as hard on yourself as possible, allowing yourself no easy solutions to difficult tasks. (See "Letting Go" earlier in this chapter.)

The following poem, by Kate Gleason, a participant in my Amherst workshop, uses an unusual and provocative form, the break in the lines of the poem visually echoing the break that is being expressed in the words:

FRACTURE

Her father would break her   Bones
arm, almost kill her, would   have
jeer, on the one hand, at the idea   the consistency
that she still loved him, the other side   of igneous rock,
afraid, knowing she was   the one
most like the boy his father had   shaped by fire.
made him into, unable to say   When
stop, I don't care what   fractures
you do, you can't make me not   heal
love you. Some fathers—   they leave
even the good times are   a space
shaky. The heart is willing   that won't
but the body is too   close,
weak. It's learned what it learned   a way
in the dark   to tell
and passes it on like Northern Lights,   weather,
ice acting as   a barometer
a mirror to the fire storms   inside
on the sun, flare-ups in   the bone
the light the color of a   now,
hidden pilot, so blue it's   an ache
a flame, tear-shaped, blazing   for storms

Fiction

WHAT IS FICTION?

Fiction is the dream of the writer, made visible on the page. It may be the writer's lived experience or it may be entirely imagined. Eudora Welty was asked in a television interview whether the source of her fiction was autobiographical or imagined. She answered, "If I tell you it is autobiography, you will be embarrassed. If I say it is imagined, you will feel cheated. So I will tell you the truth: It's a mixture."

In *On Becoming a Novelist*, John Gardner says that when we read,

> We slip into a dream, forgetting the room we're sitting in, forgetting it's lunchtime or time to go to work. We recreate, with minor and for the most part unimportant changes, the vivid and continuous dream the writer worked out in his mind (revising and revising until he got it right) and captured in language so that other human beings, whenever they feel like it, may open his book and dream that dream again.

All fiction is autobiography, because even that which we imagine is a collage of images and meanings that have come into, and have been transformed by, our minds. Fiction is *an autobiography of the imagination.*

A good friend tells me he writes his novels in order to live a life different from his own. He says that his characters and their adventures have no relationship to his own experience. Others (including myself) find that even the things we imagine are often metaphors for what we have experienced, or are a way of giving us access to working on experienced and unresolved personal history. Virginia Woolf said,

> The past is beautiful because one never realizes an emotion at the time. It expands later, and thus we don't have complete emotions about the present, only about the past. . . . That is why we dwell on the past, I think.

Fiction is story. Where it comes from—the past or the present, remembered history or utterly imagined magic—is irrelevant. Fiction is another way of telling the truth.

In a classic book, *The Forms of Fiction,* John Gardner and Lennis Dunlap list as "the most obvious" elements "shared by all good fiction, whatever form that fiction may take": *intellectual honesty, emotional honesty, and aesthetic validity.* Our unconscious mind tries to help us achieve intellectual and emotional honesty. If we refuse to write the truth of what we see and what we remember, we have to work hard to keep the door closed. We call that refusal "writer's block." I am convinced that writer's block is often a version of the story of Bluebeard and his bloody closet. If there is a secret hidden behind a door, then that door is the only one we want to open. All other doors feel boring, impossible, *blocked*. All our creative energy goes into keeping the door closed on the story that we refuse to tell. We may not even consciously know what that story is. Janet Burroway writes in *Writing Fiction*:

> It's important to realize that the great dangers in life and in literature are not necessarily the most spectacular. . . . Fewer people have cause to panic at the approach of a stranger with a gun than at the approach of Mama with the curling iron.

Once a young writer, new to my workshop, said quite emphatically that she did not want to write anything related to her own life. She wanted to write "fiction." I affirmed that goal, if that was what she wanted.

The first time she attended the workshop, I deliberately created an exercise that I considered emotionally neutral. I suggested we begin our writing with an image of someone holding a cup. She wrote a piece that on the surface seemed to be a clear and simple description of an action. A man and a woman were at a dining table. The woman had wrapped a teacup and saucer to give as a gift. The man wanted to see it; he opened the box, unwrapped the cup, dropped it, and broke it. There was not one word of overt "telling" about emotion; the writing was clean and strong and visually very satisfying. It was a brilliant piece of writing because at the end of the two or three handwritten pages everyone in the room knew that what had broken was the relationship. The young writer knew it too; she struggled to hold back tears. I suspect her writing had shown her something that she did not fully, consciously know. Fiction is just another way to tell the truth. And the truths that we have held undisclosed (perhaps even to ourselves) for a long time are under pressure and wanting to come up from the unconscious to the conscious mind. It is the psyche trying to heal itself. It is the artist in us wanting to make art. From this pressure comes the old adage repeated by so many writers: We do not choose our subject; *our subject chooses us*.

In a workshop I led at the Graduate Theological Union in Berkeley, California, there was a retired minister. The first time I had the group write, I put 30 or 40 random objects out on a cloth. Louis chose the crystal ball. He wrote a rather stiff (frightened) small paragraph about the ball itself, describing a little chip in the smooth surface and giving a sermonic moral: All of us have chips in our perfection. It was writing as usual for him; part of his life work had been finding the meanings in ordinary things and lifting those meanings up for his people. I knew that I had to jar him loose from his habitual writing patterns if he was to write beyond the limits of the traditional sermon.

In the second writing exercise, I asked those who felt comfortable doing so to close their eyes, relax, and imagine standing in a doorway. (The exercise is described in detail in the section titled "Additional Exercises.")

Louis "found himself" standing in the doorway to his sister's bedroom, looking at her bed. Her violin was on the bed, the case open, the music stand holding the music for "Silent Night." When he read this to us, he began to cry and could not finish reading. We waited quietly for a bit, and then I asked if he would like someone else to read it for him. He shook his head. I asked if it was OK for us to go on. He nodded and said he wanted us to know that his sister had committed suicide 35 years before, and he had never cried about it. Not when she died, and not afterward. He apologized for crying.

I went to Louis after the workshop session and talked with him at length. I told him that I have many times cried when I read new material; I assured him that someone else would have that experience before the week of workshop was done because, when we write, we touch on our feelings, on our own personal stories, and inevitably emotion comes up. He said he knew that it was important, but he didn't want to write about his sister again. He was not a man who could cry; this was too dangerous. I encouraged him to respect his own timing, his own way of processing things.

I had planned to offer as a writing trigger the next day a short poem called "The Takers," by Sharon Olds, about one sister who pees on another. Siblings are a terrific source of writing material! But because of Louis's decision to avoid his sister, I changed my plan and put out a large collection of buttons from my mother's button box, suggesting that people choose buttons, describe the dress of two characters, and let the characters talk to each other. Louis took one button, described his sister's dress, and wept when he tried to read.

This went on for the entire week. Every exercise I gave turned into the image of his sister's room, her absence, his grief, and finally—his anger. On the last day, I suggested that people write a letter—to someone else, or to the writer inside themselves. Louis wrote—of course—a letter to his sister. This time, we all cried.

In the course of the week, Louis taught himself how to write. He wrote honestly, courageously, and with originality. That workshop was 14 years ago. In the intervening years I have listened to thousands of prose pieces, poems, scenes from plays, portions of novels, and nonfiction fragments. Yet, as if it were yesterday, I remember a room as still as death, an open violin case, an abandoned music stand, and the music . . . "Silent night, holy night, all is calm, all is bright . . ."

ON CRAFT IN FICTION

Although we may use the mulch of our personal lives, the work we do as artists is to make of that mulch and of sheer imagination creative writing: fiction. To do that well, we need craft. We need to know how to plot, develop character, use point of view, make transitions. We need to understand and master the elements of fiction: character, action, setting. Remember, though—all of us have more of this knowledge than we may realize. We may not yet know the names for the "elements of fiction," but we use them all the time as we tell stories to our friends. What is helpful is bringing all that instinctive knowledge into conscious use as we work steadily and consistently at our writing.

There are a lot of books that say you must have an outline, character studies, and so forth. Don't believe them—unless that is your natural way of writing. Out of thousands of writers in my workshops, I've come across only two or three who have the entire book in their minds before they write it. My friend Sharleen Kapp is one of those writers. One night after workshop she said, "Pat, I wrote an entire book on my way to workshop tonight." I know how she writes; I knew what she meant. In the 35 minutes it took her to drive to my house for workshop, she had seen a plot whole and would spend the next year recreating on the page what was already in her mind.

But Sharleen is rare. Most of us write to find out where the story goes. We have no idea what is coming next, and to ask us to outline it is not only "cruel and unusual punishment"—it will kill the work of art.

Carol Bly, in *The Passionate, Accurate Story,* says, "The skills of organization are not wanted in the first draft. . . . The author should still be brooding, maundering around the material. . . . It is a great mistake at that point to start 'applying writing skills' or anything like."

No amount of craft can take the place of that creative energy that brings a raw piece of work into being. The newborn baby comes bloody and messy into the world—eventually it will be washed and clothed, but first it must be pushed out of the dark into the light. Without that intensely personal birth, there is nothing to wash.

Exercise: Breaking into Fiction #1

Writers who have never written fiction—especially those who have written nonfiction for a long time—frequently suffer a specific block. It has to do with letting go of literal "truth"—an unwillingness or inability to "lie." This may be rooted in the unconscious, in childhood admonitions to always tell the truth. Or it may simply be habit.

Here is an excellent way to move through that block: First, find a piece of autobiographical writing in your journal that you don't mind "messing with." Now choose a name with which you could be comfortable, if it were your name. Where you have used "I" in the writing, change it to that name. Where you have "me" and "my," change it to "she" and "hers," or "he" and "his." Then add one small imagined detail: a hammer on the kitchen counter; a toothbrush still damp in the medicine cabinet. An imagined coffee mug on the table. Frequently, when you commit that simple act of imagination, you open the door to the unconscious, and if you watch closely and write what you see, your unconscious mind will continue to give you metaphoric images, gold far richer than the copper and silver of remembrance.

Once I had in workshop a professor, author of several books of nonfiction, who adamantly insisted that she could *not* write fiction. "I've tried," she said one evening before our workshop session began. "I can't do it." She had under her arm the unbound book in which she wrote every Thursday evening.

I asked her to find an autobiographical piece in it and change it as I described in this exercise. When it came time for her to read, she was grinning. She read a piece that went off in a completely different direction from her original work. After the group gave her verbal responses, I asked how she felt about it. "It felt free and exciting," she said. "It was fun."

And of course, because she did not rely solely on memory, but allowed her unconscious to assist her, the writing was more compelling, more interesting, more alive than the original had been.

Exercise: Breaking into Fiction #2

This is a second exercise for breaking the block against writing fiction. Begin as in the exercise above: Write (or find already written in your journal) a short, autobiographical, first-person narrative.

Read it through, and then without looking at the first draft, write the same incident on a fresh piece of paper, but this time add a character that is completely imagined. Let the imagined character come into the narrative early in the scene, and let that coming make a difference in how it turns out at the end. But don't decide any of that ahead of time—not even who the imagined character will be—until you get to the moment in the writing when the character appears. He or she may surprise you. If so, great! Just start writing the short piece again from the top and be open to the knowledge that someone new is going to appear. Trust me—it will happen.

When you have finished, do some journal writing about how you feel about both pieces. What happened? What was different? Which is strongest, most interesting, freshest? Why? If you have a writing friend, read both to the friend and ask for feedback.

Often, breaking into fiction is just a new way of working with old material. Imagining, making stories—"lying," if you will—is one of the most primitive gifts of our human minds. How sad that so often when we grow up, we lock it away.

Novelist and short story writer Valerie Martin, writing in the *New York Times Book Review,* quotes many writers on how their work began, and then observes:

> All of these descriptions have one thing in common: they begin with an image, coming from within or without, strangely persistent in the writer's imagination. . . . The desire at the start is not to say anything, not to make meanings, but to create for the unwary reader a sudden experience of reality.

Begin with an image. See in your mind's eye a toy box, then move in closer and see the small, yellow Tonka truck tumbled on its side. Look at it closely; notice where the light falls, where the shadows rest. Now let your peripheral vision catch some other detail. Write exactly what your inner eye sees.

Occasionally I offer a chapter from Dorothea Brande's *Becoming a Writer* to my workshop participants as an optional take-home exercise. The chapter, titled "The Practice Story," follows 136 pages of preliminary encouragement and advice that is remarkable for a woman writing in 1934, before the writing process movement was even a gleam in the eye of Peter Elbow, Natalie Goldberg, Julia Cameron, Pat Schneider, and the whole generation of writing process authors and teachers who followed her. The first time I did this, I was surprised at the fiction that poured out of people who tried it. I recommend it as an exercise for beginning writers of fiction, although I agree with one of my workshop members who said, "You know, I needed the background support of this workshop in order to let go enough to do the exercise." Brande's book supplies that support as much as a book possibly can.

Great fiction has the ecstatic quality of dream as well as the practiced control of craft. Learn all you can about craft, but do not lose trust in your own deep knowing. The Olympic diver practices and practices, but finally there must be a letting go, a trusting of the practice. Let go of control and write intuitively. Let craft obey instinct, not the other way around. If you coerce your fiction, the art in it will surely die.

John Steinbeck offered the following guidelines for writing fiction, (letter to Robert Wallsten, February 13–14, 1962):

> Now let me give you the benefit of my experience in facing 400 pages of blank stock—the appalling stuff that must be filled. I know that no one really wants the benefit of anyone's experience which is probably why it is so freely offered. But the following are some of the things I have had to do to keep from going nuts.
>
> 1. Abandon the idea that you are ever going to finish. Lose track of the 400 pages and write just one page for each day, it helps. Then when it gets finished, you are always surprised.
>
> 2. Write freely and as rapidly as possible and throw the whole thing on paper. Never correct or rewrite until the whole thing is down. Rewrite in process is usually found to be an excuse for not going on. It also interferes with flow and rhythm which can only come from a kind of unconscious association with the material.
>
> 3. Forget your generalized audience. In the first place, the nameless, faceless audience will scare you to death and in the second place, unlike the theatre, it doesn't exist. I have found that sometimes it helps to pick out one person—a real person you know, or an imagined person—and write to that one. [Remember that John McPhee says he began every book with the words "Dear Mother."]
>
> 4. If a scene or a section gets the better of you and you still think you want it—bypass it and go on. When you have finished the whole you can come back to it and then you may find that the reason it gave trouble is because it didn't belong there.

5. Beware of a scene that becomes too dear to you, dearer than the rest. It will usually be found that it is out of drawing.

6. If you are using dialogue—say it aloud as you write it. Only then will it have the sound of speech.

Well, actually that's about all.

I know that no two people have the same methods. However, these mostly work for me.

As you write, trust the disconnections and the gaps. If you have written what your eye first saw and you are stopped, see again. See something else. Take a leap to another image. Don't require of yourself that you understand the connection. Some of the most brilliant things that happen in fiction occur when the writer allows what seems to be a disconnected image to lead him or her away from the line that was being taken.

Surprise yourself. Robert Frost said, "No surprise for the writer, no surprise for the reader!" Many writers have written about the strange way in which characters take over, take control, refuse to do what the writer wants them to do. John Fowles, in his notes on writing *The French Lieutenant's Woman*, describes such an experience:

> I was stuck this morning to find a good answer from Sarah at the climax of a scene. Characters sometimes reject all the possibilities one offers. They say, in effect: I would never say or do a thing like that. But they don't say what they would say; and one has to proceed negatively, by a very tedious coaxing kind of trial and error. After an hour over this one wretched sentence, I realized that she had in fact been telling me what to do: silence from her was better than any line she might have said.

Interesting—Fowles's experience is the exact opposite of mine as I described it in "Using Other Voices," where my character would not speak, but then let loose with a long speech as I stood in the shower—but Fowles and I come to the same conclusion.

When Louis, the retired minister, began to write about his sister, he saw in his mind the violin on the bed and the sheet music open on the stand. I am certain that he did not rationally think, Now, what music will I put on the stand? He did not *decide* to have it be "Silent Night" because the silence of "Silent Night" would be a metaphor for his sister's stilled voice, the silence of her absence. Rather, trusting what he saw and writing it down fast as he saw it, his unconscious mind instantaneously offered him a brilliant metaphor. This, to me, is one of the most exciting and miraculous things I know about writing.

WRITING LONG WORKS OF FICTION

When a character will not go away, or a short story will not stop coming, face it: You are writing a novel. Or, perhaps, a novella. Refusing to do it is like a pregnant woman's saying "No, thank you" to one of the twins she is carrying. I have given birth, and I have written books. The experiences have a lot in common. There is the long time of gestation—the secret inner work of a spine building and organic interrelationships being formed. In writing, for me, these are loose pages written in workshop and at my computer. The process is a lot like dreaming. Then, as the work progresses, there are seasons of doubt and fear of failure: Can I do this? How did I get myself into this? Help! I want out of here!

Write without revision if you can, until you have a complete first draft. When you have the first, rough draft from beginning to end, work through it again, revising. For more on revision, you may refer to the section titled "Revising" at the end of Chapter 7.

Somewhere near the middle you may find, as I do, that you reach a block. The first time this happened to me, I thought I was dead as a writer. The block lasted for two years. The second time it happened, I thought, Oh, this is what happens to me halfway through a book, figured out what I had done to overcome it the first time, and did it again.

I become blocked halfway through because I have set up the problems my characters face and I have no idea in the world how they are going to overcome them. What I do is go away from home for several days with nothing but living essentials, my manuscript, and my laptop computer. First I sleep and wake, take long walks, get rested. In the resting I lean toward my work, but I do not worry it. I just "tell it" that I am resting in order to give it my best attention. When I really want to, I read the manuscript through and I do not allow *any* interruption except sleep and bodily needs. I get the entire thing into my head at once, and I gently ask for an opening into the rest of the novel. It happens.

In my experience, some writers of long fiction are well served by writing in a good workshop. While others write short pieces, these writers either ignore the writing exercise or incorporate it into their longer work. Cynthia Kennison, Dick Bentley, and AnnieMae Robertson, all of whom have published both long and short fiction, have written with me for years. If the exercise I offer is a reading of Raymond Carver's poem "Drinking While Driving" one of their characters may have a glass of wine or a can of beer. If I put out some sea shells, one of their protagonists may take a walk on a beach. Occasionally they bring in a segment—perhaps a chapter—for workshop response, but mostly they come for the working companionship of like-minded people. They all write at home, alone—and once each week we write together. Recently Carolyn Pelletier brought me a manuscript that was 430 pages long, her novel about people who work in a factory. We had heard sections of the work on Wednesday evenings for two years or more. I edited the entire manuscript, line by line, at no extra cost to Carolyn, because she had written it in and out of my workshop. It was my privilege to respond to her work.

Whether you write alone or meet regularly with other writers, there will most likely come a time when you will benefit from the response of someone who reads your words and gives you a supportive, honest response.

Exercise: Someone in Shadow

Writing alone or with others, imagine someone in shadow. Keep your attention on the shadowed figure. See clearly what can be seen. Begin writing with any words that come to you. If you feel blocked, go back to the shadowed figure. Perhaps you will write what is in that person's mind. That person has a long, long history, memory, experience, loves, disappointments, fears. That person has a story. Or perhaps you will write from a different point of view, as an observer of the person in shadow. The observer, too, has a story. Begin without knowing any of that; you will discover it as you write. Trust the image that you do see, and write clearly, honestly, bravely, in your own natural voice.

Exercise: Writing a Short-Short Story

How long is a short-short story? The editor of the books *Flash Fiction: 72 Very Short Stories* and *Sudden Fiction*, says Hemingway's wonderful (and classic) "A Very Short Story" is about 750 words. He sets 250 words as the "diminutive limit."

How does a short-short story differ from a prose poem? Sometimes it does not differ at all. In her book of poems *The Country Between Us*, Carolyn Forché included the finest prose poem I know, titled "The Colonel." Years later it appeared as a short-short story in *Flash Fiction*.

How does it differ from an anecdote? An anecdote leaves you wanting to know more. The short-short story is complete. A reader doesn't need to know any more about those characters or that situation to be satisfied.

A short-short story cannot have more than one or two characters, in one or two scenes, within a short time span.

We all have countless short-short stories to tell. If it helps, pretend you are telling it to someone you like to talk to. Or go to the telephone book. Put your finger down at random on a first name. Close the book. Open it again and put your finger down at random on a surname. You know everything about this person. What he or she ate for dinner last night. Whether there was candlelight. Or did your character eat out of a pan on the stove? Who was there? What happened?

Or start with one of these opening lines:

"I never did like (*name*)."
"(*Name*) looked into the mirror."
"For once, it seemed everything was going to turn out fine."

Or start with a familiar object. Moya Hegerty, a nun who participated in my workshop in Ursuline convents in Ireland, said she was surprised by this short-short story. She started with an object familiar to an Irish country girl.

COW DUNG

Plonk! Plonk! Plonk! Down came the dung in near perfect circles, each one less full than the one before. The smell was fresh and the dung held the heat of the cow's body for a while after it hit the hard rocky path and sprawled into a lovely shaped cake, a cake that had fallen slightly in the middle and that still held the rings made by the spoon when the fruit was being folded in.

John gave Daisy the tip of the stick to remind her to move on, that toiletries were finished with, but he took note of where the cow dung dropped, as Mary would want to know. The dung would be safe there for a few days—the blue-bottles and the horse flies would have to have their share of the spoils before any further action could be taken. He looked up at the sky. Yes, a red sky at night is a farmer's delight.

Next morning as he drove Daisy to the field behind the hill he noted the progress of the cow dung. It was well set with a healthy crust all round it. Yes, it was doing nicely, but it would need another few days. He was afraid that a cart, taking the short cut to the bog, would damage the masterpiece. He ringed a few heavy stones around the dung to ensure that all would be well. His other fear was the weather, the sky was beginning to cloud.

When he had Daisy safely ensconced in the field, he ran back home and returned with three black plastic bags to cover his precious treasures. He tended the cow dung for a week until it lifted from the ground with the ease of a well baked cake. He put the three dung cakes carefully into the plastic bags and brought them triumphantly home. How to get them into the house was his next move. He knew that his mother would be doing the First Fridays and that he would be left in charge of the house to mind Mary. Yes, that would give him an hour and a half. He hid the three cakes of cow dung at the corner of the haystack and marked the spot with small stones in the shape of a cross.

As soon as his mother left to go to Mass on Friday, he raced outside and brought the presents to the back room where Mary was kept. He never remembered her being anywhere else except in that room. She sat there swaying from side to side, staring at a faraway object. His mother said that she was praying to the angels.

He knew that when he brought her the dung, there would be a quieting down as she took each hard caked piece of dung and crumbled it to pieces. The dry smell had a way of calming her as she played with it and threw it into the air. Then he waited for the moment and it always happened, her eyes would light on John and a strange earthy gaze would come upon her. She was a *duine le Dia*, a person with God.

Exercise: Writing from Something You Love

Take a stanza of a poem, or a paragraph of a book that is particularly meaningful to you and imagine it embodied in a character. Do this gently— don't try to write the entire story in your head. Just let the words of your chosen text remind you of a character. In this moment, this memory, how is he or she dressed? See your character in a setting: outdoor restaurant? seat of a Porsche? cleaning out a test tube in a laboratory? washing dishes? Begin there. With a detail of the scene, or with a thought in the mind of your character. And let the story grow out of that image.

The piece that follows is the opening paragraph from the novella *Love: A Story of Images,* by Alison Hicks, who leads workshops in the greater Philadelphia area.

LOVE, A STORY OF IMAGES

And is there one, the wisest and the best
Of all mankind, who does not sometimes wish
For things that cannot be, who would not give,
If so he might, to duty and to truth
The eagerness of infantine desire?

Wordsworth, *Two-Part Prelude*

It is true, he has always unmoored her. His form hovers, beckoning, at the vanishing point of her horizon. And pitching on his tide toward the rough open sea, her compass blindly floats and spins in his wake.

They are at their tenth college reunion, and she hadn't known he was going to be there, had pretty much assumed, in fact, that he would not, only to see his name on the final list as she checked into the dorm with her husband. The next day, she walks into the gym where rain had forced the festivities. He is playing volleyball, but stops when he sees her.

"Oh, my God," she says.

It's the classic scene every plot works toward, she thinks. Every drama, every poem, every novel, every story, every movie, every narrative playing out in your head. The return. If there is no return, then the character must be written out. If the gun does not go off in the third act, it cannot hang on the wall in the first. If your memories are to exist, they have to prove their utility, and keep coming around.

WHERE TO GO FOR HELP IN WRITING FICTION

One possibility is to join a writing workshop that includes manuscript critiques. A good group will offer suggestions and let you know where the text is confusing or unsatisfying without leaving you feeling discouraged or disempowered. Whether you are writing alone or with others, Janet Burroway's text, *Writing Fiction* is one of my favorite guides for fiction writing. Burroway is clear, helpful, and often witty. For example, she defines the difference between the novel and the short story succinctly: "Many editors and writers insist on an essential disjunction between the form of the short story and that of the novel. It is my belief, however, that . . . the distinction between the two forms is very simple. . . . A short story is short, and a novel is long." And again, discussing the basic features of the story form: "Conflict is the first encountered and the fundamental element of fiction, necessary because in literature, only trouble is interesting. Only trouble is interesting." Her book is one of those in which I start marking favorite passages, only to discover that I'm marking almost everything.

Another excellent book on writing fiction is Carol Bly's *The Passionate, Accurate Story.* The book is passionate—and helpful. I have used as a writing exercise her suggestion that "one way of character-making is putting a cast of characters together made up of your own various selves." I have asked my workshop participants to try that—write a dialogue between two characters who are differing parts of the writer's self. For instance, the self you are when speaking to your grandmother may be quite different from the self you are when speaking to the jerk who pulls in front of you in a lane of traffic. My writers wrote exceptional dialogues—and a few intense monologues because the opposing character couldn't get a word in edgewise!

Bly closes her discussion of this technique with one of the flat, honest (and, to me, funny) statements that I so enjoy in her work: "I won't speak of it further because I don't use it myself." Her book reads like a good, intense session with an excellent teacher. You come away from it *taught*—and wanting to write.

All of Peter Elbow's books are important, both in defining the theoretical bases of the writing process movement and in giving guidance to the individual writer. John Gardner on fiction and Flannery O'Connor on the short story have been particularly helpful to me, as has *Points of View,* an anthology of short stories arranged to illustrate 11 different narrative points of view, edited by James Moffett and Kenneth R. McElhen. Anthologies give you access to advice from many working writers. I especially recommend *The Writer's Home Companion,* edited by Joan Bolker; *The Writer on Her Work* (two volumes), edited by Janet Sternburg; and *Letters to a Fiction Writer,* edited by Frederick Busch. Some writers in my workshops have found Ursula LeGuin's work on fantasy writing and Steven King's work on horror writing helpful. The best periodical for working fiction writers is *Poets & Writers Magazine.*

The most important study may not be in groups or in books, however. Everything we learn in the living of our lives or in our conscious study of the work of others enriches and deepens our writing. Much of that work we do alone. Study how a man sits on a stool in the local diner, how his shirt does not meet the top of his blue jeans, how the dark hair on his back curls like a young child's hair (or bristles like the hair on a wild boar). Study how an old woman's body shrinks in the bed until the shape of her skeleton is visible under the parchment skin.

"Create and work hard on exercises of your own," John Gardner advises. An excellent suggestion—the best exercises may be the ones you create for yourself.

What about studying the classics? I'm glad I read *Ulysses*—783 pages of one day in the life of a Dublin man—but the task was painful for me and I wouldn't have completed it if Professor Hicks in my MFA program had not required it! On the other hand, I recently read Carolyn Heilbrun's brilliant comparison of James Joyce and Virginia Woolf in *Hamlet's Mother and Other Women*. Heilbrun's perspective connected to me—to my questions and my life. Such knowledge as I have of Joyce, Woolf, Eliot, Moore, and the rest, has enriched me, but no more so than knowing in the formation of my bones what poverty is—what it is to be the child of an uneducated, divorced, working-class woman in America, or what it is to walk as a child alone in an Ozark creek bed, looking for fossils and learning the ways of crawdads. No knowledge is enough. All my life I will study for the sake of my writing.

Your own life will happen to you; observe it. Read as a writer, observing what the artist was doing, and why. Form the habit of recording your observations (both from your reading and from your living) in your journal. Live your own life thoughtfully, empathetically. Listen, and watch. Write. From these practices will come the most important things you need to know in order to create good fiction.

A FINAL WORD ABOUT WRITING FICTION

Don't be overwhelmed. You already know the fundamentals—far more than you may think you know. The young writer who wrote about the broken teacup, and the retired minister, Louis, wrote with such power on the first day of a first writing workshop because they, like all of us, had practiced telling stories since they were less than two years old. It counts for something, that practice. Writing is not so far removed from speech as some would have us believe. William Blake said, "The heart knocks at the root of the tongue." Focused speech, speech that is full of emotion or clear intention is often excellent writing. All of us—even those of us who swear we cannot write—have been doing it all our lives, creating our own fictions, writing on the air.

Where to Get Help for Writing in Other Forms

There is not enough space in this book to go as deeply as I would like into forms other than poetry and fiction. Reluctantly, I limit myself to a few of my favorite resources.

NONFICTION

After a generation of being neglected, the personal essay has returned as a favorite form for many writers. There is a vigorous new appreciation for what is now called "creative nonfiction," and it includes everything from brief newspaper articles to books of history, and from diary entries and personal letters to explications of the weird mating habits of daddy longlegs. If you doubt this, check out Philip Lopate's excellent book *The Art of the Personal Essay*, and look at his table of contents by form—what a list of possible forms! It's a feast for writers of nonfiction. So, too, is the compendium of articles by leading nonfiction writers in *The Complete Guide to Writing Non-Fiction*, by the American Society of Journalists and Authors, and edited by Glen Evans. The journal *Creative Nonfiction* is a valuable resource for the writer working in this genre.

Courses in journalism at colleges and universities are excellent places to gain theoretical foundation and experience and to network. Best is to take an apprentice position, no matter how lowly, as close as you can get to the kind of writing you want to do. Magazines need fact checkers, "gofers," copyeditors, typists. If you can't get a paid position, volunteer. There is no substitute for on-the-job experience.

PLAYWRITING

The most important training for any playwright is the living theater. Unlike poetry and fiction, playwrighting is a collaborative art form. My own first play, written as an undergraduate college student, was naive but so much fun to write and direct that I was immediately hooked. A few years later I tried to direct *Aria Da Capo* and fell flat on my face—there was so much that I didn't know! That falling was the beginning of my becoming a playwright. Anyone who wants to be a playwright should be involved with a living theater. In my town there is a comedy improv group called The Villa Jidiots. They play in local restaurants and at the New Year's First Night celebration. They are fantastic! Find a group that is doing theater— any kind, every kind—and volunteer. Do anything and everything—hand out bulletins at the top of the aisle. Act. Find props. Wear black and move scenery between acts. Volunteer for every tiny job and learn what the stage and the performance and the creation of theater is all about. Go to the theater. There is no substitute for your actual involvement in order to learn what works and what does not work on stage.

When you have written a scene or an act or an entire play, what you most need is to hear it read aloud. If you are involved in a good writing workshop, the leader should provide that for you. If you do not have a workshop leader to do it for you, create such an event for yourself. Invite friends in for a potluck meal, have the play read aloud, and discuss it.

The best printed resources for playwrights are publications of the Dramatists Guild, 234 West 44th Street, New York, NY 10036. A subscription to their newsletter brings with it their journals, packed with helpful information about the craft of playwriting and markets. Good libraries will have their back issues.

SONGWRITING

Songwriting is another writing form that belongs to everyone. As I sit writing these words, I am only 24 hours past participating in a memorial service for a 94-year-old Jewish woman. The pastor, Rev. Carlos Anderson, sat at a piano and sang songs he had composed. They filled the sanctuary, rolled and tumbled and gathered us all in. He listened as family members and friends spoke, every one of them with stories that revealed a difficult and cranky old woman who was nevertheless loved by her family. At the close of the service, the pastor told us that the song he had planned to sing was not at all appropriate. He switched from slow and sorrowful to an upbeat, jazzy affirmation—both of which were his own compositions. No matter what trouble there may be, he sang, "there is love." It was perfect.

When my own mother was old, she expressed regret that when I was a baby, she didn't know "a real lullaby" to sing to me. I'm glad she didn't, because I carry in my heart her own words, sung to a hymn tune: Bye-oh, Bye-oh, Bye-oh Baby, / Bye-oh, Bye-oh, Baby Bye . . . over and over.

How sad it is that we have allowed ourselves to be deprived of singing our own songs, making them up, letting them fit the moment that calls forth from us our singing. We have almost given up all the ways of making art; so many of us believe that a writer isn't a writer unless published, a songwriter isn't a songwriter unless recorded in a professional studio.

All you need as a beginning songwriter is to sing to yourself on a long walk or as you drive alone in the country. Sing an old song that you like—one to which you don't know all the words. When words fail you, sing the melody using only "la-la-la." Then begin to use words of your own. There's no one to hear you except God, and it is rumored that God likes "a joyful noise." Sing out loud. Sing joyfully. Unless it's a mournful song—then sing mournfully and loudly enough that the song reaches your ears. Work and rework your lines until they fit perfectly. *Please don't write them down while you're driving!*

When you have the words to fit the melody perfectly, type them out and give them to someone who plays an instrument, and ask your musician friend to compose a melody. *Don't say what tune you used—it will only confuse the composer.* Just say it's a lyric for a song. If you don't know anyone who plays an instrument, call a music school. Put a classified ad in the paper: Lyricist seeks composer for country-and-western (or pop, or gospel, or whatever) songs. Make it plural. I have done this; it works. When a composer calls, be honest. Tell him or her that you are a beginner but want to learn. Don't pay for their services. Sign a simple agreement that says each of you will hold the rights to your own work and divide any money that comes to you from sale of the song.

Like all other art forms, after you begin freely using your own gifted voice and spirit, you will begin to hunger for ways to improve your knowledge and craft. *Tunesmith,* a book on songwriting by Jimmy Webb, has been called "a master class in songwriting" and "the most interesting book ever written on songwriting." It deserves every word of praise it has received. Judd Waldin, composer of *Raisin* and other musicals, cites the workshops led by Sheila Davis at The New School in New York City—and her books on songwriting—as the best resources available to songwriters today.

MUSICAL THEATER

After writing 14 plays that had been produced and several that were published, I was invited to attend the B.M.I. Lehman Engel Musical Theater Workshop in New York City. I had four children and ten thousand other reasons not to make a weekly four-hour train trip each way to and from New York, but it was terribly exciting to be invited. I accepted, thinking I would attend three times and then bow out. It was incredible. I stayed for four years. Each time, I arrived back home at 3:30 in the morning, unable to sleep even then from excitement.

SCREENWRITING

In my opinion, the best books written to help the screenwriter are by Linda Seger, *Making a Good Script Great, Creating Unforgettable Characters*, and *The Art of Adaptation: Turning Fact and Fiction into Film*. The Screenwriter's Guild also offers resources.

A Word of Caution

In all genres of writing, books, articles, seminars, or workshops that preach a negative, defeatist message are not helpful! Recently I opened a book on screenwriting in which a successful playwright took many pages to tell me that I don't stand a chance because getting into the Screenwriter's Guild is too hard, there are too many people trying already, et cetera, et cetera. A book like that is poison to the creative writer. There is always room for excellent work, and there are always generous people who will help the beginner find his or her way.

9

The Ethical Questions:
Spirituality, Privacy, and Politics

Any consideration of ethical questions in writing will of necessity touch our most primal spiritual orientation. What do we value? What are our commitments? Where do we take a stand on issues of importance to our own generation and possibly to those who come after us?

Writing as a Spiritual Practice

Whether we write as an act of personal discovery, as a form of prayer in the sense of the deepest cry and search of our spirits, or as a means of having a voice in the world, writing can be a fundamental act of the human spirit.

In 1934 Dorothea Brande put forth the idea of writing "morning pages" in *Becoming a Writer.*

> The best way to do this is to rise half an hour, or a full hour, earlier than you customarily rise. Just as soon as you can—and without talking, without reading the morning's paper, without picking up the book you laid aside the night before—begin to write. Write anything that comes into your head: last night's dream, if you are able to remember it; the activities of the day before; a conversation, real or imaginary; an examination of conscience. Write any sort of early morning reverie, rapidly and uncritically. The excellence or ultimate worth of what you write is of no importance.

More than 50 years later, Julia Cameron brought the idea of "morning pages" to countless writers through her books *The Artist's Way* and *The Right to Write*. "Morning pages bear witness to our lives," Cameron says in *The Right to Write*. "They increase our conscious contact with spiritual guidance."

Cameron stresses throughout her work the connection between a specific discipline of writing practice and spirituality. Her method of "three pages of daily longhand writing, strictly stream of consciousness . . . done in the morning" has become a way of life for many writers.

Meaningful spirituality has at its center a connection to healing the world. Often the act of writing gives the writer access to the exact center, the heart, where the inner fire of commitment sparks the necessity of action in the world. Writing and publication may in fact be that very action. Regardless of how we may wince at some of the literary mannerisms and racial stereotypes in *Uncle Tom's Cabin*, it cannot be denied that Harriet Beecher Stowe galvanized the nation against slavery and strengthened the uprising that became the American Civil War. She did that by putting words onto paper.

The writer bell hooks points out this connection in her chapter titled "Faith, Writing, and Intellectual Work" in *remembered rapture*: "I can testify that meaningful spiritual practice sustains and nurtures progressive politics, that it enhances the struggle for liberation, that it allows that integrity of being to surface in settings where we are sorely tempted to move against our vows and beliefs."

Writing is my primary spiritual discipline. Here, writing, I struggle to understand myself and my world. I write because I want to bring to myself and perhaps to my reader more light, more grace, more understanding, more delight. I write sometimes out of my anger or my concern to try to make a difference in the world. All of that, the personal work and the public work, is for me connected to what I mean by "writing as a spiritual practice." It is my vocation, and my work is my prayer. It is sometimes a conduit for an ecstatic joy, similar to my experiences of giving birth. Once in a while it seems a dialogue of light and grace.

Often, writing is where I face what for me is darkness. When I have to deal with death, with loss, with injustice, with war—I go to my writing.

The poem that follows, by Daphne Slocombe, was written three days after the terrorist attack on the World Trade Center and the Pentagon on September 11, 2001.

NOW

God grinds us with his teeth
because our hearts are hard
God grinds us with his teeth

Because we closed our eyes
to our own darkness
God swallows us
in the darkness of her belly we lie
with our eyes shut, tight shut
Behind them the tears
fall into our hearts

Because we have held ourselves separate
God smashes us into one
Now we are one people
as the wheat becomes one
beneath the millstone.

Slowly the stone wheel turns
and our hulls are cracked and ground
our eyes are unsealed
our bones are ground together with our hearts
till from our sorrow and from our thankfulness
we can make bread
to feed the children
of our enemies.

After the terrorist attacks on the
World Trade Center, 11 September 2001

Privacy and Writing

What about privacy? There is, of course, the possibility that we may to-morrow be embarrassed by what we write today. But the danger of embarrassment to the writer is the lesser half of the problem. The other half is the ethical question of whether we might embarrass others. Do we have a right to use the material of other people's lives in our writing? What about the fact that I cannot write about myself without revealing some things about those from whom I came, and with whom I live? There is nothing about myself that I can write without revealing aspects of the lives of those closest to me. Privacy for the writer is a personal question, but it is also an ethical question.

THE PERSONAL QUESTION

To the extent that I write at all, my life is "an open book." Someone, some-day, may read it, whether it is published or not. And there are some things—not many, but some—that I do not write anywhere, not even in my journal. Everyone's boundaries are his or her own; what would be intolerable self-revelation to one person is of no consequence to another. I have more than one friend who writes in journals in times of great stress and then destroys them. I know the danger in keeping a journal; someone may know who I really am. Or, more accurately, someone may know who I am in the moments of the day when I am writing, and mistakenly think that I'm like that all the time. Because sadness drives me to my journal much more than celebration drives me there, someone reading my journal could conclude that I am sad much more of the time than is true.

I know that my writing has drawn people to me, and it has pushed people away. I know that the "me" revealed on my pages is not always the "me" that is seen across a table at the local deli. I know that some of my former friends can't deal with the more complicated "me" they meet on my pages. I can't help that. From the time I was ten years old and wrote my first poem, writing has been the way that I survive, and it has been my art form.

In the short run, there are ways to protect yourself. Lock your journal up. Or put it in a notebook in plain sight, but mark it "Old School Notes" or "Genealogy" or "Great Aunt Maud's Recipes." Come to think of it, that might be too interesting! You want something that looks boring to others.

Remember that Kafka said, "Writing means revealing oneself to excess." That is as true for the writer of fiction as it is for the writer of autobiographical memoir. You cannot confine your art to what will never embarrass you. The overt lie or omission that protects you today may embarrass you tomorrow. Leave judgment to others—just do your work as truly and as honestly as you can.

WRITING ABOUT OTHERS

I received a letter recently from a woman who read my first book on writing, *The Writer as an Artist*. She said she was disturbed by my section on writing about others and questioned my insistence upon writing the truth—she said she could not write the truth about her son in prison.

I am grateful for her letter; it helped me to think more deeply about my own boundaries, my own ethics of writing. On the question of writing about her son, unequivocally, I agree with her. I do not write, even in my journal, about any painful aspect of the lives of my adult children. I may note some publicly known fact such as a serious illness, or some joyful achievement or funny episode in family life. Even for that, however, I ask their permission for anything beyond my own journal. Rightly or wrongly, I wrote and published poems about them as young children when my own life was almost entirely consumed by caring for them. However, their lives as adults are sacredly independent and have no place on my pages. (The reverse, of course, is not at all true: They may very well write about their parents, just as I have done—I tremble in my metaphoric shoes!)

Other people in my life, however, do sometimes find themselves on my pages. Some are fictionalized so much that only the person in question might guess. I have changed gender, age, description, place of residence; I have altered histories, made up incidents, distorted the truth on purpose for the sake of disguise. In my fiction there are reflections of people I know; in my autobiographical writing there are straightforward portraits of my mother and certain other people in my life. Do I ask their permission? Sometimes. And sometimes I do not. My brother's early alcoholism and incarceration by the army were profoundly formative experiences of my own. I wrote about them in my book *Wake Up Laughing*, but before I released those pages to any other reader, I asked his permission. With enormous generosity of spirit, he gave it. One friend said I could use a story that involved her if I did not use her real name. There are others not so close to me, and not likely to be identified by any reader, whom I have disguised. And there are some, living and dead, that I included without permission where I felt they would not be recognized and would not themselves be affected by it. The decision depends on *the relationship I have with the person.*

I have been asked whether I use the work of my writing workshop participants without their permission. Never! Nor am I sympathetic to teachers who use student work without giving their names and getting their permission.

Every writer struggles with the question of boundaries and rights: when does my story belong to me, and when does it belong to someone else? What about my readers who won't like it? When we published an anthology of the writings of low-income women in housing projects in western

Massachusetts and when we gave public readings, the biggest struggle the women had, regardless of race or ethnic background, was: *What will my mother think?* or, *What will my man think? Will he beat me?*

Dorothy Allison has written:

> I had been taught never to tell anyone outside my family what was going on, not just because it was so shameful but because it was physically dangerous for me to do so. . . . I didn't start writing—or rather I didn't start keeping my writing—until 1974, when I published a poem. Everything I wrote before then, ten years of journals and short stories and poems, I burned, because I was afraid somebody would read them.

There is a compelling and interesting discussion of the ethics of writing and its relation to class identity in bell hooks's book, *remembered rapture.* She discusses the pressure upon her from her own "working class" family never to reveal family secrets and suggests that pressure is less in more privileged families.

This analysis surprises me; it does not fit with my own experience. My mother certainly did apply specific and intense pressure on me never to tell how I grew up in poverty. However, wealthy writers in my workshops deal with an equal stranglehold of silence. Repeatedly, I have heard them anguish over the implications of telling the truth about families that from the outside appear ideal. I believe the desire for privacy is universal and that pressure from families to protect their secrets crosses class and ethnic lines.

Pressure to refrain from writing about one's own personal life comes not only from the writer's family. It is also deeply embedded in the attitudes of literary critics, teachers, and writers themselves.

If writing is personal, it is frequently called "confessional." Usually, the term is not meant as a compliment and is far more often directed at women writers than at men. The negative connotation is absurd. Male writers—from Job and Jeremiah to Lowell, Vidal, and Styron—have "confessed" their intimate secrets, secrets of their families, personal emotional trauma, grand sins, and peccadilloes. Who has decried their work as less than excellent because it is "confessional"? Insidiously for both male and female writers, that term is judgment of *content*, not of craft or form.

Cherrie Moraga writes in *The Last Generation*:

> All writing is confession. Confession masked and revealed in the voices and faces of our characters. All is hunger. The longing to be known fully and still loved. The admission of our own inherent vulnerability, our weakness, our

tenderness of skin, fragility of heart, our overwhelming desire to be relieved of the burden of ourselves in the body of another, to be forgiven of our ultimate aloneness in the mystical body of a god or the common work of a revolution. These are human considerations that the best of writers presses her fingers upon.

Many times writers in my workshops have said something like this: *I know that writing about myself is self-indulgent.* Or, if the subject is personal: *I don't like what I just wrote. It's sentimental.* Those statements come from a long history, and even if we don't know much about the tradition of writing in Western culture, we nevertheless are infected by it. Every generation must react against the preceding one in order to carve out new and original material. We all know that. One of my favorite cartoons shows two cavemen dragging their hands like gorillas and, in the background, a skinny cave boy, walking upright. One caveman says to the other, "Ignore him. He just walks that way to bug his parents."

My generation was taught "objectivity" as a reaction to older "subjective" or "romantic" writers. John Crowe Ransom, Lionell Trilling, Ezra Pound, and others taught us to distrust the personal voice. Now, a couple of generations later, writers come to my workshops having absorbed that literary prejudice from older teachers. "This is about me—I know it's self-indulgent," they tell me, or "I wrote about my mother—I know that's sentimental"—without knowing why they believe that to be true. It is not true. *Subjects in themselves are not self-indulgent or sentimental.* The issue is how fresh, how true, how concrete and vivid is the writing.

Political Writing

SOME BASIC ASSUMPTIONS

William Safire said, "All the ism's are was'm's." Unfortunately, although that is clever, it isn't accurate. Classism, racism, sexism, ageism, nationalism, as well as homophobia and religious intolerance—ancient demons that sicken and destroy us—still feed upon us. Writers, as artists, it seems to me, must not fail to do battle at the level of ethical foundation and moral imperative.

It might be well if every writer at some point asked this question: What would it mean for me to accept fully the implications of my life— and therefore my work—as "political"? Adrienne Rich wrote: "I did begin to resist the apparent splitting of poet from woman, thinker from woman and to write what I feared was political poetry." When I read those words I was amazed and gratified. For so long a time Rich has written what I understood to be political poetry—yet even she struggled with the very word *political.*

For many years I believed some shadowy prejudice that if a poem is political it isn't as good as if it is somehow "pure," free of political implication. Of course this was naive. Whether we like it or not, our work is political. Silence is as political as breaking silence.

Through all of my writing life I have struggled with this issue. When I was young and my husband was a clergyman, I wrote plays for the church that lifted up issues of poverty and pacifism. After we left organized religion, there was a time when I did not know how to deal with social issues of concern to me. I had not yet begun my work with women in low-income housing projects. My desire to put my writing and my concern for social justice together drove me to take a workshop with Grace Paley. I love her stories, and Paley is both a writer and an activist. How does she put those two things together?

At the workshop, the day came when I could ask my question. To me, her very short story titled "A Man Told Me the Story of His Life" was a model of political writing. With such subtlety, such art, she causes her reader—at least this reader—to think about the political implications of the lives of her characters. How does she do that? I had studied the story—it was straightforward: This happened, and then this happened. All that made it political, I thought, was her choice of names for her characters: José and Maria.

And so I asked her, "Did you give your characters Hispanic names in order to make the story have political resonance?"

She looked at me rather quizzically and answered, "No. A man named José really did tell me the story of his life."

I left the workshop grateful to Paley for her lack of pretension and her honesty. She was telling me what later I would read in Eavan Boland's words: "Just by trying to record the life I lived in the poem I wrote, I had become a political poet." You don't have to work at it. All you have to do is tell the truth.

I have come to understand, through writing about my own origins and through working face to face with low-income writers in public housing projects, that the issue is not whether our writing will be political. If we are silent, our silence is political. If we write, our writing is political. The choice, as Brecht understood, is not between the apolitical and the political. It is always between one set of political acts and another.

Martín Espada, whose book, *Imagine the Angels of Bread*, won the American Book Award, writes:

> My poetry is based on two foundations: the image and the political imagination. . . . Political imagination goes beyond protest to articulate an artistry of dissent. The question is not whether poetry and politics mix. The question is how best to combine poetry and politics, craft and commitment, how to find the artistic imagination equal to the intensity of the experience and the quality of the ideas.

The political writings of Adrienne Rich and Eavan Boland, it seems to me, rise from a necessity to address their peculiar situation of being female poets in a tradition where maleness was not only dominant in the persona of the teacher/mentor, but written into the text of the literature they studied as young poets. Audre Lorde, Sapphire, bell hooks, and other female writers express issues of race and sexual preference as well.

For me, "recording the life I lived" began with a play called *After the Applebox*, in which for the first time, I wrote personal images of poverty. When my mother saw the play, she told me she never wanted to see me again. In 1957 I was refused the graduate degree I wanted "because unfortunately you are a woman." To write the life that I have lived, it was imperative that I find a way to write "what I feared was political poetry."

When I was working on my MFA in Creative Writing, I handed in a short story to my fiction professor. It included a literal description of the two tenement rooms in which I had lived at age 13. I described the bare lightbulb that hung from a black cord, and I detailed in my character's action what I myself had done. When I was 13, I did in fact spray roach poison on a hundred or more roaches on the underside of our kitchen table. As they dropped to the kitchen floor, I (and my teenaged character after me) watched how the females dropped their egg sacs and slowly died. I kept from throwing up by pretending they were Hebrew slaves being killed by Pharaoh in front of the Sphinx. I was Pharaoh. So was the character in my story.

I know that autobiographical truth does not necessarily a good story make—and my story was flawed. But not for the reasons the professor gave. He wrote on my paper two comments: "A bare lightbulb hanging from a cord is a cliché," and "The poor don't talk about the Sphinx."

For years I have wanted to write a book called, *The Poor Don't Talk about the Sphinx*. I would ask in the book, "Is a lamp with a nice lampshade beside a Danish couch a cliché?"

Kate Murphy, a teacher in Northern Ireland, leads a workshop for blind writers as well as for writers in a housing estate. Here she writes a personal essay about that experience.

A WRITING WORKSHOP IN NORTHERN IRELAND

The pavements were painted red, white and blue, flags of proscribed loyalist organisations hung from the lamp posts marking out territory. Many of the houses were boarded up, others had broken windows and still others had tidy fronts and a well kept appearance. The parking area into which I had been directed was littered with shards of glass. Was I in the right place? Was it safe to park here? I locked the car, checked the door handles and ventured round the corner. I was standing in front of a block of brightly painted houses which the sign proclaimed to be the 'FAMILY CENTRE'.

An enthusiastic older woman met me at the door and escorted me to the room where a group of young women, one with a baby, were drinking coffee and smoking. The room was thick with smoke and the windows were closed tight.

I was introduced. They were unimpressed.—They didn't know why they were there.—They would give it a try.—A social worker had told them to come.

But, willingly, I was drawn into the conversation. X wasn't there because she had to go into hospital to get her 'operation' reversed.

'What the fuck does she want it reversed for—she's got four weans. Is she out of her mind?'

'Aye but she was very young when she had them—she's got a new partner and wants another wean.'

'She's fuckin' mad—I wouldn't do it.'

'Me neither. But I wouldn't let them tie my tubes if I had it to do again. My troubles only started when I had that op. They don't tell you that, but now I need a hysterectomy an' that snooty wee doctor told me I was too young. I said—listen dear, have you any weans?—She said, 'No' So I told her—You don't know what the fuck you're talking about, I said, It's my body, my womb, and I want it *out*.'

What had I taken on? I halted the flow of conversation by suggesting that we could finish our coffee and cigarettes—an unpopular suggestion. I promised we would take a cigarette break in about an hour if they could wait until then and explained that we would need to open the windows to let some smoke escape because I have asthma. This elicited an immediate sympathetic response and everyone took a last drag and doused their cigarettes.

We started. I explained the AWA method, talked about confidentiality and how we respond to each others work. We had a trial run with a very short exercise. They wrote hesitantly and some read but others didn't. Suddenly we were interrupted. A girl stuck her head round the door and shouted 'Samuel's mum!'

Samuel's mum leapt to her feet 'Oh God, dirty bum—they don't do dirty bums down there in the cresh. I'll have to go and change him. Don't do anything till I come back.' We continued writing but that was only the first of several similar interruptions. I did wonder why all these kids had been waiting for me to arrive before they filled their nappies. Meanwhile the six week old baby slept quietly in the corner—thank God!

Next I asked them to relax and take deep breaths. All assumed a yoga pose. I was impressed. When I ask my regular group of women to do this some of them start to giggle but these women do yoga at the centre. I asked them to think about a writing experience they had at school or elsewhere. This time no one had any problem writing and everyone wanted to read. Without exception all the women had bad experiences of writing. No wonder they weren't sure about coming to a creative writing class—I'm astonished they were there at all. One young woman wrote about a story homework assignment she had been given. She enjoyed writing it and got so involved with her characters she drew pictures of them. She read her story to her mum and dad and they were proud of it. Next day she put it on the teacher's desk and waited expectantly. She watched the teacher's face but she didn't smile. When it was returned the teacher's verdict was, 'That's too short, You can do better than that and I didn't ask you to draw pictures!'

I opened my mouth to ask for a response to this piece of writing but a voice exploded beside me, 'The oul BITCH!' There was a chorus of assent. On this one occasion I have to confess—I abandoned AWA good practice and joined in.

I thoroughly enjoyed working with this group. Not all of them stayed for ten weeks. The group was fluid—there was a baby sick, a neighbour dead, a child off school, extra hours to be worked before Christmas. Others drifted in for one session to 'see what we were doing'. Those who stayed told me they would not have missed it; one girl said it changed her life. I have promised to keep in touch and intend to bring them to meet and read with my regular group this term. I look forward to it.

WRITING ABOUT CLASS

Let me admit that I am not a person of balanced perspective on this issue. I do not claim to be, and I do not apologize for my failure to be balanced. I name my origin: As an early teenager I sat in a filthy apartment on the second floor of a tenement in St. Louis, dreaming of being a writer. I know in my blood and my bone what it takes to move from one class to another in this society. I know the terror of it, the impossibility of it without someone— several someones—reaching out a hand and dollars to help me make the transition. Helping with encouragement. Helping with patience. Helping with empathetic understanding. Helping with money.

There are too many poor people in this society. In this world. There are too many children without any way to express the incredible genius of their imaginations except by scrawling words on a subway wall or tearing down something that is not theirs. I want to change that. And so I write what follows, because I believe it.

First, about the word *poor*. "Poor" is not a bad word. Replacing it with euphemisms such as "underprivileged," and "under-served" (as I do elsewhere in this book) are well intentioned and sometimes helpful, but euphemisms are also dangerous. They can assist us in *not seeing*. They can form a scrim through which ugly truth is dimmed to our eyes. There are a lot of poor people in America, and their voices are largely silenced.

Second, the so-called canon of Western literature has been a travesty. Not because of what is included, but because of what is excluded for classist, racist, and sexist assumptions. Historically the "canon of great literature" has been identified and guarded by persons who had a privileged education, are white, and are male. We have made some progress—not enough, but some—in the areas of racism and sexism. At least there is some awareness that respectable boards and agencies related to writing and literature must have some racial and sexual diversity in their membership. However, the idea of *class* representation in the canon, or even in literary circles, has yet to dawn upon us. The voices of the poor are very nearly absent. The assumption underlying this absence is that only writers who have, in one way or another, received a privileged or cultured education can hope to be taken seriously as artists. Coupled with an ever-increasing number of people on this earth unable to gain access to traditional education, are we not perpetuating a situation in which the "canon of great literature" is so elitist that it speaks to and for only a small and privileged fraction of the human family?

This is an ethical issue. Some concrete ways of beginning to address it are explored in Part II, Chapter 13, "Using Writing to Empower the Silenced."

WRITING RACE

As I worked on this book, I took a few evenings off to watch the television premier of Ken Burns's series on jazz. There is a haunting moment in the midst of the great sounds of black jazz musicians when an interviewer asks Wynton Marsalis about *jazz* and *race*. He is momentarily startled. He looks down and you can see that he simply is without words to answer. Then he looks up and quietly says, "It's all about race."

My good friend Kate Hymes and I attended a writing conference to-gether. We sat in an open shed, listening to Sekou Sundiata reading his poem/lyrics. They were wonderful; I bought his CD. When Kate and I returned to the motel, I said, "I want to read the lyric to you that's on the back of this CD, but there's a word here that I don't recognize. Do you know what *keloid* means?"

Kate sat facing me on the other king-sized bed in the motel room. There was just a beat of silence before she said, "It's how we heal."

My friendship with Kate was new. She is a powerful educator in the state of New York. She is beautiful and passionate. I very much wanted her friendship. She is black; I am white. Something in the way she said "It's how we heal" was akin to Marsalis's "It's all about race." Quiet, un-derstated, it exploded in me. Suddenly I was a kid again in the slums in St. Louis. All the "Negroes" lived over on Washington Street, one block away from where I lived next to the streetcar tracks on Olive Street. Not one of their children went to my high school. Not one of them swam in the public swimming pool where I swam. At the movies, they sat in the balcony; I sat on the first floor. Facing Kate, I was struck with fear. Any-thing I said might be wrong. I didn't have the slightest idea what she meant, but I was too terrified to ask. I read the lyric to her, and we went down to supper.

All the while as we ate and made pleasant conversation, I felt the trouble in me wanting to bubble up. What did *keloid* mean?

When we got back to the room, I sat on my bed and asked the ques-tion, point blank. "Kate, tell me about that word."

"It's how we heal." She watched my face, saw the confusion. "When we are cut, it's how we heal. If the surgeon isn't incredibly skilled, there is a raised welt."

I saw images in my mind—African slaves with crisscrossed marks on their backs. The whole history of this nation in black and white seemed to be in the motel room with us.

"If you don't mind," Kate said. She pulled up her blouse, pulled down her bra, and there across her upper breast was a long scar. It was a differ-ent color than her dark black-olive skin. "It's how we heal," she said again simply.

Later, Kate would tell me about what she called her "close brush" with cancer. Later, I would understand that the word "keloid" can apply to white bodies, as well as black bodies. Out of that conversation Kate and I began gently and carefully to explore what other things we do not understand, what other scars we both carry. "Black people talk about race all the time," she said. "I sometimes think we talk about it too much."

"White people don't talk about it," I said. That's when I realized that there was a huge, invisible "elephant" in my own living room. In almost 25 years of leading writing workshops, hearing every taboo subject I could imagine, I had not discovered this one: White people do not write about their own personal pain and fear around racism. We may write about how terrible racism is—but we do not tell our own stories of race.

Kate and I decided to coedit an anthology of writings by women old enough to remember life before the Birmingham bus boycott. White and black. To break the silence of our own generations—mine and Kate's—to tell the stories we have never dared to tell. *Keloid.*

Only as we make ourselves vulnerable are we able to confront demons— our own, and those that threaten us from without. Each writer must find his or her own way, but of this I am certain: What is required is the courage to allow others to see our scars, the courage to look upon the scars of others, and the courage to write the truth. It may be how we heal.

WRITING GENDER

None of us is free from the knot of gender discrimination. Confronting the issue is surely as painful for men as it is for women, and making change happen is daunting for both. Gender is hugely complicated, and writers cannot escape dealing with it intimately each time they create a character. Ignorance made things seem simple to me when I was young; I didn't even know there was an alternative to heterosexuality, let alone the possibility of changing from one gender to another, until I was in college.

I did know when I was young that the options open to women were far different than those open to men. Even today that issue is complicated. Women of color and white women are writing about how sexism affects their lives and work. Audre Lorde, in *Sister Outsider*, writes, "Refusing to recognize difference makes it impossible to see the different problems and pitfalls facing us as women." Issues of sexual preference further divide women already divided by race. These divisions are exquisitely painful, but they are the legacy of deep and ancient traditions. Against all odds, both male and female writers must follow Lorde's pilgrim work, reach across barriers, build bridges of understanding across difference.

Because we have made progress in the last quarter century, it is tempting to believe that in America women—black and white—have won the sexism battle, at least in the arts. It is not so. In screenwriting, for example, at the beginning of the new millennium, 94 percent of screenwriting awards went to men. It would be funny, if it were not so sad, and so true to the history of the assessment of women's work, that in the year 2000, when the Modern Library published its list of the top one hundred twentieth-century English-language novels, it included 92 works by men and eight by women. The judging panel was made up of nine men and one woman. Only two (Virginia Woolf's *To the Lighthouse* and Carson McCullers's *The Heart Is a Lonely Hunter*) made it to the top 50.

Francine Prose, in the June 1998 issue of *Harper's Magazine*, wrote:

> Not even the most curmudgeonly feminist believes that accolades or sales should be handed out in a strict fifty-fifty split, or that equal-opportunity concessions should be made to vile novels by women. But some of us can't help noting how comparatively rarely . . . fiction by women is reviewed in serious literary journals, and how rarely work by women dominates short lists and year-end ten-best lists.

In the *New York Times,* December 2, 2001, the statistics look pretty good. Their year-end roundup of "notable works of fiction and poetry" lists 40 percent as being by female authors. In the nonfiction, mystery, and science fiction categories, the proportion of women authors dropped to roughly 25 percent, while in the children's literary category it rose to 70 percent. These higher percentages are heartening, but we must not be deceived. We will not be artists free of sexist ceilings (invisible and otherwise) until there are as many women as men in places of power at the very top of publishing houses, writing programs, editorial boards, and prize committees.

Writing and Sexuality

Leading writing workshops for 25 years has convinced me of two things: that sex is one of the funniest things on earth, and that loneliness and confusion about sexuality is rampant in American society. Sexuality, given to us for so many good reasons—pleasure, joy, procreation—is the source, too, of incomparable human suffering. Writing is perhaps the very best place on earth to tell our tales of delight and woe about our sexuality; to try on lives other than the ones we know best; and to bravely confront the dragons of homophobia and the demons of sexual hurt, loneliness, and grief.

I am convinced that a taboo is a huge billboard announcing the presence of something important. What do we not write about? Why? What are the taboos we lived under as children? What taboos operate in our minds today? People in my workshops have written (and I have included some of the pieces in this book) about: sexual discovery, rape, incest, grace, raw pleasures, physical and emotional sexual abuse, heterosexual and homosexual experiences, hilarious errors, menstruation, childbirth, wet dreams, mutilation, circumcision, pleasurable bondage games—and more. I have been surprised; I have been educated; I have been deeply grateful to have my understanding expanded and the limits of my imagination enlarged.

You can begin anywhere in your writing about sexuality—in fantasy or in autobiographical experience. Whether dealing with fantasy or lived experience, it takes courage to tell the truth. If you are aware that you need to be brave, you are probably on the threshold of writing something that matters.

Beyond the exploration of our own experiences and the taboos that keep a lid on our silences, the privilege of voice carries with it a responsibility to speak for social justice. In America, as I write these words, injustice based on sexuality is operative. Gay couples may not marry (although they may have "civil unions" in Vermont). International gay couples cannot have the privilege of immigration based on their committed relationship, as can married heterosexuals. Gay youth live in a culture that does not value them; gay men and women live with necessary secrecy and the possibility of violence. I have said it before—as writers we cannot avoid being political. If we are silent, our silence is political.

If I were to choose the single moment in the 25 years of my leading writing workshops that moved me most deeply, it might be the day David Peters wrote the piece that follows. We had written together for five days, 15 writers and I at the Graduate Theological Union in Berkeley. There were several ministers, male and female, Asian, black, and Caucasian, from several denominations. There was a priest, and a number of people who came because they wanted to study with me who may or may not have had a theological orientation. David was rather quiet throughout the workshop days; I had a sense of intensity held down, controlled. He was (still is) a Lutheran pastor. There was present in the room another

Lutheran pastor, from another part of the United States. On the last day of the workshop, in the last reading that we offered to one another, David read the piece that is included here.

Dear Bishop,

Greetings! I am in summer school at the seminary. I am in this creative writing class with a full spectrum of students. I wish I had come here last year and all the years before. This is a true seminary experience: question authority, the family, the institution, even the church, which for some is the institution most needing to be questioned. I hope you've been to summer school now and then. I recommend it heartily. Enough of that. That is not the intent of this letter.

The operative word for today is "gay." Oh, life is so gay!—for me, but not for you. For almost 40 years now, I have hidden the fact—yes, the fact!—that I am gay. For twenty-plus years of ministry, in various churches, all of which I loved very much, I was a gay pastor in a church that condemned me. Not all the parishioners, not all the pastors, not all the bishops condemned me, but certainly enough did and do. Do you have any idea what it is like everyday to go to a place that says you have no place among them? Can you feel that? Even in just a small fraction of all that I feel? I am not sure I can even fully describe how I feel.

It is too scary for me sometimes to unpack all those layers of feelings suppressed by the church and repressed by me. We're Lutherans, remember. We love suppression and repression. We're really good at this—both you and me. After all those years of encouragement in seminars and sermons, we still keep things inside—where they fester and torment like a cancer that always eats more of our flesh. I've had cancer for twenty-plus years, a churchly carcinoma, the worst kind, because it never really kills you, just wounds you again and again.

And all that pain in my neck and shoulder! That's the stress of hiding my true identity, not my only identity, but a very important identity for me, my sexual orientation: I love men, beautiful, sensual men. That stress must come out and it does in nagging, tearful pain that oozes out of my muscles every day. I get relief only when I lie down, when my body can relax. No amount of surgery will ever take away the knots in my neck and my shoulder and my back. They are constant reminders of my dishonesty, my deception, my anxiety, and my downright fear.

But then, some fear is good for all of us clergy types—some, not too much, though. What are your fears, dear Bishop? Any fears with dealing with yet another gay pastor in your synod? How many are we now? Let's see . . . there's so-and-so, and so-and-so. There are more than you think. They say there's between 8% and 10% of us scattered through every culture, but in the church culture, there are more of us, because we feel—or felt—safe in the church. But it is not so safe in the church; maybe for married, white pastors, but not for women and lesbians and people like me, for gays, for homosexuals, for queers.

I like that word, "queer," because in some sense everyone in the church is strange and queer. You're a queer, too. So what's one queer going to do to another queer? Exploit him? Take him by the balls and suck the life out of him? Well, that's one image. Queers love, too, in real, honest, and natural ways. So how can my queer bishop and I, the queer, have a love affair in a church that prides itself for grace and care? What do you think I need from you, and you from me? From you I need a parish, a place in this Lutheran, Gospel-centered church, where I can function to my best and fullest, without fear of condemnation, where I can honor my ordination vow with integrity, where I can be myself and all that my Creator and Redeemer intends for me— a place of grace, where I can say the Eucharistic words, "Given and shed for you" with great joy and boldness, because the congregation is itself gracious and caring. When will my dream become reality?

David A. Peters
Pastor, ELCA
July 30, 1999

Part II
Writing with Others

Silence is all we dread.
There's Ransom in a Voice—

Emily Dickinson

Introduction: Writing with Others

Most writers benefit from regular communication with other writers. Writing can be a lonely endeavor, much of the work must be done in solitude. However, too much solitude—or too much conversation with people who do not write, and too little with those who do—can lead to depression and despair. Having a place to listen thoughtfully to new work by others and having the option of receiving response to your own writing can be invigorating, encouraging, and tremendously helpful. On the other hand, the wrong sort of group, workshop, or class can do damage.

How Writing with Others Can Help You

There are many benefits to the writer who meets with other writers, writing short pieces side by side and sharing longer work for mutual response. Here are some of the benefits.

WRITING WITH OTHERS CAN HELP YOU LEARN THE CRAFT

In a circle of writers, when one member has written brilliant dialogue and the group talks together about how natural and unique each character's speech is, all the members of the workshop are studying dialogue. When the workshop discusses a manuscript in which the writer has used too many adjectives, all the members learn about the danger of too many adjectives. In an atmosphere of support, a writer receives help rather than judgment.

WRITING WITH OTHERS CAN HELP YOU CORRECT YOUR MISTAKES

In a good workshop, other writers read your work thoughtfully and, having told you what they like, also tell you where they are confused, unconvinced, or dissatisfied. Questions and suggestions are offered in a tone that does not assume superiority. Complete honesty and thoroughness in critique, and the necessity of revision, do not have to mean humiliation and embarrassment for the writer. In fact, good response often sends a writer back to the work encouraged and helped through blocks and uncertainties. There are practices that can help writers to be good responders. Those are discussed in the section on manuscripts, Part II, Chapter 12.

WRITING WITH OTHERS CAN HELP YOU TAKE RISKS

Each time one member of a workshop tries something new, all the other members are invited by that risk taking to try new forms, break old taboos, write with increased courage. I have seen this happen in many forms: When one writer is funny, comedy springs up in others; when one writes an erotic piece, others dare to do so too; when one writes in response to pain, others become braver; when one writes a sestina or a villanelle, others dare try. Writing with others and listening to the writing of others can give you courage to take greater risks, to tell more truth, to trust your own instincts. Writing with others can strengthen your nerve.

WRITING WITH OTHERS CAN HELP YOU PUBLISH

A good workshop leader will have knowledge and resources to help you know when and where to send a manuscript for publication. In my workshops, each ten-week session closes with a "Sending-off Party." I lay perhaps a hundred sample journals on a table and we assist one another in choosing appropriate markets. Newcomers are encouraged by watching more experienced members send off manuscripts. For more about this, see the section titled "Help in Getting Work Published" in Part II, Chapter 12.

WRITING WITH OTHERS CAN GIVE YOU PERSPECTIVE

Once you begin to offer your own work for publication, the workshop can help you deal with rejection slips, and it can be a place in which to celebrate accomplishments. In my workshops I frequently ask if anyone has received a rejection. I sometimes read my own out loud with groaning and gnashing of teeth. We celebrate rejection slips as evidence that the writer is keeping his or her work out; we groan together, laugh, console.

Don Fisher received the following rejection letter from a Canadian journal, *Dead Tree Product*.

> Dear Don Fisher,
>
> Thanks for your poems. I really disliked "A Poem About Love and Astronomy," and I liked the other two enough, more so "A Bit of Conversation . . ." due to the strength of the image. But it doesn't really matter, because *Dead Tree Product* has folded due to financial difficulties. Sorry for this inconvenience.
>
> Good luck writing. Thanks for your material. I liked the Laurel and Hardy stamps, but, you fool, U.S. stamps in Canada are like Canadian money in the States . . . pretty worthless. Nice try. Buy an IRC next time.
>
> I apologize again for the inconvenience.
>
> Gabino Vidal Travassos
> Ex-fiction editor, *Dead Tree Product*

Our laughter and teasing at this rejection eased the sting of it for Don and reminded us all to buy International Reply Coupons (IRCs) when offering work to Canadian journals. We all experience victory when an acceptance comes to one of us. We correct each other when someone talks about "submitting" a manuscript, remembering Marge Piercy's advice, "Never say 'submit'! Say offer." Don subsequently received a number of acceptances, and one appears in this book following the exercise "Ransom Note," in Part III.

WRITING WITH OTHERS CAN HELP YOU NETWORK

By meeting together, writers form important relationships that may result in collaboration, or in contacts with or introductions to editors or agents.

WRITING WITH OTHERS CAN HELP YOU
BELIEVE IN YOUR OWN ART

Most of us have been taught that we cannot write. That was not the lesson intended by the good men and women who were our teachers, but it is what happened to most of us. When you put your soul onto the page (and that's what writing is)—when you "write your heart out," anything less than A+ hurts. The message is, You could have done better. We learned the lesson well: We believe in our inability. What we need to hear—and believe—is our ability, our facility, the effectiveness and strength of our own peculiar and inimitable voices.

WRITING WITH OTHERS CAN ASSIST IN
PSYCHOLOGICAL AND PHYSICAL HEALING

Major attention is now being given to writing as a methodology for healing not only psychological wounds, but also physical illness. *Poets & Writers Magazine*, national news magazines such as *Newsweek*, and even some major health organizations are giving careful attention to the connection between writing and health. Writing is inextricably linked to working on one's own inner life and outer relationships. Whether we work alone or in a supportive group, writing is good for our body and mind. Chip Spann, who is making the intersection of writing and physical health his primary vocation, says this:

> The emerging field of the medical humanities is being fueled by modern scientific articles like that of Joshua Smythe and associates in the *Journal of the American Medical Association* (*JAMA*, April 14, 1999, Vol. 218, No. 14) where patients with asthma and rheumatoid arthritis showed objective clinical improvement over four months when they engaged in reflective writing related to their illness.

Novelist Alice Hoffman, in an article in the *New York Times*, August 14, 2000, describes her experience with cancer:

> An insightful, experienced oncologist told me that cancer need not be a person's whole book, only a chapter. Still, novelists know that some chapters inform all others. These are the chapters of your life that wallop you and teach you and bring you to tears, that invite you to step to the other side of the curtain, the

one that divides those of us who must face our destiny sooner rather than later. What I was looking for during 10 months of chemotherapy and radiation was a way to make sense of sorrow and loss. . . . I wrote because that was who I was at the core, and if I was too damaged to walk around the block, I was lucky all the same. Once I got to my desk, once I started writing, I still believed anything was possible.

WRITING WITH OTHERS CAN COMPLETE THE ARTISTIC ACT

Writing is an act of communication. As a writer/artist, you give your art into the mind of your reader or listener when you read your work to someone else, or allow it to be read. It is received; you have communicated. That is the fundamental work of the artist.

Some Options for Writing with Others

FIND A WRITING COMPANION

For many writers, the first step in writing with others is finding one other writer with whom to talk about the work they both are doing. This may or may not include writing together; it may simply be sharing writing that each has done separately.

Finding a person who can be your primary writing companion may be difficult, but it is worth the effort. Family members and close non-writer friends are usually not good candidates. They care too much, want too badly to please or correct us, have different versions of our stories, recognize our source material—for all kinds of reasons they are usually the very last persons you should ask to be your writing partner.

Perhaps the best place to find a writing companion is in a workshop or class. There are several writers who have been members of my weekly workshops for ten years—two members have stayed for more than 15 years! Cynthia Kennison has written more than one novel in the workshop and has taken national prizes in both fiction and poetry. The other writer has not published and has not sought publication. She is a gifted writer, but very private. We gather weekly in the circle to write together, read aloud, offer response.

JOIN A CREATIVE WRITING CLASS

Your local school system or area college may offer writing classes as continuing education. I have suggested earlier that there is one sure test for choosing a writing class: After you have attended, do you feel more like writing or less like writing? If you find a class that sends you home wanting to write, wonderful! If you feel put down or discouraged about your own work after a class meeting, don't go back. It's that simple. There is no value to be gained from humiliation. On the other hand, there are gifted and generous teachers who can become your mentors in the craft. You just have to seek until you find a teacher who is right for you, as you would a physician, a psychiatrist, or a clergyperson.

JOIN A COMMUNITY-BASED WRITING GROUP OR WORKSHOP

In most areas there are writers who work together in a support group or workshop. You can locate these through your library or perhaps through local bookstore owners. Free workshops are sometimes advertised in the newspaper. The advantage of no-fee is often offset by a disadvantage: The skill and energy of wise, experienced leadership doesn't usually come gratis. A leaderless group tends to be short-lived unless it is a small, closed membership of established friends.

When you choose a workshop for which there is a fee, remember that you are the consumer, the purchaser, of a service, whether the "vendor" is Harvard University or your next-door neighbor. In most university and college workshops, there is a trial period during which you can change your mind and get most of your tuition back. You should be able to do this with a private workshop as well.

Ask if you may visit once, either for a fee or as a guest. Ask if after three meetings you may choose to drop out and receive a refund for the remainder of your tuition. Give it a trial of at least three meetings, and then make up your own mind on the basis of the "one sure test" described above. What is important is that you understand what you need, and claim it. Sarcasm and put-downs, though they may destroy the confidence of one student, may cause another's adrenaline to rise. He or she may think, I'll be damned if I'm going to be destroyed by this (bleep), and go home to write.

Most writing workshops are led by people who are published writers and have completed formal training such as certification in the Amherst Writers & Artists (AWA) method, or an MFA degree in Creative Writing.

AWA certification means the person has completed a 30-hour intensive training in workshop leadership and, in the judgment of the AWA leadership, is qualified to lead a writing support group or, if published and adequately experienced, a writing workshop.

An MFA indicates that the person who has received it has completed an academic program of two years or more and has completed work that passed an academic committee. The focus will usually have been on improving the student's own writing and knowledge of literature more than on leadership skills appropriate to leading workshops or writing groups.

There are gifted teachers and excellent workshop leaders without any formal credentials, and there are teachers and leaders with formal credentials who will not help you. As you look for your primary writing community, trust your own intuitive response.

START YOUR OWN WRITING GROUP OR WORKSHOP

If you cannot find a workshop or writing group that meets your needs, you can start your own. Leadership is not easy, but this book gives you a step-by-step method. Beginning this work with others who want a community of writers will give you energy and encouragement. If you want formal training in the Amherst Writers & Artists Workshop method, it is available, as are writing retreats and workshops where you can deepen your own writing skills and experience in the AWA method. These are led by trained affiliated workshop leaders who themselves offer workshops throughout the United States, as well as in Ireland, Peru, Mexico, the Isle of Iona, and other places. A list of AWA-affiliated workshop leaders is available on our website, www.amherstwriters.com.

Basic Principles of a Healthy Workshop

The Amherst Writers & Artists method for writing classes, groups, and workshops has developed in a community of writers that had its origin in 1979. Teachers, workshop leaders, and several thousand workshop participants have helped create these practices. They are deeply rooted in the writing process movement whose pioneers have called for and have brought about reform in teaching writing since the 1930s. That reform has been most fully articulated by Peter Elbow.

Perhaps there is very little that is new in what we propose, but we have brought together, out of practices used throughout the writing process movement, a concrete plan for how to write with others in a group setting, whether it be in a classroom, a living room, or a social service setting such as a hospital or housing project community center.

Chapter 12, "Creating Your Own Workshop or Writing Group," describes in detail a workshop as I lead it in my home in a college town. The participants are writers who come together to write for possible publication and/or for personal fulfillment. This method is exactly the same whether I use it in graduate school classrooms in Berkeley, California, or in a convent in Ireland. It has been widely adapted for use in public elementary schools, high schools, and colleges.

Chapter 13, "Using Writing to Empower the Silenced," details this method adapted to a population that has been denied higher education. Based on our work with low-income and other under-served populations, these workshops are designed to raise the consciousness and self-esteem of people whose voices have been silenced by poverty or other hardship.

Whether in a graduate school classroom or in a housing project living room, writing together and reading aloud to one another brand-new work and experiencing having that work received only with affirmation of what stays with the listeners, revolutionizes the teaching and learning experience. Everyone learns by listening and by withholding judgment until the proper time, when the work is presented in manuscript form. Experienced and beginning writers teach each other. We learn from one another. Often, the least formally trained writers are the freshest, if they can be helped to write without affectation in the voices that they use with friends and family. Writers who are publishing regularly and those new to writing work side by side with mutual respect, and the variety of voice, subject, and genre in the workshop gives permission to everyone to experiment. Supportive community is the setting in which significant writing is most easily and effectively accomplished.

Underlying this workshop method are five essential affirmations and five essential practices.

The Five Essential Affirmations

These affirmations rest on a definition of personhood that is nonhierarchical, and a definition of writing as an art form available to all persons.

1. Everyone has a strong, unique voice.
2. Everyone is born with creative genius.
3. Writing as an art form belongs to all people, regardless of economic class or educational level.
4. The teaching of craft can be done without damage to a writer's original voice or artistic self-esteem.
5. A writer is someone who writes.

The Five Essential Practices

1. A nonhierarchical spirit (how we treat writing) in the workshop is maintained while at the same time an appropriate discipline (how we interact as a group) keeps writers safe.

2. Confidentiality about what is written in the workshop is maintained, and the privacy of the writer is protected. All writing is treated as fiction unless the writer requests that it be treated as autobiography. At all times writers are free to refrain from reading their work aloud.

3. Absolutely no criticism, suggestion, or question is directed toward the writer in response to first-draft, just-written work. A thorough critique is offered only when the writer asks for it and distributes work in manuscript form. Critique is balanced; there is as much affirmation as suggestion for change.

4. The teaching of craft is taken seriously and is conducted through exercises that invite experimentation and growth as well as through response to manuscripts and in private conferences.

5. The leader writes along with the participants and reads that work aloud at least once in each writing session. This practice is absolutely necessary, for only in this way is there equality of risk taking and mutuality of trust.

Fundamentally, these practices guard against hierarchy and keep the individual writer safe. They take growth in the craft of writing seriously, and they ensure a commitment to critical response that is offered without condescension or arrogance. Honest response to written work is crucial for the growth of a writer, but that response is given only when the writer brings in a manuscript and asks for response. Every writer, no matter how young or how inexperienced, is treated with kindness and respect.

The three stories that follow were told to me by people in my workshops.

A young woman in her twenties, recently graduated from college, joined my workshop. She was quiet and found it difficult to read her work aloud. After some time, she told us that years before she had written a short story in a high school English class and had received the paper back with no mark on it except these words from the teacher: "This is monkey feces on canvas." She said she had not written one word of "creative writing" from that day until she joined the workshop.

Another woman, middle-aged, joined a workshop led by a famous poet. He asked the workshop to "talk through" their poems before writing them (a practice I would personally find very difficult). The woman said she preferred not to talk about her poem before she wrote it. He insisted. She said that she was thinking of writing a poem about her own beginning of menopause and her daughter's first menstruation, occurring at the same time. The poet answered, "Oh, my dear, I wouldn't! It's so clichéd!" The woman stopped writing.

A third writer, a young man in his first year in college, was a student in a remedial writing class, where he had been placed because he had so much difficulty with spelling. The teacher asked the students to write a short story. At the next class session, she said, "I am going to read one of your stories out loud and I want you to tell me what grade I should give it." She read the story, and the young man listened to his own words, amazed at how good the story seemed to be. When she was finished reading, she asked the class what grade it should receive. "A! A!" they responded. "I'm giving it an F, she said, "because there are 107 misspelled words in it." And she handed it to the writer. This young man was brilliant; he was also dyslexic. The year was 1952, before much was known about the different ways in which people learn. He believed for 40 years after that experience that he could not write, until he joined an AWA workshop led by Kathryn Dunn. Now he is a published poet and an outrageously good short story writer.

In the first case the judgment was on *the writing*; the teacher called it "shit." In the second case the judgment was on *the content* of the writing (and, more damaging, on the writer's personal story), called "clichéd." In the third case, the judgment was on *the spelling.* There are countless ways to make a writer feel stupid. Hierarchical classrooms breed contempt and abuse of authority. They have at the head of the table someone who reinforces ideas such as: I know and you do not know; I am the expert and you are the novice; I will judge you, and if you are a real writer, you can take it!

All three of the writers in these true stories are middle-class and college-educated. They are all three articulate people, successful in their professions: social worker, teacher, businessman. If they were silenced by an insulting and ridiculing comment by a teacher, how much more are those whose education has not been completed, whose work lives have been frustrated, whose origins are in poverty or in some under-served segment of the population? It is not difficult to imagine what happens to young artists when classrooms are overcrowded, teachers overworked and exhausted.

My experience is that there are an astonishing number of stories like those. I sometimes have an image of a battlefield littered with dead and dying bodies. What a lot of pain we have caused in trying to do a good thing—just teaching someone to write!

It is imperative that the leader understand that many people who return to writing after a long silence carry pain. A writing group is not a therapy group—it is concerned with liberating the artist in the person. But the artist in many persons has been wounded. They have been graded and found lacking. They have been embarrassed publicly and they have been shamed. These fragments of a longer poem by Jean Wood, written after she allowed the workshop to respond for the first time to a manuscript, express fear that is not at all unusual:

I was afraid . . .
Afraid of the silence . . .
Afraid none would speak . . .
Afraid if they spoke,
Their words would be kind . . .
Their words would be caring.
I was afraid . . .
Afraid if they cared,
The tears would come . . .
And never stop.
Afraid if I cried,
They would turn away . . .
And not hear my words again.

. . . as each one began,
I turned my head . . .
Turned my eyes to listen.
Their words were kind . . .

Then I realized . . .
I hadn't cried.
Yet they saw my pain . . .
I let them come closer,
Closer to knowing . . .
The person I am.

Writers returning to their writing after a long silence are frequently distressed that so much pain comes up and out onto the page. But usually when we open the door to memory it is pain that will come first because we have been pushing it down for so long. It is under pressure. I reassure the writer that under the pain there will be other kinds of images: playful, joyful, even forgiving, if he or she faithfully takes whatever comes and doesn't try to rush through long-suppressed painful images. Sometimes cleaning out the old stuff takes a long time. Sometimes in the "old stuff" there is some of our best art. Remember Michelangelo's angel in the stone?

I think of pain in the writer that way. Inside all that suffering there is an angel, and writing chips away accumulated resistance to find the essential meaning—the angel—in the stone. When I turned back to confront poverty and orphanage in my own childhood, it took me 14 years and three complete books to begin to find spontaneous images of my mother that were not painful. The old saw "Forgive and forget" has it exactly backward. It should be "Remember and forgive." Remember fully, in detail—perhaps many times. Feel all the stages of grief, denial, anger, resignation, acceptance. Perhaps then forgiveness will come up when you least expect it, in the middle of a piece of writing, like a flower out of the muck. It did for me. I was writing one of the final pieces to be included in *Wake Up Laughing*. It was about my mother selling eggs to her neighbors. Suddenly I realized something I had not seen before. "Ah, Mama, you never told me that!" I wrote, and a frozen part of me cracked open, melted.

Not everyone, of course, comes to a writing workshop or class with a need or a desire to write out of unresolved pain. Even those who do can't write about pain all the time. Writing exercises (triggers, prompts) should invite a variety of responses. For example, in offering a line from a poem as a prompt—"Something has ceased to come along with me . . ." (Jon Silkin) or "Those who are dead are never gone. . ." (Birago Diop)—would likely trigger some memory or imagined scene quite different than would "Be sure to use firm, hard cucumbers" (Angie Leydon) or "Her nipples want to drive all night to Alabama" (Ellen Doré Watson). Or how about this one? "An artist who paints the sky green and trees blue should be sterilized" (Adolph Hitler). For a list of other quotes to use as possible prompts, see the *Oxford Book of Quotations* or any good anthology of contemporary writing. Look for these qualities in the quotes: surprise (as in "sterilized" and "nipples"); concrete images (as in "cucumbers" and "nipples"); emotional triggers (as in the Diop and Silkin quotes). Avoid general language, vagueness, or "preachy" quotes.

I have written at length about voice. Let me say here just this: A writer's voice is an incredibly delicate instrument made up of all the places he or she has been, all the persons loved and lived with, all the cultural nuances of original neighborhood, workplace, home, country, continent, historical period, and personal story. The cadence, the rhythm, the lulls and ecstatic explosions of a writer's voice belong only to the writer, and no teacher or workshop leader, no matter how gifted, can say what that music ought to be. Neither is it possible for one person to dictate when the time has come for another to break free of fear and learned constraints. Freedom, and its power, comes to the writing voice out of the writer's own necessity (need) or out of the writer's own security (safety). Those are profoundly personal areas and cannot be coerced, bullied, or judged into being.

The Writer's Workshop

We write together—leader as well as participants—in response to a suggestion (a "trigger" or "exercise") given by the leader. The leader's participation in writing and reading brand-new work aloud is absolutely central to this workshop method. If the leader of a group stays safe, there is hierarchy, and the group members' safety is compromised. When the leader reads aloud, is honest about fear that "this one doesn't work," the members of the group are empowered and the leader is even more powerful than if he or she keeps a safe distance. In our workshops, leaders share their rejection slips as well as their acceptances. We tell the stories of what is happening to us as writers, and in every meeting of the workshop we read our first-draft, just-written work at least once.

We are all free to ignore the leader's exercise suggestion, and there are always some writers who do, choosing instead to write on a work already in progress, or on something that was on their minds when they came to the meeting.

Writing together is an experience entirely unlike any that I ever had in elementary or high school, in college or graduate school. I certainly never experienced a teacher's or professor's reading aloud work that he or she had just written! I don't know how to express the almost ecstatic experience that rather frequently happens when people write together and affirm one another's new work. There are so few places in our normal social lives where we are privileged to meet one another so vulnerably—to laugh and cry and laugh again.

Because there is no critique or discussion of first-draft work, we venture out with our words, often prefacing them by disclaimers, but daring to read them anyway, and hearing that they are accepted and respected. When we are funny, we get to hear the reward of our listener's laughter. Sometimes when we grieve, someone else weeps with us. We never discuss that work, not even to mention it at break over coffee and brownies. It belongs to the writer. But each of us has been heard and affirmed. We go home empowered to type up our words, revise them, and maybe prepare them in manuscript form to bring back for group critique.

I sometimes think there isn't a fresh writing exercise under the sun. And then I have a new idea that I've never tried before. For example, recently I suggested that we all write about being "under something." One person wrote about being under his car. Another wrote about being under her bed, and still another wrote a lovely erotic poem about being under his wife! Steve Johnson, who is a plumber as well as a writer, wrote this remarkable prose poem:

> Laying on my belly reaching up to the work at the bottom of this kitchen floor. Always I have had to quell panic in these nasty places. Crawlspace work. Dirty. Belly work. In Monterey, black widows and raccoon mummies, snakes, scorpions. New Mexico crawls had the standard spiders plus Hanta viral mice and rats. In Monterey, I would light up these three foot short, three thousand square foot caves with a dozen halogen work lamps. Light it up to daylight that erased the dark but showed clear every furry corpse, every spider's home, every rusty 1959 Brew 102 can. Years of standing in front of entrance hatches taking slow breaths, muttering oaths, trying to remember some forgotten tool so as to delay the entering. Now, back in New England, celebrating standing up in dank cellars, wet basements, stone lined holes under houses. Three thousand miles across this country to escape crawls, and today, my chest in a frozen Leverett puddle, in darkness, avoiding the mouse mummy against my chin.

On a usual workshop evening we begin by writing for 20 to 30 minutes, then those who choose to do so, read aloud what they just wrote. All readings are brief, because we do not read aloud anything written outside the workshop. Writers come from varying levels of experience and confidence: Some have already published widely and may have a manuscript in progress; some are returning to writing after a silence of many years; some have done very little writing outside of school. We all have in common, however, a need for safety and a need for a workshop leader who can help the group keep appropriate boundaries.

When we write together in workshop, we do not have time to revise or even read over to ourselves the words that we read aloud. To read under these circumstances is a powerful and sometimes emotional experience, both for the writer and for the listener. Our practice, upon hearing work that has just been written, is to mention "what we remember; what stays with us." This saves us from too much sweetness and the temptation to dishonest praise. We don't have to like what we have just heard. Writing is an act of communication: Offering back to the writer images that remain with us completes the artist act. I have written; I have been heard. If I write about being a teenager in St. Louis when Elvis was on every teenager's mind, I don't need someone to tell me the writing is good. I need someone to tell me, "I see that kid putting the nickel in the jukebox."

Later, when I have typed the piece and revised it, I will want to hear the problem in the poem—that I mention Hitler and the Allies as if they were contemporaries of Elvis's greatest hits. (*Oh! Just because they are both back there in my memory bank doesn't mean they happened at the same time!*) The group discussion may help me understand whether the character is believable, whether the setting is sufficiently vivid, whether there are grammatical errors in the text, whether the ending is effective. When the time comes for critique, it should be honest and thorough, but balanced with affirmation of what is working well.

Traditional teaching of writing has too often emphasized what is wrong. Most of us understand instinctively how to encourage and assist a child to do creative work. If a child brings you a picture of a bird in flight she has just drawn with a blue crayon, and you see that the left wing is hanging awkwardly down the page, but the right wing is soaring, you do not say, "By the way, that crooked left wing looks really stupid." You say, "Oh, look! Look how that right wing is lifted by the air! I can just feel the flying!" The child looks at the picture, and what does she do? She goes immediately to her crayons and draws the left wing so it, too, soars.

A good workshop leader will be able to teach and guide the participants. When I teach, as I frequently do in a workshop setting, I try to let teaching come out of response to work that has been done well. Julia Cameron and I discussed and celebrated together how similarly we have written about being a writer. Without knowing one another or reading each other's books, we have written almost the same passages, such as this one of hers on feedback:

> As a writing teacher, it is my experience that if I praise a student's strengths, the weaknesses eventually fall away. If I focus on the weakness, the strengths, too, may wobble and even vanish. Just as we would not give over a valuable young horse to just anybody to train, we must not give over our work to just anybody to critique. And by this I do not mean that we must go only to professionals. Too often professionals have their own ax to grind.
>
> An amateur reader can give very valid feedback. (Remember the word "amateur" comes from the verb "amare," to love.) What you want to find in a reader is someone who loves to read and is friendly to the idea of your developing as a writer.

In this method, as in traditional workshops and classes, a good workshop leader offers group response to work in manuscript form. We do not, however, critique work that has just been handed out and read aloud. We insist on waiting until the writer puts it in manuscript form and all workshop participants have had time to read and critique it outside of workshop sessions.

In this way we honor the writer's own sense of when he or she is ready for critique. I had one young woman in workshop who wrote for a full year, twice every week, and would not read her work aloud, let alone bring it in for group response. She wrote—I could see her pencil moving furiously across her page. Finally, after one year, she brought me a manuscript—"for you only," she said. After I read it and wrote in the margins what delighted me in the work and made some suggestions, she brought in a new draft, gave it to everyone, and participated fully in the workshop from that time on.

While I would not have the full freedom of my independent workshop in my graduate level classes in Berkeley, I would do there everything I could to preserve the writer's safety and privacy for as long as possible. Each person has his or her own inner timing for moving out of the stage of gathering strength privately and into that of receiving public feedback to private effort.

In the workshop session, with a manuscript in hand, we enter into a thorough discussion of its strengths as well as raise questions and discuss problems. At that stage, as in immediate feedback to new work, we treat all work as fiction unless the writer asks us to treat it as autobiography, thereby keeping the focus on the work as literature and protecting the privacy of the writer. At the end of the discussion, the writer receives all copies of the manuscript with notes from readers and a letter of response from the leader. We encourage the writer to bring in a revised manuscript for further discussion, or suggest that the writer send it out as a manuscript for possible publication by journals and magazines that we recommend.

Twelve Basic Principles for a Healthy Workshop

1. Write together in workshop and invite, but do not pressure, members to read what they have just written.

2. Do not allow the workshop to critique or correct first-draft work that has just been written in the workshop.

3. Allow great diversity in age, experience, style, and genre in your workshop.

4. Assume all written work to be fictional unless the writer volunteers that it is autobiographical.

5. Encourage workshop members to be honest with both praise and critical suggestion in responding to work in manuscript form. Be rigorous and honest in your own responses.

6. Give your workshop a wide variety of exercises.

7. Write along with your workshop members, read that work aloud, and invite response.

8. If one person is making the group unworkable, ask that person to leave.

9. Do not be thrown off center by anyone else's expertise; be realistic and without defensiveness about your own limitations and strengths.

10. Stress confidentiality.

11. Help people try out new forms.

12. In moments of genuine crisis, be ready to abandon all "practices"; follow your own instinct.

Writing in a Classroom

I have not, to this point, said enough about good teachers and exciting classrooms. Every year I have the privilege of "kicking off" a summer writing program for teachers in public schools in Connecticut, under the supervision of Mary Mackley, the visionary director of the Connecticut Writing Center, University of Connecticut. My responsibility is to provide a model workshop in which teachers experience writing in the ways described in this book.

I love leading that group because it puts me in touch with how committed, how caring, and how desirous of doing good work most teachers are. Most of the problems are not with the people doing the teaching, but with the old methods that have made teachers themselves afraid to write, and therefore often unable to evoke good writing from their students.

Good teachers everywhere have intuited and invented ways to encourage young writers. My own life as a writer began on that day in the summer following seventh grade (described in the Introduction) when my teacher, Dorothy Dunn, climbed the stairs of a tenement to give me her book. She believed in me, *I believed in her belief*, and I climbed out of an impossible childhood on the rope of that belief.

I imagine young writers, children, high school sophomores, freshmen English students, graduate students—writing in a classroom without fear and trembling. The chapters before this one have made abundantly clear, I hope, what the dangers are in the old models of teaching writing.

I began teaching writing as a graduate student in my final year of study for my MFA at the University of Massachusetts. I taught as I had been taught: Students brought in manuscripts, and we all sat discussing the problems the manuscripts presented. The writing was usually stiff, and I believe now that the discussions helped very little if at all. More likely, they contributed to the deep freeze of the students' writing voices.

My own breakthrough as a writing teacher (and the beginning of the development of the method that we now call the Amherst Writers & Artists method) occurred one evening after I had graduated and finished my student teaching. Poet Margaret Robison, who had been an MFA candidate with me at the University of Massachusetts, and I had started an independent writing workshop. For several weeks we used the method that we had been taught—no writing together, just discussion of work done at home and presented for discussion. One evening, after everyone had gone home from the session, Margaret sat back in her chair and said wearily, "Pat, I can't stand it! This writing is so bad! Next week, I'm going to just bring in a bowl of seashells and set it in the middle of the floor and see what happens."

She did, and we saw what happened. Each writer took a shell, held it, and we wrote together. What a shock! The writing that we heard people read was rich, deep, full of metaphoric reference and surprising turns. None of the freshness of voice had been edited out by anxious writers preparing for critical feedback.

Margaret and I never looked back. And in the year and a half that we continued to teach together, much of the foundation of the method in this book was laid down. There was no critique of brand-new, first-draft writing. As leaders, we wrote together with our students, taking the same risks they took. Work in manuscript form was given thorough critique in group discussion and in notes and a typed letter from us.

Peter Elbow's essay "Inviting the Mother Tongue," in *Everyone Can Write,* is a crucial exploration of the possibility of inviting students to use their mother tongue while maintaining a profound respect for the reasons they may have to resist that invitation. He draws deeply upon his own experiences as a writer and as the director of a university writing program, committed to teaching standard written English because he feels "an obligation to invite all my students to use their own language and not to make them conform to the language and culture of mainstream English," while at the same time he also feels "an obligation to give all my students access to the written language of power and prestige." His essay argues persuasively for an *invitation* to students to use their own languages of home:

What I love is the mother tongue. Most people cannot really feel comfortable or at home writing, and cannot use writing as naturally as speaking, unless they are taught to write in their home voice—that is, in whatever language comes naturally to hand and mouth. People can't learn to write well unless they write a great deal and with some pleasure, and they can't do that unless they feel writing to be as comfortable as an old shoe—something they can slip into naturally and without pinching.

After all, we experience our language or dialect not just as something we use but as a deep part of *us*. Our home language is not just inside us; we are also inside it.

He discusses the fact that "the mother tongue is more deeply connected to the unconscious than any dialect or language we learn later"—a subject that is extensively dwelt upon in the early chapters of this book. And yet, with the honesty that I value so much in his work, Elbow looks unflinchingly at some of the reasons for reticence, fear, and resistance that may cause students to protect their original mother tongue. His "Vernacular Englishes in the Writing Classroom: Probing the Culture of Literacy" is essential to any discussion of the subject. He describes ways to welcome the mother tongue of the student, while inviting experimentation in academic and/or artistic options.

Let me stress my earlier phrase, "*invite students to experiment.*" That is, we need to *invite*, not demand or even pressure; and our invitation should be to *experiment*—try out options, not settle on a single approach. We need to recognize and respect (and talk about) the various reasons why vernacular speaking students might *not* want even to try out a vernacular "home" dialect in writing—particularly if it is stigmatized. Some may not want to use a home dialect for *any* classroom task; some may not want to use it for those academic rhetorical tasks that they experience as impersonal, abstract, square, or clunky—alien to home rhetorical traditions; and some may not want to use it because they want to develop fluency in *producing* SWE [standard written English]—and therefore are willing to pay a price of reduced comfort, fluency, and power at the stage of putting words on the page; and finally, some may feel that they have too few allies in the class and so will need to use vernacular dialect only for private writing (if at all). A few may actually disapprove of their vernacular—just as Jesse Jackson called Ebonics "trash talk." Nevertheless I maintain that we should *make* this invitation to experiment.

As teachers, we need courage—the courage to look clearly at the risks we ask our students to take, and a willingness to take those risks ourselves by writing and reading with them. We also need hope—the hope that in time all mother tongues may be valued, encouraged, and welcomed as an enrichment of literature, and as refreshing alternatives to the necessary standard language of power and prestige.

If You Are a Student

Recently, my granddaughter, who is a university sophomore, complained bitterly about the courses she is currently taking. "From now on," she said, "I'm going to find out who the good teachers are before I sign up for classes!" How does one find a good teacher? Not so differently from how one finds a good doctor, or therapist, or priest. Ask others who have studied with that teacher—do they respond with enthusiasm and excitement?

It is all right for you to ask the teacher or a school administrator (or better yet, a former student of that teacher) what you can expect in the classroom. You (or your parents or taxpayers) are paying for a service provided by an institution. You have a right to ask polite questions and to do your best to find the teachers who will most effectively mentor you as an artist.

If the method used by the teacher is simply to have students bring in manuscripts of work done at home and to lead class discussion of the text—be cautious. Ask about the grading system; on what basis are grades given? If grades are given on the "excellence of the writing"—be cautious. Art, and the critique of it, is hugely subjective. If grading must be done, it should be on the student's timely and regular attendance, fulfillment of assigned work, and class participation. It should not be based on the teacher's evaluation of the artistry of the student's work as compared to that of other members of the class.

Once you are attending, be attentive to your own responses. Apply my one sure test: After being with your teacher, do you feel more like writing or less like writing? You should never be made to feel embarrassment or shame in the classroom. If that happens, there is something wrong with the way writing is being taught. Drop the class. Take auto mechanics or geometry! Then write about fixing cars, or about the perfect problem.

Here's a bit of counter-advice: You can learn a lot by watching how something is done wrong. As long as you don't allow anything to undermine your confidence in your own voice or your enthusiasm for writing, you can learn from anyone. I would never have written this book if I had experienced only wonderful teachers of writing in school. I did have some great teachers, but I learned how *not to do it* from the not-so-good classes.

Now and then you will happen into the classroom of a great teacher— a teacher who invites you to be honest and brave; a teacher who believes in you and wants your words; a teacher who makes the learning of craft exciting and rewarding; a teacher who teaches you to believe in yourself and in your own art.

"A good teacher," Peter Elbow says, "can be a perfect audience." He says in *Writing With Power*:

> I think I got much of my original deep feeling for writing because of one of my high school teachers, Bob Fisher. He took me seriously. He wanted me to write. He asked me to write about things that were important to me. He opened me out. He assumed that I could write creatively in ways I never would have thought of, and I could. He assumed I would be deeply interested in topics I had never thought of, and I was. With him as a teacher I came to like writing, to look forward to it, to feel I was doing something important when I put words on paper.

If you are a student, the ideal is that you sign up for a class and experience companionship with other writers led by a guide who is wise and compassionate. The setting is a workshop, rather than a class, although it may be called "a class." By that, I mean that everyone is learning—the teacher included. You will write together and share first drafts aloud in class, and the teacher will write along with you and will read that first draft to you, modeling courage and undercutting hierarchy. You will be invited to use your own natural voice in your writing, and it will be honored even when you may move away from it to experiment with academic and artistic forms.

You are an apprentice working at your craft, and in a good class you are respected and protected from embarrassment or shame. As much as your teacher can possibly manage, given the school's rules, a significant portion of your work will be free of grades, and you will know that as you write. At the end of the class you are glad you took it, because you know more certainly that you are a writer. You know that you will be learning about your art form as long as you live, but you are a writer already. You are a writer *now*—respected by your own peers and by your teacher.

If You Are a Teacher

If you are a teacher, the most important preparation for your teaching is the liberation of your own writing voice. If you know how to feel reasonably confident and safe when you do your own writing, you will be most able to help your students. If you know in the privacy of your own mind that writing brings up fear for you, use that knowledge as you teach. Talk about that fear to your students and admit that it still plagues you. What a liberating thing for a student to hear! *You mean I'm not alone in this? I'm not a freak because I'm scared?* Let writing time be one place in the school experience where teacher and student are "in this together." When you write with your students and you don't like what you just wrote, be sure to read that piece and complain ahead of time that you don't like it. Then let them tell you what they like, and let them know you feel better about it. This will not undermine your authority as the teacher. It will actually strengthen it, because you dare to be real, honest, vulnerable.

An example of a teacher writing with her students follows the exercise titled "The Scramble" in Chapter 8.

Most of us begin our writing alone, somewhere in childhood or adolescence. We come as students into classrooms with our hidden and continuing passion on pages tucked away *just in case* we might feel safe enough to show it to the powerful person who stands before us in school. If we are among the blessed, that powerful person says *yes* to our effort, believes in us, and teaches us without breaking our spirit. Blessed or not, everyone with even a modest education has experienced writing with others in a classroom. Many come into the class clad in a solid suit of armor. Teachers who still wear that armor—who are still afraid of writing—unconsciously teach that fear to their students.

If you are a teacher, allow yourself to teach out of the vulnerable place in yourself where your own writing voice lives. Follow Peter Elbow's guidance for classroom teachers; use some of my writing prompts and exercises both for your own writing alone, and for writing with your students in class. Above all, have fun with your students. Give up being an "expert" and just be yourself. Teaching writing invites the creation of community—it is the wildest and most wonderful adventure I know.

Exercise: Free Writing in the Classroom

Make clear to the students that if you read what they have written during free-writing time, you will not correct any mistakes. You will write, too, and may share what you have written by reading it aloud when writing time is over. Others are free to read or not read aloud what they have written.

Ella Rutledge, who has taught writing in university classrooms in Japan and at Kingsborough Community College in Brooklyn, offers this suggestion:

In my classes, I have found it helpful to get topics for free-writing from the students at the beginning of the term. Everyone writes on a small slip of paper a word or a phrase or an idea that they would like to write about: "winter," "eating," "terrorism," "how to improve this school's registration system." These papers are collected and kept in a small colorful bag. At the beginning of each class, I shake the bag and ask someone to reach in and pull out today's free-writing topic. I write it on the board. I put on some gentle background music timed to last ten or so minutes. "Write until the music stops," I say, and most everybody does. The students enjoy all writing on the same topic. I enjoy reading each student's individual take on it, and this reading helps me get to know them better, too. In the course evaluations I hand out at the end of every term, many students always say something like, "I wish we could spend more time on free-writing. That's what helps me most of all."

CHILDREN WRITING IN A CLASSROOM

The writing process movement has already brought about a revolution in the way young children are taught to write. Rather than having writing come after reading, little authors are creating books of their own stories and are learning to read in part by reading their own words on paper. What a difference that would have made for me—a kid who had no father, no house of our own, reading "Dick runs. Jane runs." In that story, Father comes home every day and reads the paper while Mother cooks. Nothing in that story was familiar to me. What if I had been helped to write my own book—what stories would I have read aloud to the other three children in our one-room school in the Ozarks?

Peter Elbow writes, in his "War between Reading and Writing" (in *Everyone Can Write*):

> It has been demonstrated over and over that children get quicker understanding and control of literacy—language and texts—through writing than through reading. . . . Tiny children can write before they can read, can write more than they can read, and can write more easily than they can read. For small children can write anything they can say—once they know the alphabet and are shown the rudimentary trick of using invented spelling.

He added in an E-mail letter to me the following:

> This process of writing into reading is going on in countless schools around the country, and it can produce a deep change in a child's relationship to literacy. Writing puts the child into *active* relationship to literacy where the emphasis is on the child's own words and on the child as a builder of meaning—and

where the central question is, "What's on your mind?" Reading puts the child into a passive relationship with literacy where the emphasis is on other people's words—and the central question is, "Did you get it right?" This new emphasis on writing as a gateway to literacy strikes me as the biggest change in the culture of literacy in at least a century—much longer really.

It is not too much to say that Peter Elbow, in his consistent and careful work on behalf of a revolution in the teaching of writing, has brought freedom of expression to more people—young children, students, adults— than anyone else *in at least a century—much longer really.*

Enid Santiago Welch has been the principle pioneer in adapting the AWA method to teaching writing to young children in public schools in Chicopee and Amherst, Massachusetts. She has moved me greatly with stories of the children's commitment to their own work and to each other as they grow in confidence and experience themselves as writers. Even the youngest children follow our workshop practices. They learn the difference between autobiography and fiction in the very first exercise: "Tell us ten things about yourself, but make one of the ten a lie. We will try to guess which is the lie." Following this funny first exercise, the children learn that no one knows for certain what is true and what is fiction, and the teacher helps them treat everything that is written as fiction unless the writer wants to say that it is autobiographical. I have been amazed to hear tiny writers refer to "the narrator" or "the girl," understanding in essence, if not in these words, the difference between a first-person narrator and a protagonist.

Their ability to keep confidentiality has been awesome! If one child weeps while reading a story about a parent on drugs, the other children respond respectfully, tell what they like in the writing, what is strong, and understand that no mention of this story is to be made outside the classroom. What is written is sacred, Enid tells them. It belongs only to the writer. Young students are told that they may write about anything at all, but if they write something that indicates they are in danger, the teacher will talk to the student about it. After that conversation, if the teacher is still concerned, he or she will get help for the child.

In Northern Ireland, Protestant and Catholic children are educated in separate schools. Heather McNeill is a teacher in a Protestant state controlled primary school.

My name is Heather McNeill and I am a teacher at Portrush Primary School in Northern Ireland. I have 25 years experience teaching a wide range of subjects to children aged 8–11.

I was first introduced to Pat Schneider through my local women's writing group and then when I attended one of her workshops in Northern Ireland. Immediately I saw the potential of using her methods with young children, especially those inhibited due to pressures of spelling and grammar.

I decided to introduce a creative writing club into the school, "Scribblers." Over the last three terms I have had two different sets of children in my weekly workshops, ranging in age from 8–11 years, both male and female.

I place emphasis on the writing rather on mechanics, in other words "get your ideas down and we'll worry about spelling and punctuation later!"

The children create poems, stories and sometimes even jokes. They are more enthusiastic, are less inhibited than in a normal classroom situation, and they enjoy the teacher writing along with them.

Here are a few exercises I have used with the children:

a) My goody bag: a collection of items suitable for children such as little animal ornaments, small toys, birthday candles, jewelry, shiny things.

b) Postcards: pictures of landscapes, portraits, children, animals, funnies.

c) Word association: "Write anything that comes into your head when you hear the word sad" (or happy, or rain, wind, Christmas, Halloween). "Now choose one of your thoughts and write about it."

I vary the time for each writing activity and we always have "read back." During "read back" I have encouraged the children to be positive about each other's work. What do you remember? What did you like? What stood out for you? The responses are honest and adult-like, discussing language used, rhyme and rhythm etc. I am amazed at how well the children respond to each other and how they are eager to read out their work. In fact there's often an argument as to who goes first. Their concentration span tends to be better than in normal class situations. A less formal atmosphere exists when we sit around tables in a circle.

We have invited other classes to readings of our work, some poems and stories have been sent off to competitions and we have created Scribblers poems together mixing our ideas. . . .

. . . children are motivated, uninhibited and write from the heart on all topics, personal thoughts of an upsetting kind are also forthcoming such as death of a loved one, a pet etc. I have also introduced these methods into my own classroom teaching with the less able children.

A WRITING WORKSHOP IN A HIGH SCHOOL CLASSROOM

Jane Schneeloch, who teaches English at East Hartford High School in Connecticut, has observed the following:

[This method] works better, at first, with the lower ability student—the student who has not had the five-paragraph essay tattooed on his/her brain. (When I hand out a selection of abstract Picassos as a prompt, the academic student wants to tell me all she knows about Cubism. In my "basic" class Izzy writes, "She was a blazin' blond with blue eyes, the type you holla at.")

It can be adapted successfully for use in the more academic classes. (Students studying SAT words will remember a story about a "charlatan" and those he "dupes" better than flash cards. An assignment to create a dialogue between Mama in *Raisin in the Sun* and Ma in *The Grapes of Wrath* will teach more about character development than a list of examples.)

It provides the first opportunity for success and recognition for some students. (Tamisha, who does poorly on "book tests," suddenly has students asking to read her story about the dog that she rescued from the pound.)

It can open up communication beyond the classroom. (Mindy wrote about the father who deserted her family when she was small. When he came back into her life, she shared with him what she had written in school.)

Preparing a piece for publication provides an excellent opportunity to present the grammar and mechanics part of the course. The student is motivated to make the writing look its best when it will have a real audience.

Because using this method develops students' confidence in expressing themselves, they will ultimately improve their performance on more traditional forms of evaluation, i.e., the standardized test.

Students who use this method develop their own unique voice that they will then be able to use in other places, i.e., the college entrance essay.

Facing a stack of writing assignments written using this method is far less daunting than facing a stack of five-paragraph essays. A teacher may, believe it or not, even look forward to reading these papers.

For several years Kathryn Dunn has led a remarkable workshop at Amherst Regional High School for a deliberately mixed population of students. The intention was to put together young people who had little reason to know one another in the normal course of their days: Cambodian refugees, low-income students, minority students, students with special needs, students at risk of dropping out, and mainstream students. Here is Kathryn's report of her experience:

A HIGH SCHOOL WRITING WORKSHOP

"I look at all . . . that people are doing here and I wonder why it is so hard for me. I do not understand what the teacher in A Period was saying. . . . I think of my home; I hear the . . . voice of my father, the sounds of the children playing. . . . But now [at school], I am lonely and confused and worried."

". . . I didn't know that."

The semester begins with these words from a young Cambodian student and a response from her classmate. We go on to discuss what makes this writing strong, how it impacts us as listeners and readers. Another student reads a dialogue between a "redneck" and a "punk." The language is clipped and provocative; it is so full of electricity that many students speak at once in response.

"What's working in this writing?" I ask, over and over. A word; colors; a dream; metaphors; abrupt changes in a conversation; the juxtaposition of scenes: television against a memory of war; sounds: a mother calling her son's name as he leaves his home and country. In this way, students begin to identify the writing strengths that each member brings into the classroom.

In this high school classroom we have students for whom English is a second language; we also have special needs students, students at risk of dropping out, and mainstream students. We work in two spheres. The first focuses on each person as an individual. I ask them to give me the memories they carry, the sounds and smells and tastes of their homes, the music of their parents' words, their cultures, their histories, their morning at school. From these sources come words, poems, stories, and dialogues. Some write plays. Some write journal entries. Some use the rhythms of their native language. Writing becomes the medium for exploring and understanding the fabric of each person's life.

Sharing these lives—moving from private to public—becomes the second sphere of our work. A young Korean woman reads about her experience in a Catholic boarding school in the Midwest; a young man reads a journal entry about Palestinians in Israel. Another student describes how it felt to be arrested. I bring in apples and they write about Malcolm X and immortality and blood and Cracker Jacks and Red Sox and sanitariums and—yes—apples. Then they share their words and each person's story becomes part of a larger, collective fabric. In this process, students learn about each other. They also learn about their abilities to communicate with the written word.

Within this project, I strive to create a setting where each student can turn away for a few minutes: from the teacher, the blackboard, the lessons, the peers—where an individual can focus on herself or himself, in order to tap the resources each one holds. Their lives are rich and troubled and earnest and funny and despairing and hopeful. This is the source of their stories, and it becomes the force behind their writing.

If I am doing my work, this setting offers students the time and support to explore their own stories, as well as the encouragement to share them with others. If I am doing my work, they will come to understand that they are already capable writers; and from this understanding, they will begin to ask the questions and pursue the paths that will lead to increased and more complex writing skills.

The AWA method of writing is based on the conviction that we are all story tellers, and that anyone who can talk to a close friend can write. This method works for the group, because it builds on the strengths of individuals, and it values the inherent diversity of the class. It works for the school because it provides a setting in which populations that rarely cross paths are actively engaging each other on a weekly basis. It works for me because I get to use a medium I love, and I have the privilege of sharing writing with ten students who work hard and give us wonderful stories. And it works for the students, both as people learning about themselves and each other, and as writers who gain confidence and ability in their use of a lifetime tool.

The poem that follows is by Sophal Chhoun, one of the young writers in Kathryn Dunn's workshop:

WAKING FROM A NIGHTMARE

Working on the farm picking strawberries,
hands moving leaves.

       Like when we moved among trees and bushes to hide.

People talking out loud, laughing.
I listen to them.
The wind blows; I hear it.

       Like when my mom and dad whispered in my ear
       to tell me to be quiet.

One tray is full;
one man runs to the truck to get paid.

I am still picking.

       Like I was still hiding from the soldiers: Khmer Rouge
       and Vietnamese.

I hear him running; I hear his boots making sounds.

       I heard the boot of the soldier running to kill a man
       holding hands with his son to hide.
       The man fell down.

Like the man puts down the tray of strawberries.
The strawberries roll down off the tray.

       Like the boy ran away from the soldier.

I hear a man say, "I will never forget where my parents
got killed."

I hear a woman say, "I will never forget where my husband
got killed."

A man watches his wife working through the field.
I hear him say, "I will never forget the day I fought
with the Khmer Rouge."

My tray is full and I walk carefully to the truck.
Hoping that the strawberries will not roll down off my tray.

Hoping that there will be peace in my country, Cambodia.

TEACHING WRITING IN COLLEGE

Ali Lichtenstein teaches Composition 101 at Keene State College in New Hampshire. She writes:

> English 101: Essay Writing is KSC's first year composition course. Each semester I walk into a room of twenty college students to teach this mandatory writing course. Very few students in each section are confident about their writing skills—most are terrified. They dread this class, and their anxiety is palpable. To reassure them, I talk a bit about how I will be teaching writing in workshop format and how the Amherst Writers & Artists method works.
>
> This is a rigorous course. Studies show that a college student's success or lack of success in a first-year composition course is a strong indicator of her/his future ability to succeed in college studies. I want my students to succeed in college, to gain the skills and confidence needed to write academic papers for the next four years, but beyond that, I want them to love writing and trust their own voices as writers and thinkers.
>
> During the course of each fifteen-week semester, students bring several pieces of their writing to a polished, well-crafted stage. . . . We (I write with the students) begin each cycle of writing an essay in the same way: we write in response to various prompts designed to help tap thoughts and memories. Similar in format to an AWA writing workshop, I offer a prompt (which may be used or ignored) and we all write for a set period of time, from 10 to 20 minutes, depending on the length of the class. Then we break into small groups of five and read our work out loud, pausing between readers to give positive responses about what is memorable and strong. Students love this process. They begin to find common themes with other students, they develop a strong sense of community, and they begin to trust their ability to write their own stories as they begin to lose their fear of writing.
>
> After the class has written several pieces, I introduce an academic essay assignment. Often students will choose a piece of earlier writing to begin their first draft, but I always give one more prompt at this point because sometimes reading the written assignment itself triggers new ideas. Because the course must cover certain material, students write expressive, affirming, persuasive, and informative essays. They always begin with their own thoughts and ideas and experiences, and they always write for several sessions before beginning the next assignment. My one steadfast "rule" for each assignment: it must be on a topic that interests and is important to the writer.

When Ella Rutledge came to Amherst for training in our workshop method, she spoke out of long experience teaching college writing courses in Japan and America. I asked her to reflect on that experience. This is what she wrote:

Many of my students have hoped, at the beginning of a writing class, just to be given the proper format so they could safely fill in the blanks with "correct" answers. Indeed, many instructors and many writing textbooks do use the five-paragraph format (introduction with clearly stated thesis statement, three-paragraph body providing support for the statement, and conclusion, a restatement of the original thesis statement). I dislike this format because it puts the student and his or her thoughts in a straitjacket or a cage. No piece of writing in which the writer can rehash at the end what was said at the beginning can be an experience of learning for the writer. But the successful essay will be just that: an experience by which a student organizes his or her thoughts on a subject, comes to a new understanding concerning that subject, and at the same time provides evidence to others of that learning process.

Of course thesis statements and the logical thought process by which an essay is developed are important. Students in the traditional classroom have to be taught these things. But other things are also important. I once tutored a student at a writing center who had been assigned to write a description of a busy supermarket. She had gone to the supermarket and sat at the entrance for half an hour and recorded everything she saw, heard, smelled, and had successfully captured that chaotic, vibrant scene. "But," she moaned, shoving the paper at me, "I can't find a thesis statement anywhere!" This is need for format out of control. It is also important for students to learn just to sit quietly and observe what is happening around them, and to record that in accurate language. It is even more important for them to learn that skill before going on to thesis statements, for if they do not, the chances are good that they will construct such statements not from their own minds and experience but from the ideas and opinions of others.

Even in the traditional grade-propelled classroom, and especially in the developmental or ESL classroom, room needs to be made for allowing the students to first find their own voices. The use of many of the exercises described in this book for writers working alone or in workshops where the participants attend voluntarily and where neither teacher nor student needs to worry about a final grade can be adapted to the college classroom.

TEACHING WRITING IN GRADUATE SCHOOL

For years my own experience of classroom teaching has been at the graduate level, in a classroom where there is a wide diversity of national and ethnic backgrounds. Every one of the participants comes with a strong professional background and an excellent education. Nevertheless, most of the participants are terrified of writing. Most of them have completed masters or doctoral programs. They have written term papers and professional papers—even books—for publication for years. And still they are terrified. I have many, many times sat vigil in a circle of writers as a professional man or woman broke down with joy at hearing his or her own voice affirmed for the first time. At this moment I am remembering a woman with a doctorate whom I described in chapter 6. She was from New Orleans, of mixed Mexican, Indian, black, and white heritage. She began writing in her academic voice, cultured and exquisite. She needed no help to do that, but there were other stories that could not be told in that language. After several days of listening to others write, sometimes about childhood, I sensed her frustration, and specifically asked her to write a piece about her childhood, inviting her to use any voice that wanted to emerge. She wrote a piece about her father's death, in the rhythms and the cadence of southern black church folk. The voice that poured out of her was incredibly beautiful—full of the culture of her ancestors. When we talked about it, rejoicing in its power, she cried and said, "Nobody ever wanted that voice from me before."

Teaching creative writing at the college and graduate level is essentially no different from leading writing workshops in a living room or in the community hall of a housing project. The fear is the same. And the antidote to fear is the same. The fear is that our own most intimate, most real voice will be rejected. The cure is to have it welcomed and affirmed. When the writer has grown in confidence in his or her own voice, the teacher/leader introduces lessons in craft, form, and technique. New genres may be introduced; the poet is encouraged to write a play; the short-story writer is stretched to try a sonnet. On a foundation of acceptance and celebration of the original voice, innovation will be welcomed.

USING WRITING IN COURSES OTHER THAN WRITING COURSES

Dr. Genevieve Chandler in the School of Nursing at the University of Massachusetts uses this writing method as an intervention technique with adolescents at risk. She sees the loss of voice in adolescents as a public health issue and trains nursing students to use writing with youth at risk, working to prevent their dropping out of school and ending up in the court system. She has also developed and published a methodology for evaluating the progress of students in AWA method workshops. Reprints are available from Amherst Writers & Artists Press. The following is from her article in the *Journal of Child and Adolescent Psychiatric Nursing*:

> To date, the majority of interventions with adolescents have been problem focused and administered through verbal techniques such as lectures and discussion, with the content determined by adults.

[In the workshop based on Schneider's method] "Writing came easily, students were very eager and excited about sharing. I was impressed with the sensitivity to each other's writing and feelings of closeness that came through when commenting on their peers.". . . The writing was affecting not only the individual, but also the group dynamics.

The piece that follows is by Dr. Linda Meccouri, who uses the AWA method in computer courses and diversity courses.

TEACHING WRITING IN A COMMUNITY COLLEGE

I am a teacher of Computer Information Systems and Diversity Studies. (Yes, they really do go together—especially in these times.)

This past semester, I taught a course called CMC for the Global Village—a combination of teaching Internet technology and computer-mediated communication using Global Studies topics for discussion. The discussion took place in an online "discussion board." I have used the skills and techniques in Pat's method extensively, although the actual content and "triggers" came from the discipline. So bruised are some of my students that we actually did not refer to what we did as "writing"—we used words like "discussing," "listening," and "communicating." It just convinced me that we can never underestimate the fear and risk involved in writing. This was the year of the September 11 terrorist attack on the World Trade Center, and the topics in this class were exquisitely sensitive, so writing rather than discussing verbally took on a new dimension of risk. By writing, we were going to "own" our opinions, stereotypes, gifts and horrors.

We wrote in response to a "trigger" which was the discussion board forum, each member writing their response in a separate thread with everyone responsible for reading all entries and responding with what they liked, learned, and were curious about. Students took turns in teams of two "moderating" the online discussion—this is a process of learning to facilitate "conversation" in a virtual community. From the introductions to the final questions, the culture of encouragement and the "method" was used to handle the painful/joyful learning with such a diversity of students writing about culture, religion, technology, gender, class, war and peace.

What about Grades?

I hate them. I am not alone. Good teachers everywhere understand the damage that is done by grading a young artist's work. And they try in every way imaginable to avoid them, mitigate them, soften the blow. Grading hurts the creative process.

The question from those who defend testing and grading is, What about standards? We are all concerned about standards. We all want student writers to grow in craft as well as in confidence. Our differences lie in the way we use to get there. By what method do we achieve the desired standards? Ideally, standards would come up from student writers themselves, working for their own "personal best," rather than having standards handed down through tests and grades.

The problems with teaching writing in our educational system cannot be fixed by mandated tests. It can only be fixed by the true commitment of all of our people to the education of all of our children. Setting up special schools "for the gifted" is a new mask for a very old practice: the cynical abandonment of the poor. Too often government-funded private and charter schools siphon off the most intensely committed parents and critical financial support from public schools. Our nation was built on a foundation of public education, equal opportunity. That foundation has never been more at risk than it is now. The issue for public education is not tests, but money. Money for the schools. Adequate salaries for the teachers. Smaller classes. And writing understood as an art that belongs to every person.

In teaching writing, the problem with "standards" is their subjectivity. Historically, they have weeded out the voices of difference, and narrowed the channel of those who reach professional acceptance. In most school systems, teachers are required to give grades. Sometimes a teacher can push to change the practice in teaching the arts. When I was first invited to lead my annual workshops at the Graduate Theological Union in Berkeley, California, I made, as a part of my contract, the agreement that I would give an A to everyone who took my course, *so long as they attended all sessions and participated in class work.* I remember that the dean looked at me with serious and questioning regard, and I promised him my students would work hard. And they do. And they all get A's!

Ali Lichtenstein did not give grades at Keene State other than the midterm and final grade. "The lack of grading individual papers," she writes, "did not mean a lack of evaluative feedback. Students received many comments from me giving feedback on their work, and I met with each student several times during the semester. The final grade in this course was based on the portfolio, journals, and all in-class work, including participation and writing."

As far as it is possible, grading of student writing should be avoided. Similarly, schools should not sponsor contests. For every one student who is chosen as excellent, there are many who come out of the contest having learned that their work failed—the opposite of the learning we want.

Rather, schools should sponsor open-mic readings where many students have an opportunity to read their work and be applauded, and there is no "voting" on who is "best" or any system of placing one above another.

Some Practices for Teaching Writing in the Classroom

From first grade through graduate school, the method described in this book is appropriate for use in the classroom. Here are some basic practices (never call them "rules") for teaching writing in the classroom:

1. Remember that every student already uses beautiful, passionate, effective language somewhere, speaking to someone. No one's original voice is "wrong." Your task is to evoke and welcome the voice that already exists, and to give the student confidence enough to sustain him or her through learning additional skills in using that voice and experimenting with other voices.

2. Use the exercise prompts suggested throughout this book, and dream up new ones of your own.

3. For the most part allow *subject matter* to come up from the unconscious reservoir in your students' minds. If you must assign subjects, encourage them to engage their own unconscious minds through free association. Encourage innovation in form even while teaching standard forms. ("Write an essay that imitates this one, then write the same subject in any form you want to create.")

4. When you are teaching academic forms, such as the term paper or essay, train your students in the use of free-writing techniques for getting into their subject and breaking down blocks. For example, you might encourage them to begin each writing session with ten minutes of free writing. Suggest that they begin free writing with a concrete image. For example, if students are writing book reviews, ask them to begin by holding the book in their minds and finding one concrete image, either from the book or from their reaction to it. Write down that image, and write freely for ten minutes anything at all that comes to mind. Just keep the pen moving. Then turn to the term paper or essay and feel free to use anything that might have come up in the free writing.

5. With young children or other writers who cannot type, allow them to use phonetic spelling and help them to bind their stories into attractive books without correcting spelling. Or use volunteers who will type their work so they can see it in a printed form free of spelling errors. Don't teach spelling while teaching writing; it can be taught separately. Do not write on a student's handwritten page. Treat it as if it were a work of visual art (it is!). You would never draw on a student's drawing, or mark it with a grade. Make your comments on a separate piece of paper, or on a typed copy. Teach children how to give positive feedback to brand-new material and how to offer suggestions later when it is in "manuscript form."

6. Ask students who type to create a typed first draft before offering any suggestion or critique.

7. In responding to a typed manuscript, be certain that both your verbal comments and those in the manuscript margins are weighted on the side of affirmation. There should not be more suggestion for change than there is appreciation and praise.

8. Do not grade writing. If you must grade, let it be on attendance or on number of assignments completed, but grade the writing only if you can give all your students an A.

9. Write with your students, and read your own brand-new work aloud to them as they read theirs to one another and to you. Be honest about how you feel as you do this—if it feels scary, tell them so. Your own power and authority will only deepen as they experience your willingness to risk along with them.

10. Don't let a student leave your mentoring until work has been brought to a place where you can affirm it in some way that is honest for you and empowering for the student.

Creating Your Own Workshop or Writing Group

In 1973 Oxford University Press published a groundbreaking book titled *Writing Without Teachers,* by Peter Elbow. It powered a revolution that was already simmering. From a child's first year in school all the way through graduate MFA programs, teachers and students of writing began to focus on the creative *process.* How does art happen? What is needed to make good writing happen?

It was a shocking suggestion, that writers might write without teachers. Perhaps it is now a shocking suggestion that you might start your own workshop or writing group. It's an idea whose time has come.

A workshop or a writing group? What is the difference? Usually the term "workshop" implies that the leader has either professional training as a teacher of writing or professional experience as a published writer. He or she has knowledge of literature and an ability to guide others through manuscript development and the process of submission of manuscripts for possible publication. If you feel that your own experience as a writer, teacher, and/or workshop leader is adequate, call your group a workshop. Follow your own experience and/or training, and use the guidelines offered in this book. If you want to take further training in this workshop method, you may want to attend writing retreats or leadership trainings sponsored by Amherst Writers & Artists.

If you do not have much experience writing and/or publishing, but are skilled in group dynamics and can creatively and effectively lead a group, then call it a writers' group and see yourself as the group facilitator. Follow the guidelines offered in this book. Allow knowledge about writing and publishing to arise from the members themselves as you study and work together.

Starting a new workshop may feel daunting, especially if it is independent of an institution. Believe me, I know! When I started, in the late 1970s, there was no book like this one to tell me what to do. I learned by inventing as I went, and so will each workshop leader, finding what fits her or his own personality and gifts of leadership. It does help to be part of a network of support. Pat Craig, whose humor lightens the load for all of us who are affiliated leaders in the AWA network, sends us all occasional reports. This excerpt was written early in her experience of leading workshops:

> I am in some kind of transition and it is driving me crazy. I have my elder son's room, always before known as "Aaron's room," torn apart. It seems to be called "the writing room" now, and I have no patience at all for it being kludged and half-assed. I have the floor and all the surfaces covered with paper that needs organization, and I have run out of steam, but it needs to be done by group on Sunday, and I am having wild and expensive fantasies of putting in clerestory windows and a window seat, a Hopper print that I love, a Craftsman floor lamp, a blue velvet couch and foot stool. I have plants and rocks all over the patio, awaiting the beginning of this season's last leg of gardening, none of which I had time for but all of which I have put off since 1977 and all of which seems instinctively and metaphorically important. I have two stories in shambles, and son-of-a-bitch if I don't seem to have started a novel. Plus I am in the middle of the visioning stage for that new career class for artistic and creative students that is to start in August, which is starting to feel like tomorrow. I'm beginning to get the possible vision of a new job, and of course the group is in shnibbles too. Honest, this is not at all like me. I am targeted, focused, methodical—or I guess I was.

Pat's humor is one of her greatest gifts as a leader. Over the years, I have come to believe that taking ourselves with a grain of salt, especially when we are in a position of leadership, is a survival skill that will keep us from quitting, no matter how "kludged" we may sometimes feel.*

Even if you feel that you do not have any skills as a group leader or as a workshop leader, you may want to meet with one or more friends with-

---

*NOTE: Just in case you don't recognize "kludged," as I did not, and can't find it in a dictionary, as I could not, here's a note from the author: "It's a computer term that means thrown together out of spare/mismatched parts, i.e. kludged together."

out a leader. Just follow the guidelines in the next chapter and do the exercises that follow. A writer is someone who writes; a writing group can simply be two or more writers who meet and share their wisdom and their knowledge of craft in a spirit of collegiality.

Many of the lessons that I learned "by guess and by gosh," as my grandmother would have said, you do not have to learn the hard way. Answer the questions below step-by-step, and follow the guidelines. They will help you avoid many of the pitfalls I could not foresee as I began my writing workshops without any appropriate models to follow.

From this point on, I will use the word "workshop" to mean any creative writing group.

What Kind of Workshop Do You Want to Create?

WHO WILL THE MEMBERS BE?

Will you invite both men and women? For years I led two workshops each week for men and women, and one for women only. Unfortunately, I cannot offer one for men only, since any group I led would always have a woman present, but I think a workshop for men only would be a fine thing. However, I have been told by more than one man that he preferred a group that includes women, and at least one male member of my workshops has said that he believes many men are most comfortable writing with women. This is an interesting possibility. Some people are more creative in mixed groups, while some do best among their own gender. Your decision should be based on your own interest and comfort as leader.

WILL YOU INVITE ONLY EXPERIENCED WRITERS, OR INCLUDE BEGINNERS?

In my experience, it is best to mix experienced and inexperienced writers together. Some of the freshest, strongest writers I have worked with come free of preconceptions about what "literature" is. And some of the wisest, kindest workshop members have been those who have written and published widely, are willing to share their experience, and are able to receive encouragement and support from others. A wide variety of participants in a workshop gives a writer a rich range of responses to his or her work. I have had a 75-year-old woman who was a retired physician and a 14-year-old junior high boy writing side by side in workshop. She wrote about being a doctor when women were rarely allowed into medical school; he wrote wildly imaginative science fiction stories. Their support of one another was beautiful to behold.

WILL YOU REQUIRE A WRITING SAMPLE BEFORE ADMITTING SOMEONE TO THE WORKSHOP?

I never do. The work that writers will do in a supportive workshop is almost always far better than what they have written previously. Also, I don't want to limit my groups to writers who have been handpicked, and I don't want to be prejudiced ahead of time by reading something that may have been written in terror under pressure of receiving a grade.

HOW WILL YOU GET TRUE DIVERSITY?

A mixed population—not only in race and ethnic origin, but also in age, economic and educational level, writing experience, and preferred genre—makes a rich mulch of images, forms, possibilities in the group. Everyone brings some unique gift of life experience and perspective. Working in a diverse group helps us to be generous, to share what we know, and to learn from everyone else. I have to work constantly to achieve diversity. I live in a college town where rents are high and there is not a balance of racial and ethnic populations. In my own community the only way that I have been able to achieve the depth of diversity that I want is by specific recruitment and offers of financial aid. Since I am an independent entrepreneur, this means a direct loss of income, but it is an ethical question for me, and a test of my commitment to my own ideals. And it makes for a better workshop.

WILL YOUR WORKSHOP BE FOR ONE GENRE ONLY?

I prefer workshops that are not genre-specific. That is, poets and fiction writers, playwrights and librettists, nonfiction and songwriters are all mixed together. I myself write in many different forms, and I think doing so makes writing less arduous, more fun, full of surprise, and ultimately more effective. All writers are strengthened by hearing and responding to work in various forms; many beginning writers do not know what they write best; and many experienced writers will surprise themselves by writing in a form they have not tried before.

Practical Matters

HOW MANY, AND WHEN?

I suggest a three-hour workshop meeting with enrollment limited to 12 persons, or a two-hour workshop with enrollment limited to eight. Some AWA workshop leaders offer three-hour morning workshops, occasional all-day Saturday writing retreats with lunch included, weekend writing re-treats, and six-day intensive retreats. Any of these options can be adapted to your situation. Leaders who come to Amherst Writers & Artists for train-ing receive sample schedules for these events and resources for leading them.

Twelve is an ideal number of participants for three-hour workshops, and eight participants for two-hour workshops. That will give you a good gathering at meetings when several are absent, and a manageable work-shop even when all are present. I suggest that you wait until you have at least five participants before beginning. In the early days I recruited friends to be "warm bodies," coming free of charge until I had enough paying participants to make the group effective.

WILL YOU CHARGE TUITION? IF SO, HOW MUCH?

Yes, you should charge tuition. People will value your workshop accord-ing to how you, yourself, value it. When I come to this question in our trainings, I tell this story: Once when my children were in elementary school, my daughter Laurel had a registered Sheltie. She sold the first litter of puppies and was looking forward to breeding a second litter when the dog got out. When the puppies were born, I put an ad in the local paper that said, "Free puppies. Half sheltie, half handsome stranger." We did not get a single call. A week later the breeder called to set up an ap-pointment for the dog to be bred, and I told her it was too late. "What are you doing with those puppies?" she asked. I told her about my ad. "You can sell them," she said. "Place the ad again, and charge $25 per puppy." I placed the ad again: "Puppies. Half sheltie, half handsome stranger. $25." Within a week, the entire litter was sold. We are strange creatures, we humans. Charge for your workshop. You will be more likely to fill it.

How much to charge should be based on two considerations: your own professional level, and the market price for similar services in your community. As a teacher with an MFA in Creative Writing and years of experience in group work, I began by basing my workshop fee on the amount paid by a special student taking a comparable number of classroom course hours at our area graduate schools. I advise leaders without academic credentials, but with experience in writing and publishing or group work, to research the cost of comparable services (group therapy, art classes, yoga and exercise classes) and charge accordingly.

This workshop model is equally effective for groups that gather informally, with no leader and no tuition.

When you have made these decisions, you are ready to publicize your workshop.

PUBLICIZE YOUR WORKSHOP

You will need three kinds of publicity to begin a new workshop: a poster, a brief community calendar announcement, and a news release. Most beginning workshop leaders may find paid display ads too costly. They may in fact be less effective than regular news releases and calendar announcements.

The text of the poster and the calendar announcement are basically the same. My own poster might read:

Amherst Writers & Artists
CREATIVE WRITING WORKSHOP
Beginners & Experienced Writers Welcome
Leader: Pat Schneider, MFA
Poet, Playwright, Author
Tuesday evenings, 7:30–10:30 P.M.
77 McClellan Street, Amherst, MA
For more information call 413-253-3307

When I began this work, all I could say was "MFA" and "Published Author" (a few small journals). There was no book to guide me, no model of community workshops for me to follow. Some of our affiliated AWA workshop leaders don't have the "MFA" to put on their posters, but do have "Certified in the Amherst Writers & Artists Workshop Method." Whatever your qualifications, put them on your posters and news releases: "Published"; "Certified"; "MFA"; "Experienced Group Leader."

The news release will give more information. Put at the top of your page "For Immediate Release," the event date, and your name and telephone number as contact person. Always use full double-spaced lines, and put the most important information first; newspaper editors like to chop off the ends when they lack sufficient space. Mail your publicity to your local paper, radio stations, libraries, schools, community centers, and churches. Take copies of the poster to area grocery stores, laundromats, and bus stops. The success of Amherst Writers & Artists in the early days was completely dependent on the hard work done in publicity. A friend and I began together, which is much easier than beginning alone. We went to our local radio station and volunteered a regular program in which we interviewed area writers (and plugged our workshop). We talked a local printer into making beautiful posters for the program in exchange for free ads on the radio station, and our feet beat the sidewalks of Amherst and surrounding towns taking those posters everywhere.

WHAT TO SAY WHEN PEOPLE CALL

Until you have five prospective members, thank them for calling, take their names and addresses, and tell them you will call back when you have five people. I do not require a mailed-in deposit for my workshops, but some other AWA workshop leaders do. Your decision will depend on the community in which you live. Large urban areas seem to need the financial commitment in order to have people actually show up; I don't find that to be necessary in the small college town where I live.

After you have met once with your first interested people, tell callers that it is possible that you may have an opening soon, and they may come once as your guest. This immediately establishes you as a generous and secure person; it also gives you an opportunity to see whether the person is right for your group.

When you have done all that is suggested above, you are ready to open your door and welcome your new workshop members.

THE PREPARED PLACE

It is Thursday evening, almost 7:30. I have prepared a place. There are 12 comfortable chairs arranged in a circle. The house smells of chocolate, hot coffee, and tea. On the table I have placed a plate of warm brownies. There is also a dish of carrot and celery sticks and a bowl of popcorn. Beside them, I have laid out an array of announcements, several literary journals that are advertising for manuscripts, the latest copies of *Poets & Writers Magazine*, the *Dramatist's Guild Newsletter*, the *American Poetry Review*, and the *Chronicle*, the newsletter of the Associated Writing Programs. There is a copy of the *Directory of Literary Magazines* compiled by the Council of Literary Magazines and Presses and a loose-leaf notebook full of recent guidelines from journals, and current contest announcements.

Place is important. I prefer to lead workshops in my own home, an old farmhouse near the center of town. We gather in a circle until I have given an exercise, then people spread out into several rooms to write, coming back together to read that new material and critique manuscripts.

When I lead a workshop in an academic setting, I arrive early, arrange the chairs in a circle, put some kind of printed handout material on each chair, and have some refreshments on a side table. (I have seen two studies reporting that generating new writing burns as many calories as running, bicycling, or making love! This is not absurd; the brain uses enormous energy—in fact, one quarter of the body's basal metabolism.)

The piece that follows was written by Deene Clark in my Wednesday workshop one evening as I was writing this book. It says, better than I can, how important is the leader's careful preparation of place.

> I open the front door and walk into the house. Already, in the hallway, I can smell it, and walking down the hallway and into the living room, the odor is strong: brownies, freshly baked brownies, warm and waiting for us. Such a delight. Such a welcoming, beckoning house to walk into. It says, "welcome"— the brownies do. But of course, if brownies, then a time to eat them, and to chat and laugh and thereby to be at home.
>
> There is other food on the table awaiting the mid-evening break: melon, raw carrots, freshly washed grapes, coffee, tea, soda, orange juice and, as I said, chatter and laughter. At the break, we will have been writing together— the ten or twelve of us—for an hour or so, having been invited to respond to some lines from a poem or a book, or to some pictures or to several articles: ancient kitchen utensils, old fashioned toys and children's books, a line from a song, the song itself. That's how Pat begins the evening.

If you want to, close your eyes, relax your body, clear your mind, be open . . . Let your thoughts travel back to a time before this time and come upon someone who was very important to you and see where it takes you in the writing—or write whatever is on your mind right now.

Brownies are on my mind tonight. Walking into the living room after two years of these weekly sessions feels quite familiar and comfortable as does the presence of our teacher and guide: Pat Schneider. In this brownied gathering-place, we will be invited to remember a death, a sin, an ecstasy, or whatever else comes to us out of the unconscious in response to Pat's invitation: *See where this takes you, in your writing.*

I will be quite full when I leave the group three hours later, whether I am possessed by brownies, melon or my own wistful memories and yearning. And I will have received some feedback from the members of the group, including from Pat, if I choose to read aloud the pieces that I will have written. It will be positive and encouraging feedback on this initial response. Later I may choose to print up enough copies to hand out to all the group members . . . [when] I would like some critical response: what worked and what didn't? What sticks out as awkward? Things like that. . . .

"Hear what people say and then decide for yourself what is helpful and useful, then write it the way it works for you; it's your story or poem or whatever," Pat often says. Writing this way is new to me: no lectures, theories, rules, "right way" or even a theme or text. I guess you'd call it writing with the right brain—letting ideas, words, pictures simply enter your imagination spontaneously, as a surprise perhaps, to you as much as to your fellow writers. I suppose, it's all been there, tucked away in the unconscious, but now it's called out.

How else would I remember the determined look on my mother's face, almost as if in battle, as she hand-whipped a large pan of potatoes, except that someone invites me to do so? Where was the thought of Marsha—dear, dear Marsha, whom I loved so earnestly when we were six and back together at Lake Ossipee for our families' summer vacation, before Pat invited us to *remember a time before this time and a person who* . . .

And how could I avoid re-entering the Radiation Oncology Department at the Brigham Hospital, once Pat has brought me there with a picture post-card among many post-cards she has laid out on the coffee table—a card showing a kid with bandages around his head?

But tonight it is brownies that remind me of the Cushman bread man who used to come by our house each week in Concord, New Hampshire, delivering his wonderful Cushman brownies and cakes and breads and donuts, every week of my adolescence, so that now I begin to taste the brownie and to remember my mother and me, after I've come home from school, full of some story, complaint or delight—and she listened.

Then I would have gone riding on Duke and—there, it's happened again: I'm on Duke, cantering across the cinder road in Concord, New Hampshire. I'm 14, my life is open and beckoning, safe and private and, on an evening fifty-five years later, in a comfortable living room full of the smell of fresh-baked brownies, I will mount and ride again, and it will be wonderful.

A Sample Workshop: Meet the Members

The 12 workshop members I describe below are imagined composites created from my experience. All names and characters are fictional with the exception of Eva Brown, who asked that I use her real name and tell her actual story. Each workshop member illustrates one suggestion for keeping a workshop healthy.

If you are already a member of a workshop, you will find familiar problems and perhaps some new solutions described. If you are a workshop leader, the suggestions outlined here will help you strengthen and maintain a supportive community of writers. If you are a solitary writer, I believe you will enjoy the stories in this chapter and find some useful information for your own writing life.

The first four people to arrive at this imaginary workshop are the least experienced. I meet each person at the door, welcome him or her, offer refreshments, and help get conversation going.

JEANNE, INEXPERIENCED AND AFRAID

The first person to arrive is Jeanne, who is the mother of four children, a woman who left high school without finishing and never went back. She has always wanted to write but is frightened of spelling, punctuation, and grammar, and is insecure about her West Virginia accent. She is certain that everyone else is far more accomplished than she is and she comes to the workshop only on the strength of great courage.

Jeanne does not know she will do her most powerful writing about her family in a coal-mining town, the baths she took as a child standing shivering in a galvanized tub near the wood stove, the struggles of those who wanted to form a union.

For many weeks Jeanne has not read anything to us, but she has been writing in her notebook, and when I have asked her how she's doing, she says, "I'm OK, but I'm not ready to read anything yet." I have told her she may remain silent as long as she wants and I have encouraged her to begin by writing about her childhood. Tonight, for the first time, Jeanne will take the risk of reading, and for the first time she will hear others telling her what they like and what they remember. She will go home with her confidence strengthened and her voice a bit more free.

Suggestion 1: Invite, but do not pressure, members to read what they have just written in the workshop.

Only in an atmosphere of utmost safety can language flow freely. I believe that people can be trusted to know when it is safe to read and when it is better to remain silent. Once I had a young woman who, for more than a year, could not read aloud in the workshop. After weeks of silence I began to feel that the workshop needed to hear her voice, and privately I told her so. "Can you now and then just make a comment on someone else's writing?" I asked, and gently told her that having someone who never speaks can begin to feel like a judging presence. She seemed to understand that, but said she was afraid she didn't have anything worthwhile to say. I suggested that she could just "second" what someone else had already affirmed, by saying "I also liked . . .". It was a good step forward for her, and not long afterward she brought me a manuscript to read. I wrote many affirmations and a few suggestions for change. She worked on it with me and then finally handed it out to the entire group for critique.

EVA, WHOSE NATIVE TONGUE IS NOT ENGLISH

The next person to arrive is Eva. She was born in Germany in 1938 and heard only the German language spoken until she was four months old, when her family fled to France and dropped German entirely, fearing they would be sent back to face concentration camps. She heard only French spoken during those two and a half years. When Eva was three, her family moved to New York City and spoke English, although she thinks her father probably still spoke German at home. Eva works as a psychologist and writes professional documents. She wants to learn to write in a way that is more creative, less formal. She feels overwhelmed by the ease and freedom others seem to have in their writing. Eva's written work seems always to have a slightly heightened formality, as if there is a trace of accent that you cannot quite identify. She does not yet guess that the voice in which she speaks will be exactly right to tell the stories of displacement by war and that they are her deepest resource.

Suggestion 2: Do not allow the workshop to critique or correct work that has just been written.

Writing that has just come from the pen of a writer should not be critiqued by other people. A piece of writing, newly born, is as fragile and raw as a newborn baby, and should be treated as respectfully, as tenderly. When my workshop members write together side-by-side, and read that new work to one another, I do not allow anyone to make overt or subtle suggestions for change. What is helpful is giving back to the writer what the listener remembers, and what the listener likes. Each writer is finding his or her way to voice. It cannot be coerced, and it cannot be given form or shape by anyone else.

ANDY, WHO IS YOUNG

The next workshop member to arrive is Andy, a junior in high school. He comes on a bicycle, wearing a huge plastic helmet and a backpack. He writes science fiction, amazes us with his constant invention, and wants more than anything in the world to be a writer. Andy is a great asset to the group. His energy and inventive imagination are good for us all. He will write for several years in my workshop, and he will resist my every effort (and I will try!) to get him to bring anything in on paper to hand out for workshop response. For four years I will grin and give up, encourage him, tell him my honest delight in the incredible worlds he creates and reads aloud to us. Then there will come a day when he will take a writing class in college and will be able to work with deadlines. My role in Andy's life is the same as for every other writer: This is your time; do in it what helps you as a writer. I trust that you know what is best for you.

Suggestion 3: Allow for great diversity in age, experience, style, and genre in your workshop.

It breaks down competitiveness, increases compassion, and allows more learning to happen in everyone. The elderly writer learns from the slang of the young; the young writer learns from the experience of the old. The sophisticated writer is given courage to be plain and earthy; the plain and earthy writer is enabled to write with sophistication. The skilled writer teaches the unskilled about form; the unskilled writer invites the skilled writer to trust his or her own instincts.

FAYE, WHOSE SUBJECT MATTER IS CONTROVERSIAL

Faye is in her twenties, dresses in jeans, T-shirt, and sneakers, writes graphic first-person stories about life as a prostitute in a neighboring town. She writes in the first person about Johns and one-night stands and fear of AIDS. No one in the group knows whether Faye's work is fiction or autobiography. A retired public health nurse in the workshop tells me I should privately ask Faye questions, offer counsel. With some inner ambivalence, I say no, that is not what Faye wants from me; if it were, she would ask. I tell the nurse to follow her own instincts if she feels like intervening. I feel it is my task to protect Faye's boundaries by providing her with a good workshop and a safe place to speak the truth of her imagination or of her life. It is none of my business which is which.

Faye will write her stories and listen to us tell her what we like and what we remember. She will receive our comments on the pages of her manuscripts. And then, suddenly, she will disappear from my workshop, from my life. And I will grieve, and I will always wonder how she is, where she is. But I am not a therapist or a social worker or a minister. Whether her work is fiction or autobiography is irrelevant to the strength of her writing. Fiction is just another way to tell the truth.

Suggestion 4: Assume all written work to be fictional unless the writer volunteers that it is autobiographical.

Even if the writer is moved to tears as he or she reads, respond to the written work using "the narrator, the child, the mother" and so forth, rather than "you, your grandmother, your lover." In *Tell Me Something I Can't Forget,* the documentary film about my workshop with low-income women, there is a scene in which Robin Therrien breaks down as she reads about the suicide of her mother when Robin was a child. We wait in silence as she struggles to read. When she cannot, I offer to read for her. When she says no, I say, "OK. Now. We're a writing workshop, and we love each other. But the way we protect each other is to deal with this as writing. So what can we say about what we've been given in the piece of writing? What's strong? What stays with you?" The workshop members slowly and carefully name images that moved us, and Robin listens.

Your task, as workshop leader, is to protect the writer by keeping the boundaries clear. I always discourage responses that begin "That makes me think of the time when . . ." The sharing of related experiences by other members of the workshop moves attention away from what has been written and disappoints the writer by removing the focus from discussion of his or her manuscript.

GEORGE'S ATTITUDE GETS IN THE WAY

George is a medical doctor who is working on a novel. He has no difficulty writing chapter after chapter—he loves writing, and when he writes about an emergency procedure in the operating room, the work is intensely interesting, fresh, believable. But when he tries to write about women, everything goes flat. He has two women in the novel; he refers to them as "the fair Jeanette" and "the ravishing Nona." The fair Jeanette has blond hair and bright blue eyes that "twinkle"; the ravishing Nona has black eyes that are always "snapping," and black hair. Neither woman has a wrinkle, a blemish, a wart, a hair out of place. George knows he has a problem here; he is shy, and working on this part of his writing is very difficult for him.

As I sit trying to find a way to help him, I remember the traumatic experience I had in graduate school when my professor, Andrew Fetler, told me flatly that my writing was terrible. His words float into my mind, "The problem is not with the way you write. It's with the way you think."

As is so often true with teaching, I suddenly realize that I am learning. For the first time I really understand what Andy was trying to tell me. For the first time I can accept that he was right, even though it was terribly hard for me to hear.

I tell George the story—how I was so angry I dared in a white heat to tell my own story, the real truth in all its complexity and confusion, in order to prove to my teacher that there was another way of thinking in me, a way that he had not yet seen on the page. George looks at me and smiles. "What you're asking me to do is change my life," he says.

We are silent together for a moment, and then I say, "George, that's what writing does to all of us. That's one reason why it's so scary. It shows us how we think."

George says he has to work on the way he thinks about women. Until that changes, he can't write about them in a way that will satisfy a reader (with the possible exception of readers who share his point of view!). I ask why all the doctors are called "Doctor Brown" and "Doctor Filmore" while all the nurses and secretaries are called "Sally" and "Anne." "That's not my problem," he says. "That's the way it really is in a hospital."

Suggestion 5: Encourage workshop members to be honest with both praise and critical suggestion in responding to work in manuscript form.

Every writer has prejudices, blind spots, inadequacies. If the narrator's attitude in the written text is sexist or racist, ageist or classist, compassionate acknowledgment of that fact will help the writer. Every writer makes mistakes and typos, is sometimes vague, awkward, or derivative. Getting back 12 copies of your manuscript with all those things marked is of great assistance to any writer. I suggest to workshop members that they read manuscripts twice: first noting anything that stops or disrupts their reading, then in the second reading noting what they particularly liked. It is important to balance a critical response.

JOAN WRITES FOR FUN

Joan is a weaver, a member of the town government, active in her local Quaker meeting. Writing has always been easy for Joan. She loves language, is a natural storyteller, and writes for the fun of it. She has a collection of manuscripts: short stories, poems, three novels, and several plays. She wants help to start publishing her work.

Joan is one of the few writers I have known who "writes" an entire book in her head (sometimes almost instantaneously) before committing a word to the page. This is unusual. Most writers, like myself, don't have any idea where a piece of writing is going; it reveals itself as it goes along. But Joan always knows the ending before she writes the beginning.

Her strength is in plotting. She is a natural storyteller; suspense seems to be instinctive in her talking and in her writing. But the back side of our strength is almost always our weakness: Joan needs to slow down, allow complexity of character to develop, allow moments of silence to occur. Anne Tyler says in the introduction to *The Best American Short Stories 1983,* "Almost every really lasting story—*almost*, you notice—contains at least one moment of stillness that serves as a kind of pivot." When Joan slows down, she will discover that there are poetic moments of stillness in her as well as driving, electric plots.

Suggestion 6: Give your workshop a wide variety of exercises.

This will enable you to evoke each writer's strengths and address each one's weaknesses. Some people will respond best to a suggested image, as described in the exercise "Remember an Image" in the "Additional Exercises" section, while others will respond best to objects or pictures placed in their hands or chosen from a coffee table. Encourage experimentation; invite people to "play."

Surprise is a major factor in exercises. When I bring objects, I keep them hidden in a paper bag until the moment when people are ready to write, and then I don't allow them to talk after I reveal the objects. A man's shaving brush may cause one person to write a funny account of the first time he tried to shave, and may evoke deep grief in another who remembers the death of a father.

MARIA BELIEVES HER WORK HAS NO MERIT

Maria is in her seventies. She has been an administrator in a research firm, is retired, and lives alone. She has written and published professional articles. Always dressed up, she writes fiction elegantly and frequently tears up her manuscripts. She does not believe in her own gifts, which are great. If someone suggests that one of her short stories be offered to a literary journal for publication, Maria laughs and says, "Aren't you nice!"

Maria has always wanted to write, but she is instinctively very competitive. She needs to succeed. Under a mask of bravado and good cheer, she is terrified of being embarrassed, terrified of failure. She asks the workshop for severe critiques, but she responds to even gentle critical suggestions by deciding that her work is "shit." Maria's work is witty, urbane, sophisticated, and wise. She is a private woman; her writing carefully conceals her own life.

She is astonished that I reveal in public my rejection slips; that I say truthfully I am frightened to read brand-new writing aloud; that the writing life continues to be risky. As the writers in the circle tell stories of their successes and failures, I hope that Maria will gradually realize she is not alone in her fear and will dare to join us in the risky business of sending work out for possible publication.

Suggestion 7: Write along with your workshop members, read that work aloud, and invite response.

Model for your workshop the truth of the writing life. To do so will be liberating for them and for you. I take the same risks I am asking my workshop members to take. I write along with them in every writing time, and I try to write courageously. I read autobiographical work of my own sometimes. In every meeting I read my work aloud at least once, even when it doesn't please me. When I feel afraid to read, I tell them so. Occasionally I give my workshop members a manuscript of my new writing to critique. I do not take workshop time to discuss my manuscript, but I ask them to write their comments and return the manuscripts to me. Often, when I receive a rejection slip, I read it aloud and invite others to do the same. When I have a triumph, I talk about the details of publishing contracts, agent percentages, promotional appearances. In other words, I take my workshop members in, make them my writing peers. And they are. In this kind of atmosphere, success abounds.

PHYLLIS, NOT A GOOD GROUP MEMBER

In leading creative writing workshops, I have experienced many small, human, sometimes comical problems: Someone falls asleep and snores resoundingly during writing times; someone chews gum and pops it loudly; someone smells bad; someone sits with a skirt hiked up so far those sitting across from her are embarrassed; someone comes late every time; someone leaves early every time; someone is a therapist and doesn't want to be in a workshop with a client, and on and on. There have been people who have left because personalities—my own included—did not connect creatively. Once a woman left because she was offended when I read as a writing exercise the first sexual fantasy in Nancy Friday's *My Secret Garden*, and once a man left because I refused his invitation to take the whole workshop skinny-dipping in a local hot tub!

Only twice have I had to ask someone to leave. One was a man who was so defensive he saw even my *compliments* as an attack on his writing, his manhood, his mother's great-aunt Sarah. The other was a woman whom I shall call Phyllis.

Phyllis had been leading a writing workshop in a neighboring town and called to ask if she might come once as my guest. I said I would be pleased to have her visit. When she arrived she brought with her two other women whom I was not expecting. That evening, one of my writing exercises was to play a portion of a beautiful recording of wild wolves howling. At the end of the evening, Phyllis took me aside and told me that it was irresponsible of me to play the sound of wolves—I might upset people too much. However, she wanted to join the workshop, and since I had an opening, I said she could join.

From the beginning, Phyllis could not live within the boundaries I tried to maintain. She would not—could not—keep from telling people what was wrong with their writing, although I explained and explained that we wait until work is in manuscript, that we do not critique first drafts. Forty-five minutes after we finished responding to someone's work, Phyllis would interrupt whatever discussion was going on, almost always beginning, "I just have to say . . ." and would attack the work we had finished discussing.

Finally I told her I needed to refund her money and ask her not to come back. That was one of the hardest things I have ever done. My own regret was eased somewhat when Phyllis told me, "It's all right. I've talked to my sister about you, and she told me what's wrong. In a former life, I was your mother, and you have a problem with authority."

Suggestion 8: If one person is making the group unworkable, ask that person to leave.

Your responsibility to the group—to keep it healthy, to protect it—may necessitate your asking someone to leave. The bottom line is that you, as a workshop leader, have to be able to work with the people who have gathered. If you can't work with someone, you have a right and a responsibility to protect yourself as well as the group.

AMY, AN ACCLAIMED WRITER

Amy is a writer whose plays and short stories have received critical acclaim. She teaches writing at a college in a neighboring state, and drives two hours each way to attend the workshop. She is one of the funniest writers I have ever had in a workshop; her dry wit makes every session a party for those who come. Amy comes to the workshop because she finds it a stimulating focus for her week of writing. The writing she does in response to exercises I offer become the germinating center of short stories, plays, poems. When her play wins a national prize and is performed halfway across the nation, she brings a video of the performance and we set up a separate evening for the viewing. Afterward, we talk about playwriting, and the next week another workshop member begins to write a scene for a play.

Suggestion 9: Do not be thrown off your own center by anyone else's expertise; be realistic about your own.

If we lead our groups without pretension, being open about what we know and what we don't know, we can welcome the participation of very experienced writers. It takes skill and a quiet spirit to be able to keep a group from taking on subtle hierarchies. Not only can your own ego be rattled by someone with considerable experience and skill—your other workshop members can be insecure, too. Treat all workshop members equally; in your own heart value one as much as the other, and that will level your workshop to the highest, not the lowest, common denominator. Remember that what you are providing is a context in which good work and good learning can happen. Everyone teaches everyone else. I have at this time in my workshop a physician named Tom Plaut whose books on asthma have sold more than 100,000 copies. Tom certainly does not need my help in knowing how to write medical books! However, in the workshop I provide a community of writers where he experiments with new forms and shares his wisdom in the areas of his own book publishing and marketing expertise.

CONNIE, A WRITER WHO IS SUFFERING

Connie is a beautiful young woman who has been in the workshop for several years. She is a gifted poet, has published two books of poetry, and is regularly published in literary journals. During the course of the workshop, Connie discovers that her four-year-old child has leukemia. Over a period of months the child is dying, and Connie goes through denial, rage, grief. She cannot write about anything else. Often, as she reads her written work, Connie weeps.

Another member of the workshop comes to me complaining. He suggests that I refer her to a therapist and ask her to leave the workshop. I refuse to do this; I tell him that Connie's subject—like all of our subjects—really "chooses her," and in every other respect her participation in the workshop is comfortable; she responds sensitively to the work of others; she laughs when someone writes a comic scene. I try to tell him gently that if he finds it too uncomfortable and needs to leave I will refund the remainder of his tuition. He does choose to leave.

Soon after Connie's child dies, she becomes pregnant again, goes through a brief period of joy, and then loses the pregnancy in the third month. She is inconsolable. She writes one evening in workshop that her mother, with whom she has a difficult relationship, has said, "Why in the world don't you just forget it? That fetus wasn't any bigger than a nickel!"

This time my own heart feels broken. The workshop is made of 12 people who have been together for a long time. We have listened to Connie's images of nature, her joy in the natural world before the illness and death of her child and her miscarriage. Now the cruel insensitivity of her mother feels like too much. Suddenly I know that the workshop is more than a workshop to Connie—and to all of us. It is a community; we are companions; we are family in this moment.

I ask Connie if it would feel good to her for us to have a little ceremony for the lost baby. I say that if she would like it, we will all sing a lullaby and then, since it is a simple and natural thing for me to do, I will pray for the journey of the baby. She nods her head. In my voice that is good only for lullabies, I begin, "Sleep, my baby, peace attend thee, all through the night . . ." The workshop joins, some sing, some hum the song quietly, gently. And then I pray a simple blessing on the life and on the journey of the baby.

Suggestion 10: In moments of genuine crisis, be ready to abandon all established practices, and follow your own instinct.

MICHAEL, WHO WANTS TO TRY A DIFFERENT GENRE

Michael is an engineer whose book on designing bridges has sold out in three editions and has been translated into Spanish and Japanese. He is working on a second, related book and already has a contract for its publication. Michael's mother died this spring, and the farmhouse in which he grew up was put up for auction. Images have been coming up that don't fit into his bridge books. He brings me several short journal entries about the barn, the tools, the hired man, the jersey cow, the spider in the corner of the haymow. What do I do with these? he wants to know.

Suggestion 11: Help people try out new forms.

Often, the need to move from one form to another is the source of a writer's block. To try poetry may seem "pretentious"; to try fiction may seem like "lying"; to try dialogue may seem "voyeuristic"; to try autobiographical material may seem "self-indulgent," or like "betrayal." Yet one form is seldom adequate to any writer's lifetime work. First encourage a writer to try a new form, and if that fails, offer to change (just once!) a paragraph of prose into a poem or a bit of autobiographical first-person narrative into third person for him or her. Sometimes you may help a writer break through the wall of seeming impossibility.

JIM NEEDS CONFIDENTIALITY

Jim is a teacher in the public school system in my town. He is a favorite teacher of many young people. His classes in history are the hardest, most challenging, and most loved. It is common knowledge that students hold him in high esteem, remarking on how fair he is, how he does not play favorites, how he makes World War I come to life in ways they can never forget.

Jim writes in my workshop for many months. He is working on a novel about a young man growing up gay in a strict, conservative religious environment. Sometimes, as he reads about the family, how the boy was rejected and made to feel shame, Jim has to sit silently for a moment until he can resume reading.

Although we treat everything as fiction, it is clear to all of us that we may hold knowledge about Jim that could cost him his job, cost him great suffering. We will listen to his written work and respond with appreciation for the narrator's courage and integrity as well as for the writer's exact images and psychological insight. When he brings in a manuscript we will edit it carefully and give him back 12 copies with our comments on its strengths and its problems. In time, Jim will decide whether to publish his book under his own name or a pseudonym. But for now he doesn't have to worry about it. What he writes in the workshop will never be discussed outside the workshop.

Suggestion 12: Stress confidentiality.

All writing is in some sense autobiographical—even imagined images reveal how our minds work. All writers reveal themselves to some extent in their work, whether they intend to do so or not. Especially in reading our first drafts aloud, we allow others access to our personalities, perhaps even to our secrets. This is a holy experience; this is revelation. It must be taken with the utmost seriousness, and that which is revealed must be kept confidential.

The Workshop Meeting

We begin promptly at the announced hour. In my experience, if a group begins five minutes late two meetings in a row, almost everyone will arrive five minutes late to the third meeting. As leader, I respect those who have arrived on time by beginning on time. Latecomers quickly learn to arrive on time. My weekly workshops begin at 7:30 and end at 10:30 P.M. Set your workshop at the time that is comfortable for you. It will most likely succeed if it fits your own preferences.

THE FIRST WRITING EXERCISE

Members have been thinking about their writing on the way to the workshop. If we make announcements and do business first, that valuable, solitary centering can be lost. I don't want to waste it, and so I start with an exercise immediately after calling the workshop to attention.

My first exercise tonight is a collection of random objects. I place a cloth on the coffee table in the center of the circle and bring a covered basket of objects to it. The objects are hidden from view because the element of surprise helps to jump-start the imagination. I kneel with my basket beside the coffee table.

Then I say, "Now if you already have in mind what you want to write, just ignore my exercise. I'm going to put out some objects. I want you to choose an object—just choose something you'd like to hold in your hand. If you don't know why, that's good—it's best that way. Take the object with you to your chair, hold it in your hands, and see what memories or images come to mind. Then write anything that comes to you. Be free to stop and start. Remember, you are making an artist's sketch."

I take my objects out of the basket. There are perhaps 50 items, including a man's shaving brush, a seashell, an old whiskey bottle, a rusty horseshoe, an onion, a ball and jacks, a skate wheel, a baseball, a red silk bra, a crocheted doily. Someone starts to joke about the bra. I stop her, saying that everyone is now searching for a memory, an association, so we must be silent.

People choose objects and take them to favorite places in my house. Maria goes to the big chair in a corner of my study; Andy settles down at the far side of the kitchen table close to the brownies and the latest issue of the *American Poetry Review*. Amy goes to the pantry and sits on the floor with her back against the refrigerator, near the cans of tomato sauce, the salt, the pepper, the jars of beans. Eva curls up in a corner of the big couch. George eases his back by lying belly down on the rug. Joan does not move from her place in the workshop room where she sits at the end of the sofa. Always.

We write together for 20 minutes. Then I call out to the group, "Please take just two more minutes to bring it to a place where you can go back to it later."

In two minutes, I call out again, "If you need to go on writing, feel free to do that. Otherwise, let's gather here for reading." Even though some members have been with me for years, I say these same words each time. Little rituals make us all safe, and some members are newer, and need the repeated permission. All but two of the workshop members gather in the room where we first met. Two stay in other rooms, continuing to write. They may join us at any point in the reading time.

"Who would like to read first?" I ask.

READING ALOUD WHAT WE HAVE WRITTEN

Joan says, "Oh, I suppose I can, but this time it is *really* garbage!"

We laugh, because we all do this. We call our warnings "apron wring-ing," as if we have wept into our apron so much it needs to be wrung out, or as if we are nervously twisting an apron between our hands.

When I first led workshops these apologies bothered me, and I tried to get people to stop prefacing their reading with put-downs of their own work. But gradually I have come to believe that even in the safest environ-ment, reading our inner thoughts aloud is a vulnerable act, and discourag-ing people from expressing their anxiety can also be a subtle form of group censorship.

And so, as time has gone by, I have come to acknowledge that apolo-gizing, "apron wringing," serves an important function, though of course I rejoice when writers are able simply to launch into their reading. Often an apology precedes a particularly vulnerable piece of work. We have come to anticipate that the larger the apology, the more important the work. "Wringing one's apron" seems to make the way safe, as if we our-selves want to the say the worst that anyone could possibly say, so there is nothing to fear in what others might think. Observing each other "apron wring" has become a game in one of my workshops, and we jokingly compete to see who can apologize most creatively.

Kathleen Moran, a member of that workshop, made a "Collection of Classic Apron Wrings"—the "best" apologies given by members of our Thursday night workshop. She divided them into five categories:

1. Apron Wringing that Is Pure Self-Deprecation:
    "It's kind of messy, so you'll have to bear with me . . ."
    "I think this may be an exercise in obscurity . . ."
    "I enjoyed writing this, but I don't think you'll enjoy listening . . ."
    "This is really, really awful . . ."

2. Apron Wringing with Concern for the Group:
    "O.K., but you people are going to be really disappointed . . ."
    "I didn't read this over, so you all are going to be in trouble . . ."
    "After what I have heard here tonight, I shouldn't read, but since I spent my time writing, I guess I will . . ."
    "I'm too intimidated tonight. You guys were great!—Oh, all right . . ."

3. The Sadistic Apron Wringer:
    "I suppose I should read this, because you people deserve to be punished . . ."
    "So, you like trivial? I can give you trivial . . ."

4. The Apron Wringer with a Sense of History:
    "I'll read while I have a voice, then I won't ever read again!"
    "The all-time great failure . . ."

5. The Paradoxical Apron Wring:
    "I am not going to say my usual apron wring tonight, but . . ."

Our apologies are like a diver's testing the board just before jumping, or an animal's turning around and around before lying down. They are a way of preparing the way, preparing the place, reassuring ourselves, testing our voices before fully letting go. I do it myself—why not? Mine usually takes the form of "I don't like this thing at all, but—oh, well! Here goes!"

I have learned that one of the greatest gifts a leader can give to the group is to read aloud something he or she has just written, and hates! "I don't like this thing at all," I proclaim, then read the stops and starts, the half sentences, and the lines that say "Oh, shit! Why can't I write tonight?" I can't say how many times group members have thanked me, have said, "I thought only I felt that way!" By being honest, being open, you empower others. One lovely thing about leadership: As you appropriately give power to others, you gain power yourself.

In this sharing time, the only work that is read aloud is work that has been written during the workshop writing time. This keeps all of us on an equal footing; we are taking equal risks; none of us has had the opportunity to revise. Also, it controls the amount of time each person takes—reading work that was written at home is much more difficult to keep within the bounds of available time.

Joan has chosen a strip of yellow plastic with the words "Police Line—Do Not Cross" printed on it in bold black letters. She is writing about a murder. She reads to us part of a chapter in her mystery book. As she reads, we see in our minds the dark storeroom of a huge business building; we feel fear. When she has finished, I ask the group, "What did you like? What stays with you? What do you remember?"

RESPONDING TO NEW WORK READ ALOUD

A number of people speak briefly, mentioning the sense of danger, the image of the stacks of unused office furniture, the overwhelming sense of dark, and the silence that surrounds the narrator. Joan nods, smiles, thanks us. And then another workshop member reads—this time a poem, very different in tone as well as in form. Usually I ask the group the same questions after a writer reads: "What do you like? What do you remember?" It isn't necessary to "like" something that has just been read—what the writer most needs is to have made connection. To have been heard. An excellent response after a story about a man and a truck is simply to say, "the man getting into his truck," or "the child's face when the father drives away," or to quote a few words, "grief wasn't what he expected to feel."

One of the central practices of our workshop method is this: We treat all work as if it were fiction, unless the writer specifically asks us to treat it as autobiography. I cannot stress too strongly how important this is. Only when all work is given the dignity of being treated as literature, as separate from the life story of the writer, can a group of writers be truly free to write about anything.

This practice is awkward at first; some people find it easier to do than others, and the leader has to give gentle reminders and be persistent in a gentle manner. It helps to call this "our practice" instead of "a rule," and to explain as many times as necessary why it is a helpful practice. It keeps discussion of a piece of writing on track. It prevents digression into personal exchanges that are not centered on the written work. In short, it keeps the writing workshop from becoming a pseudo-therapy group.

We have proven that all writers can keep this boundary if the leader consistently insists upon it. It is fine to use the word "you" in talking about how skillfully the writer has written ("You described so clearly the child sitting on the step!"), but it is not OK to identify the child on the step as the writer ("I could just see you sitting on the step . . ."). Even in our workshops for children in housing projects, very young writers learn to say "the child," "the mother"—even "the narrator"—instead of "you," and they correct one another if someone forgets.

The story that follows is an example of what can happen.

The most dramatic experience I have ever had with this practice happened in Ireland. (I tell it with permission and have changed the name.) After I had been leading workshops in Ireland for several years, a regular writing group developed that met every two weeks throughout the year. A woman I shall call Mary was new to their group; she had attended their meeting only one time and was persuaded to sign up for my five-day intensive workshop. On the third day of our workshop, Mary wrote about being sexually abused as a child. She was weeping as she read. "I can't tell anyone, because if my husband's family knew I had been abused, in Ireland, I would be considered an unfit wife. But I am having flashbacks, and I need help. I saw an advertisement in the newspaper—a man who said he could help with problems of childhood abuse. I saved up money each week from my grocery allowance until I had enough to go. When I arrived at the address, it was a motel. He took me into a room, and he told me to lie on the bed, and he locked the door. Then he kept getting closer and closer. When he got really close, I jumped up and ran to the door, but he wouldn't let me out until I let him kiss me."

Mary sat with her head down, crying. I responded with some words about what a terrible situation that was for the narrator, and how clearly the problem was described. Others spoke about the narrator, too, giving feedback that affirmed and encouraged without once referring to "you."

After my workshop was over, I was invited to attend their regular workshop meeting before I flew home. I was pleased to do so. They had no specific leader, but one of the members offered an exercise, and we all wrote. Mary was the first to read. She read a very strong, graphic piece about a husband who insults his wife in front of the children. It was written in first person, and again, she wept as she read. The first group member to respond said, "Your husband is doing terrible things to your children!" Person after person responded to Mary's writing with personal comments—"You wrote the dialogue beautifully, you really captured your husband's voice," and "Your writing was powerful—you let us see how your husband is hurting your children . . ." and so forth.

I was stunned. Several other people read, and the same sort of responses were given. When the workshop was over, the group turned to me and asked, "Well, what do you think?" I gulped and said truthfully that the exercise was excellent and the writing was wonderful, but "I'm surprised that you are treating all the work as autobiography. You aren't treating it as fiction."

It was their turn to be stunned. Clearly from the expressions on everyone's faces, they simply did not know they were ignoring this crucial practice. But the moment I said those words, Mary got up from her chair and reached for her coat. "I'm never coming back," she said, fighting tears. I have just been sitting here waiting—I can't wait to get out. I'm so sorry I read what I read. I thought it would be like Pat's workshop—I will never come back."

That is the difference. I can promise that if you do not hold this practice absolute, you will not hear about taboo subjects. You will not hear the deepest secrets, the greatest vulnerability. And therefore you will all be kept from writing your greatest art. Not that art has to be telling our secrets—but it does have to be free to go wherever it needs to go, and usually our pain comes out first.

It is simply nobody's business whether what we write is factual or imagined. A workshop is not a therapy group. Healing does happen, but it happens because we keep appropriate boundaries. This is one of the reasons that leaderless groups have difficulty lasting very long. If you are a leader and your participants are having difficulty with this practice, I suggest you read this passage out loud or copy it and hand it out in your meeting. Often, treating work as fiction will not seem important—for instance, who cares whether a piece about a child playing with a puppy is autobiography or fiction? But *if you do not practice it when it is unimportant, it will not be in place when it is important.*

ANNOUNCEMENTS AND OFFERING MANUSCRIPTS FOR CRITIQUE

Reading and responding to the work of all those who want to read, including myself, takes about an hour and a half for a workshop with 12 members, which brings us to the midpoint in the three-hour evening session. We have announcements of upcoming readings and our own writing news. (I don't encourage personal stories or political announcements here, simply because I need to protect our time for writing. People may put announcements on the coffee table if they wish, and personal stories are welcome during the break.)

TAKING A BREAK

After announcements have been made and manuscripts for next week's discussion have been handed out, we take a break for coffee, juice, brownies, carrot sticks—all of which have been available throughout the evening. The break is important because the writing and reading portions of the workshop are so structured that there is little time for getting to know people beyond the written word. Usually we take 15 minutes for the break.

MANUSCRIPT CRITIQUE

After the break, we take out our copies of the manuscript that Michael gave us last week. It is five poems. They are dense and full of subtle innuendo. We talk long and deeply about two of the poems, telling him first what we like, what we think works well, and then telling him what troubles us. Two people disagree about one image: One person says it is unclear, the other says it is perfectly obvious. We do not try to decide between these two responses. We find out how many people agree that it is unclear, and how many people understand it. I tell the group that all of their responses are "right,"—that is, all are honest responses—just what a writer needs. What is helpful to the author is knowing how people respond. He will decide whether or not to change anything.

Everyone has written on his or her copy of the manuscript what they like as well as what troubles them. When we finish discussing two of the poems, all the copies are returned to Michael with the letter I have written giving him my general response in addition to the specific comments I have noted on my copy of his manuscript.

It is my hope that Michael will take all of our copies home, go through them, and take the suggestions that he finds helpful. I hope he will disregard and discard any suggestions he feels are wrongheaded, including my own. I hope he will do another draft and, if he wishes, bring it back in for another response. Or if he feels it is done, and would like to try for publication, I hope he will send it off for consideration. I encourage him to do that, and mention a journal or two that he might try.

For more specific guidance on responding to manuscripts, see the section below titled "Responding to Manuscripts in a Writing Workshop."

THE SECOND WRITING EXERCISE

This workshop has been meeting for several weeks, and trust has been established. I choose, tonight, to offer an exercise that I know may bring up emotional material for some writers. When everyone has settled again with writing pad and pen after the break (or after the manuscript discussion, if there has been one), I ask my workshop participants to take a moment to center back into their own bodies. I ask them to be aware of their breath. After a moment I say quietly, "Now find in your memory a snapshot or a photograph of someone close to you, someone important to you." After a moment of silence I say, "When you are ready, begin writing with these words: *In this one you are*," and say gently, "So you are writing to the person in the picture. *In this one, you are . . .*"

People sit quietly for a moment, and then some move to other places— the big couch in the piano room, the chair in the study—and write. This time we have only 15 minutes of time, but by the end, there are beautiful, moving things that are read aloud. We respond by saying what we like, what we remember. We encourage each other to go home, type the piece, work with it to revise, expand, cut, rethink, and then bring it in manuscript form to the workshop where we can read it on the page and make our comments of appreciation and of suggestion for change.

CLOSING THE WORKSHOP SESSION

I keep to our schedule faithfully, starting on time and ending on time. If we are not finished at our closing time, I announce the time and give permission for those who must leave to do so. "The rest of us," I say, "will stay until we are finished." I know people who have left workshops where there was not a clear adherence to the announced time of closing. Some have babysitters or other reasons to leave on schedule, and no one likes to get up and disturb a session.

If we finish a bit early, and there are ten or 15 minutes left at the end of a session, I excuse those who want to leave and offer a short exercise for the few who remain. We may write for five minutes and share with no responses at all, rather than dismiss early. My writers appreciate this, and it is amazing what jewels can appear on the page in five minutes! Some ideas for short exercises are offered in Part III.

AS PEOPLE LEAVE, AND AFTERWARD

As people prepare to leave, George and Connie stop at my chair to make an appointment for a private conference during the coming week. I encourage all of my workshop members to have at least one private conference with me during each ten-week session, so we can talk at length about their writing. In that way I can become better acquainted with them, and they can have an opportunity to tell me any concerns that they might not want to bring up in the group.

Eva is the last to leave. We talk for a moment in the doorway, and then we say goodnight. I take my workshop notebook and jot down the exercises I chose for tonight on the page where I keep that record. If I do not do it immediately, I will forget and next week I won't know whether I am repeating an exercise I offered recently. As I straighten the room and put out the lights, I allow myself to "come down" from the high energy of the evening.

I will put the pages I wrote tonight into a desk drawer to wait until a day when I can rework them; Andy's writing may remain forever in his spiral notebook; Joan will stay up until the wee hours, typing, revising, preparing her manuscript to bring in to the group next week. Maria, I am sorry to say, will tear up the prose poem she wrote about a woman in a huge ocean storm clinging to a porthole, looking into the churning water as her children sleep in their bunks. But she cannot completely destroy the vision that she created. I will remember it.

Responding to Manuscripts in a Writing Workshop

As leader of a workshop or writing group, you have been given a manuscript by one of your participants. It has also been given to the entire workshop. In preparation for the group discussion, you read. As you read, you are listening to a voice from a country other than your own—the country of that person's childhood, youth, lost loves, commitments, wounds, disappointments, ecstasies, achievements, intuitions, courage, cowardice, sorrows, sufferings, imaginings—the foreign country of that other life.

Nothing can equip you for the journey you are required to take when another human being trusts you enough to allow you to pass judgment on his or her attempt to communicate. He or she is naked before you. Revealed. Seen. But you, too, are naked and ignorant in the face of that trust. No human person is good enough, wise enough, experienced enough, excellent enough to pass judgment on another person's vision, and that is what writing is—the attempted expression of a vision. All that you have to give in response is what I am calling your "nakedness"—your own raw, honest, human response—*this is what it means to me; this is what I hear; this is where I was confused.* If you are not able to recognize, and more than recognize, to *acknowledge openly* the fact that every opinion you entertain is subjective, is limited by your own taste, age, and condition, then you will more than likely damage the writer who has asked for your response. The more he or she trusts you, listens to you, the more damage you are able do.

If, on the other hand, you put aside fantasies of superiority and the temptation of the sweet taste of power, if you respond as just one more life, not assuming to hold *the* truth of how a manuscript should be changed, rather assuming only the utter validity of your own response as *one reader's reaction*, you may be of great assistance.

I like the story of the little girl who cries when her mother tucks her into bed, and begs not to be left alone. The mother answers, "But, honey, you're never alone! Don't you know God is always here?" The child says, "Yes, Mommy, I know that, but tonight I need somebody with skin on!" When I am responding to a manuscript I like to remind the author (and myself) that I am a person with a particular "skin" on: age, life experience, taste. "Consider the source," I say, and then I freely offer all of my responses—the *hurrah* and the *but* . . . mixed up together, and balanced. My workshop participant already knows that my "skin" includes my graduate degrees in writing and many years of experience. The danger is that the writer will give the critic too much power rather than too little. We would all be better off if we believed what Barnett Newman said: *Art criticism is to the artist as ornithology is to the birds.*

In our workshops, no work receives critique until the writer has typed it and brought it as a manuscript. Most writers cannot type a manuscript without making changes, and so, if the work is typed, it has probably been revised. That means the writing already has been translated from its first pure outpouring of imagination or memory. Vulnerability is not as acute as it was when the images had just emerged from the unconscious. The sheer passage of time may have lessened the writer's vulnerability.

We do not ever read an entire prose manuscript out loud in workshop. To do so is an unwise use of other workshop members' time. They can be expected to have carefully read and written notes in the margins of manuscripts before coming to workshop. Also, when a writer reads aloud, he or she *performs* the work—some to its advantage, some to its disadvantage. It is a good idea to have the writer read one page of prose, or to read a poem aloud. This gives members who were absent a chance to glimpse the work and perhaps enter into the discussion a bit. It also refreshes the memory of those who read it earlier, and it gives a sense of the writer's own intonation and rhythm. More than one page of prose, however, should be avoided. Poems can be read aloud before discussion, but usually not more than two or three poems can be critiqued in one session.

What follows is a description of the way we respond to manuscripts brought in by a workshop participant.

RECEIVING THE MANUSCRIPT AND PREPARING THE GROUP

Each person who joins my workshop receives a paper that includes instructions for what we can handle in manuscript response: number of pages, prose double-spaced, number of poems, frequency of offering work for group discussion.

My practice is to ask the person who brings in a manuscript to distribute it by laying it on people's chairs during the break. This keeps to a minimum the moments taken up by handing things out. It is the writer's responsibility to get a copy to everyone; if she wishes, she can mail the manuscript to absentees, but I don't assume the responsibility for doing that.

The first time someone hands out a manuscript to a new workshop, I talk a bit with the group about what we will be doing, encouraging them to write honestly both their questions and their praise, asking them to balance those responses. I reassure them that their comments do not need to sound like an English teacher's, although if someone has those skills, they will be appreciated by the writer (you don't want to hurt or offend the teachers in your group). I tell them that the responses that are most helpful are just the human responses, "I love this" or "I'm confused here," and so on. Every writer needs to know how the piece will feel to the reader who picks it up off a coffee table. That may be even more important than the response of a professor.

THE LEADER'S WORK ON THE MANUSCRIPT BEFORE GROUP DISCUSSION

As leader, my preference is to prepare the manuscript on the day of the workshop, so it is fresh in my mind. There is some danger in this, however, because if my day gets unexpectedly full, I can be too pressured to do a truly careful job—so the day before is probably the best time. Editing a manuscript is perhaps the most concentrated work I do. It is harder than my own original draft writing, I think, because the task is twofold, to try to understand the writer's intent, and to help the writer fulfill his own intent.

I read the manuscript through with an erasable pencil in hand, paying particular attention to any moment when I am "popped out" of the writing by something that gets in the way of the flow of my own imagination as it follows the narrative or the poem. Such an interruption might be an awkward sentence, a change of tense, or a transition that doesn't work for me. This first reading is crucial for catching those places that jar me, because the next time I read through the work, I will already know things about it that may obscure problems. So the first reading is not primarily for making notes on what I like and appreciate, although I do jot those down if I want to. I just watch for places that trip me. I don't worry about balancing my critical comments with appreciations as I read through a manuscript for the first time.

My effort is always to teach through my critical comments. Therefore, if a person uses a semicolon incorrectly, and I know the rule for semicolon usage, I write a little note (using the back side of the page if I need to) explaining how the semicolon is supposed to be used. However, in my case, I am not a grammarian. I do not have a comprehensive knowledge of the names of parts of speech, and so I could not do exhaustive teaching of that sort, even if I wanted to. But I do have a finely tuned ear as to what works and what doesn't, and I am good at identifying why it doesn't work, even if I don't have the technical word for the part of speech. I am still learning as I go. For example, I took a workshop years ago with poet June Jordan, in which she bore down on us as white female writers, saying that white women write in the passive voice. My memory was that she included in that critique the use of words ending in "ing." And I decided she was right. I caught myself doing it a lot, and I caught a lot of other writers using "ing" endings rather than verb forms that were stronger, more definite. After I had written on countless manuscripts that writers were using "passive voice" (too many "ing" endings), someone in my workshop recently corrected me, saying that "ing" endings are not passive voice, but "present progressive tense."

I cannot emphasize strongly enough that knowing or not knowing the names of parts of speech is not what makes you a brilliant editor. It helps. And, incidentally, it helps your ego a lot to avoid being told in front of a workshop that you have just made an error in your own area of expertise. However, even that is an opportunity. I immediately thanked her, asked her to repeat it, wrote it down in my notebook, in full view of the workshop, and said that I am not a grammarian and appreciate "all the help I can get"—after which she said that using the "present progressive tense" is very close to passive voice, and that in fact June Jordan may have included that as one of the habits to avoid. Which June Jordan most certainly did.

What makes you a brilliant editor is that sort of careful reading where you are listening, not only to the manuscript, but to your own response. It is catching your own difficulty in understanding the text, and jotting down where you have trouble. Often the writer can and will want to fix his or her own problems. Your job is not to teach grammar—unless you love to do it and it is a skill, in which case, do give it to your writers, but do so gently, so as not to overwhelm them or make them confused about equating writing well with knowing the names of parts of speech. Your job is not to teach grammar, but to reflect back to the writer where his or her reader loved and moved freely with the work, and where the reader had difficulty. The more specific you can be, the better. A global comment such as "You have awkward sentences here" helps the writer very little. In fact, it will probably panic and block the writer. But a comment like "Reading this sentence, I am confused" is helpful because it targets the problem and it makes it a message about *me, the reader*, not about *you, the writer.*

In making suggestions or raising questions, I most often add a little question mark, circled, or I say "Maybe," "In my opinion," or "If this were my poem, I might . . ." As much as possible, I qualify my comments, soften them. Remember, the writer will magnify every criticism ten times. No matter how softly you express it, the writer will hear it loudly.

One of the biggest dangers lies in inserting your truth into someone else's work and thereby getting that person off the track of their own voice, their own vision. I learned a lot about that when a poet whom I respect volunteered to "critically read" a manuscript of my poems. When I got the manuscript back, I was very confused and troubled, because it seemed to me that what she suggested would simply destroy my poems. And yet, she is a good poet. How could she be wrong? Perhaps I am wrong, I thought. Perhaps I am not a good poet. But, in time, I came to understand that what she was cleaning out of my poems was *Missouri*. All of the idiom of my own country origins were being cleaned up, erased. She is a native of New York City—her voice is very different from my voice. And she did not perceive the difference.

Be very careful in your suggestions for changing someone else's work. Try to keep your comments stated in ways that acknowledge your own subjectivity. I will say more about that later when I discuss the letter that you will write to accompany the manuscript when you return it to the writer.

I believe we honor writers by telling the truth. However, I think we need to be wise in assessing how much of our criticism a writer is able and willing to use. The first time I respond to a writer's manuscript, I am extremely careful to have more affirmation than critique. I need to learn more about this writer. I need especially to learn what the writer is going to do with the comments she receives from me. One writer will take the comments home, work on the manuscript, and bring it back to me in two weeks with many of my changes made, some ignored, and some new development of the work that had nothing to do with my comments. That is ideal. The next time that writer brings me a manuscript, I will know she can *use* my ideas, is able to disregard suggestions of mine that may be off base, will likely not be blocked or hurt by questions. However, I am still and always will be careful to express fully and generously on every manuscript from this writer what I love and appreciate in the work. The ideal reaction does not always happen. I have had writers go home pained and less able, no matter how sensitive and careful I tried to be; I had one writer destroy an entire novel. If the worst happens, do not be too hard on yourself. You are not responsible for all the ancient wounds to self-esteem that have accumulated in your writers' lives.

Remember, too, that the ability to respond to critical suggestions immediately or at all is not a signifier of a more advanced writer. It has to do with the writer's history of being "criticized"—it has to do with family, friends, elementary school teachers, Ph.D. committees, lovers, you name it. And so it is wise, oh, good and gentle workshop leaders, to be very, very careful the first time you respond to someone's manuscript. And the second time . . . and . . .

After the first reading, in which I have jotted down my problems and questions, I read it through again and write what I love, underline favorite places, note with "Wow!" or "Wonderful" or more specific comments on the places where the writing most moves or delights me. This must be honest. It must be full of your own integrity. Every work has something beautiful in it, if you look at it through the lens of this human being's wanting so badly to write that he would come to the workshop space, give the time and effort, and, trying and longing, would risk the exposure. If I could not find, as well as the dross in every manuscript, the gold of a writer's artistry—if I could not identify strengths in every manuscript with honesty and integrity—I would find another line of work.

I always write my comments in pencil, because I may change my mind in light of what I read later. I may even change my mind during a workshop discussion and sit there saying to everyone, "I've just changed my mind about what I wrote here," and erase it in front of them, as everyone giggles and I model that nothing is written in stone and even the leader's opinions can be dead wrong.

Having written my comments on the manuscript page, I finish my response by typing a letter to the writer, summarizing important issues, and going into more detail if there is something that was too large for the pencil notes. I almost always urge them to ignore any comment that does not meet with an answering "yes" in their own minds. And I begin and end this letter with thanks and praise. I keep a copy of the letter in a file so I can go back and look over what I have given as response over the course of a person's work with me.

GROUP RESPONSE

I do manuscript responses (I try not to use the word "critique" very much) after the break at the middle of the three-hour workshop session. Each manuscript gets no less than 20 minutes and not more than 30 minutes of group time. We can do two manuscripts in one evening—never more. In order to end the evening in a gentle and unified spirit, I try to have a brief writing after the manuscript response, even if it is only five minutes of writing, after which we read to one another aloud "as a gift"—that is, with no verbal response.

The writer reads the poem, or one page of the prose manuscript, aloud. He chooses, if the work is prose, which page to read. We do this in order to have some sense of the writer's voice; this practice also functions to remind the group members what the manuscript is about if they have read it, or to clue them in a little bit if they have been lazy! It focuses us as a group on the work at hand, without taking up too much time.

The writer remains silent, allowing everyone to talk about the manuscript in his presence, without joining in or answering questions. He will learn more this way, because if, for example, one person is confused about something, the writer will lose the opportunity to know if others are confused if he answers the confusion before the leader can ask whether others were confused. The writer has an opportunity to respond at the close of the discussion.

Unless there are no new members, and everyone knows the process well, I ask the group to remember that we will talk first about the strengths of the piece—what we love, what is strong, what is working well. I tell them that our practice is that anyone who has a suggestion or a question must first have expressed something positive about the work, because if we can't identify the strengths, we have no business talking about what mitigates against the strengths of a work. I am very serious about this. If someone starts to "criticize" without having first named something as a strength, I ask her to first tell us what she appreciated.

We talk as a group about the strengths of the piece, and if the group is a bit slow to respond or if one person has given a long list of the most obvious strengths, I suggest that the writer doesn't mind hearing the same thing twice—others can name the same spot as a favorite in a manuscript. I usually save my response to the end of the appreciations, and then repeat comments with which I agree and add anything that wasn't mentioned.

Then we talk about questions or problems. There are several aspects to this process:

1. Allow—even encourage—people to disagree. The point is not to come as a group to consensus. In fact, it is more helpful to the

author to have a split opinion, because it gives the author more room to make up his or her own mind and find an original solution to the problem.

2. If there is a strong negative opinion offered, find out how many people agree or disagree. Tell your group that disagreement is important, and tell them why.

3. Be careful not to let the discussion get into a "chewing over" of a problem and how to solve it. That process can damage a writer. What you want is to name the problems, not necessarily to solve them.

4. Save your own responses to the end, and then agree or disagree or name the division of opinions in a summarizing kind of way.

5. Finally, and very importantly, summarize what is strong, what was liked. Ask the group to help you do this if you have the time and inclination. Don't take a long time, just leave the writer with the words of affirmation rather than with the words of criticism, and encourage the writer to bring it in again in a new draft if he or she wants to.

AUTHOR'S RESPONSE AND MANUSCRIPT RETURN

Give the author an opportunity to respond, but try not to have that develop into a discussion. (Almost always the author will simply thank the group, or maybe clarify some point that was confusing to the group.) If someone wants to discuss, tell them they can continue privately if the author wants further discussion.

Ask everyone to write their names on the manuscripts so the writer will know who's talking to her. Give all copies back. Occasionally mention to the whole workshop that hanging on to other people's manuscripts is not all right, so if they miss a session when there is a response to a manuscript, they must be certain to get their copy back to the author.

Finally, in a good writing class or workshop, there is a great effort to affirm and strengthen the writer's own voice and to allow it to grow from the inside through practice and through listening to others' work. Writers should be invited and encouraged to bring in manuscripts, and responses to them should be detailed and thoughtful. The leader and participants raise questions, but refrain as much as possible from making decisions about what the writer should do. The writer keeps silent, listens as the group discusses the work. At the end of the discussion, he or she is invited to respond or ask questions.

The leader's role here is to assist the writer. I believe what is most helpful to the writer is having information about *how many* of her readers heard opposite meanings. By listening to the discussion, the writer learns far more than if someone were to ask her directly what she meant. If she were to give the answer, she would lose the opportunity to learn what all of her readers think, and who they are. Sometimes the age, temperament, or experience of the reader influences his or her response.

Once I received in workshop a beautiful erotic story (later published in *Yellow Silk*) about an old woman who masturbates. The group that night was made up entirely of people under 40, except for myself and one other woman who tended to be rather elegantly quiet in workshop. I listened as the entire group agreed that the character's severe judgment on herself for masturbating was unrealistic. "She wouldn't feel like that," someone said, and everyone agreed. The elegantly quiet member was elegantly quiet. I made certain that everyone did agree, and then I asked my quiet member what she thought. "It's absolutely realistic!" she snapped. And it was. She and I could remember how terrible a thing masturbation was thought to be when we were young. Our parents believed it would make us "feebleminded." Peggy Gillespie, the author of the story, was a grief counselor in an oncology program at our area's largest hospital. She knew her character, and in this case the response of most of the workshop members was valuable only if the leader helped the group to see that the character was accurately drawn, but the author will need to decide whether she wants to give more information for the benefit of her younger readers.

Your task as workshop leader is to draw out your participants' honest response and try to balance their opinions with differing opinions whenever possible, because differing opinions enlarge the freedom of the writer. Of course, if everyone agrees, the writer's options are clear!

Helping Workshop Participants Publish and Read in Public

The workshop leader who is most helpful in this area is the one who sends his or her own writing off regularly. Staying in touch with the changing world of literary journals and publishing houses by frequently browsing through market sourcebooks and periodicals will make you more able to respond helpfully when someone reads a piece that seems perfect for a particular journal.

You can stay current with what literary journals and forthcoming anthologies are looking for by reading each issue of *Poets & Writers Magazine* and *The Chronicle*. Keep those periodicals and a good current market reference or two available for your workshops.

At the end of each ten-week session, my workshops bring potluck supper and usually (the workshop decides) we have a "Sending-off Party." All those who wish to do so bring multiple copies of manuscripts ready to send out, along with envelopes and stamps. I put stacks of sample journals out on my coffee table (you may ask your workshop members to bring samples of what they have at home, or perhaps your library will allow you to borrow some). It's a good idea to build up a collection yourself by buying sample copies from journals that interest you. I also put out books of marketing resources and a loose-leaf notebook of journal guidelines. Workshop members who prefer to write, or do not wish to offer work for publication, go into other rooms with an exercise I have prepared, and write during this time. Those who have already been published help those who have not; everyone shares knowledge and ideas.

Occasionally we sponsor a reading for a writer who has published a book, or for the entire workshop. This is an important time for workshop members, because they have an opportunity to share their writing and/or their community of writers with friends and family. Sometimes we add a potluck supper to the event, or hold the reading in a restaurant. Readings are also good public relations for your own business. The public announcements and the event itself raise awareness in the community.

It is important to help your workshop participants get perspective on what happens when you start sending out your manuscripts. Seeking publication is a process that will always involve more rejection notices than acceptances. Novelist Jay Neugenboren says that he received 537 rejections before his first short story was accepted for publication and a thousand rejections before publication of his first novel. He wrote eight novels before one was published! Even when you are no longer a beginner, you are not protected from rejections. I tell my workshop participants when I receive a rejection. I tell them that I average about 15 rejections for every acceptance! Be *real* with your workshop participants.

Valerie Leff, who teaches writing in North Carolina, wrote a letter to me that included this:

Tell this to your students—my last story was accepted after I received 150 rejections on it over 5 years. I kept working on the story and kept sending it out. I always liked it. In this business, the tenacious stubborn mules get ahead.

This business of becoming a writer has been some wild ride. First the cracking open, the freedom of putting thoughts to paper, emptying the busy brain. Then the marvelous discovery that this stuff entertained other people—that I could make a roomful of fellow women-writers laugh or weep—that it was something more than the most effective psychotherapy I'd ever had. Then the first few attempts at professionalism—publishing a story or two, leading a workshop—having an answer that felt meaningful when someone asked "What do you do?" Then there was a whole lot of guilt—all that investment in myself, my thoughts, my work, when there was such a need for activists in the world. How could I go to writing workshops when the environment was being destroyed? When children were hungry, illiterate? When there was still so much prejudice and discrimination everywhere I looked?

Then came more outward success, publication in top journals, teaching at a university, better answers to that question, "What do you do?" Just lately, I am having a glimpse of some new level: Getting to have a platform, a voice in the world and getting to use that voice to say something meaningful. This is the level that wipes out the guilt and the fear of leading a self-indulgent life. Like it's more than just "bully for me" that I've had some stories published, but the satisfaction of knowing that those stories really say something about class and race and politics and human nature and compassion. I never really expected them to—it was always just enough for me to try to hone my craft and entertain. But now this feels like a serious, and even generous, occupation. An activist occupation.

You will have in your workshops persons who publish easily and quickly, and you will have some who do not have the tenacity to keep trying, or who will not find commercial publishers for their work. Encourage those latter writers to self-publish. Help them understand that the prejudice against self-publication is elitist and old-fashioned. The publishing world has changed radically; new technologies make self-publication or the use of print-on-demand services available to everyone, and that is a good thing for writers and a good thing for literature. After all, if it were not for self- (or family) publishing, we would not have the work of James Joyce, who agreed to pay 60 percent of the printing costs of *Portrait of the Artist as a Young Man*. Neither would we have Henry Miller, Virginia Woolf, Anaïs Nin, Mark Twain, and on, and on. Walt Whitman published his own poetry, promoted it, and even reviewed himself under a pseudonym!

A controversial word of advice: I encourage writers to send work to several journals at a time unless they are sending work to a journal that publishes monthly or to an editor with whom they already have a relationship. I myself am editor of a literary journal, *Peregrine*; I know the woes and problems of the editor. Nevertheless, it is unfair and unreasonable to ask writers to send work to only one journal at a time. Most of them pay zero for the work, sending the author one or two copies. They hold it for a long period of time (*Peregrine* publishes only once a year, and so if work is sent in the spring, it will be held a full year. And none of our staff is paid—we can't afford to pay the writers.) What right does a journal have to require that work be sent to only one place at a time? None, in my opinion. The writer is the owner of the work; the journal is seeking good work. It's none of the journal's business whether it is being offered elsewhere. If the editors want a manuscript, they should eagerly take it before someone else does. Why should it be any different than selling any other merchandise? As writers we must value our own work and our own time. With courtesy and sympathy for the problems of editors, we must claim our own rights. Once again, remember Marge Piercy's advice: "Never say *submit!* Say *offer!*"

Ethics in the Group Setting

In addition to the issues discussed in "The Ethical Questions: Spirituality, Privacy, and Politics," a leader of a writing workshop might also consider the following issues.

VULNERABILITY OF WORKSHOP MEMBERS

It is the responsibility of the workshop leader to recognize the vulnerability of his or her clients. Even in the workshop that is beautifully and brilliantly nonhierarchical, the leader is responsible for keeping workshop members safe. The same rules that apply in other settings apply here: Clients need clear boundaries in relation to the leader.

One of the most upsetting events that occurred for me as administrator of a network of workshops happened many years ago. Someone attending one of our workshops came to me reporting that an affiliated workshop leader (who was a brilliant writer and quite charismatic) was carrying on simultaneous sexual relationships with three members of the workshop. For the record, it's not a good idea to have sex with three members of your workshop, simultaneously or otherwise. Needless to say, the community was in a shambles.

No matter how excellent the leader may be as a writer and a teacher, if he or she doesn't respect boundaries and understand the vulnerability of those who reveal themselves and their imaginations through their writing, that person does not belong in the role of a workshop leader.

DIVERSITY AS AN ETHICAL IMPERATIVE

I believe that a writing workshop leader must do everything in his or her power to create a community in which there is diversity of voice. It is not always possible—I have led good workshops for groups like one in Detroit, where all but one of the members were therapists, and several at the University of Connecticut where all the members were teachers. Many times my workshops have been composed entirely of white people, and I have always felt that to be a serious loss.

In cases where I am invited to come into a group, I have no control over the situation. However, I can do something about my own workshops, and through all the years of leading workshops and writing retreats, I have given partial and full financial aid to persons who would bring diversity of voice into the group. Those have included persons of color in my almost entirely white community; low-income persons in my predominantly college-educated community; lesbian and gay writers in this town where the majority is heterosexual; persons with disabilities; and recently, a dynamic, funny, gifted woman from a nearby city who is a working professional prostitute. Boy! Did she teach me a lot in that retreat—and with such good humor!

One word of advice: It is wise to offer scholarships for one period at a time, rather than offering it without any ending date. Your own ability to offer support may change, or you may want to pass around the financial aid.

ETHICAL BUSINESS PRACTICES

Perhaps it goes without saying, but I want to note briefly that a writing workshop leader must be ethical in his or her business practices. In my workshops, participants may pay weekly if they find that easier than a lump-sum payment. A number of persons pay cash, and it would be easy to keep that money as secret income. Unethical practices of that sort are like a cancer; if we allow them to live in our system, we endanger the whole organism. Keep good and honest records; your business will be much more likely to thrive than if you try to cut corners.

Another, less obvious, matter in relation to business ethics is the importance of taking care of yourself. Value your own worth, and charge a fair price that is consistent with comparable services in your community. If you are able to give your time as a volunteer, wonderful! Give that gift through a social service agency or in a context where it will do good. However, if you are leading a workshop as a business, do not set too modest a fee. Strangely, people believe us—if we say by our fee that we are not worth as much as the workshop around the corner, clients will likely go around the corner.

It is important—even, perhaps, an ethical imperative—to take good care of yourself; otherwise you will not be able, in the long run, to take adequate care of others.

A number of other ethical issues such as the protection of privacy are treated at length in other sections of the book.

Using Writing to Empower the Silenced

*The reason I came was
what I had to say
was important to someone.*

Lyn Goodspeed
Original Chicopee Workshop

*At one time or another, we all have felt other. When I teach writing,
I tell the story of the moment of discovering and naming my otherness.
It is not enough simply to sense it; it has to be named, and then written
about from there. Once I could name it, I ceased being ashamed and
silent. I could speak up and celebrate my otherness as a woman, as a
working-class person, as an American of Mexican descent. When
I recognized the places where I departed from my neighbors, my
classmates, my family, my town, my brothers, when I discovered what
I knew that no one else in the room knew, and then spoke it in a voice
that was my voice, the voice I used when I was sitting in the kitchen,
dressed in my pajamas, talking over a table littered with cups and
dishes, when I could give myself permission to speak from that intimate
space, then I could talk and sound like myself, not like me trying to
sound like someone I wasn't. Then I could speak, shout, laugh from a
place that was uniquely mine, that was no one else's in the history of
the universe, that would never be anyone else's, ever.*

Sandra Cisneros
The House on Mango Street

When I met for the first time with a group of low-income women, at night in an office building in an old mill town in Massachusetts, I had no idea that my life and their lives were about to change. "*Big time,*" I can almost hear Robin say. She was homeless in that first year, but too proud to let any of us know that she and her three small children were living in her old car, getting food and showers at various shelters. Robin later said she was planning to kill the children and then kill herself. Things were that bad. And she might have done it, too—after all, her own alcoholic prostitute mother had killed herself when things got too bad to bear.

Now, after 15 years, Robin has her Master's degree in Social Work. She is the author of a book of resources for leaders of writing workshops for youth at risk, titled *Voices from the 'Hood,* and is the primary co-trainer in Amherst Writers & Artists Institute, offering training in workshop leadership.

Writing is an incomparable tool for empowerment. Before a woman who is a low-income single parent can resume an interrupted education, she must believe in the integrity and power of her own voice. Before an abused or neglected child can entrust painful secrets to a caring adult, he must experience having his story honored. In the silence of bereavement, or being a developmentally delayed adult in a group home, or being an incarcerated man waiting out his time, or a battered woman in a shelter, writing can be the bridge out of isolation into community. In community there can be hope and help.

Using my original workshop for low-income women as a model, Amherst Writers & Artists Institute certified leaders have led workshops for all of the following groups. These have met in cities and towns across the United States, and in Ireland and Northern Ireland.

Children of migrant workers
Children in public housing projects
Children in public schools
Children in summer camp
Youth in public schools
Youth at risk in housing projects
Youth at risk of AIDS
Youth: dancing and writing
Gay youth
Homeless youth
Pregnant teens
Veterans
Incarcerated men (Ireland and the United States)

Incarcerated women
Low-income women (Ireland and the United States)
Residents of a battered women's shelter
Irish nuns (Ireland)
African American women
Women of color
Breast cancer survivors
Alzheimers patients
Caregivers
Latina women
Single mothers of young children in housing projects
(Dis)Abled women
Battered women
The San Francisco writing group (for queer women survivors of sexual
    abuse who want to write about sex)
Blind men and women (Northern Ireland)
Families in summer camp
Bereaved parents
Family members of victims of AIDS
Teachers and teachers' aides
Nursing students
Theological students
Undergraduate students
Elders (still active in community affairs)
Elders (in nursing homes)
Elders and youth together
Residents in a lock-up substance-abuse program
Persons with life-threatening illness
Residents in a group home for the developmentally delayed
Sexual abuse victims
Church groups
Wilderness campers

How This Work Began

All of the groups listed above use our workshop method, with some variation as is appropriate to each population. My own deepest experience has
been in leading free workshops for low-income women in housing projects.
In the pages that follow, I draw primarily upon that experience. All of the
women whose stories and words are included in this section have read it
and have generously given their permission for these things to be told. In
our training sessions, as we prepare others to lead workshops, they tell
their own stories, only a few of which I could include here.

I had been leading creative writing workshops in Amherst for five years when Deb Burwell, a young social worker, asked me to lead a workshop for a group of low-income women in Chicopee, a mill town with public housing projects along the Connecticut River. I wanted very much to do it, but I was also afraid. Would I be adequate to the challenge? How would it be different from my regular workshops? Where could I get help in learning how to lead a workshop for low-income women?

I couldn't find any resources. Where were guidelines for teaching writing to adults caught in poverty? How should it differ from workshops for graduate school students in California, or for college-educated men and women in my living room in a tidy college town?

I learned by going forward and by the grace and patience of the women in the writing group. There were eight members who stayed for many years, another four who came occasionally. We met for weekly sessions over ten weeks, took a short break, then met again for another ten-week session. Some time in the second year, under the Reagan administration, all funding for projects like ours dried up. No agency sponsorship. No pay for me. No child care for them. We kept meeting.

We have been together now for more than 15 years. At first we tried meeting in the women's homes. Impossible! Children banging in and out; neighbors in the projects yelling to or at one another; old cars screaming in and out of parking lots. We tried meeting in a library basement at night—too spooky, too scary. Finally we settled down in the Bellamy House, an old home of a writer that housed the Chicopee Chamber of Commerce. There we had quiet, and we wrote our hearts out.

It is never possible to know the deepest meanings and results of this work, but there are some signs. All eight of the central members have been published in national literary journals. Six of them lead or have led workshops of their own and work with me as co-trainers of people who want to lead similar workshops. They train social workers, writers, teachers, clergy, and others.

Two women in the original workshop have received master's degrees: Teresa Pfeiffer an MFA in Creative Writing, Robin Therrien a Master's in Social Work. Lyn Goodspeed has completed her undergraduate degree; Enid Santiago Welch is close to graduating from Mount Holyoke College. One of the women has taken the high school equivalency exam 15 times. She has not given up.

Not all of the women have been able to continue their education, but all have become strong, effective leaders and trainers in the AWA Institute. Mary Ann is on oxygen for emphysema. In the Florentine Film about our workshop, *Tell Me Something I Can't Forget,* she reads a piece about her lifetime work in a factory, how she had five-minute breaks— just enough to "puff, puff, puff on the old cigarette."

Evelyn, our oldest member, collapsed in the office of the Housing Authority two years ago. She was fighting them, protesting an eviction notice for her refusal to allow a second spraying for roaches in two days on a Fourth of July weekend when her adult children were visiting. She had lived in that apartment for most of her adult life. Her aorta ruptured as she pleaded to keep her home; she died the next day.

Two of our longtime members still struggle with substance abuse and other problems, but they continue to participate as trainers, helping potential leaders understand the problems of low-income women. Karen Buchinsky coleads a workshop in a women's prison.

Teresa teaches writing at a junior college; Enid leads writing workshops at Amherst Regional High School and for adult women of color. Robin has been head of social services in a huge nursing home. She left that position for one that pays half as much, choosing to work with the poorest families in the town where she grew up.

Goal and Purpose

These workshops are not literacy groups and they are not therapy groups. They are writing workshops. In that, there is no difference between this workshop and one for the general population. The purpose is to free the voice of the writer. Whatever follows upon that freedom is unique in each participant, but it is always good. Keeping clear the distinction between therapy or literacy goals and the goals of a writing workshop is crucial to the success of the work.

What we offer is respect for the workshop participant *as an artist.* Certainly the work is about healing, and the workshop is a profoundly effective setting for healing, but it does not achieve that healing through the teaching of literacy or through therapy.

The goal is something that most low-income adults have never experienced in their lives: to be respected as an artist. To have their own voices honored. To have their own stories received as important and beautiful. The goal is self-esteem.

Huge life changes are likely to occur in a person who for the first time truly believes in the worth of his or her own words. But our goal, as workshop leaders, is simply to evoke and welcome each writer's voice. The life changes will take care of themselves as people begin to believe that they can go back to school, that they are not "failures" or "stupid" or without worth.

Self-esteem is the primary stumbling block for people whose educations have been interrupted by the culture of poverty. They have internalized messages from TV and from unfortunate popular attitudes: "lazy"; "don't care"; "irresponsible." When I began working with ten women, mothers of young children—all but one of them second- and third-generation poverty—there was a litany that I heard over and over again: *I can't write. I am stupid.*

These women are brilliant. They colead with me now; tell their stories; read their poems; challenge and guide the teachers, social workers, clergy, and writers who come to us for training. They were brilliant before I ever met them. They just didn't know it.

Writing workshops for low-income women, men, and young writers can increase self-esteem, enable empowerment, and evoke healing through the achievement of personal voice and the creation of supportive community. At the heart of this method is the conviction that all human beings are artists, and capable of writing in their own voices work that is strong and true. Out of that achievement, people grow in their desire to resume inte.rupted education, to develop as artists, and to claim their rightful place in the world.

Sue Ann Adams's poem states our goal and purpose perfectly. She came to our workshop for low-income women in Chicopee—not the one that I led, but its offspring, a workshop led by former members of my Chicopee workshop, Lyn Goodspeed and Julie Benard.

KALEIDOSCOPE VISION

Through my kaleidoscope vision I see them
Swirling about me
Like black tar paper
They wrap my soul
And block out the light
My mother, mommy:
        You stupid, fat cow,
        I'll give you something to cry about

My brothers:
  Fucking brat just go away disappear
The man's face—gray at the temples:
  Better not tell, they won't believe you anyway
  They'll say you're the bad one
  Bad girls burn in hell
My husband:
  You good for nothing bitch, you made me hit you
The lady behind me at Big Y:
  It must be nice to get food stamps and get paid to do nothing
  Should of kept your legs closed

Through my kaleidoscope vision I see them
Floating around me, encircling
Engulfing trying to force ME to fade away
In the center I see an unchanging image
Created from a mere drop of ink,
Released from its own captivity
Seeping outward through every crack in their smothering wall
Bringing awareness, spreading courage

NO I say
I am not these things

I AM A WRITER

The Question of Healing vs. Therapy

In these writing workshops, healing happens. It happens in good workshops for MFA students on a university campus, in good workshops for
teens at risk in a housing project, and in writing groups in living rooms.
Writing images from your memory and your imagination is a healing act.
That which was broken or only dimly understood comes clear as you
write. Many famous writers have said that they discover what they mean
as they form it into words. The essential act of making art recreates the
artist as it reforms the world.

Nevertheless, *the writing workshop is not group therapy*. In a good writing workshop, this healing occurs individually, often secretly, and in utmost privacy. There is no pressure on the participant to read what has
been written. The leader of the workshop may never know the effect of
the writing workshop on the lives of its members.

In traditional group therapy, a person shares by telling his or her story
to others who sit facing the speaker in a circle. The speaker watches

everyone's facial expression and body language, and may subtly alter the story in response to others' body language. In workshop we write our thoughts before sharing, our faces turned down to our pages, having no input whatever from anyone else's facial or body expression. As a result, the words that we share are pure self-revelation. Reading aloud is an intensely inner and personal sharing. It is far more vulnerable than storytelling, where the speaker watches the listeners as he or she creates a story.

Because of that vulnerability we keep to our strict practices of response to manuscripts (described below) and to new work that is read aloud in the group. If these practices are allowed to slip, a workshop can become a dangerous place where even more damage is done to those who have already been hurt when they tried to write. If the practices are observed, the workshop setting can be a context for deep healing of wounds to self-esteem, to memory, to the physical body, and to the artist that lives in every person.

Although these workshops are not therapy groups, there are therapists who have adapted our workshop model for use in therapy groups. For example, Rob and Andrea Zucker have used it for bereaved parents at Bay State Medical Center in Springfield, Massachusetts. Because their group members gather for the specific purpose of sharing memories of children who have died, Rob and Andrea do not use the practice of treating all work as fiction.

In work with very elderly patients in nursing homes, the writers simply refused to follow our practice of offering positive feedback. Instead, they responded with "That reminds me of . . ." and launched into a story. Finally, we "got it"—all they wanted to do was tell their stories. They didn't want to be bothered with any young whippersnapper's "method."

Sharon Bray, however, leading a workshop for younger elders, reported a very different experience. Her writers enjoyed sharing, and found our practices helpful in setting boundaries. Sharon wrote to me about "the utter joy and fun that has emerged from doing this work with senior citizens. It is heart-warming and always brings a smile to my face. Bill, for example, a retired architect, aged 80, came to our 'Awards' dressed in a rented tuxedo and a Clark Gable mask! What can I say?"

Who Should Work with Low-Income Writers?

Can you work with low-income people if you are not a social worker or a therapist or a teacher?

Yes, you can. The overwhelming majority of those who are caught in poverty cannot find a way out by themselves. I say this out of my gut experience of having been saved from poverty by a few brave people who were willing to cross the tracks from privilege to poverty to find me where I lived. I would not be here today and you would not be reading these words if a bare handful of people had not, at different times in my life, *saved me* by first *seeing me* and second, *coming to where I was* and giving me some of their time, some of their wisdom, some concrete help in getting scholarships, in having the courage not to drop out of school when my family demanded it, and on and on. It doesn't take a social worker or a teacher or a therapist to make a difference in someone's life. Although it may sound clichéd, it is still true: What it takes is love and courage and incredible patience.

CAN YOU DO THIS WORK IF YOU HAVE NEVER "BEEN THERE"?

Yes. The issue is not whether you have been in prison or been physically disabled or have lived in a public housing project on welfare, but whether you are able to be honest about your own privilege. It is uncomfortable to admit that we have privilege. Along with that admission may come feelings of guilt or embarrassment. If our privilege is great, if we actually come from wealth, we may have been hurt and even abused by others who are angered by evidences of money in our families. The hurt of the child happens in all walks of life.

Nevertheless, it is not true that "we are all the same under the skin." The truth is the opposite: We are all different. The hurts are different, the angers are different, the strengths are different. Never, never tell your writing group that you understand because "we are really all alike." They know better. They will be patient; they will not contradict you, but they know better. What we need to do is celebrate our difference. Name it, accept it, and honestly explore what it means.

Write with your people the exact truth of your own growing-up experiences. Do not dwell on your privilege, but do not disguise it. If you are white, write sometime about the privilege of being white and maybe about the pain of being one of the race that perpetrated harm. If your parents had college educations, don't brag about it, but don't pretend it isn't a huge difference in the story of your life and the stories of the lives of the people you lead. If one or both of your parents held a steady job, name that as privilege, and be honest about the things that cause pain even in situations of privilege. You want from them the honest revelation of their homes and their lives, because that is where the power in their writing lies. It lies in the same place for you, and your honesty about your privilege as well as your honesty about the pain in your life will give them permission to be honest in their own writing. When difference is acknowledged and respected on both sides, trust will grow.

THE RIGHT REASON

Those of us who do this work must be led by our joy, not by guilt or by "ought and should." If we do "the right deed for the wrong reason" it will not work. We will burn out or our workshop participants will fade away.

In the early days as I drove the 35 minutes from my comfortable home on a tree-lined street in Amherst to the projects in Chicopee to lead those first workshops, I would think, *Why am I doing this? I'm tired. I'm gonna quit doing this every blessed Sunday night!* But on the way home I often sang at the top of my lungs the whole way, full of such joy and power, I felt drunk on it.

That's what I mean by being led by your joy. If you are empowered by the work, if after a session you are full of joy, full of spirit, then it is your vocation. You are in the right place. If not, it isn't what you should be doing. Don't feel guilty about it if it doesn't work for you. Ask yourself if there is some other population that would be right for you.

Carolyn Benson and Karen Buchinsky have each told me many times the joy they feel in leading workshops for women in prison. Loren Jacobs gave her permission to include the following:

Loren is an African-American woman, 47 years old, who has been in and out of prison since age 12. She earned her high school equivalency degree in jail, but she had never thought of herself as a writer. In the prison writing workshop she began to listen to her own voice: "The workshop has opened up a door for my inner self to be expressed. It has given me inspiration and encouragement to tell my story and to hear it myself."

Others in the workshop began to wait eagerly to hear what Loren had to say. She wrote the following poem in the third meeting of the first workshop she attended. "I'm a writer!" she said, with an enormous grin. She submitted the poem to the Springfield Library Poetry Contest, and although it did not win any prizes, just to apply was a wonderful affirmation of the strength she was claiming for her own.

I AM FROM
(after "Where I'm From" by George Ella Lyon)

> I am from the Alley,
> dirt roads an' collard greens.
> I am from the Sixties, Woodstock,
> Afros and Free Love
> where there was no love.
> I am from confusion
> and racism with no identity.
> I am reborn.
> I am from ashes.
> I am from dust.
> I am from tomorrow. I am
> a torch in the dark.
> I am from valley lows
> and mountain heights,
> I am from Light.
> I am from the four corners of the earth.
> I am from the mountaintop
> and I am Good News.

WHAT IF YOU JUST CAN'T DO IT?

Occasionally someone starts a workshop, or perhaps takes the intensive training that we offer, and says, "I can't do this." If that is true for you, I beg you to accept that with self-respect and even joy. Not everyone is called to this work, and that is all right. We don't always know that we can't do something until we try.

We need to be realistic about what we can and cannot do.

Where Do You Find People for a Writing Group?

It's very hard to go door to door in a housing project and stir up a writing group. We have tried it. Enid Santiago Welch and a volunteer student from Smith College went door to door in the Chicopee projects, handing out a printed invitation and talking to people about workshops. No one came.

There are many reasons that people don't respond, and most of them have to do with fear. We had more success in enrolling children and young writers than adults, for obvious reasons. The adults want educational opportunities for their children, and they want them off the streets in areas where there is almost nothing for young people except gang activities. But there is resistance by some low-income men who may not want to stay home with the kids and may distrust those who encourage the women to join a group. Poverty brings with it other ills: justifiable fear, paranoia, and homophobia. Some of our workshop leaders received threats from men, taking the form of "Leave my woman alone. You're all a bunch of 'lezzie's!'" One fear in some men is that they will lose their women, and it can happen. A woman who learns that she has a voice and a story, that she is smart and able to make changes, may leave the man who abuses her.

Most of the low-income women with whom I have worked have suffered at the hands of men, and so have wanted their groups to be for women only. There is too much fear, too much unresolved anger, too many memories held in silence to make it possible for many women to write freely in a mixed group. Some of the women are afraid to take their written work home, and ask us to keep the pages for them. In rare cases a couple has managed to stay together and the man supports the woman in her writing—drives her to the workshop, attends her readings, and is proud of her accomplishment.

Men who are caught in poverty are perhaps those with the greatest needs. If they are abusers, it is usually because they themselves were abused and watched other men abuse their wives and children. Women have access to their own tenderness through giving birth, nursing, and caring for young children. Unless men prevent them from doing so, women tend to tell their stories to other women. Men in the projects and other situations of poverty are desperately in need of the kind of experiences writing workshops provide.

We have many little boys and teenaged boys in our AWA Institute workshops—more male than female participants, in fact. But we have not had many men come to take our trainings, and we have not solved the problem of how to offer workshops for men, or how to get them to be willing to participate even if we had the leadership for them. An exception is work with men in prisons—we have trained men to do that work and have also had female leaders of workshops for incarcerated men.

Practices

Our practices are essentially the same as those for writers in the general population. There are, however, some subtle differences. The beginning of Part II of this book describes the basic method. What follows are some of the differences.

WRITING TOGETHER

In the beginning, when a group of low-income writers first writes together, many of the participants will not be able to write more than one short paragraph in response to a writing exercise. Therefore it is important for you as leader to be prepared with several writing "triggers." There will be exceptions. Out of eight writers, I had three exceptions. The first was Teresa, whose childhood was spent in a middle-class home; she had exceptional language skills and wrote freely. At first she prefaced each reading with put-downs of her own work, but she did not have difficulty in putting words on her page. Robin, who had written in notebooks all her life as a personal survival technique, was from the first day an unstoppable fountain of words. Enid (the Latina pronunciation is *ehn-need*), who was bilingual and very articulate, wrote but was very shy about reading. All of the other workshop members had been so shamed by school experiences they would not venture more than a few sentences onto the page and needed a lot of encouragement to read.

HANDLING EDUCATIONAL DIFFERENCES IN THE GROUP

Much more than in a regular writing workshop, there may be vast differences in the linguistic and educational levels of your participants. What you want to do is give each workshop member full freedom to use her own voice. That means, in my own workshop, that Teresa is writing side by side with Diane. Teresa came into the workshop with considerable mastery of the English language. Her parents were college-educated professional people, but through a series of misfortunes Teresa landed in the projects, a single mother. Diane, on the other hand, comes from many generations of poverty. She is one of 11 children. Her father was abusive, functionally illiterate, and absent. Her mother, Native American and French Canadian, was a first-generation English speaker and had no time for Diane and no formal education to pass on to her. Diane is intensely bright, but very limited in vocabulary. She dropped out of school at an early age.

Other writers in the group fall between these two in their skill level. How do you, as leader, make it a good experience for everyone?

The answer, as always, is by being honest. You celebrate Teresa's work in the same tone and with the same respect that you celebrate Diane's work. You name Teresa's gifts, but with no more praise than when you name Diane's gifts. These women are not supposed to sound like one another, but they are called by you to write with equal courage in the voices that are uniquely and brilliantly their own. Enid's vocabulary offers Spanish words that everyone can learn; Evelyn's offers Polish words; Teresa's offers English words; and you ask them to define unfamiliar words for the group. (You will need to be acutely aware of the distance between your own vocabulary and theirs. In my group, words that would need defining for some of the members would include common middle-class vocabulary like "agenda" or " imply.") Lyn's courage in coming to the workshop against the odds of a giant physical handicap, and the raw truth of what she writes, are exemplary in another way. You lift up her work as brave and important, being always careful to avoid the error of most classrooms, where one person's work is valued more than another's, and there is subtle pressure for everyone to sound more like each other.

Stories That Heal

There are many stories that I tell in my workshop for low-income women, but two seem especially effective. The first one concerns something that is obvious to most of us who have the advantage of an education and a profession. But in my opinion it is absolutely not understood by many women caught in poverty. In our training sessions as they colead with me, members of my workshop retell the story, saying, "This story changed my life." Here it is:

Two babies are born on the same day. One of the babies is born to two professors at Amherst College. She grows up taking ballet lessons and piano lessons. There is a room in her house that is a library. Every wall is covered with books. When she is ten years old, her parents have a sabbatical year. (Stop and tell the group what that is.) They go to Israel for a year, and the little girl studies Hebrew and visits Masada. (Stop and tell the group what that is.) This baby learns all day, every day. She learns the English language and she learns dance and she learns piano and she learns a little bit of Hebrew. She learns how to be a woman in a professional world.

The other baby is born to parents or a mother in Hampshire Heights Project. Her daddy is out of work and drunk most of the time. He's not home much, and when he is he puts his fist through the bedroom door and beats up the baby's mother. When he's not drunk, he's nice. The baby's mother has three other kids. She sometimes works at night as a bartender, but she's afraid to leave the kids with their father because a couple of times he didn't stay, and there are drug dealers in her courtyard, and if anyone tells that the kids were left alone, the Department of Social Services might take them away. This baby learns, too, all day, every day. She learns how to keep quiet when her daddy is drunk. She learns how roaches crawl up walls. She learns how a woman acts when a man is beating her. She learns how to be a woman in a public housing project.

Both babies are born on the same day. They are equally brilliant.

Having told them this story, I passionately and repeatedly tell them that they are brilliant. They have learned well—perfectly—the lessons that their lives have taught them. Now they can write about it.

My second "story" engages them in a dialogue. Someone says she can't write because she can't spell—she always got bad grades on papers in school.

"Who do you think corrects the spelling of five-hundred-thousand-dollar-a-year executives," I ask.

(Silence.)

"Think about it. The big executive behind his desk. He has to write a letter. Who corrects his spelling?"

"His secretary!"

"Right! And I'm your secretary. I'll correct your spelling. Good writing is not about spelling—it's about telling the truth of what you imagine or what you have experienced. Forget about spelling! That's my job!"

And it is. Until their confidence has grown. Until they hear for themselves the power and passion of their own voices. Then they will begin to work at spelling themselves, because it no longer feels overwhelming, and because it has become fun instead of a terrible test always resulting in failure.

THE VERY FIRST WORKSHOP MEETING

Your first meeting needs to begin with something that helps people relax. After some words of self-introduction and welcome, tell those who have gathered, "Because this is a writing workshop, we are going to introduce ourselves in writing. This is just a little game—it's not about how we write. After all, we're all a little scared, including me! So this will help us get acquainted."—Or something like that.

Opening the First Workshop Session

"Everyone make a list of ten things about yourself. They should all be true things, like 'I was born in Missouri; I have one brother,' etc. But hide among these ten true things *one lie*. A fiction. Something that's not true. When we all have our lists, we are going to try to guess which one is not true—so be sneaky!"

Give the group only three guesses, and if the group fails to guess right, playfully exclaim that the writer is the winner! "You won! We couldn't guess!" Then the writer tells which one is the fiction. No fair guessing if you already know!

Notice that I say "lie" first, then add "fiction." This is an example of the teaching you will be doing in a workshop for writers whose educations have been interrupted. Some of the writers in my Chicopee workshop would not have immediately understood if I had said, "Make one item on your list fiction." "Fiction" is not a word that is commonly used in Diane's world. It might mean a novel. By the time she figured out what I meant, she would have lost the next three sentences, and I would have lost her attention.

I never want to leave anyone out—and so I always speak at a level that reaches the *least able* participant, without ever calling attention to that person in a way that embarrasses or "grades" her. The more able participants understand what you are doing and soon they, too, begin to participate in the compassionate teaching by pausing in a reading to gently define their own big words. You can assist this by asking, "What does the word synchronistic mean?" after one of your more advanced writers uses it in a sentence. As you define words as you go, never looking at the individual who might need that definition, the writers begin to do the same thing, and everyone teaches everyone. It is a lovely way to break down hierarchy and create community.

After we have written together for a while, when they are ready to puzzle out a poem by a famous writer, I bring in Sharon Olds's poem, "I Go Back to May, 1937," in which the poet speaks to her parents:

I want to go up to them and say Stop,
don't do it—she's the wrong woman,
he's the wrong man, you are going to do things
you cannot imagine you would ever do,
you are going to do bad things to children . . .

The poem wishes for the parents a better, wiser, life, but ends with the line, "Do what you are going to do, and I will tell about it."

Bringing the work of outstanding contemporary poets and fiction writers introduces the women to work that touches on their own lives and gives permission to "tell about it."

Exercises for Writers with Limited Formal Education

At first, keep most of your writing exercises very simple and very clear, and state them as direct suggestions:

The First Time . . .

Write about your first job.

Write about first grade or kindergarten.

Write about the first time you drove a car.

Write about the first time you noticed race. Or a memory that includes racism. (It is important to give opportunities to write about dangerous and difficult topics, interspersed with the chance to write about gentle and funny topics.)

Write about the first time you kissed a boy or a girl. (It is important to subtly offer exercises that invite them to break down the walls of homophobia, even if it is just in the way you offer the exercise.)

Write about the first time you saw the ocean, or write about never having seen it, and imagining it. Or write about a river, or a lake, or a swimming pool.

Write about giving birth, or write about not giving birth, if you never have.

Write about the first time you experienced death (an animal? a relative? a friend?).

Write about your first menstrual period.

Write about your first date.

Write from Remembered Feelings

Write about a time when you felt angry.
Write about a time when you were happy as a child.
Write about a time when you felt sad.
Write about a time when you felt afraid.
Write about a time when something funny happened.

Random Objects

Put out several objects. Always have the objects hidden in a basket or other container until the moment when the participants are ready to write. Have them keep silence as you put the objects out, telling them gently that someone may already be thinking of a story they need to write, and talk may make it harder to find the story. Tell them to pick up one object and hold it. Then see if any memory comes to mind, and write that memory. Be sure the objects include some that may suggest problems, such as an empty bottle of cheap wine or whiskey, a cheap sex toy (like the ones available in some public bathroom dispensing machines), a piece of frayed rope, a package of cigarettes, a bottle of pills with the label scratched so the pill inside can't be identified. I include things that I hope may evoke memories of significant experience: a rosary, a page of scripture written in Hebrew, an old piece of jewelry, a box of condoms, a well-used rattle or baby bottle, a small teddy bear, a beat-up softball, a handful of jacks, a seashell, a mirror, a bit of crochet, a broken dish, a man's pipe, a shaving brush, and, if I can, something funny—a sexy bra?

I was startled the first time I tried this exercise with my low-income writers. I had used it many times in my regular workshops, and no one had ever seemed to hesitate to take an object—two or three if the writer was so inclined. With my Chicopee writers, I laid out the same objects in the same way on a nice cloth on the floor. No one moved from her chair. After they finished writing, I asked, "Why didn't anyone take an object?"

One gave me the answer, and the others agreed: "You never said we could touch them!"

It moved me deeply, because it seemed to me to be exactly the disempowerment, the lack of entitlement, that I wanted to erase. I take care now always to say in my exercise directions (for everyone, middle-class, too, just in case): "Please take one and hold it in your hands."

The Same Object

Give everyone a mothball. A piece of penny candy. A railroad spike. A nail. A screw. (Almost no one will write about a metallic screw!) A potato. A pill. (Make it harmless—a vitamin—but don't tell them what it is.) An acorn. A long stem of grass or wheat. A torn bit of map. A slice of carrot (The design is elegant and beautiful). A rock. A small piece of sandpaper and a bit of cotton. Have them close their eyes and receive the two objects without looking at them, just have them feel the textures until they are ready to write. It's fun to think of new things to stimulate writing—obviously the list is as long as the world is various.

Smells

Anything smelly makes a good exercise. Use discarded film cartridges to hold small amounts of odoriferous material—preferably the black containers, so people don't use their sight for identification. Try Vicks Vaporub, or a strong cleaning solution, or whiskey. Give everyone a container and ask them to "bring a smell next time." You'll get laughter and some good writing too! Always bring a few extras, because some people will forget.

You can also use one larger batch of smelly stuff. Once a woman brought a covered bucket of straw from the floor of a horse stall. She opened it and we all wrote with the smell of horse manure in our noses.

Pictures

I go to secondhand book stores and find collections of photographs that suggest stories. I take a razor blade and cut out the pages, then use the book cover as a folio for the photographs. In workshop I spread them out and let people choose a picture. Sometimes, for fun, turn the pictures over and have them choose one at random. Sometimes suggest they take two and have the two people talk to one another, or alternate paragraphs about one and then about the other.

On the closing night of a ten-week session, I say, "Please choose two pictures for the person on your left and two for the person on your right." Each writer then has four pictures chosen especially for her, and she is free to use only one, or all four, or none at all. (See the section below titled "Language: The Danger and the Opportunity" for more about this exercise.)

Exercises That Teach Gently

When the writers have been together for some time and I know their skill levels, I begin to use exercises from other sections of this book and those that come to mind in response to the writers' needs. I begin to introduce poems written by well-known poets to gently broaden their knowledge of established writers and their understanding of written forms. Some of my favorites for this work are prose selections by Grace Paley and Dorothy Allison, and poems such as Sharon Olds's "The Takers," an excellent trigger for sibling stories and poems, or Cheryl Savageau's "Crazy Ol' Baker" to evoke stories of relationships with people who are not "normal," or Raymond Carver's "Drinking While Driving." I use pieces like these by reading them aloud slowly, twice, just before people write. I don't say the name of the writer before I read and they write—rather, I just ask them to "listen just as you would listen to music. Don't try to hold on to the meaning—just let the poem flow through you, and then write whatever comes to you to write." After they write and read their own work, I hand out copies of the poem or prose piece and we may talk about it. Savageau is a native American poet, and mention of that fact gives Diane a deep connection to her work. I would want to introduce writers of different ethnic and racial backgrounds, as well as gay writers, disabled writers, both male and female writers, in the same way to help my own writers deepen and broaden their sensibilities.

As I write this, I notice that the poems coming to my mind are those that invite the readers to deal with painful subjects. I balance those exercises with pictures, objects, or something deliberately designed to trigger humor. Some very funny writing came out when I gave everyone an egg and refused to tell them whether it was hard-boiled. And a little book I found of photos of men's bare butts is a favorite for hilarious writing. I found it in a used bookstore, and cut the pages out to spread on the floor of the room where we write. One of the women cried out, "Nasty! Nasty!" (she was serious) when I first offered the pictures—but she wrote up a storm!

In the second or third year of my work with low-income women I tried to do more specific "teaching" about poetry and grammar, and I got instant rebellion. "We can get that in school," they told me. "What I need to do here is just write whatever comes up." For most of them, that was true. We were fighting much greater enemies than grammar. We were fighting against failure and hurt, abuse and neglect. For the first time they were drinking a regular draught of praise and affirmation. They didn't want to muddy the waters with what felt too much like school.

A few wanted more concrete and specific help, and I gave that to them through responses to manuscripts that they gave me. In time, all of them wanted it, but it never changed the nature of our workshop sessions. Those were for writing. Grammar and other lessons belonged to manuscripts. There will be more about that below.

READING OUR WRITTEN WORK ALOUD TO ONE ANOTHER

After a time of writing together, we read aloud. (The leader writes, always. She or he reads aloud at least once in each writing session. The reason? We have no right to ask our people to take risks we are not willing to take ourselves. To me, that is a moral imperative.) The goal is to create complete safety for the writer through an insistence that no correction or suggestion be made in response to brand-new, first-draft writing. Only statements of what is liked and what is remembered are offered. This practice makes possible a great range of teaching opportunities through praise of what has been done well. It also heals the damage done by a lifetime of "grading" and negative feedback on writing that is so often experienced in school. In our workshops we do not discuss manuscripts in the group except to offer praise for what has been done well. In that context, with the author's permission, a piece someone has written may be lifted up as an example of "metaphor," "dialogue," "character development," or good use of rhyme. Using the language of literary criticism as *praise* is a brilliant way to teach it!

In our workshops for the general population, critical response to manuscripts is an ongoing and helpful part of our group process. In workshops for low-income writers, however, critical correction of written work is offered privately, and only when the writer wants that kind of feedback. There are never assignments, although optional take-home suggestions may be offered now and then, but only with a dash of humor and freedom not to take it home at all. The work that the leader does on a participant's manuscript is carefully done according to practices that build up, rather than tear down, the confidence of the writer. There are guidelines below for handling the manuscripts of writers with limited educational backgrounds.

PROTECTING EACH WRITER'S PRIVACY

All writing is treated as fiction, unless the writer asks that it be treated as autobiography.

This practice is of crucial importance. It ensures the privacy of the writer and greatly increases the sense of safety and the possibility of risk taking. As I have said earlier, writing is vulnerable work. I have been amazed to discover that even the youngest children in a living room in public housing quickly learn to treat everything as fiction unless the writer says it is autobiographical. In that safe place they can write what they cannot say anywhere else, and the workshop leader will keep the paper, if writers don't feel safe taking it home.

THE LEADER WRITES AND READS ALOUD

The leader writes with the group and allows the group to respond to his or her work. This is absolutely essential. The leader takes risks, makes himself or herself vulnerable, writes honestly—in every way, works to break down the walls that older, hierarchical models of leadership have built between participant and leader. Whatever you ask of your writers, you must be willing to do yourself. Even more than *willing*—you must *do it.*

HOW TO HANDLE MANUSCRIPTS

A leader of a workshop for low-income writers must tailor manuscript response to each individual writer. Unlike workshops for the general population, it is not a good idea to do group critiques of written work. There is too much history of public embarrassment and shame in adults who have dropped out of school. Manuscript critique here should be done privately, between the leader and the writer. There is no group discussion of mistakes made—ever! There is, however, constant lifting up of success, and successes are used to teach, as I described earlier.

We have had writers in our groups who are completely illiterate. They talk their writing into a tape recorder while others write, and we bring their stories and poems back to them typed, clean of spelling errors, and with correct punctuation. We do not change any of their words without their permission.

The few who type do so. Suggestions are written on typed pages in pencil (never in red ink!) with frequent "maybe," "perhaps," "If this were mine, I might . . ." The leader should never use put-down words such as "awkward" or "cliché." Instead, use the positive form: "Maybe this could be said more simply" or "Maybe a fresher word here." Those participants who can type may be enlisted to help type work for others.

I learned a shocking and important lesson one night in Chicopee when I first asked my writers if anyone would like me to take her work home and type it. Dorothy, a fiercely bright and severely language-impaired writer, said angrily, "I had a tutor once. She wrote on my paper!"

I felt like the comic strip character who says, "DUH!!" Why didn't I ever understand before? The writer's handwriting is *holy.* I would never draw on someone's drawing—surely words are as sacred as visual images. And so for writers who cannot type, I take their handwritten pages home and make of them a little three-page booklet consisting of (1) their original copy with no writing on it from me, (2) a typed copy as they wrote it (mistakes intact) with my praise and appreciation written several times— as many positive comments as suggestions for improvement, always, and my suggestions for change, explaining why, teaching as I go. My comments are in black pencil (never red). The final page (3) is a finished copy in professional manuscript form, with the author's name and address in the upper left corner.

Many times the women have said to me that seeing their own words in print for the first time, free of spelling errors or teacher's comments, changed their lives.

Each special group of writers needs special methods of response. A leader must work intuitively, empathetically, making adaptations, rejecting what is not appropriate in his or her own setting and inventing what will work.

Sample Manuscripts

See samples on the following pages.

Note: Lyn Goodspeed is a founding member of the original Chicopee workshop for women living in housing projects in Chicopee, Massachusetts. She is now a co-trainer with Pat Schneider and other members of AWA Institute workshops, training persons who want to lead similar workshops.

[handwritten manuscript of the poem, reproduced below in typed form]

Lyn Goodspeed

Note: Lyn, this is exactly as you wrote it, with my suggestions marked.

Repeating, Repeating Push, Push, harder harder Breath Breath deep deep   my

mother would say or they will take the gas away and you won't be put to sleep and you

will feel everything all the pain. Give me that mask and I will take a long deep breath and

there will be no more pain pain Again Again Lynn, Lynn, push push we we are are

all most there there. Force Force what what is happen happen to me Two two of them

them. Sleep sleep wake thank thank only only one one baby baby.

Lyn — maybe I'm wrong,
but I think this is
a poem —
— a terrific poem!
Love,
Pat Schneider

AGAIN AGAIN

Repeating, repeating
Push, push
Harder, harder
Breathe, breathe
Deep, deep
My mother would say
Or they will take the gas away
And you won't be
Put to sleep
And you will feel
Everything
All the pain

Give me that mask
And I will take
A long, deep breath
And there will be no more
Pain, pain
Again, again.

Lynn, Lynn, →
Push, push
We, we
Are, are
Almost
There. There.

Force, force.
What what
Is happen happen
To me, me
Two, two
Of them, them
Sleep, sleep

Wake

Thank thank
Only only
One one
Baby baby.

    -- Lyn Goodspeed

[Handwritten margin notes:]
Lynn, I really like the repetition + the rhythm - it feels like childbirth!

Good work!
Excellent dialogue!

Lynn, in your manuscript, you spell your name two ways - maybe they should be the same on the poem?

If you like it as a poem, I'll make another copy + fix the name problem. all the words are exactly as you wrote them.

13 ■ Obesity

Eyes stares mouth
stab with sharp words
the light is bright and cold
hard cold. They
don't like me.
I don't like me.
They say that I am different.
I say that I am different.
I don't like this. I don't
like that they don't like this.
They don't like that. Hurt
comes running back.
It didn't go far.
It is always there.
Go back. Go forth. All
the same. Back hurt
carry heavy load back
then and now.
Looking down at the judges.
They don't like anything
of myself. Wishing
things were different
now. I see eyes
eyes looking at this thing
that I am not happy with
wish were gone
gone.

Published in *Peregrine*, Vol XV

Lyn spelled her own name two ways on her handwritten manuscript. One of the effects of this method is a slow, and profound, development of a sense of self-identity through the affirmation of voice. Lyn offers this sample of her early work, along with a later, published poem, as an illustration of the results that can occur in this kind of writing workshop.

As explained in the text, the leader of the workshop takes the original manuscript (with the writer's permission), types it, makes affirming comments and only a few suggestions on the typed copy. In this case, I also typed it out as a poem—Lyn's first poem! The final page of her work given here was published in the literary journal, *Peregrine*.

CONFIDENTIALITY

There is careful and consistent attention given to maintaining confidentiality in the workshop community. This is important for all writers, but in situations where the group members live close to one another in a project, a prison, or some institution, the disclosure of information may have severe consequences.

We have discovered that there is a great capacity for confidentiality, even in the youngest children or the most troubled adults, if the leader is consistent and careful in reminding the writers of the sacred trust that is involved in listening to one another's first-draft work.

Language: The Danger and the Opportunity

I offer these suggestions out of my personal experience on both sides of the poverty line. Some of them are no doubt controversial. They were hammered out in the existential setting of a low-income workshop without funding, without child care, without agency sponsorship or, at times, even a place to meet. As hard as that was, it did give me freedom to invent my own way, without pressure from some agency staff to do the workshop "their way"—with standard curriculum, testing, evaluations, and so forth.

The women's commitment to the workshop, even if it meant meeting in tiny project living rooms surrounded by kids and noise, brought about our independence, and my stubborn insistence on what a writing workshop ought to be brought about the development of this method. We created it, the women and I, writing together for 15 years (so far). There has been hell and there has been high water, but we have come to some practices that we all believe make for a strong writing community for under-served populations.

THE DANGER

Perhaps the most important thing for leaders of this sort of workshop to understand is the gulf that exists in vocabulary between many low-income writers, and those who live and move in middle-class society. This is not a problem if you are working with children or youth; they are accustomed to adults, having large vocabularies, and not understanding does not carry with it a cloud of shame. But with adults whose formal education has been interrupted by poverty, there is usually a history of failure or a feeling of failure. There is pride that makes it impossible to ask, What does that word mean? And there is the silence of incomprehension and the reinforcement of feelings of failure and stupidity. It is of crucial importance that you avoid embarrassing or insulting the intelligence of mature people who do not know the meaning of the words you speak.

In our experience, this is the subtlest and often most disturbing problem that middle-class people face when they cross the poverty line to work face-to-face with those who have dropped out of formal education. If we talk to someone just off an airplane from China, for example—someone who speaks very little English—most of us immediately and intuitively change our vocabulary to accommodate their level of knowledge of our language. We do not assume that because they do not know English, they are "dumb" or lack knowledge of some other kind.

However, in talking with a person who looks just like us, and who uses the same base vocabulary, we do not alter our language. Therefore, we sprinkle our sentences with words that an average person having dropped out of school at age 12 or 13 will not have in their working vocabulary. We use words like: "intentional"; "peripheral"; "substantial"; "curriculum"; "agenda"; "priority"—perhaps half of our working vocabulary is made up of words that my workshop participant, Diane, does not ever use and does not understand. She has become the primary expert in our Intensive Leadership Trainings in the area of vocabulary and the low-income woman. She talks about how she feels in school conferences about her children when teachers and school psychologists talk and she cannot understand anything that is being said to her. "I feel stupid," she says. "I tell them I don't understand and they act like I'm stupid, and they don't talk different. They just go on, and so I just tune out. I don't mean to, but I can't help it. And they think I don't care about my kids."

The workshop leader must have a great deal of empathy and willingness to let go of all the big words. If a workshop member like Teresa has a big vocabulary, she can be encouraged to use it, occasionally defining a word that we need to understand. But the leader must never use language that the least able person in the room cannot understand. It is common sense. If she can't understand you, she will drop out. She's already had enough of feeling stupid. Gradually, if you are compassionate and patient, her vocabulary will increase and you will learn how to intuit, evoke, and strengthen her great giftedness, her brilliance, in ways other than by the size of her vocabulary.

In the above section on suggested exercises, I describe one that invites writers to choose pictures for the persons sitting next to them on their right and on their left. I want to "walk you through" my own mental process as I present that exercise, as a way of demonstrating what goes on in my mind in any workshop where one or more participants have limited vocabularies.

First, I explain that we all have grown to know each other's voices, each other's personal metaphors. (The word "metaphor" just slips out of my mouth, and instantly I realize that not everyone in the room really understands what a metaphor is, although we have talked about it when someone wrote a particularly nice one. Once again, I gently explain what a "metaphor" is, avoiding meeting the eyes of the ones who need it, never singling them out even by where my gaze falls. I don't ask if everyone understands—I know that some don't, but they will gradually come to understand if I go over it again and again as praise for good metaphors in participants' writing—sometimes in the writing of a person who has no idea of what a metaphor is!) Continuing with the exercise, I say that since we know each other's voices so well now, we can affirm (too big a word— I catch myself before it comes out of my mouth and substitute *celebrate*) each other by giving each other images (oops! I said it, and realize someone in the room doesn't know what I mean. Instantly I add *pictures*).

This is hard—maybe the hardest part of your work. It is crucial that you give directions in a way that is fully understood by the writer who has the most limited vocabulary, and that the writing you do in workshop never leaves her out. As a writer, a member of the community, I do write with my low-income women honestly and with risk. But I choose to do that with language that is simple and clear. Amazingly, sometimes that strengthens, rather than weakens, my writing.

I am almost always asked in trainings, "But isn't this condescending?" No. Emphatically no. It is being in touch with reality, and it is being kind. If you speak in big words, you speak in a foreign tongue. It's OK to use big words when you are talking to children and youth—they expect adults to know more words than they do; it doesn't hurt their self-esteem, and besides, you know instinctively when to define for them the words that you use. But if you are leading a workshop for women your own age or older, it's a different story. In many ways they know as much as you do. In many ways they know more than you do. A lack of knowledge of middle-class English is more or less invisible. As leader, you may be tempted by their wisdom and their patience to assume that they understand what you are saying. They are more than likely faking it, nodding their heads, seeming to understand when some of them do not have a clue! There is too much history of believing, I don't understand, and so I am stupid. Obviously, they will hide what they consider their "stupidity" until they trust you profoundly. Diane Mercier and Robin Therrien, in my workshops, are now full of fire and conviction when they speak about it in our trainings. "I don't understand a word of what you just said, and so I drift off. I just go 'la-la-la' in my mind. I don't mean to, but I can't help it, because I don't know what you're talking about," Diane says, looking the social workers and teachers, the ministers and published writers in the eye. Then her voice chokes up, and those we are training "get it." As Robin frequently says, "Big time!"

Another pitfall with language is the danger in critical comments. Beware of words that have traditionally been used to "correct" writing. As I said in an earlier section, no workshop leader, regardless of the educational level of his or her writers, should use critical comments that shame, embarrass, or put down the work. Some examples are: "awkward," "cliché," "redundant," and "sentimental." Instead, phrase your comments gently and positively, like, "Maybe this could be said in a fresher way," or "I think this word has been used so much, maybe a fresher phrase would be better," or "Can you show me this instead of telling me, so I can feel it more deeply?"

Do not have any "rules," have "practices." Do not call your group a "class," call it a "workshop." Instead of being the "teacher," be the group's "leader" or "facilitator." Try to meet in a place that does not suggest a schoolroom. For a short time our original workshop met in a library where the table and chairs in the basement room reminded the writers of school library furniture. The women still, years later, express revulsion at the thought of that room.

THE OPPORTUNITY

When you understand clearly the problem of language, working with it in this context can be exhilarating—even fun! There is a sense of giving amazing gifts: the word *metaphor*—the words *simile, line break, plot development, narrator, character, protagonist*.

That is done by pointing out and discussing what has been done well—your most powerful teaching. Lift up strengths. For example, a writer who brings in a rhymed poem that sounds very much like a Hallmark card will possibly not try again if you respond by saying it is "sentimental and clichéd." What can you say that is true and positive? I would talk about how exactly the writer accomplished end-rhyme. I wouldn't mention that *what was rhymed* could be fresher. I would talk about the writer's excellent sense of rhythm, and read a few lines, stressing the beat. Then (not the next week, but soon) I would bring in a copy of Robert Frost's "Stopping by Woods on a Snowy Evening" and I would talk about the same things—excellent end-rhyme, excellent rhythm. Then without drawing any comparisons I would talk about how surprising and fresh the images are—and ask whether the group thinks Frost meant exactly and only what he says, or whether the poem is a metaphor for the coming on of death. And once again, I would talk about what a metaphor is, until even my most beginning writer talks about her own and others' metaphors.

For a long time, Evelyn Fitzpatrick, the oldest member of our original Chicopee workshop, wrote only very short, very humorous pieces of memoir. She took very little risk, revealed very little of anything but her positive feelings. She was a wonderful member of the group, a mediator, and a support to everyone. Shortly before she died, Evelyn wrote the following poem. It was a profound breakthrough in her writing. For perhaps the first time she dared to write in a way that let the unconscious move into the conscious act of writing, and I held my breath. What she wrote was a work of art, and it was a profound use of metaphor.

THE CROWS

You wake one morning and you are expecting
the sameness you always feel.
You awake instead to a strange feeling
of loneliness. There are no crows
squawking their morning rituals.
The rain is silent and invisible
but the wetness on your skin is real.
This morning is left over
from your ancestors.
It has come to claim you,
but you resist.
You can feel the pull,
trying to suck you into itself.
If you lose, you are gone,
and you don't even know your ancestors.
You twist your body and struggle
to stay on the edge.
And then you hear the crows.

Be patient with your writers. Their breakthrough writing will come in their own time, not yours. It will surprise you—it will take your breath away, and you will find yourself singing all the way home.

Who You Are and Why You Are There

"WHY ARE YOU HERE?"

As I have said earlier, no matter who your workshop participants are, it is important that you not pretend that "we are all the same." We lead workshops now in prisons, with survivors of AIDS, groups for women of color and women with disabilities. What we need to learn to celebrate is our difference, the beauty of it, rather than our sameness. We all suffer illness, death, and disappointment, but trying to cover our differences by talking about where we are alike sometimes rubs salt into a very old wound.

Economic poverty adds suffering on top of suffering. Where it is several generations deep, where education and social services are minimal, there is a trapped quality to life that many persons with more privilege have a hard time truly understanding. I can tell you from my own experience that a low-income person doesn't want to hear "we didn't have much money" from anyone who had one parent with a steady job, food on the table at every meal, and rent paid on time.

There is one perfect answer to all of this: honesty. Everyone is not the same. You do have privilege, that's why you are trying to give and they have come hoping to receive. What you cannot know in the beginning, and what they probably do not know either, is that you are going to receive at least as much as you give, and they are going to give as much as they receive. My own life has been changed by the women of the Chicopee writing workshop, and all of the change has been for the better.

Not immediately, but sometime, especially if you are challenged as I was challenged the night Dorothy asked me, Why are you here? you may need to say or write something like, I am here in this workshop because I have privilege. I come from a house where there are no drug dealers on the corners, no roaches in the walls, no condoms in the gutter, or discarded hypodermic needles against the curb. I want you to have safety and privilege and education. That's why I'm here.

If you are honest, they will believe you. If you open, they will guide you. If you are compassionate, they will love you. If you are brave, they will stay.

LETTING YOUR WORKSHOP PARTICIPANTS TEACH YOU

If you are genuinely humble, understanding that the people you work with are as intelligent as you are, and are wise with their own lifetime of experience, you will be all right. Admit to them early on, I will make mistakes. I hope you will tell me when I do. I want to learn from you. And practice that with every breath you take. They will teach you, and they will love you for being willing to be taught. Freely apologize when you have "stepped in it," as you will. I promise you, you will. Laugh at yourself if you can. Swear at yourself if you must. And go on.

HAVING FAITH THAT YOU ARE MAKING A DIFFERENCE

More than once I have been asked by a middle-class person, "Are you certain that we should be here? Maybe we are just giving hope where there is no hope. Maybe they are worse off because we have been here. After all, they have to go back home to things just as they were."

My answer is passionate: Yes! Yes, we should be here!

When I was 12 years old and in the orphanage, a young student social worker took me home with her for one overnight, once. She took me into a solid, sensible midwestern home on a nice street. Up some clean, wooden stairs and into a bedroom. There was a bed, nicely made, and one of those old-fashioned vanity dressers, with the low shelves on each side and the long mirror in the middle, with two narrow mirrors on each side of it. I walked to the mirror and stood looking in it.

After a moment of silence, she asked, "What is it, honey?"

"It's just that I've never seen my whole body before."

"Well," she answered gently, "You just go on and look as long as you want, and when you're ready, come out. I'll be waiting for you in the hall." She went out and closed the door, and I looked at myself. And I looked at the room. Clean and spacious, and for one wonderful night— mine! I had never in my life been in a room of my own.

The young social worker disappeared—I don't even remember her name. She has no idea that she made a categorical difference in my life. I saw myself in a room of my own. I saw myself.

It is not usually given to us to know what we give, or how it will bear fruit. But it will. An ancient prophet told us to scatter our seeds. Some will fall on stone, some on hard ground. But some will fall into the warm soil of a human heart, and a child or a woman or an old man somewhere will look into the mirror of his or her own story, and will say, "I see myself!"

Part III

Additional Exercises

*I don't have nothing to write today—maybe never. Hammer in
my blood a giant river swell up inside me and I'm drowning.
My head all dark inside. Feel like giant river I never cross in
front of me now. Ms Rain say, You not writing Precious. I say
I drownin' in river. She don't look me like I'm crazy but say,
If you just sit there the river gonna rise up drown you! Writing
could be the boat carry you to the other side . . .*

Sapphire, from *Push*

Additional Exercises

There are many exercises woven into the text of Parts I and II. These additional exercises are designed for the writer working alone and for the leader of a workshop or writing group. If you are working alone, I suggest you wait until you are ready to write before reading the exercise, because surprise is a part of the effectiveness of the triggering image or suggestion.

There are three kinds of writing exercises—those designed to get writing started, those designed to improve craft, and those designed to take the writer into deeper significance or broader perspective. Until the emergence of the writing process movement, most books that included writing exercises were heavy on perfecting your craft and short on getting writing started. The question of deeper significance was assumed to be embedded in craft. I am convinced that the best way to learn craft is to practice—to write, write, write. (A variety of good exercises helps!) And, if possible, to have honest, sensitive, and thorough response from a supportive community of other writers. Significance and perspective are matters of the spirit. Good exercises can help the writer be open, listen, and write more deeply and fully.

Words begin to flow when the writer is no longer thinking about words themselves, but rather is seeing in his or her mind some concrete image. An image, not an abstraction, is the deepest wellspring of writing. When you are beginning to write, be faithful to the image—abstract meanings will reveal themselves to you through the images more powerfully than if you work the other way around.

Writing exercises (sometimes called "triggers") should stimulate the senses. That is how the world comes to us, through our senses, and memory of sensual experience is how we recreate what we have experienced or imagined. I have therefore included exercises in this chapter that involve sight, smell, taste, touch, and hearing.

The exercises described below are designed to trigger images, to get you started writing, and in some cases to assist specifically with some aspect of craft. In several exercises I have suggested how discussions following the exercises help the workshop to consider matters of craft. This sort of discussion can follow any of these exercises, as issues of craft arise within the members' written work.

These exercises are suggested for use in a workshop in which people are free to write in any genre, but all can be used effectively by groups limited to one genre, and almost all of them are also excellent for use by a writer working alone. Similarly, the exercises in Part I, "The Writer Alone," are also useful when offered to a group.

Guidelines for Good Exercises

MAKE YOUR EXERCISE SPECIFIC AND CONCRETE (FOR YOURSELF OR FOR YOUR GROUP PARTICIPANTS)

Dick Bentley, a workshop member who had just completed his MFA in Writing, complained about exercises he had found in a book on writing. "The exercises are too cosmic," he said. "The author tells you to write a 35-page story on God. I'd much rather describe God's hat." Dick's point is well taken. The best exercise is one that is clear, simple, and concrete. It triggers a memory, an association, an image. An onion pulled out of an ordinary paper bag and placed in a writer's hand will work magic; it may evoke dinners in a childhood home, weeding in a garden, walking through a farmer's market; or, ironically, the globe of onion with its layers and mystery may very well evoke a 35-page story on God!

USE SURPRISE

If you are writing alone, try opening the book at random and writing from the first exercise you find. Open a book of poetry or prose, a play or a newspaper, and write in response to the first image or the first word that your finger touches.

If you are a workshop leader, do not reveal your exercise until the moment of writing has come. Surprise is very helpful in triggering images. If you are using objects, bring them in a bag or a basket covered with a cloth; if you are using pictures, do not set them out until everyone is seated in the circle, and quiet. Then spread the cloth on your coffee table or on your floor quietly, and arrange your pictures. The moment is "theater"—you are setting a scene, calling your people to attention and to meditation, as an actor or a priest might do. If your exercise is verbal, call your writers to silence before you read the exercise. If they seem excited and scattered, you may need to invite them to close their eyes for a moment and become aware of their own breath. (I always use these words: "If you feel comfortable doing so, close your eyes—I will close my own." Some people do not feel safe with their eyes closed in a group, especially if the leader may be watching.)

VARY THE MOOD OF YOUR EXERCISES

Choose exercises that call forth different sorts of responses: serious, playful, outrageous. And let your own mood be your guide. If you are working alone and you are feeling quiet, rest into that quietness and give it voice. If you are feeling high and full of energy, allow your language to have the sparkle and zest of your own feelings in that moment.

As a workshop leader, I have learned that the best exercise to offer to your workshop is the one that interests you at the moment you are offering it. We are all much more creatures of the atmosphere than most of us realize. Workshop groups arrive already subdued, or noisy, or tired, or funny. As you wait for the group to arrive, the only clue you have is how you yourself feel. If I am feeling quiet, wanting exercises that are inner and meditative, I frequently find the workshop arrives in a similar mood. Similarly, when I am feeling excited and happy, often the door bursts open with people laughing and joking as they come in.

It is wise to have two or three things that you can use when your own "writing temperature" is different from that of your group, however. I keep two card files—one of exercises and one of single provocative lines from poems and prose—in small file boxes close at hand. I also have a shelf of books of pictures that have been cut from their covers and so are like folios of photographs or works of art. And finally, available to the workshop participants at all times, I have a plastic box of black-and-white postcards. If an exercise does not interest someone, he or she may go find a postcard image and work from that. A very shy young woman named Kate used only those pictures for over a year, while other writers worked from the exercises I suggested.

Writers working alone often create this sort of resource for themselves by having boxes or jars where they place pictures, phrases, handwritten notes, or even single words for use as writing "jump-starters" at a later time.

ALWAYS OFFER YOUR EXERCISE AS AN INVITATION, NOT A COMMAND

Whether you are a leader of a writing workshop, or a solitary writer wanting to move your fingers to write, offer the invitation gently. The writer may ignore the exercise if there is already something in mind to write. Even the best exercise can be a block, if the writer needs to write about something pressing at that moment.

RELAX AND TRUST YOUR OWN ENERGY, OR THE ENERGY OF THE GROUP YOU ARE LEADING, TO SPARK IMAGINATION

Not every exercise will work for you. One that does not work today, when you are sad, may work tomorrow when you are happy. No one writer in a group will find every exercise helpful. Now and then someone has expressed dislike for my "go back in time and remember . . ." exercises; recently someone said, "I can't write in response to a picture." But those very people come up with an alternative idea of their own, because I have made it clear that my suggestion is only that—a suggestion.

In leading a workshop, trust your writers, and try to have variety in your exercises. Something that surprises me, but has become undeniable, is the fact that images pass in silence from mind to mind in a workshop setting. Too frequently to be coincidence, several people will use the same image even though no one has mentioned it prior to the writing time. I first noticed this phenomenon one evening when three people wrote about an armadillo, and no armadillo had been mentioned. Since then, I have come to realize that it goes on all the time; the room is charged with imagery when people write together. I don't have to do all the work.

SOMETIMES TAKE A RISK—USE SOMETHING FOR
OUTRAGEOUS HUMOR OR TO BREAK A TABOO

In the first few years of my workshop in Ireland, we met in a convent, and the participants were nuns. Taking a lead from my friend and Ursuline Sister Máire O'Donohoe, who invited me there and has a wonderful comic gift, I went each year prepared with something that I hoped would be funny, as well as my usual exercises. One year I had difficulty finding a good idea and then thought of the new shop in our college town that sold nothing but condoms. Perfect! I had a very funny conversation with the young man who was selling them, trying to figure out which would be the best model for an exercise with nuns in Ireland. In the workshop, I had them all in a brown paper bag, and handed them out solemnly, one to each Sister. I did tell them ahead of time that this object might arouse humor, anger, or some other emotion. That would be fine for writing— just write anything that comes, I said. Sure enough, most of the women wrote very funny pieces after they opened the packages and examined the contents. One wrote a bitterly angry piece about contraception, and one ignored the exercise entirely and wrote about something else. But she didn't give the condom back.

Máire now leads workshops for low-income writers and for teachers in Ireland.

USE A GOOD EXERCISE MORE THAN ONCE

Ruth Bolton Brand has been in my workshop for several years and has written a number of times obliquely about the experience of a young girl at the time of her mother's suicide. Recently I suggested as an exercise the image of standing in a doorway. Ruth has written in response to that exercise before, but for some reason this time she was ready to tell the story. The young girl stands at the closed door behind which was the bed her mother had left to go drown herself. I will not forget: the writing was devastatingly clear, perfectly in the voice of a child.

Don't hesitate to use a good exercise more than once. Remind your writers (or, if you are working alone, remind yourself!) that it is important to write the same story over and over. You are looking for the tiny unresolved nuance that you have never seen before—the glitter of that secret is what brings it to the surface of your mind. Accept its invitation. Write it again.

How to Use the Following Exercises

If you are writing alone, most of these exercises will be helpful ways to begin a writing session. If you are leading a class, a writing group, or a workshop, use drama and surprise by waiting to reveal the exercise until your participants are settled, ready to write. Then present the exercise aloud, slowly and clearly. There is an element of ritual that is helpful in beginning to write. If you are writing alone, be aware of your own rituals and honor them. If you are leading a group, create a kindly but slightly formal atmosphere as you present the exercise; in this way you will help your writers move away from ordinary conversation into the silence and solitude of their own writing.

I have included sample writings in response to some of the exercises. They are for the writer alone, not for use in a class or workshop. Wait to read the response until after you have written. That writer may act as a companion or even trigger another writing for you.

Exercise: What Matters?

This is my own favorite way to start writing. I ask myself, What matters? Right now, this minute, what matters?

When I ask myself that question, the answer often comes as a concrete image. If it surprises me, if it seems inconsequential—good! It's best if I don't know what the meaning of the image is. If you try this, begin writing whatever comes to you in response to your question, no matter how small or meaningless it might first appear to be. Describe how light plays on the rim of a glass of water, how the frayed edge of a man's jacket touches his chair. Your mind has given you that image as something that matters; as you write, you may discover why.

Margaret Robison wrote a book-length poem made up of images of one small town: Cairo, Georgia. These lines are from that book, *Red Creek: A Requiem.*

> What matters, then?
> Poetry matters, and the line
> that will not break
> under the weight of history.
> What matters then?
> A single gardenia broken
> from the dark-leafed bush.
> What matters then?
> The dark-leafed bush.
> What matters then?
> The gardenia.

Notice how the poet hones in on the detail of the leaf, the blossom. Margaret is from Georgia—where gardenias grow profusely in the yards. In the poem, she is writing about what she knows intimately. Her writing becomes more and more concrete and, as it does so, the poem gains power. This is a poem about how to write a poem—how to come closer and closer to the truth. She relies on what Nabokov calls "divine details." In doing so, she teaches us how to write "the line / that will not break."

When I use *What matters then?* to start writing, I invite something as simple and inconsequential as a leaf on a dark-leafed bush to come to me. But for me, the image would not be a gardenia. If I go back into my childhood, it might be a leaf on a persimmon tree or a huckleberry bush. What would it be if you went back to your childhood? Or to last week, or to the last time you watched the movement of water?

The following poem, written in response to this exercise, is by Paula Sheller Adams, who uses this workshop method in a school for troubled or delinquent teens in Indiana:

ARMISTICE

What matters now
is that you are here as I am here.

What matters now
is that there is still a now for us
in which we stand together,
though closer to the edge

of that mysterious sea—
far closer than in those days
when we worked in the sunny inland,
somehow raised the children,
and fought our battles
in open fields—
far, it seemed, from the crash of wave on shore
and the path's drop-off at land's end.

Though it was in our tears,
we were heedless, still, of the salt taste on the winds
already blowing inland from that sea—
too vast,
too final,
for any crossing
but by love . . .

Exercise: Choosing from a
Group of Objects

If you are writing alone, choose an object that has some meaning for you. Hold it in your hands (or, if it is too big, sit where you can see it) and begin your writing with a detail of that object. Flannery O'Connor, who is perhaps America's greatest short story writer, took drawing lessons to help her *see* more clearly the detail she wanted in her writing. Describe your object in detail until something else occurs to you, then move to whatever your unconscious is giving you.

If you are leading a group of writers, wait until they are quiet, then spread a plain cloth and put on it a collection of objects that represent various kinds of experience: a spool of thread with a needle stuck in it; an old, scarred wooden spoon; a man's shaving brush; a whiskey bottle; a horseshoe; a small crystal ball; a dog whistle; a hand mirror; a rosary; a baby rattle; a used baseball; a jump rope; a mean-looking knife; an artificial rose; and on, and on. I suggest you offer at least 30 or 40 small objects, as various as possible.

It is important that these objects be things that suggest memory or story. Lay them out on the cloth with a sense of ritual—handle each object with respect. As you place the objects, you might quietly say something like this: "Every object here is full of story—what it was before it was made into this object, and where it has been, and the stories of all the people who have used it. Objects give us the world—they are how the world comes to us."

It is a good idea, however, to say nothing about specific objects. If someone asks what something is, or where it came from, tease a bit and say, "Write what you think it is, and I'll tell you later, after you write." And if the group gets giggly or chatty, ask them to be quiet because someone may already be forming an idea of what to write.

This is an excellent exercise for the first meeting of a new workshop, because a variety of objects gives a range of choice of subject matter. One writer may choose a wrench and write a section of his science fiction novel. Another may choose an empty whiskey bottle, and write an emotionally charged piece about an alcoholic parent. Objects are what I call a "cool" exercise (as opposed to "hot"). That is, this exercise does not suggest tone or content because there are so many options.

In the writing example that follows, Deborah Campbell Softky, in my workshop at the Graduate Theological Union in Berkeley, California, chose an old door key.

In order to write, first you have to know that you exist.

Before I met my husband, I never knew what color my skin was. I didn't know that my skin was brown and smooth and shiny. I was BLACK. A social political concoction that I was dipped in. But I wasn't *too* black. No one ever called me Chocolate Drop. No one paid me any mind until I was ten or eleven and some boy said, "She has a nice body but put a paper bag over her head." My best friend whispered this to me in my ear and I disappeared.

I never knew that I had breasts until my husband pointed them out to me. I mean, I knew that two things hung off my chest and they were big, and once, in Junior High, when small breasts were in, I wanted to cut mine off. But I never knew that they were *my* breasts until I was thirty-four years old and I walked by a store front window and there, sticking out through my blue Gap shirt, were these breasts! And they were nice ones, too. I went home and told my husband, "Look, I have breasts!" and he said, "I already told you that before. You're always forgetting."

I turned thirty-five and I discovered I had a body. A very nice body. It curved in at the waist and out at the hips. I found it early in the morning. The raging Furies weren't up yet. There it was in the full length mirror. I went into the kitchen to tell my husband. I said, "Bill, I have a body," but he just looked at me and kept drinking his coffee.

My Old Testament teacher told me that I have a brain. He gave me a B+ and I had never read the Bible before. I love him. He is like my father— getting bent out of shape over things, but he is also loving and compassionate, unlike my own father. I cry when I ask my teacher for a letter of recommendation for seminary. He puts his arm around me and says that everything will be all right. He has hairs growing out of his nose but I forgive him.

The black man is trying to drown me in the deep, dark sink. I slash at him with the jagged edges of a broken champagne glass. I escape down the driveway. It is covered with dead leaves. The phone is ringing in the bushes. It rings and rings and rings. I answer it. It is the police. "Help me, help me, I've been raped!" They won't answer me. "O.K." I say, "Will you come out if it's only aggravated assault?" The black man has buried a piece of glass in my knee. I wake up. I can't write if I don't exist. It's o.k. to write if I'm not on the covers of magazines everywhere. Does this end? No, it doesn't end. Not until the phone rings and rings and rings, rings and rings and rings, and rings and the voice on the other end answers and says, "May I help you?"

Variations on This Exercise

1. Each writer chooses five objects and arranges them in an interesting relationship to each other, as if creating a kind of abstract sculpture made of the objects. Then all members of the workshop look at each other's arrangements and write whatever comes to mind.

2. Give all writers identical objects. I have used buttons, cinnamon sticks, feathers, potatoes, screws, keys, dried grape tendrils, eggs, seeds, acorns, eggs, railroad spikes, a single grain of rice, mothballs (in plastic sandwich bags to protect skin)—and on, and on.

3. This variation on the objects exercise comes from fiction writer Corinne Demas Bliss: Pass around a container of ordinary objects, and have writers close their eyes and choose one object. Ask them to feel it with their eyes closed and replace it in the container without looking at it. Have them write descriptions of the object sight unseen. Then have them describe another object that they have seen but not touched. To their surprise, Ms. Bliss says, they find that the objects they "saw" with their eyes closed are always the most fully described.

Exercise: "I Am From . . ."

Paula Adams, a workshop leader in Indiana, wrote to me, "In the second meeting of a new group, I've used the 'I am from . . .' exercise. It continues the get-acquainted process (and trust—especially crucial with my incarcerated girls) and has produced gorgeous pieces from the entire workshop with almost unfailing consistency—more than any other exercise I've used."

The exercise begins with reading aloud the following poem by George Ella Lyon, from her book by the same title:

WHERE I'M FROM

I am from clothespins,
from Clorox and carbon-tetrachloride.
I am from the dirt under the back porch.
(Black, glistening
it tasted like beets.)
I am from the forsythia bush,
the Dutch elm
whose long gone limbs I remember
as if they were my own.

I'm from fudge and eyeglasses,
            from Imogene and Alafair.
I'm from the know-it-alls
            and the pass-it-ons,
from perk up and pipe down.
I'm from He restoreth my soul
            with a cottonball lamb
            and ten verses I can say myself.

I'm from Artemus and Billie's Branch,
fried corn and strong coffee.
From the finger my grandfather lost
            to the auger
the eye my father shut to keep his sight.
Under my bed was a dress box
spilling old pictures,
a sift of lost faces
to drift beneath my dreams.
I am from those moments—
snapped before I budded—
leaf-fall from the family tree.

Follow the pattern of Lyon's poem by writing sentences that begin, "I am from . . ." This is an excellent exercise for anyone who thinks she or he can't write a poem. This one, by Gina McNeely, was written in my Amherst workshop:

WAKING UP FOUND

I am from clothespins . . .

—*George Ella Lyon*

I am from a life turned around

I am from going to sleep lost
and waking up found

I am from one day at a time

I am from indescribable love
in one small house
among four living souls

I am from surrender and forgiveness
and giving back

I am from the dead
from a world without mercy

I am from blood spilled
and whiskey worshipped

I am from nuthatches, goldfinch
and waxwings at my window

I am from a hot shower
into a soft, bright towel

I am from under the man next door
whose three small girls I babysat for

I am from the puke that I slept in
with my face on the floor
before I learned that 15 year olds
can't be whores

I am from a horse barn
each one fed and kissed goodnight
I wish my parents
could have treated me as right

Exercise: Imagining a Place

This is a common way for a writer alone to begin writing, and it is a powerful tool for the workshop leader. Have people close their eyes. (Always add the words "if you are comfortable doing so.") For a few minutes lead the group in relaxation. My way of doing this is to suggest, slowly, with pauses: "Be aware of your own breath—how it brings refreshment to every part of your body. If it is comfortable to do so, stretch out your feet and legs and let them be at ease. Now your belly, let it relax. Now the muscles of your back. Remember the organs inside, doing the body's work . . ." and so on throughout the body, ending with, "Now as you take in a breath and let it out, let all of the parts of your body come back together and be at ease."

Then I say, "Now travel back in your own life to some time before this time, and find yourself in—a doorway. (Or in an old car, or in an upstairs hallway, a big chair, a front porch, a swing, a secret place, looking into a mirror, waiting in line, at a work place, in the dark, on a city street, school yard at recess, outside a closed door, in a bed . . .)

After you name the place, allow a few seconds of silence, then quietly ask two or three questions to help the writers become located there, giving them time after each question to silently find an answer.

1. "What is the quality of light?" (If it is a doorway, ask: "What is the quality of light in front of you?"—then pause—"What is the quality of light behind you?") Again, a brief pause—You just want them to "see" the light, not think about it.

2. "Is anyone near you, or are you alone?" If you have suggested a bed, ask whether the covers are smooth or wrinkled. If it is a doorway, ask, "How tall are you in relation to the door handle?" Do not ask more than three questions in all. Then say gently, "Stay there as long as you want. If something begins to happen, let it happen. When you are ready, very quietly pick up your pen and paper, and write whatever comes to you to write."

The first year I led my workshop in the convent in Ireland, I used the doorway innocently, having no idea what a powerful image that would be for nuns, all of whom had entered the order when they were very young, and before the huge changes of Vatican II. Every single Sister wrote about the doorway through which she had left home knowing she could never return, even if a parent died—or she wrote about the doorway through which she entered the convent. It was profoundly moving.

Catherine Swanson wrote the following poem in response to my suggestion "Find yourself in a bedroom."

NIGHT FEEDING

In a dark room
where thin white curtains
bend and dance
in the evening breeze,
two beds stand side by side,
but only one child sleeps
under the eaves.
Beyond long windows
that face a pine-shrouded lake
the moon casts an arm of light
across tiny waves
softly touching against
a stone dock.
Alone in the house she sleeps.
The revelry at Auntie's next door
does not disturb
the rise and fall
of her small, flat chest.
Nor the cry of the lonesome loon
calling for his foraging mate.
Nor a fisherman in search of a catch
trolling his motor
past the stone dock.
Only the squeak
of the screen door below
and the sound
of heavy footsteps
on the stairs
open her eyes.
Awake now, she waits
to suckle the stick
thrust into her mouth,
and sip the sour semen
from its tip.

Exercise: The Photograph Collection

Lay out a collection of pictures and allow people to choose one or more as
a trigger for their writing. An excellent source of photographs is secondhand photography and art books. I look for photos that suggest a story:
The best turn out to be collections by several photographers. Magritte
paintings are wonderful writing stimuli: The strangeness stirs up subcon-

scious imagery. Cut the pages from the spine with a razor blade or stationery knife, and use the cover as a folder for the pictures.

Variations on this exercise include the following: Hold a container of
black-and-white picture postcards over the writers' heads as they sit in a
circle and have them pick one—or three—at random. Or, if the group
has been together a long time (excellent for the final meeting of a ten-
week session) have them choose two postcard images for the person on
their left and two for the person on their right, affirming as you do so
that we all know one another's voice now and may choose images for our
neighbors.

Rebekah Boyd-Owens chose a postcard photograph of two people on
a motorcycle leaping over a deep ditch and wrote:

LOVERS' LEAP

They hadn't really thought about it. They hadn't really calculated. They just
hinged themselves together with her thin arms. Hinged themselves atop the
sputtering motorbike.

"We can make it!" The heat swung from their torsos up into their faces
while the bike spat, spat. He kicked a rock and she hinged her body, breasts
flattened out against his back, hinged herself to his coat, grasping her fingers
together just above his belt buckle. "We can make it, up and across!"

The snakes and small rabbits were gone, out of sight. And they hinged
themselves. Excited.

The trees were points; reasons for stopping, for turning back.

"It's not that far," he shouted as they hinged and he twisted and revved
and finally her feet came up and his feet came up and the bank across the mouth of
the gully, the bank at the other side looked fluffed up with dead grass.

Their feet came up and they saw the dead grass while the trees were pointed
but they didn't hear the echo, long and bellowing. They didn't hear the echo
of the sputtering bike, the echo in the gully, in the opened jaw of earth before
them. And they hinged and their feet came up and he turned to kiss her. He
kissed her and twisted the black to rev and he kicked it to gear and they went.
And they flew.

Exercise: The Fragmentary Quote

Use a fragment of a poem, a sentence from a prose piece, or a few lines of
dialogue from a play to trigger an image for your own writing. I have
suggested elsewhere that quotes used as triggers should have one or more
of the following qualities: concrete image, emotional trigger, surprise, or
humor. Sometimes the quotes I give are simply everyday things we say

that may have caught my attention: "You've done it again!" "If you promise you won't tell." "I know I left it right here." "Don't touch that!" "You
opened my letter!" Sometimes the quotes are lines from my own poems
or prose—most often, I give fragments of lines by other writers.

Following this exercise I often give my workshop members a page of
examples of how to give credit when you quote someone else's work—
copies of several poems and prose pieces that begin with a quote by someone used as an epigraph. You can find those by flipping through several
books of poems—it's a common practice among writers.

I never hand out printed quotes. They don't seem to work that way.
Make them brief, and offer only a few at a time. Dictate clearly, including
punctuation, line breaks, and if the sentence is incomplete, say "dot, dot,
dot" at the end.

A young writer in r .y workshop in Berkeley, California, told me that
her writing group keeps a paper bag of quotes, and members reach into
the bag for a quote to trigger their writing. My own workshops have
created a shoebox full of "first lines of stories never written." It sits on a
shelf in my library. Whenever someone feels in need of a little help, they
dip into the box for a fresh idea.

When I am alone and want to be surprised into writing, I sometimes
open a novel or a book of poems at random, close my eyes, and set my
finger down on a page. Whatever phrase my finger touches, I use as a
trigger for beginning to write.

I have used hundreds of quotes in workshops: phrases from works of
fiction, single lines of dialogue from plays, lines or partial lines from poems. Some lines of my own from poems in my books *Long Way Home* and
Olive Street Transfer are offered here as writing triggers. Every book on
your bookshelf is rich with possibility. Here are a few lines from poems of
mine. Each one alone, or several at a time, can be offered as the stimulus
for writing:

"Rain moves over the garden . . ."
"Your death is a hole in the universe . . ."
"A hickory nut falls to the footpath . . ."
"I am a small man without a head . . ."
"You were the gentle one . . ."
"I won't go back there this time . . ."
"We were young together . . ."
"I've read your letter again . . ."
"Right before you disappear . . ."
"I told you when I left . . ."

"There was something that I asked of you . . ."
"Don't go. Don't stay . . ."
"She got quieter as she got old . . ."
". . . the lake was still . . ."
"Here I cross a river . . ."
"I am still a long way from home . . ."

Here are some of my favorites from other writers:

"Come into animal presence . . ." (Denise Levertov)
"Her nipples want to drive all night to Alabama." (Ellen Doré Watson)
"I am from . . ." (George Ella Lyon)
"And the body, what about the body?" (Jane Kenyon)
"I've always hated hospitals, dentists offices, and jails."
    (*New Yorker* cartoon)
"If I had not known you / I would not have found you." (Pascal)
"If I had no memory / I would say this is perfect." (Jane Rohrer)
"When anger was in, / I was officially angry . . ." (Penelope Scambly Schott)
"It was the fear of losing him that kept me silent." (Joseph Conrad)
"The burly son of a bitch . . ." (Carter Revard)
"The earth says have a place, be what that place / requires . . ."
    (William Stafford)
"Nothing your mama tells you / across rivers / suffices."
    (Penelope Scambly Schott)
"I stand on all fours, my fur . . ." (Nancy Willard)
"Every angel is terrible . . ." (Rainer Maria Rilke)
"The untamed sea is human . . ." (Susan Shoenblum, age 11, in *Miracles)*
"There are names for what binds us . . ." (Jane Hirshfield)
"I've been sitting in this phone booth for half an hour, pretending to
    make a call." (Truman Capote)
"I want things whole but I love things broken." (Ellen Doré Watson)
"How we drift in the twilight of bus stations . . ." (Martín Espada)
"Grandma, come back, I forgot . . ." (Carolyn Forché)
"Dear Mrs. Pearson, I am writing to you on a matter which is personal
    to us both . . ." (Doris Lessing)
"Mama, I always see you there . . ." (Sharon Olds)
"Something happened." (Joseph Heller)
"Please do not call to me, mother, / while I am making pancakes . . ."
    (Nicholas Stix)
"To know ourselves as we are, we must know our mothers' names."
    (Alice Walker)
"Because I do not hope to turn again . . ." (T. S. Eliot)
"Of all the Souls that stand create / I have elected One . . ."
    (Emily Dickinson)
"O mother what have I left out? / O mother what have I forgotten?"
    (Alan Ginsberg)

"To do something very common, in my own way . . ." (Adrienne Rich)

" . . . my fourteen year old penis in his tight, unhappy lips."
(Norman Mailer)

"'So you're saying you had an orgasm?' asked Ida. 'Is that normal, having an orgasm during exorcism?'" (Jennifer Ashton)

"There was old sex in the room and loneliness, and expectation of something without a shape or name." (Margaret Atwood)

"She could hear them living all through the house." (Ray Bradbury)

"We see in the old photos / the women we have become . . ."
(Penelope Scambly Schott)

"If you do not come too close, / If you do not come too close . . ."
(T. S. Eliot)

"The things I did, I did because of trees . . ." (Marvin Bell)

"I think I know what water dreams . . ." (Penelope Scambly Schott)

"No one owns the old road . . ." (Larry Laurence)

"What a long, strange trip it's been . . ." (Jerry Garcia)

"Am I the bullet / or the target / or the hand / that holds the gun?"
(May Swenson)

"I know the feel of his hands on me . . ." (Cheryl Savageau)

"Dear God, I am writing you a memory I hope I will have . . ."
(Donna Gates)

"With a hook and / a hook and a hook / you took territory."
(May Swenson)

"Today it is quiet in the Holy of Holies." (Jay Schneiders)

"Too bad people change and forget to tell each other—too bad . . ."
(Lillian Hellman)

"Any minute now, something will happen." (Raymond Carver)

Exercise: Writing Dialogue (Group Exercise)

Number the people in your group off, 1,2; 1,2 around the circle. Tell the group that everyone is going to participate in writing a dialogue. Ask each number one to decide who the character is for whom they are speaking, and then to write on a piece of loose paper (not in a bound book) a provocative comment in the voice of that character. For example, I might decide I am a cranky old woman who says, "Dammit, you've done it again!"

When all the number ones have written their provocative statements, have them pass their papers to the number twos, without telling them who the character is.

Now the number twos decide who the character is who will answer this comment, but they do not tell their partners. For example, my partner might decide his character is a teenaged kid who is tired of being scolded. He might write, "Fuck it, then! I'm outta here!"

Without each person's knowing who the other's character is, allow the couples to write dialogue. Continue back and forth with the dialogue for 15 minutes, then have each pair read their own characters' lines.

My experience has been that this exercise completely changes some people's attitudes about writing dialogue—it is so much fun, and so easy to do.

Exercise: Writing in Response to Music

Play music to trigger images for writing.

I try to vary the music, both in style and in the generation it represents, so on different evenings, different people are served. When I play an "oldie," I try to choose something familiar even to young writers.

In the following example, playwright Tanyss Rhea Martula believes she wrote this scene in response to music that I played. I think she wrote in response to a line about perfection in a poem of Jane Rohrer's that I found in the *American Poetry Review*, January 1985. The fact that we can't be sure pleases me because it illustrates the way the "trigger" works—it disappears once the imagination of the writer takes over.

I think I have never laughed harder than in the production of this scene, where the actor and actress were doing an exaggerated dance to increasingly florid music, while the woman talked and the man's expression became increasingly stoic.

ANNIVERSARY

Stage setting: a bare room except for a metal folding chair leaning against one wall.

A MAN and A WOMAN in their early sixties enter, dancing to the "Tennessee Waltz." The couple, dressed in their "anniversary" clothes, waltz around the room once or twice. The WOMAN begins to speak to her husband as they continue to dance, and as she speaks and her thoughts change and build, the music/dancing changes and builds, from waltz to tango to polka.

WOMAN (as they waltz)

You say this is perfect? This is in no way perfect, Henry. If you had any kind of memory, you'd know this wasn't perfect. In fact, this is the worst anniversary I've ever had. And, remember, it's your anniversary, too, Henry. Thirty-nine years of anniversaries and not one perfect one yet as far as I'm concerned. Do you remember our very first one, Henry, our Wedding Day? Far from perfect, wouldn't you say? Your gabardine suit was wrinkled, you forgot your spectacles so you couldn't even sign the marriage certificate, Father Blinosky had to do it for you, and you threw up all over me and Mama's wedding dress as soon as we were in the car. Remember, Henry? I should've married Charlie. I mean, then my memories would be different. They'd at least have a chance of being perfect.

(The music slides into a tango.)

No, I haven't been keeping track of Charlie all these years, but who knows, as smart as that guy was, he probably runs a liquor store or at least a funeral parlor by now. And look at you, Henry. Small repairs and lamp shades. I mean, who can make a decent living on coffee grinders and lamp shade fringe?

(The tango gets wilder with lots of dipping by the couple in the next section.)

And it's not that I don't forgive you for the throwin' up, Henry. We all throw up every once in awhile. Why, I even threw up once, on our tenth anniversary, remember, Henry, when we drove the Studebaker all the way down to Holyoke for the big Bingo binge right before Lent, but you had to go that roundabout way and get lost? And I had my head in the map and got all woozy and threw up all over the car 'cause I missed the ashtray? Guess we were lucky to have the Studebaker, though Charlie probably would've at least had an Oldsmobile or Pontiac by then. Undertakers do alright, and liquor's always been sky-high.

(Music bursts into a polka as the couple struggles to keep up.)
Perfect? No, I wouldn't say Charlie woulda made a perfect husband, I'm sure he woulda had his faults. As I recall, he used to pick at his fingernails in church. But, then, you used to do worse things than that in church, Henry, far worse than dirty fingernails. So don't talk to me about a perfect anniversary, or a perfect marriage or a perfect life or a perfect anything.

(They stumble and stop dancing, but the music continues. The WOMAN is upset.)

Just give me one perfect day, that's all I ask for. I've told that to Father Blinosky more than once. Just have God send me one perfect day and I'll be contented. One day when the septic doesn't back up . . .

(A phone rings offstage. The music stops.)

. . . one day when the kids don't call for money . . .

(The woman starts to exit as if to answer the phone.)

. . . one day when some dog doesn't shit on the lawn. Then, I'll say, yes, this is perfect.

(The WOMAN exits. The MAN is alone on stage. He starts to whistle very softly as he carefully takes out assorted pieces of a broken coffee grinder from the various pockets in his suit. He sits down and repairs the coffee grinder in a very slow, but patient way as he talks to the audience . . .)

Exercise: Writing about Sex

A first experience of sex or sexuality can be a vivid source of images for writing. First experiences of all sorts are fruitful: first job, first religious experience, first date, first menstruation/first time shaving, first cigarette, first car accident, and so on.

First sexual experiences are only the beginning of what is possible in writing about sexuality. This piece was written in my Amherst workshop by actress/playwright Ruth Bolton Brand for a book she is writing about a grandmother's adventures with a man named Hank.

SIXTY-SEX

He called and said, "I'd like to come and spend the night with you."
   I didn't stop to think about how a feminist-oriented woman should react to this. I reacted as I reacted and said, "Oh—spend the night?"
   "Yeah."
   "Uh—sleep with me?"
   "Yeah, I want to come and make love to you."
   "Oh—well—uh—yeah—okay."
   "Okay, see you in a bit."
   "Where are you now?"
   "In Boston—I'll be right out."
   "Boston? Boston is sixty miles away."
   "Yeah—at a pay phone—my time is almost up."
   "Oh—okay, see you."
   "See you later." End of phone call.
   It's eleven at night. My cat and I retire early. We hardly ever have visitors. My little grandson comes down and we have make-believe tea. The grand-daughters don't come. Hardly anyone comes. I lie still, thinking non-thoughts. Make love—make love—to Hank? My mind flips, my cat purrs. I still lie still. I won't get up and run around the apartment screaming for joy. This will upset my cat. She's very nervous. I pet her, thinking of how she broke the antique wedding plate when I got so hepped up over the married dentist coming to visit. That fiasco—what a fool I was. She knows it, my cat. She lies still, thinking everything's okay.
   But I hop out of bed and start straightening up. I look in the mirror to examine the circles under my eyes. I go to the bathroom to wash, all the time thinking, why should I wash? Make love? Make love with Hank? Oh my god, don't get worked up, keep cool, calm, collected. My cat is digging in her box trying to find a decent place to do her business—at least it's not on the rug. I will not be a doormat. I will not allow myself to be made a doormat of. I rub cream, then make-up under my eyes, I brush on mascara. No need for a dia-phragm, no more of that.—I'll be dry. I haven't done it in so long. Shit, who

cares. Well, I'll put a little cream down there.—He's going down there? Oh, my god. I'll put on a sexier nightie.—I don't have one. It's too cold for the long slinky sleeveless second, with the mended rip in the bottom, that I bought for the dentist and never wore. How silly! Kitty and I go back to bed and wait. I leave my old flannel gown on. To hell with it. Hank's only been here once before. Will he find the place at night?

After an hour or so I hear a loud radio, a car driving up beside my apartment window, the radio switching off. Suddenly silence. There's a knock. Oh my god—a knock on my door! Kitty braces herself. I rise from the bed, brace myself, and go to open the door. Hank is standing in the flesh, all six feet of him, bald in the doorway.

"Hi," I say.

"Hi," he says.

Many writers find it challenging to write erotic scenes, and yet good fiction requires that our characters be embodied, and that the experience of the body be fully believable. In the example that follows, two women make love. It is from a novel by Bridget Bufford, titled *Minus One: A Twelve-Step Journey*, published by Alice Street Editions. Bridget leads writing workshops in Columbia, Missouri.

I come in to candlelight and smoldering music, k.d. lang's sultry sound. Holly takes my hand, pulls my hips against her. I breathe in Obsession, a little sweat and beer.

"We need to talk," I say. My voice is low, faltering.

"Not yet," she whispers. "Be with me, Terry."

I surrender once again, my body hot and wet on hers. We dance, on and on. Desire scorches my skin, Holly feels as ripe and bursting as a plum under my hands. We kiss, still swaying to the music, until my lungs burn and I have to break away for air. Holly peels away my sweaty shirt, strips me to the waist. Runs her tongue from my throat to the top of my jeans, and I'm witless, stoned.

There's a blanket folded on the couch. Holly shakes it out and spreads it on the carpet. I unbuckle my belt, kick off my shoes, slide my pants to the floor. The candles flicker with the stir of our undressing; Holly's body glows surreal and radiant. She lies upon the blanket, and our full contact shocks me like a dive into an icy spring. Holly rolls from under me; her hands and lips travel my length. She trails her fingers over my flesh until I become liquid, makes love to me with an aching sweetness and attention. I come slow and full, waves surging and ebbing until ripples die away and tears spill down my cheeks.

Alongside me, she pulls my head to her shoulder. Wipes my tears with a gentle hand.

I wake with a start, sweat cooling on my legs and back. "Holly! I—"

"Hush. You went to sleep."

"Oh my God. I'm sorry. I never do that. I—"

"It's all right, Terry. It's enough. What we did was enough." She kisses my forehead, then gets up. Comes back with some pillows and a sheet, arranges herself on her side. "So you need to talk?"

Exercise: Religious Tradition

Use images from your own religious tradition in a fresh way. These images are a rich source of metaphor.

In the example that follows, Teresa Pfeifer, a member of my Chicopee workshop, uses images of communion and of Moses in a natural, understated way to give depth and perspective to her poem about her son.

FOR MY SON ROBERT: NOVICE, AGE FIVE

You break bread into the center
of your large green net,
preparing your gift for the lake
as though a part of this communion
for centuries.

Pumpkinseed after pumpkinseed
finds its way to your offering. You
place each fish into your orange bucket
with the hands of a surgeon.
What a delicate operation!
You slip a large piece of bread
into the bucket.

The armies of children move in.
You defend these fish, insisting,
"Don't touch, don't hurt them."
Like Moses, you empty them back
by the parting of the waters.

Exercise: Cut and Paste

This exercise was created by Jack Meyers: Write a short poem or prose piece in a gentle, happy, or peaceful tone; write a poem or prose piece of the same length in an angry, sad, upset tone; cut and paste the two together, alternating lines without trying to make sense of it at first.

Patricia Lee Lewis, who leads workshops and retreats in sacred sites around the world, wrote the following in response to this exercise:

TWO HUNDRED WINGS

You are pregnant, the doctor says, I am sorry, leaves
float golden orange, he turns away, his white coat, his big
shoulders, between twig and ground, are you sure, the girl says,

a hundred starlings, it's all she can think to say, light
among red oak branches, except then she cries, their voices
like the voices of the thousand leaves, what else to do

with shame and sin and no one will forgive you now, beyond
the trees, you little whore, she can hear the baby's father, a
woman stands, except then, she says, inside the sobs she says,

she raises both her arms in salutation, is there anything you
can do, it being 1954, it being Texas, two hundred wings,
and this being unforgivable, he turns and says, a single

bellows whooshing, No, I'm sorry, and when her mother
slams her hands against the steering wheel, pushing air,
and says, what have you done to me, in close formation, and

when her father says, like a cloud, I will have to resign
from the ministry, she breathes the risen wind, she knows
there was nothing anyone could do, and she enters
the small cottage among trees.

Exercise: Details of Direction

Write a piece in which you give a detailed description of a lesson, either from the point of view of the teacher or the learner. This is an excellent way to work on clarity of detail.

The following example is a fragment of a longer piece by Maria Black written in an all-day Saturday writing retreat in my home. As so often happens when a writer is faithful to detail, this piece at the end becomes about much more than the making of a dress.

I pinned the delicate onion skin paper to the material, my mother showing me how to line up the arrows with the grain of the fabric, the weave of the fabric. She held it while I wrestled with the pins, awkwardly. She was always a good teacher, patient, encouraging, letting me struggle. When the pieces were all pinned, she pulled out her scissors, the special ones, pinking shears, and I held the heavy things along the line of material marching up, sawing up, chewing cleanly up and down the lines of my blue dress, around the curves where my neck would be, my arms, all the while my young mother, younger than I am now, watching me, well aware of the occasion, marking my face, smiling I'm sure to see the rapt concentration.

I especially remember the feel of finally turning over the clipped and notched facing around the neckline, pinching the seam with my fingers, smoothing the thick blue, as solid and substantial as any summer day could be, as normal and routine as any mother's love, folding it over and watching my mother show me how to whip it down. Her fingers moved so surely, the needle's tip so close to them. She didn't use a thimble, said it got in her way, but she gave it to me to wear when I took over. It was a silver thimble, Lallie's, her mother's, already dead, dead and cold and gone forever: that mother.

I remember the hot dry grass of the hill leading down to the Guadalupe, the shady bank and the scrub oaks, their roots exposed and white with the wear of little feet. I remember the swing, held back on a nail until used, then standing up high on that tree's roots, higher than the others with the stick of the swing held out before me, in front of my new pale skin, and my conversation with myself before I pushed off, a conversation alone inside my head yet self-conscious as if the world was watching, then no thoughts but the body deciding when to let go.

Exercise: Making the Unfamiliar Familiar

Begin by describing a scene you know very well, that others may not know.

This may be an intimate scene, such as shaving in the bathroom, getting undressed in the high school gym locker room, or a place where you have lived—a house, a kitchen, a closet, a bedroom, a familiar store or church or school.

I have used a variation of this exercise as a "teaching exercise," to demonstrate the value of writing about what we know and to stimulate discussion after we write. It worked particularly well when a new woman who had lived for many years in China as the wife of a member of the United States Foreign Service joined my workshop. No one in the workshop knew this fact but me. Without any previous announcement to Sherry, I asked the workshop members to write for just five minutes a description of a street market in China. They howled in dismay, but I teased them into trying it—just for five minutes. Then I had us all read our descriptions (my own included) and when we were finished, I asked which of us had really been to China. There was no doubt. Everyone in the room had written awkward, stereotyped images of naked chickens hanging upside down in shop windows and lacquered dishes like the ones we had seen in Chinatowns in the United States. Only Sherry's description was rich, colorful, and surprising, full of Chinese words and images, the scents and sounds of a street market.

Then we all talked about the fact that each of us comes from a place of intricate, interesting detail, if we will just write it so others can see, taste, smell, touch it.

The example that follows was written in a workshop by Sharleen Kapp. It is about a place where she lived for several years:

THE SUBJECT IS FLIES

The subject is flies, and dry dust blowing across the crusted earth—its surface crackling open like a large yawning mouth hungry for moisture.

The subject is babies with stomachs swollen—mud caked, crouching down to poke at the bursting, baking lizard—it, too, packed in mud.

The subject is leather thongs, and spear throwers, and billabongs, and brown skins and black, pink freckles, deep browed foreheads and loneliness.

The subject is Dreamtime, the source of all understanding; a direct connection to God (pale skinned flying man), a Dreamtime journey with the hammer thrower.

They gather together before the rainy season and create strange music, throaty lingering passages that travel down seven foot long horns, carved wooden instruments—treasured—sacred, passed from father to son.

The men gather in the evening to share rude jokes and join in the games, the rabbit kill.

The women, blond curls or black, thin breasts loose, long sinewy muscles, balance the youngest child on one hip, standing by the one hut, outback trading post.

Dusty children, boys and girls, dancing around the edges, chewing loudly on wichity grubs, happy. They take their places at the fire waiting for the lizard to burst, hot and juicy out of its mud blanket.

The men rest their instruments and talk slowly, gutturally. The subject is flies.

Exercise: Taste

Offer bite-sized pieces of something to eat and see what this food for thought stimulates. I have used thin slices of lemon; a loaf of uncut, fresh home-made bread from which workshop participants broke off bite-sized pieces; ripe cherries; strawberries; slices of raw carrot, apple, and so on.

In my workshop at the Graduate Theological Union a young writer named Ali Hall wrote a prose poem—or perhaps it was a recipe for a brilliant cookbook! Here is the closing portion:

HERE

Here. This is how you do it . . .
. . . And if you pick the raspberries yourself, try and get there when god does, just before the birds and the sun, when the berry kernels' hair stands out and the skins are strong enough to hold as many dew drops as your tenderly grasp-ing fingers. Also, take enough to freeze for later. When you mix some sugar with your berries, check and see if they are as sweet as yesterday's, listen as you taste, one-two-three, and if the sweet has pleased its way off your tongue, they're probably just about right. Remember, you've got the cream cheese trick on your side. And sometimes when you scrape it all into a pan you like for bubbling and bursting the berries around the golden pads of dough, its got the tum-tump-tumping of a Bach oboe concerto. But only sometimes.

Exercise: Ransom Note

Kathryn Dunn suggested that her Amherst workshop members begin with the discovery of a ransom note. An exercise like this one will be an utter puzzlement to some writers, but some will have great fun with it, and everyone knows they may ignore a suggestion if they prefer to write something else.

Here's what Don Fisher wrote that evening:

RANSOM NOTES

Poems like ransom notes
lie around my apartment.
One of them has my cat
says revise
or I'll never see her again.
Suggests I start with the fifth stanza.

Another one's holding my mail
until I make the metaphor work
and chuck the third stanza all together.

The one about my mom
now that's a pickle
but, the thing is
I want my Cuisinart back.
I need it to make Pesto.

They're all around me
I can't take a leak
without being forced
to send something to Ploughshares
or the Georgia Review.

I miss my cat
my Cuisinart
my mail
and my privacy
but that one about my mom
that's still a pickle.
Don't know what I'm gonna do there.

Exercise: Biography

Have the group call out answers to several questions about each of two characters, then have everyone write using some or all of the answers. Peggy Gillespie used this exercise in a workshop at the Hampshire County House of Correction. Some of the questions Peggy asked, and answers given by the writers, follows:

Character's name?	Tom-Tom	Amanda S.
Place of residence?	Albuquerque	Maine
Pet?	piranha	cat
Favorite item of clothing?	cardigan	spandex
Strangest item of clothing?	elevator shoes	fake fur
Hates?	electric can openers	false teeth
Favorite food?	pork fried rice	Oreos
Religion?	Hindu	Jehovah's Witness
Collects?	old cars	beer can tops

This exercise is fun for a group and is especially good for evoking humorous writing. Almost always there is surprise and laughter as people share the many different ways a single image has been used. And often a writer goes on to develop a piece into a successful short story.

James Gryszan, a member of Peggy's workshop, wrote an imaginative, jazzy piece in response to the images he and other writers had called out, from which the following is excerpted:

It was an acrid and hot day. A dust storm was developing out in the suburbs of the New Mexican town of Albuquerque. Tom-Tom had to interrupt Jack's game to feed the piranha school. The tank was aburst with clicking, hungry man eaters. Tom-Tom said he was a Hindu. No meat for him. But to stay in touch with the compromises of reality's many swinging doors, he enjoyed the devouring of meat flesh substitutes.

He had an idea. He would get dressed and go to the Hippy Shoppe Cafe and read some poetry. Getting dressed in his cardigan sweater and elevator shoes and obsessively clean machine, his 1952 Sunbeam-Air amphibian vehicle. Out here in the desert it doesn't rust, he said. Yes-sir-ree. There he was stemming a proud stance and a glint of amusement in his eye. He arrived downtown.

First thing through the door. All the Mothers of any kind of invention were all gathered in one. He was on top of the list. He sat down at a table, ordered from the waitress pork fried rice and a copy of Along the Watchtower by Jehovah. The head hip hop in this place. The Branch Davidians were doing their set poetry reading and then Tom-Tom could sign.

Just then he spotted on the rug beside him a group of girls all dressed in black; top to toe was spandex riddled with holes. She was eating Oreos as she smiled she spoke. Hi, my name is Amanda S. Pleased to meet you Mr. Where you from? Well I'm down from Maine. I saved beer can tops which sponsored my Fish Out Of Water Poetry Series.

Exercise: Dream Image

Images from dreams are already works of art, metaphors for meanings we ourselves often only dimly understand. Begin with an image from a dream, and write freely, letting words and associations come as they will, without imposing any necessity of order.

An anonymous writer in my workshop in Japan wrote the following poem using a dream image.

TO AN UNBORN CHILD

I have never dreamed of you
except in my dreams.

So many unspoken words ring
like noisy bells in my silence:

"Sorry, I have no intention to marry."
"I have to finish college."
"I've got to get myself a job."
"I want to go to grad school."
"I need a career."
"Oh, I hate my husband."

After all these years of
bleeding in vain,
you appeared in a dream one night.
I am not sorry and I won't be
sorry for not seeing you in person.
But you may stay in my dreams as a
guarding angel,
if you want to.

Exercise: The Sense of Touch

Write in response to something that has a characteristic texture. I have used cotton balls, sandpaper, modeling clay, pieces of silk cloth, samples of Braille, chestnut burrs, cockle burrs, smooth stones, and other things. Have writers close their eyes, then give the object into their hands and ask them to allow themselves to experience the sense of touch without looking, before they begin to write.

I have heard of writing groups that put people in pairs and have them close their eyes and touch one another's hands or face, then write a description of the other person. I myself have not used this exercise. I think this kind of thing should not be attempted unless a group agrees to try it. Keeping your group safe, keeping boundaries clear, is the workshop leader's responsibility. Perhaps the reason I have not tried it in my workshops is my own sense that it would not be comfortable for me.

Exercise: Writing Directly to Someone

Write in your most personal voice, directly to someone. Perhaps the person to whom you write is no longer in your life. Or maybe, like Emily Dickinson, you could pour your heart out on paper to the person who lives next door to you. The Psalmist in Hebrew scripture wrote many of his psalms as personal addresses to God. Many poets write in second person to a named or unnamed "you." "Call me Ishmael" at the beginning of *Moby Dick* makes it one long personal letter from the narrator to the reader. Direct address is one of the most powerful forms of writing.

The following poem is one I wrote in a workshop that I was leading in my home in Amherst.

PERSONAL ADDRESS

To you only I speak,
although you are forever
changing names, places
of residence, appearance,
affect. Reputation.

When I was a child
you hovered in the rafters
of the tabernacle, above
the visiting evangelist's head.
My mother said I should repent,
and so I did. Of what,
I have forgotten. I was
five years old. I do remember
how the tree, under which she knelt
and prayed with me for my salvation,
bore a single peach that year:
the hard, green bud of it. How
all the summer long I watched it grow.

There was something that I asked of you
in that worn-out orchard.
Although I don't remember what it was
I asked, I do know
I took the peach for answer.

Exercise: Daily News

So much is coming at us through the media that stirs us to pity or delight, anger or laughter—and all of that is fodder for the writing animal in us to chew upon. Write in response to an item from the news, police reports, personal ads, swap columns, television.

Recently, in our town, which is home to three colleges, there was an item in the newspaper with the headline "Mother Climbs in Dorm Window." A national paper carried the news "Man Keeps Dead Parents in Attic." Headlines like that are begging to have fiction written in response. A retired doctor in my workshop wrote a beautiful story based on that headline, in which a gentle but strange man keeps his parents' bodies, and the family doctor and police find a way to take them from him while preserving his dignity. Just think of what might unfold from this want ad that appeared recently in our local paper: "Sadie the Cleaning Lady, call

Mrs. Finch." Or this notice taped to a telephone pole near the center of town: "BILL! WE KNOW YOU TOOK IT. PLEASE! RETURN IT NOW! WE WON'T GO TO THE POLICE! IT IS AN HEIRLOOM! PLEASE, BILL!"

Exercise: The Fearful Scene

Write a scene using fear that you have felt. You may give the fear to a character, or write in first person, autobiographically. Make the details so clear, so concrete, your reader will feel the same fear. In this example, Dee DeGeiso wrote a memory that she had "carried around in her head for thirty-two years." Dee is a playwright who helps all of us in the workshop think about good dialogue. This piece is the powerful beginning of what may become a short story.

Everyone got quiet when the boy walked down the street. He was about fourteen years old, wore a Brooklyn Dodgers baseball jacket and carried a navy blue briefcase. He was black, a colored boy, probably from down below 18th Avenue.

"What's that coon doing here?"

It was a hot August night, sunset. A gang of kids of all ages was hanging out on the Costellos' porch. The older boys were smoking cigarettes, the younger ones were sucking Popsicles. Darlene and Rae-Anne sat on the top step polishing their nails.

"Hey, jungle-bunny, where d'ya think you're going?"

The boy stiffened slightly but kept his gaze straight ahead. He increased his pace but didn't run.

"Hey boy, didn't you hear me? Where the hell d'ya think you're going? Wise-guy nigger. Aren't you gonna answer?"

"Let's go after him."

Billy, Swaf and Johnny T. stubbed out their cigarettes and slowly moved toward the boy.

"Leave him alone. He's probably just cutting through."

"Pipe down, Rae-Rae. You want him messing around your house when you're sleeping?

"Maybe he's lost."

"Well, we'll just help him find his way, won't we?"

"Need a little push, boy?"

The boy started to run then, slipped slightly, then regained his balance and took off at full speed toward the brook at the end of the street.

"Let's get him."

The younger kids cheered as Billy, Swaf and Johnny T. began the chase.

"What are they gonna do to him? Billy has a knife."

"Yeah. And brass knuckles too."

"He didn't look dangerous to me."

"Yeah. Well, I guess we can't have them coming around here."

Rae-Anne and Darlene looked down the street but the boys were out of sight. Mr. G. called out from his upstairs window, "I hope they get him. We don't need no niggers around here. They'll teach him a lesson. You girls oughta go inside. It's getting late." And he was gone.

"Rae-Anne, let's go down there."

"I'm not going anywhere."

"He may need help."

"Are you crazy?"

"They could kill him."

"They'll just beat him up. They'll kill *us* if we show up. I'm going in. Wanna come?"

"No. I'm gonna let my nails dry first."

The younger kids had drifted across the street and Darlene was alone on the porch. She wondered what was in the boy's briefcase. A composition pad. A pencil box. A large soap eraser. Maybe some ballpoint pens. He liked the Dodgers. Her father said the Dodgers were bums. What did his father say? She had been taught to stay away from the colored, but was never given a reason. Her mother told her never to look at them, to encourage them. They lived in dirty houses on dirty streets, drank too much and didn't work. Except for some of the women who were maids for the rich Jews on Mount Vernon Place. Why did he have to come here? He must have been scared. Did he think he could just sneak by? What were they doing to him? Darlene had been Billy's victim since she was five. Swaf's too. They had thrown lit matches at her feet, pushed her face into the snow, bumped her too hard when she was roller-skating. And she was white. And a girl. What were they doing to him?

She decided to go down to the brook. It was almost completely dark. She had never gone down to the brook in the dark.

Exercise: Something You Know by Heart

Take a text that you know by heart—the words to an old song or a fragment of liturgy from your religious tradition, and use it to start your writing. You might use fragments of it throughout a piece, allowing it to be a kind of refrain. You might begin with the first words of a verse and end with the last words, with your own images interwoven between lines of the song or the liturgy.

Or you might give the words you know by heart and then write your own free translation of them, as in this powerful translation by Sue Swartz of my Indiana workshop:

This is the first full paragraph of the Sh'ma, a central prayer in Jewish liturgy:

V'ahavta Et Adonai Elohecha b'chol l'vav-cha u-v'chol naf'shecha u-v'chol m'odecha.

V'hayu ha devarim ha'elah asher anochi m'tzav-echa hayom al l'vavecha.

V'chinantam l'vanecha v'dibarta bam, b'shivitcha b'veytecha u-v'lechtecha va-derech

U-v'shochbecha u-v'kumecha. U-k'shartam l'ot al yadecha v'hayu l'totafot bain eynecha. U-k'tavtam al mezuzot beytecha u-vi'sha'arecha.

And you shall love the Lord, your God, with all your heart, with all your soul, with everything you have. Take these words that I command you this day to heart. Teach them diligently to your children. Speak of them when you sit inside your house or walk upon the way, when you lie down and when you rise. Bind them as a sign upon your hand, and keep them set between your eyes. Inscribe them on the door posts of your house and on your gates.

Here is Sue's free translation:

You shall love the Breath of the universe, that which unifies all creation, the Unknowable, Always-Present One, with each beat of your heart, with each rise and fall of your chest, when your belly is full and when your belly is empty, with every muscle that contracts and expands, with your consciousness and your dreams, your rational and your animal, your blood and craving and anger. Hear the sound of these words spoken by the Breath of the Universe. Hear and envision and taste the lightning crackle, the sound of creation, and know that there is no other truth, no other reality. Do not hold them tight to your heart, but live them. Live them in your words and in your sighs, in the way you hold your children and in the way you hold a stranger. Repeat them to your children in all you do until they are as solid as stone, inescapable as death. Your children will know when you really mean them. Take these words, these pieces of connectivity, and keep them with you always: when you are home and no one is there as witness, when you change diapers and talk to teachers, when you go to little league and when you iron clothes. Take them with you out into the world, into each interaction, every time you shake a hand and buy your groceries, rush to a meeting and greet a friend. Let them be with you in your open-eyed morning and in your 3 A.M. nightmares, when there is dawn and dusk, when you are moving and when you are resting, when there is energy and when there is exhaustion. Wrap them in your hands, in the very marrow and tendons so that every object you touch bears their imprint, so that the poetry you create bears their seal. Bind them between your eyes and you will see the world as it is: broken and holy both, awaiting human touch, everything equally perfect, nothing left out. Inscribe them on your door posts, in the public places, on the boundaries and in the corners. Write them on your gates to remind yourself and to comfort the stranger with My words: be now a nation of priests, of those who delight in God.

Exercise: The Absolute Relative

Write about a family member—one of those stories that is repeated when the clan gathers. Every family has legends, tales of adventure and/or horror. It is a rich source for the short story writer. Variations on this exercise include writing about a family event: birthday party, picnic, funeral, anniversary. Cynthia Kennison has taken prestigious prizes and awards both in the short story and as a playwright. She leads a workshop in Worcester, Massachusetts. This is one of her family stories that she swears is true!

A FATAL ATTRACTION

Mosquitoes will hate this smell. We light the citronella candles on the picnic table, and mosquitoes will fly away and break their stingers on the black birch trees and fall onto the floor of the forest. The candles smell good to us. Really. Comforting, like something you rub onto pulled muscles. Only you don't have to put any onto yourself, and that is very important.

My Uncle Randall still attracts moths in the summer. They fly out of the evening air, indoors or outdoors, into his hair, his ears, up his sleeves, his shorts. Sometimes in the afternoon, when he carries the *New York Times* from his cottage to my father's, when the odor of the hemlock needles he walks on rises and surrounds him like Christmas, my uncle arrives with a white moth or two clapping slowly on his white crew-cut.

It was in the *New York Times* he read about eradicating gypsy moths in a way that wouldn't hurt the environment. The idea was to keep them from mating with each other, to decrease their numbers through birth control. My uncle wants to do the most harmless thing, always.

My aunt and uncle came up from New Jersey for the summer with a crate of little golden plastic cages that looked like lanterns. They were sex traps. Uncle Randall assembled these traps before he hung them in the branches of the hemlocks, the spindly oaks, the white birches whose silver leaves trembled like moths flocking. He had to place in each trap a receptacle of a potent potion. The potion's job was to mislead every male gypsy moth in the forest to believe he would mate with a trap. Instead, of course, he used up his sexual energy, and that was that in the procreation game for him.

My uncle, on a short wooden ladder, hung his sex traps and climbed down and waited. The first swarms of moths beat themselves to death—or ecstasy, we couldn't tell—in the traps. My uncle rubbed his hands with glee and thumbed his nose while my father wrapped tree trunks with electrician's tape and watched caterpillars climb to the cottage eaves. The moths loved my uncle's potion.

The moths also loved my uncle. They still love him. The instructions on the trap crate said you mustn't touch the sex potion. Even a tiny drop on your skin, anywhere on you, will be absorbed into your own chemistry, your soul maybe, and never leave. You will forever attract moths. Not only gypsy moths, they are gone for now. But other kinds.

"You won't need to mark my grave," Uncle Randall tells my aunt. "Save the money. Just look for moths diving for my spot in the earth."

Exercise: Face-to-Face with an Animal

Close your eyes and imagine yourself face-to-face with an animal. Then write what you saw in your inner eye.

Brooke Sullivan wrote the following poem in response to this suggestion.

> God watches as each sparrow falls
> and they do, myriads of them,
> from the cold; frozen;
> clenched in a cat's jaw,
> flickering, fighting to stay alive.
> They are in the abandoned barn,
> above the cornice down the street.
>
> This fall as all color left the fields
> the leaves fell, sumac standing
> like soldiers along the ridges
> guarding the slope up from the river.
> Little birds: chickadees, tanagers,
> lit on the sumac, raced
> around the wounded oak torn by lightning
> in the tangled yard of the abandoned barn.
>
> What I mean to say is that
> there is no stopping the fall.
> Swift and sad
> and a prickly cold over the legs and arms
> as birds are discovered,
> fallen, gray tufts of down
> matted in the cracked bones
> washed up with the wooden debris
> littering the river bank.
>
> And in the fields, ridged
> and plowed away for winter, the dog
> hunts in the mud clumps for remains
> of birds.

VARIATION: WORK ON AN UNRESOLVED RELATIONSHIP

This suggestion also puts you face-to-face with an animal, but the intent is personal self-discovery. It is from Ira Progoff, whose books and workshops on keeping a journal have been helpful to many writers.

Think of someone with whom you have an unresolved relationship. Imagine that person as an animal, taking the first animal that comes to mind. Now imagine yourself as an animal, again taking the first animal that comes to mind. Imagine yourself moving through a forest. You come to a clearing, and in the clearing is the other animal. Let the two animals approach one another. They may speak, or not. Write what happens.

Exercise: Magical Realist

Write without making "sense" in the usual way.

This is a wonderful exercise for springing the imagination out of its usual tracks. Try writing a paragraph of nonsense, making the second half of each sentence *not fit* the first half in its meaning. When you have finished the paragraph (if you are leading a group, let them write nonsense for three to five minutes), begin writing in your usual way, but allow something impossible (maybe magical) to happen in the midst of realistic narration. Remember that John Gardner said the single most important quality of great fiction is an element of "strangeness." The piece that follows was written in workshop by Jim Eagan:

> Seth stabbed the floor with his cane, trying to maintain balance on his wobbly old shanks. He careened across the room toward the third story plate glass window, unable to slow his momentum. There was a deafening crash as he hit the glass with his cane-side shoulder. He was airborne, dropping at an ever-increasing speed.
>
> He opened his eyes and closed them immediately. In that moment he glimpsed the shattered glass suspended like crystals in the air all around him. He saw the street coming up to meet him. When he closed his eyes he saw his father standing before him, arms outstretched, with a glow of light around him. In the light that surrounded his father, Seth saw shadows of other people; they seemed familiar in some way, although he couldn't see them clearly.
>
> "No, no," a loud voice shouted in his head, "I can fly. Don't you know I can fly?" He tightened the muscles all over his back and began to breathe deeply. Flinging his cane away he raised his arms like giant wings that caught the evening sun and shot a crystal clear blast of white light into the eyes of the people in the street below.
>
> They covered their eyes for a moment and when they looked again the street was strewn with shattered glass. An old man's broken cane lay against the curb stone and three magnificent, silver tipped feathers drifted softly to the ground.

VARIATIONS ON THIS EXERCISE

If you are using this exercise in a group, tell your writers that they are going to "mess with" what they write next, and so you suggest they write something they won't mind changing. (In other words, you don't want the deepest self-revelation, in case changing it would be upsetting.) Have them write for ten minutes on paper that you pass out. Tell them to write on only one side of the page. Use as a trigger some pictures or objects, or four short quotes that include one or two serious lines and a potentially funny one, like "Be sure to choose firm, hard cucumbers . . ." (Angie Leydon) or "Her nipples want to drive all night to Alabama." (Ellen Doré Watson).

When they have finished writing, give each person a page of colored construction paper, a bottle of glue and a pair of scissors. Have them cut their sentences apart and arrange them out of order on the page of construction paper, to make a poem. They may use phrases or complete sentences, but may not write anything new. If they balk, read aloud an abstract poem by James Tate and one by Charles Simic, and remind them that both authors won Pulitzer prizes for poems that do not always follow linear patterns of thought.

"Use Random Words" and "The Scramble"(Part I, Chapter 8) are also valuable exercises to help writers in workshops break out of habitual ways of writing.

Exercise: Giving or Receiving Advice

Write some advice, or write about receiving it. Heather Davis wrote this beautiful poem in my women's workshop in Amherst.

ADVICE

Save your coins. Know how to work a hammer,
a shovel, a pen. Know which way is north.

Don't offer explanations. Possible and impossible
are both ways of saying "today".

Keep extra blankets for travelers. Feel the shape
of words in your hand, follow them

to your tongue, and watch as the other hears them.
Notice twigs and feathers, the width of the moon.

Resist when necessary. Neither blue jay, nor beetle,
nor bellowing bullfrog would offer anything less

though they know nothing of war. Remember
what you already know. Remember where

you have seen this before. Hold your children.
In time they will learn, but for now

be in your own shoes. It's o.k.
if everyone sees it, your sure heart scared to death,

your unsure heart loving again and again.

Exercise: Writing What You Don't Know about What You Know

This suggestion comes from Eudora Welty—take a familiar subject and find those aspects that are still unresolved in your mind. Explore those edges, those shadowy places. For many of us who write, it is this exploration of what is not yet fully understood that makes writing so satisfying. We write "what we know and do not know we know," T. S. Eliot said.

Exercise: Writing about Writing

Suggest that everyone write how they are feeling about their writing or about questions that have come up in relation to their work. Once in a while—not more often than once in a ten-week session—it is a good idea to give a group the opportunity to reflect out loud together on their own writing. I do not mean by this an invitation to evaluate the workshop—that is best done one-on-one in private conference. I have tried evaluation discussions in the workshop and have found that people come to workshop to write, and at least some of the writers resent taking time from writing to discuss group dynamics. Problems are best dealt with in private conference with those concerned.

This exercise is for the purpose of talking about writing and our experience of writing. I give ten minutes of writing time, then have each writer read or talk from written notes, without response. This allows everyone to have equal "floor time." I take notes to be certain that we come back to something each person has said before we open a general discussion. This exercise is a good way to include those persons who tend to be shy about sharing their questions or problems with writing in the group. Often just hearing that others are struggling gives heart to the timid.

Sometimes one of the writers in a group will write something that opens concerns for everyone and gives the leader an opportunity to teach. Sarah Browning raises a very difficult question for writers (below). After she read, the workshop responded with an excellent discussion about personal and political writing. When this happens, it is good to relinquish your planned agenda and allow the group to take its time in examining a question of craft or conscience. To assist our discussion on this occasion, I introduced Carolyn Forché's overtly political poem "The Colonel" and Grace Paley's subtly political two-and-a-half-page story "A Man Told Me the Story of His Life." Here is Sarah's piece, written in response to my inviting workshop members to write for ten minutes on how they are feeling about their writing, or suggestions they may have.

> Maybe this exercise will work for me another time. Sometimes when I'm distracted and I force myself to focus on the exercise I do come through the other side to an interesting piece of writing. But tonight I'm cluttered. I'm not receptive.
>
> I came home and read the *Boston Globe* and talked about the defense budget with Tom. I'm making arguments in my head about the possibility of further cuts in the military.
>
> I wonder how possible it is to write about that kind of rage. Sometimes my rage at injustice in the world absolutely consumes me. I am physically torn to pieces. I can't even now seem to say what happens to me when I think of women living on welfare checks of $375 a month.
>
> Why is it simple to write about suffering on a personal level—or rather about the pain one has experienced from others—but not about the pain one experiences at knowing about systemic injustice? Is it that the pain people inflict on each other is always complicated? That there are ambiguities? Is it that only writing about specific, personal experiences, even if they are not one's own, is the only kind that "works"?

Exercise: Writing a Response to Another Writer

Frequently, reading a good story or poem will stir in your mind a response, a desire to "talk back" to the author. Those responses can be excellent work of their own. I wrote a poem arguing with Richard Hugo. It appeared in a literary journal and then in my book of poems, *Long Way*

Home. In Sue Walker's book *Blood Must Bear Your Name,* the poem "Hammering Virgins: The Dream of Female Signs in James Dickey's (Un)Broken Hungering" is addressed to Dickey. The first line is two words: "Listen, Jim, . . ."

The poem that follows was written in my women's workshop by Deb Pond, to Rumi, a twelfth century Sufi poet whose mystical poems are loved by many people.

RUMI, MY LOVE

Rumi, my love,
(may I call you that?)
I long for your embrace.
You would look undaunted
at my same coat, even my
lonely meditation cushion—

past all my failings;
I know this. And I would
not mind your vernacular
nor be jealous of your 3
friends. No, I would let
you lie underground, the

sun and wind blowing across,
free of walls and visitation.
And I would have watched
carefully and listened perfectly

But what about the dance?

Exercise: Writing in the Style of Another Writer

In the prose poem that follows, Sarah Kavanagh writes a response to Virginia Woolf's novel *To the Lighthouse*. She captures beautifully the cadence of Woolf's prose, but it is, after all, Kavanagh's voice, and her vision.

Sixteen years old, reading a paperback *To the Lighthouse*, I suddenly knew that I existed in this world: "because she knows me, because Virginia Woolf somehow knows me." But turning the page I realized that, no, she didn't know me; she was trying to know herself.

And there we were, Virginia and I, in our own little boats, floating on top of a sea of reality, drinking the water as it leaked into our boat, gurgling up reality page after page. And looking around, I saw boats about to be launched, boats underneath me, sinking slowly to the bottom, filled with mirrors of myself and Virginia trying desperately to drink as much reality as we could before it consumed us. And those others were tied to me, and I was tied to Virginia, we were a web of little boats, shells filled with history. Each one waiting to be consumed by reality, drift to the bottom of the ocean, and be brought back out to shore by the tide where our driftwood lives are made again into another boat, into another body waiting to consume as much reality as she can until she becomes so heavy that she sinks to the bottom, to be spat back up again and again and again.

And writing now, I am collecting this water, these words, in my hands. I am watching it slip through my fingers, but here in my palm a drop remains, and I will keep still enough to carry it to you. I am trying to let you see this vast ocean, this eternal cycle. But how can a drop of water help you to understand the ocean? Take it, hold it in your palm and feel it on your skin. And know that at least since you can feel it, and I can feel it, that we are both alive. And for a moment, stop desperately trying to guzzle up the ocean, and notice a drop of water. And maybe when we look up, we will see a million boats, a million bodies floating on a drop of water, in the palm of Virginia, in the palm of Virginia, in the palm of Virginia.

Exercise: Writing in Answer to Another Writer

Elise Turner, who has led workshops in New Mexico for various populations, writes a response to a poem by Pablo Neruda:

EVOCATIONS ON READING NERUDA'S *ODA AL DICCIONARIO*

capsula
hueca, esperando aceite o ambrosia . . .
storage
a hollow word, waiting for olive oil or ambrosia . . .
Ambrosia in pewter bowls in dark inns
        on sea coasts centuries ago
Graceful lamps of brass holding oil
        to burn when dusk turns to dark
Ox in a door frame blocking
        view to the next room, opening
        out into pages,
        its spine the binding, its blood the script—
                but not dying with the spilling
        or the syllabary, but living.

In the beginning was the word,
now not the void and no longer the silence
    but beauty in bees swarming
    to their hives, drawn deep in
    to spin tendrils of golden liquid,
to store white comb.

No longer the silence but the
 chants of men rising through them
  from the earth to praise stars and flint,
 songs of women to drive the dark away,

  comfort small children snugged up
      against their bodies
and protect ones nearby tracing ochre lines
 on soft earth floors in sunlight filtering through
 openings in shelters of saplings and hides.

One who brings the gem from the dark depths
places it in my mouth, between front teeth, gently . . .
    Who are you?
    and should I
carefully,
 slowly,
with a forefinger and thumb,
take the gem from my mouth . . .

  and place it . . . where?

Your gift an offering
for which I find no place.
What place to match its beauty?
What place could be to hold its crystal color
    its eons of life condensed
    to a vibration in the palm
    of a wondering hand?

Who are you who finds your
    form in the dictionaries of
        Spain or Pakistan
            Indochina and Swaziland?
And are you there among
    the peoples who write no lines
    but preserve their lineage in
     memory

 body
        story
  song?

Exercise: A Series of Images

Usually I give three at a time: "A cracked mirror, winter ice, a lightbulb." "A lollipop, a dirty comb, a fishhook." "A wild flower, a sidewalk, a doorknob." Workshop members are free to use only one, two, or all three images in their writing.

VARIATIONS ON THIS EXERCISE

If you are writing alone, allow yourself to be surprised by images. Get ready to write, then open a magazine or book of pictures and take at random objects that you see: a man's scarf, an apple, a child.

In a workshop, ask the participants to provide images. I give people three minutes, ask them to list at least ten images, then have individuals call the images out at random, inviting others to write down any that are of interest. People then choose one or more images and write.

Another idea: Have a number of images written on three-by-five cards or slips of paper and draw one from the container when you want to write; in a group, allow writers to choose three without reading them first.

Exercise: Writing to an Imaginary Relative

Sue Walker, a professor of English at the University of South Alabama, began to consider searching for her birth family. She invented this exercise by writing a series of poems to an imaginary brother. Those poems and two long, quite amazing poems, became her book, *Blood Must Bear Your Name.* Here is one of her poems to Martin:

YOU AIN'T JESUS, BROTHER

Dear Martin,

You ain't Jesus,
and you ain't Elvis either.
You're a veritable hound-dog.
It's cruel calling my house near midnight,
and when my husband answers
saying you want to speak
to your sister Sue.
I hadn't told him about you.

Who in the Jesus H. Christ
is this Martin guy, he asks,
and what am I supposed to say to that?
Answer he's some freak from Graceland
who wears blue jeans and suede shoes,
a boy-man who walked into my life
before Christmas sucking on wafers,
and drinking Gallo wine.
You've blown it, bro;
now I have to try and explain how
some creep with mutton-chop sideburns
straddling both sides of the Mason-Dixon line
rode your mama and mine. A family
is more than the blood in one's veins,

but I didn't want my husband
to know about the man you call
father and all that rock and roll.

Exercise: The Uses of the Ordinary

Read a nursery rhyme, a recipe, a school yard chant, or a set of directions
from one place to another, an advertisement, or a provocative want-ad or
item from the personals column or police report in the newspaper to get
the writing started. In my opinion, reading the material aloud (unless it is
a visual stimulus, like a map) is better than handing it out, because images move across the listener's mind and open images that are already
there. The printed word has a finality about it that is not quite so evoca-
tive. (However, working alone at my writing, I have often dipped at random into *Pilgrim at Tinker Creek* and allowed whatever words my finger
touched to act as a trigger for my writing.)

Exercise: An Animal Speaks

Write in the voice of an animal. Perhaps you will choose an animal you
know very well, or one that you see in a picture and do not know at all.
    In the poem that follows, Peggy Reber writes in the voice of an animal
she lives with and talks to and listens to, every day.

I DREAM, THEREFORE I AM

I hear rustles and whispers.
I hear the slow drip of gravy
and the squirrel raising its eyebrow.
I hear the humans thinking,
always thinking, about how many
tax deductions they'll make this year,
about wars in distant places and
whether to buy a new washing machine
or have the roof re-shingled.

I wonder where it gets them,
all that thinking. Pretty useless, I think,
unless she's thinking about what
she'll make for dinner.

I mean, wouldn't they rather be lolling,
napping, dreaming, even snoring,
because being alive is good
and sleeping is best, because then
you are your deep true self,
whole and shining,
and the world spreads its teeming fields
and sweet green woods before you like a giant menu.
So many scents! So many scampering creatures!
A thousand luscious things to roll in!
One ecstasy opens to the next and the next and the next!
World without end!

They laugh when they hear me yipping in my sleep.
What do they know?
They're always only thinking.

Exercise: Stream of Consciousness

Sometimes it is good to write without any particular external stimulus. Many of us do this in our solitary writing as a way of getting started (priming the pump!) or as the way to work on a manuscript. If you are leading a workshop, it is sometimes helpful to allow your writers to have a "warm-up" by allowing a free flow of images onto the page before you offer an exercise. This is often called "free writing" and is highly recommended by Dorothea Brande, Peter Elbow, Natalie Goldberg, Julia Cameron, and me! Without stopping, write everything that comes to your mind. Let it be incomplete sentences, fragments, full sentences, whatever. Julia Cameron, a delightfully funny writer, says, "You simply move your hand across the page while writing down whatever comes to mind: 'Dad's cough is getting worse . . . I forgot to buy Kitty Litter . . . I don't like how things went in yesterday's meeting . . .'"

A therapist in my workshop informed me recently that we each have 70,000 thoughts a day. What a steady stream of material for writing!

During a workshop Jennifer Bryan, a psychologist, wrote this moving response to her work life. The absence of periods and the breathless pace communicates the intensity of the experience as well as the sense of an ocean of human need in which the doctor is trying to steer her own course.

Rape, she's fifteen I didn't ask about her ethnicity or culture she's so different from me yet I know her I know her see her did she wear that orange lipstick for me, is her hair always so neat and clothes so clean or did she fuss over herself for me for coming to the doctor for talking about the dirty rape the horrible touching and tearing and lies he told, did she bring a ten year old friend because she knew how white I'd be, how tall, how rich-looking and smart-sounding, how my heels would click click on the hospital tile as we walked to my office, the ten year old who she's looking after who she wanted to have wait when her own sister wouldn't, when her grandmother wouldn't come at all, and my needing a signature on the forms and my needing the insurance card and grandmother's got no phone and Ladeeta's just fifteen and the man was forty-five and she cried when she told me but I didn't start there because I knew how it would hurt and so she told me other things about her father dying and it was five years ago and she went to live with her grandmother because her father said that would be best, Ladeeta said my mother do drugs and he didn't trust her, but grandmother was good and she took care of Ladeeta and her father both because the father got sick and stayed at home and went to the hospital and stayed in the hospital and died at home because he got the sickness and I said the word, not like a question—AIDS—and she nodded and the tears were there before we even got to the man to the neighbor who said he was taking her and Treneese to eat out but he lied and it was a bar in Chicopee and Ladeeta said we was minors; I knew not to be at no such place, and I've got a history to gather a thorough history presenting problem psychosocial family school medical previous psych contacts suicidal homicidal Axis I Axis II Axis III Axis IV Axis V, she was thirty minutes late, I'd almost gone home and then she was there and the twenty year old sister who didn't want to stay and the ten year old friend and no grandmother to sign the papers and the secretary asked me do you still want to see her and I said yes even though a place inside had called out no, no I do not want to hear this story, I do not want to sit across from dark Ladeeta who is so beautiful and too grown up and awkward and graceful both, I don't want to hear how he drove to the woods and locked all the doors and told her she'd like it and told her she'd be feeling good, like a woman and I want to lift up my pen right here and stop the writing of this story and stop the telling and stop the feeling of fire and sickness in my gut that no pen can douse no telling can fully cure no sleeping will erase because Ladeeta is fifteen and he hurt her and he gave her diseases more than one and maybe the one that killed her father I can say the name, I can say it—AIDS—and Ladeeta, she can't read, she told me that, she can't read, had such a hard time in school always something taking her mind from the books or the sound of the teacher's voice and she doesn't want to go back to the grandmother's house where she's lived since her father died in 1987, she lives with her sister, the one who didn't stay because she had a baby to go to, and Ladeeta is afraid now of grandmother's house because he is a neighbor almost across the street and he said he'd kill her if she told and even though the police came and picked him up she thinks he will be back, he got big drug money to pay that jail bail, and his wife say, watch your back you asked for it, and so Ladeeta can't read and she wants a better life and her grandmother says she must go to school to have a better life and since February Ladeeta goes to school and stays at her sister's house and she doesn't go out and hang and she minds the baby washes the clothes and stays inside, keeps the house neat and clean, neat and clean, neat and clean

Exercise: What's Going On

Write a response to world events. It might be something on the evening news, or something you feel strongly about. It might express a political opinion, or just tell the story of some people caught up in a confusing world. The piece that follows was written in my workshop in Amherst, but it has now grown into a short story that is forthcoming in *Carolina Quarterly*. Valerie Leff, the author, teaches creative writing at the University of North Carolina–Ashville.

THE WAY THE WIND IS BLOWING

The phone rings in the afternoon, and it's my mother. She tries to sound cheerful, but she is depressed. She says everyone in New York is depressed. Even uptown. "Every few blocks, there's a funeral. You hear bagpipes, old Irish ballads—those poor firemen!" She says Margie Menuchin broke down twice yesterday at the Bridge table. "You know, her children are in their thirties. They have two friends who were killed, bond traders. Young men—both married with small children." My mother and father spend as much time as possible up in Westchester. They listen to music. They are on a Prokofiev kick. "No wonder we're depressed, right?"

She tells me a story. On the morning of September 11th, the neighbor who lives two houses down kissed his wife goodbye and left for the World

Trade Center. His wife watched the buildings collapse on TV and received no call from her husband. By mid-afternoon, friends and family were gathered in their living room. They made calls to city hospitals, reported him missing. At four o'clock, the husband phoned. "Well, I'm leaving the office now. I'll catch the 4:32 train and see you soon." He had no idea that anything had happened. He was shacked up all day with his mistress in Scarsdale.

Exercise: Dream House

Write the dreams of all the people who are sleeping in a house.

It might be a house where you lived as a child, or it might be the house of a character about whom you are currently writing. Gene Zeiger, who leads workshops in Shelburne, Massachusetts, responded to this exercise by writing the following poem:

> FAMILY
>
> Their daily house is filled with fuss
> over what is solid, with no room left
> for the colored world which sits, lips
> pursed, beyond the far away mountain.
> At night, however, all lips part
> and in the growing darkness
>
> Mother dreams of figurines,
> white China, and damask. An Arabian
> merchant dusts her mahogany and, smiling,
> kisses the red nails of her left hand.
>
> Father dreams of wealthy stallions,
> sleek and brass-belled. On a flat
> vast plain without moon or cloud,
> they pound and pound the shifting earth.
>
> Little sister dreams of blue balloons
> and the biggest one is hers. She picks
> it up and flies to Paris. There she sits
> in a sunlit room where everyone is breathing.
>
> Older sister dreams of jungles
> where she is wild, slim, and tragic.
> Trees gleam with water and she can fly.
> When the prince finds her, she never needs to smile.

The house dreams of animals:
cats stalking wildebeests, birds
preening on chairs. Cups and saucers
shatter to the floor as peacocks
stalk the sodden rubble, move slowly
out to the stunning trees.

Exercise: Sense of Smell

Write in response to a strong odor. When I am leading this exercise for a group of writers, I sometimes use the same odor (a mothball or a dab of Vicks Vaporub, for example) in discarded plastic film containers. These are excellent because you can ask the workshop participants to lift the lid and smell without looking.

At other times, I have a variety of odors in small bottles: spices, motor oil, perfume, sachet, liquor, and so on. There is a certain Thai fish oil that has been preserved underground for years before it is brought to the table— it has a powerful smell that to Western noses suggests decaying animal matter. Excellent for evoking strong memories! Once one of my writers brought in a covered bucket filled with straw from a horse's stall. When she removed the lid, the room filled with a wonderful odor of barn and animal. The sense of smell is said to be the most acute awakener of memories.

Joan Marie Wood leads workshops in Oakland, California. This poem, from her book *Her Voice Is Blackberries,* was written in response to the odor of perfume:

ROSE COLOGNE

No cork on the stopper
Her red glass bottle
with the silver filigree
that she polished polished
Now I'm suspended
in the aroma of her suicide
Perfume of gone-like-that
gone-like-that, O-Rose-
can't-you-bring-her-back-
and-I-will-tell-her-
not-to-do-it

Exercise: Taboo

Write a list of things that you consider taboos in writing—things people don't write about. When I have asked workshop members to do this, they have included such things as incest, aging, gay sex, being poor, being rich, masturbation, unwanted children, unpopular political positions, religious faith that is not currently "cool," and many other topics. After each writer has created a list, we call out ones we are willing to share, and everyone extends their original list. Then we write, using the topic that is hardest for us to write about.

This piece by Sue Swartz surprised me, and taught me. It takes me into an experience—and celebrates the experience—that I have had no way of understanding.

WRITING ABOUT THE TABOO

Here is what the whip feels like: icy tentacles flashing on your skin like sudden sunrise, turning into hot metal pouring across your body like oil, smooth, electrical, hungry; stinging like an army of insects, tender as a baby's kiss, suspended in time until you burst like a thousand bits of glass. Here is what the blindfold feels like: darkness, a cutting off of yourself, a constriction of breath, the knot at the back of your head pressing into its hollow valley. Darkness and then panic that you will never see light, that the world will disappear, will spin on its axis further and further away. But you know this is not real, cannot be real, has never happened before and you relax. You breathe in the silk and the perfume, you hear your lover moving around, circling, picking up an object, contemplating, and you sink into the surrender, glad for the darkness and the suspense. Here is what handcuffs feel like: soft velvet against the inside of your wrists, circling you like a bandage. You are cared for, wrapped up like a gift, and the metal closing around you holds you prisoner and you melt, the connection flowing from one hand to the other, blood leaping across an imaginary highway, fingers on the left sure that they belong to the right, swaddled in a long line of silver, release dangling from the bedpost, from your signal, your secret chosen word.

To be submissive is to have all the power. The power to entice, to seduce, to allow; to be the one who decides to give yourself up in absolute trust to another, to give them the gift of showing just how much they love you, how much they want you. To give them the gift of letting out their hidden side, the side that wants to punish, to inflict, to lash out with leather and wood and metal. Here is what it feels like to be held afterward, the orgasm wrung from your body: like you are a precious jewel whose perfection could only be seen through the revelation of its small flaw, like the favorite child who was punished a bit more than necessary and then given a warm bath with Epsom salts and lavender, like one who has been imprisoned for years and given release on the day scheduled for execution, who is surprised when the warden shows up shuffling his feet and forcing papers into your hands, papers that have been signed at the midnight hour pardoning all your sins, granting you freedom. There is no more fire, no more bending of your will. There is no darkness, no movement, no hunger. The insects are gone and there are only kisses, warm and wet at your throat, your lover's kisses, God's kisses, your lover's whispers, God's whispers. Amen, you say. Amen.

In the chapter on ethical questions in writing I discussed the powerful taboo in the white community against telling or writing any of our personally painful experiences of race. It is important, I think, for the workshop leader to open opportunities for writing about the hardest topics in our society. It can be done subtly, by putting out appropriate pictures or reading something provocative with no specific direction for writing. Or it can be done openly, by naming certain taboos and asking people to write anything they want in response.

Beth Hook wrote the piece that follows after I said that I had never heard a white writer in my workshops write about his or her own personal pain around racism. I did not overtly ask the questions she names, but her piece makes clear how intense are the questions that lie under the surface of this taboo.

You're asking me if I know what it's like to be dark-skinned in this society, if I know what it's like to meet someone like me: white. Have I ever noticed the subtle signs I give off that let you know how much guard to keep up? Are my eyes open? Do I cross the street to avoid passing you by? You're asking me if I can talk comfortably about my reasons for being here. Do I feel comfortable working with people of color? Why am I here?

Can I say it to you without feeling self-conscious, without sounding like a mealy-mouthed do-gooder? Why didn't I join that White Women Against Racism group or insist more strongly that we form one of our own? I want to talk to you honestly, but I hesitate because you might judge me too slow or ignorant. (There's the curtain; I want to run off stage and wrap it around me. No I don't. I stand there certain in myself but uncertain if I can express myself clearly to another.)

This is the most important work there is, the reason for going on. The hope of healing voices too long denied and silenced into permanent retreat. The beginning is hearing someone else say what you would have uttered if you had a voice and felt you were important enough to listen to. It's a slow thaw but something in those words touches you and you feel a warmth somewhere inside. Then more words. And seeing someone who is not you look into your eyes with the recognition of sameness. A wall of clear ice shatters around you. And then breathing. Suddenly you are aware of the sound of your own breathing and though it frightens you at first, soon it becomes reassuring like a lullaby at night and you like the sound of your own breath.

I can't say exactly how it happens but one day you're adding sound to your breath and then music. And that holds you. For a long time. And then another day the sound becomes words and you are speaking, this voice, the one banished to the hinterland, the interior, you're not sure where it comes from. But you instantly claim it as your own.

You ask me why I'm here and I tell you, I wouldn't miss this for anything in the world.

Exercise: The Neighbor

One of my favorite poems is Cheryl Savageau's "Crazy Ol' Baker" in her book *Dirt Road Home*. I sometimes read that poem aloud and invite writers to use an image of a remembered neighbor. This was written by Karen Buchinsky, who leads workshops in a women's prison. I like the fact that I am left with uncomfortable questions at the end of the piece.

THE STORY OF THE CHILD MOLESTER NEXT DOOR

I want to tell you the story of the child molester next door. I want to tell you how we confronted him with sticks and bats, circling him, and drummed him out of town. He left in shame, never to be seen around here again. But that's not the real story. I'll tell you how we all glare at him when he walks by. We stop talking and give him the evil eye, we toss our heads at him and spit on the ground, shaming him, so he stays in the house all day and never comes out until we've gone in, but that's not true either.

The others are too nice. I glare at him and don't say anything. Except yesterday I said something. I had a petition to restore Megan's Law. I knocked on his door and, earnestly, politely, with big innocent eyes, I said, "Fred, I'm collecting signatures." I held the petition out so he could read it, waving the pen right next to it. "We want to restore this law so the public can be informed if there are sex offenders in the neighborhood, so we can protect our children. Would you be interested in signing this," I said, "so we can keep our children safe." I gently waved the pen around, hypnotically I hoped, so he'd grab it, he couldn't help it.

I saw a strange look on his face. He was sure I knew, but if I knew, why would I ask him? If he didn't sign it then he's saying it's okay for child molesters to be in our neighborhood, maybe even right here! Maybe even admitting he is! A small uncomfortable grin, and he took the pen. "Sure, I'll sign it," he said resignedly.

"Thank you," I said, looking at him with my big innocent do-gooder eyes. We were a team now, keeping the neighborhood safe from bad strangers.

Exercise: Freshening a Fragment

Take a small bit of writing—a page or so—from your journal. Or write a straight narrative account of something that happened to you. (Give yourself only five or seven minutes to do this, and write fast, without editing.)

When you have finished, put it aside, and without looking at it, begin again to write the same narrative. *Do not look back!* Allow yourself to say exactly the same words if they come to you, or to change it in any way you wish. After a bit, introduce into the narrative an object that was not there in the first draft, and that was not there in your memory. Make it completely imagined. Go on writing the narrative for a bit, and then introduce a character (again, completely imagined) that wasn't there, and give him or her a significant place in the narrative.

This is fun—and for many people it simply magically erases the big problem of how to break out of literal memory into imagined scenes and characters.

Here's an example, by Hedy Straus, in my workshop in Berkeley, California. Notice that as soon as Hedy begins to imagine, the writing is deepened and enlarged by metaphor.

LITERAL MEMORY, five-minute write:

The cardiologist will come out to talk to you. You can wait out in the waiting room.

I was still breathless from the treadmill, though the treadmill test had ended—been stopped, really, by the nurse. Her look of mild boredom had changed in an instant with a frown and pursing her lips, as she pushed the button on the EKG machine and caused a strip of paper to be printed out. She grabbed the paper and dashed out of the room while the technician stopped the treadmill belt and eased me onto a chair while she deftly pumped up the blood pressure cuff at the same time.

BEGIN AGAIN & INTRODUCE AN IMAGINED OBJECT:

Now I'm outside the waiting room, waiting for the cardiologist to give me the results of my treadmill test. On the table next to my chair there's a Family Circle magazine with a color photo of a chocolate bundt cake, frosted red, white and blue for the July issue. I'm tempted by an article promising "Lose Ten Pounds by Labor Day." Next to the magazine sits a plastic model of a heart. I know it's the exact one we used in my nursing school class—I remember the name Eli Lilly printed on the base. I pick it up and hold it against my hot cheek. The plastic feels cool on my face.

INTRODUCE A FICTIONAL CHARACTER:

When Dr. Stephens appears at my side as suddenly as if he'd surfaced from under water, I startle and drop the heart. It comes apart, the way it was meant to for study. Now he and I are on the floor on our hands and knees together, picking up the pieces. I hand him what I am absurdly proud to remember are the left ventricle and the right atrium. He has the superior vena cava and the aorta in his hand.

"I'm sorry," he begins.

"Oh, no, it's my fault."

"No," he continues, "I mean I'm sorry to have to tell you we found a blockage."

"A blockage?" I look at the heart fragments in our hands and on the floor.

"A blockage. You'll need to come in."

Exercise: Writing about Illness

Sharon Bray leads specialized workshops for cancer survivors, as well as regular writing workshops, in northern California. "I wrote this in Pat's workshop at the Graduate Theological Union in Berkeley," Sharon noted, "just after I had finished radiation therapy for breast cancer. The phrase Pat offered as an exercise was, *the hospital corridor was dimly lit*."

The hospital corridor was dimly lit—or was it? Maybe it was the cast of the yellow walls, making the room eerie and unreal. Any moment now I hoped I would awaken from this yellowed, faded dream.

I turned left into the waiting room, a montage of faces before me: men, women, a teenage girl, a grade-school boy. Some with hair; others without. We were all members of a private club, meeting each day at 3 P.M. We wore the uniforms of anonymity: pale blue hospital gowns, our common bond in the 15 minutes of daily radiation, stilling the invasion of cancer in our bodies.

I sat down slowly and offered a silent prayer of thanks. I would be spared the ordeal of chemotherapy. I self-consciously pulled at the blue gown, closing the opening at my chest. A bald woman across from me smiled knowingly. I nodded and averted my eyes. Maybe if I pinched my arm, maybe then I would awaken. I held a piece of skin between my thumb and forefinger and pressed.

"Ms. Bray?" The cheerful voice jolted me into awareness. Someone was calling my name. I looked up and smiled woodenly. This was no dream. Holding the sides of my blue gown together, I stood and followed her down the yellow corridor.

Exercise: Writing a Ballad

All writers, after all, write alone. When we go home from workshop, when we sit with our note pad at lunch, when we burn the midnight oil writing, we write alone. At least once in each ten week workshop session, I offer an optional take-home exercise. I try to vary the form; for instance, I might hand out Dorothea Brande's chapter "The Practice Story," from *Becoming a Writer*. Another time I hand out take-home "kits" for writing a sonnet, a sestina, a villanelle, or such, as described in the section on writing poems. When I hand out the exercise for a villanelle, I spend a little time talking about iambic pentameter, counting out the stresses in exaggerated form, pointing out how deeply familiar it is to us from Shakespeare and so much of English poetry.

Poet Peter Viereck believes that iambic pentameter is based on the relation of the human heartbeat to the breath. He points out that lifeguards are taught to breathe into the mouth of a person pulled from drowning, one breath for each five heart massages: Five to one. Ta-TUM, ta-TUM, ta-TUM, ta-TUM, ta-TUM. "How Shakespearean of nature!" Viereck laughs during an interview reported by the *Valley Advocate*. "Our very life depends upon this rhythm. Now, knowing this, would you want to be in the hands of a free-verse lifeguard?" Iambic pentameter has five stresses to one line. If you have not been writing in form, it is a good idea to try. Writing a scene for a play, a story that is a mystery or uses magical realism, or a poem in a classic form will stretch you as a writer, deepen you as an artist. We cannot know too much about our art form, and the best way to learn is to try doing what we have never done before.

In response to my "ballad kit" (Miller Williams's definition of ballad form and several ballads, including one by Langston Hughes, one of my own, and the lyric to "Frankie and Johnny"), Carol Foster wrote this ballad:

EVE'S BALLAD

The water-gazer peered and paused—
"You had a son who died?"
Eve blinked, "No, no. No son at all,"
And tried hard not to cry.

She searched and searched to find the truth,
Learned Voudou, science, lies,
What might be known of oak or owl
Or children's open eyes.

There must be exits, answers, choice
In what we don't command:
The things we have that angels crave,
Webs etched inside our hands.

The only time Eve cast a spell,
For passion in her bed,
Her teacher warned, "you must want change."
"Amen," Eve bowed her head.

She wet her hair with oil of rose;
The moon was in its sign.
Her husband left when lightning came
But could not tell her why.

The answer is that there is none,
Sweet secrets layer deep.
She was relieved to end the quest,
Be rid of restless sleep.

Late love found Eve—she rocks her babe
and senses fate's not fixed.
She wonders if Achilles' mom
Drowned faith down by the Styx.

Exercise: Father and/or Mother

Perhaps there is no richer material for us than the stories of our lives with—or without—our parents. The material is primal and universal, available to every writer. For some of us it is inescapable. Kim Chernin, in her book, *The Woman Who Gave Birth to Her Mother*, could as easily be speaking of the father:

> Mother-stories have to be told over and over. Repetition is part of their nature. They have come into existence because, like a Chinese box, or a Russian doll, they contain secret drawers, dolls within dolls, stories within stories in a sequence that must be explored, until the heart of the matter, the smallest doll, the innermost drawer of meaning, has been reached.

The poem that follows is written by ten-year-old Robert Hastings, a participant in Enid Santiago Welch's workshop for children in a housing project in Chicopee, Massachusetts.

WEED

It is life.
It grows from the ground.
It is ground up like meat.
It gives him a sharp and good feeling,
that gives me a sharp and painful anger.
He rolls it like a red carpet
and licks it like a lollipop.
My anger gets deeper
as the smell gets worse.
As he smokes me
I get hotter and hotter.

Some Five-Minute Exercises

When there are any extra minutes at the end of a workshop, or the writer alone has an additional brief window of time, it can be surprisingly fertile ground for writing. Having little time sometimes releases our sense of the importance of our words and allows a refreshing freedom to slip in.

If your work, or your workshop, has been serious and you need a short writing exercise to close without changing the mood, do free writing for a given number of minutes without stopping.

Another use for these short exercises is to help a workshop "loosen up" a bit—laugh. The following exercises are for fun—and for the natural humorists in your workshop, who need to have their funny bones tickled now and then.

Dictionary

Pass around a dictionary, and have each person in turn close their eyes, and point to a word and read it aloud. Each person writes it down. Writers may use all the words, or as many as they wish. This is fun working alone too.

Imaginary Definitions

Give everyone the same three or four obscure words and five minutes to define them. Just read the definitions and enjoy the laughter, giving the real definition at the end. The dictionary is full of words that most of us would be hard-pressed to define.

The Imaginary Source

Everyone writes an imaginary source for one commonly used phrase, the source of which is obscure. A couple of books of origins of words and phrases on your library shelf can be a great resource. For example, the phrase "rule of thumb" evoked many interesting and funny imaginary origins in my workshop, not one of which was accurate. Cynthia Kennison suggested this definition:

> It was King Wilfrum the Gauche who ordained that the length of his own left thumb would be the standard unit of measure for all things. It was a difficult standard to maintain because he often had difficulty telling his left from his right, and in winter both his thumbs shrunk slightly, and he could not be everywhere at once in his kingdom. "Rule of Thumb" has come to mean a rough, probably inaccurate guideline.

In fact, the phrase may have originated in law—there is at least one reference in early American law that indicates a man could legally beat his wife, as long as the stick with which he beat her was no bigger around than his thumb!

The Accidental Name

Writing alone, open a telephone book and put your finger down on a first name. Close the book, open it again, and put your finger on a sur-name. In a workshop, give everyone a three-by-five card. Have each person write a first name on the card, and pass it to the person on the right, who writes a last name. Then collect the cards and give them out at random, not letting anyone keep a card on which he or she wrote. When everyone has the card he or she will be using, tell them, "Now, you know everything about this person. You know what he or she dreamed last night, had for supper, fears, loves, hates. You know this character's favorite food, worst habit, and every secret. Just begin with one detail, and let it flow."

The example that follows gives the first three paragraphs of a complete (very funny) short story written by Paul Barrows about the name that he received on a card.

> In September of 1975, Mr. Palermo and one hundred ninety eight other passengers disappeared while flying over the Bermuda Triangle. Subsequently, Mrs. Palermo discovered she could communicate with her husband by tuning

her television to channel 28, a station unused in her local area. It was for this reason that Mrs. Palermo resisted getting cable TV, although she could tell by the tone of the salesman's voice when she explained this to him that he didn't believe a word of it. Well, what did she care?

It was Elaine's reaction that bothered her more. She had thought Elaine, her sixteen year old daughter, would be overjoyed when she said, "Sweetie, I've just talked to your father, he comes in now on channel 28." But instead, Elaine had just looked at her in horror. Well, Mrs. Palermo had finally decided, what else could one expect from a teenager?

This had all happened almost twenty years ago now, and after so much time, Mrs. Palermo was quite used to the whole thing. Of course, she had been afraid to get a new television—what if he would only come in on this one? He did not always come in clearly. Sometimes there was static, sometimes his voice was very faint. She often had to repeat her questions and occasionally she had to shout. But then, it had been like that even before he disappeared . . .

Exercise for a New Workshop: Seven-Minute Autobiography

As I have said earlier, this is an excellent opening exercise to use the very first time people meet to write together. Have all workshop participants write a seven-minute autobiography in which at least one detail is fictional. At the end of seven minutes, the workshop tries to guess the fiction. Give them only three guesses—that heightens the pressure, and the fun! In introducing the exercise, tell the group not to worry about how well they write—this exercise is just a game.

This opening exercise accomplishes several things: It warms up the group and gets everyone reading, responding, and laughing. But there is a subtle and more important teaching: It demonstrates the fact that listeners can't tell whether the reader's story is autobiography or fiction unless the writer volunteers that information. Point this out to your group after they have finished reading to one another. The essential practice of treating all our writing as fiction is so important for creating an atmosphere of safety that I recommend this exercise on the first day of any new workshop as a way of teaching that practice.

Exercise: A Reflection

In the week following the loss of seven astronauts when the *Columbia* broke apart, it happened that I offered as a writing exercise, these words: "You might include in your writing some reflection, perhaps in a mirror, or in water, or some other sort of reflection." Carol Booth, in our 30 minutes of writing time, wrote this beautiful poem. I include it here as the last poem in this book. May it be so for each of us, as we live, as we die, as we write:

IN HER EYES

> *I could then see my reflection*
> *in the window and in the retina*
> *of my eye the whole earth and sky*
> *could be seen reflected . . .*

—Columbia *astronaut Kalpana Chawla*

In her eyes, the world.
In the glass, her eyes see themselves
as dark as nothing
holding the tiny globe,
carrying it, delighted, through space.

In her eyes, in the parched, crevassed pockets
that hold them, the echoing footsteps of women.
Dark, they left desert Africa
to cross a transforming land.
Birthing generations, they arrive light-skinned,
where the rare sun touches,
but does not warm the frozen earth.
They give birth again.

In her eyes, a feast of colors.
A world reflected back through the lens
of her growing excitement. She looks up
to the Northern Lights, and down through
the open sky. She has drawn it all in;
now she breathes it all back.

Briefly Stated: 50 More Exercise Ideas

Remember that an exercise is just the diving board into the "dreaming place." Start with the suggestion, but always be open to the delicate appearance of something else—something deeper. As soon as that something else appears at the edge of consciousness, abandon the exercise and keep writing what an inner vision offers.

1. Write about an obnoxious kid you once knew. Or someone scary, or strange.

2. Jot down your father's age at your conception. Then your mother's age. Write a brief description of the house where you were born, as you remember it or as you imagine it. Then write to one or both of your parents, or about them.

3. Muriel Rukeyser, in *The Life of Poetry*, suggests beginning to write with the words "I could not tell . . ." "For in what we cannot say to anyone," she writes, "in our most secret conflicts, lie curled our inescapable poems."

4. Write about having too much or having too little.

5. Kathryn Dunn suggests writing a childhood story without using the letter "a." Do it playfully—shake up your usual habits of writing!

6. Write a description of a character sitting in a straight-backed chair. Remember sitting in one yourself. Try it with a soft armchair. A pew. A park bench. A seat on a bus or train.

7. Write about a quietest time in your life or in the life of a character.

8. Describe a person using one idiosyncratic detail. Sharleen Kapp wrote in response to this exercise that a man's protruding eyebrow hair was "a cellular shout of independence!"

9. List five things you have feared and five things that have comforted you. Choose one and write.

10. Begin by describing a small room.

11. Bente Clod, a writer and teacher of writing in Norway, suggests beginning with a familiar piece of writing and substituting as many words as possible, then going on with your writing.

12. Write about having sex or giving birth or being childless.

13. Write about loving someone of the same sex or the opposite sex.

14. Write in great detail about something you do often (shaving, washing dishes, mowing a lawn, washing a dog, folding clothes, cooking a favorite dish).

15. Write about the death of a real or imagined person.

16. Write about a creature (insect? reptile? animal?) that frightens you or your character.

17. Write about the profession you know best, perhaps give it to an imagined character.

18. Write beginning with "If I were the woman (or the man) who lives next door . . ."

19. List things one might be proud of and things one might be ashamed of. Choose one and write about it.

20. Begin by writing down a bit of ritual or an old song that you know by heart. Then intersperse those lines with paragraphs— anything that comes to mind, allowing lines from the remembered piece to act as a refrain throughout the piece.

21. Use the word "cow" (or "orange," or "ghost," or "fuck") in what you write.

22. Write a scene or a story with one color as a motif—like a "white story" or a "red story."

23. Name yourself: "I am water," or "I am (?)." Write out of that sense of self.

24. List the names of everyone with whom you have ever been in love. Then write.

25. Imagine looking through a keyhole. Write what you see.

26. Write about a walk that is really death. A hello that is really good-bye. An argument that is really foreplay.

27. Write from an image: a broken mirror, a horse shoe, a tombstone, a door needing paint.

28. Write about a sound: a baby, breathing; a teakettle; a hammer. Write about silence.

29. Write a thank you to things you don't usually thank: a skillet, a lightbulb, a bedsheet.

30. List three things you want to keep and three things you want to lose. Then write.

31. Write about a time when you escaped. (Give the experience to a character if you want.)

32. Write about something you have no idea how to do, as if you did know.

33. Write about a familiar ritual. Interrupt it.

34. Write about fixing something that is broken.

35. Begin with an unflattering detail of appearance.

36. Write a fight.

37. Patricia Lee Lewis suggests, "Make up an elaborate lie about yourself. Be so specific you yourself believe it."

38. Richard Hugo suggests writing a description of a barn seen through the eyes of someone who has lost someone.

39. Write about a machine you have loved or hated.

40. Patricia Lee Lewis suggests, "Find a mad person in yourself. Write from that place."

41. Jane Hirshfield suggests the following, which she calls "the importance of the negative." List three to five colors like "blue" or "the color of rain on the tin roof." List three to five animals, sounds, and charged emotions. Use one from each list and include "This is about . . ." or "This is not about . . ."

42. Begin writing with the words, "Have you forgotten me?"

43. Write about giving three things away to three people, telling them why you are giving each gift.

44. Write after thinking about "the kindness of inanimate objects." (Pat Schneider)

45. Choose five words. Set a timer and write in response to each word for one minute. Then take something from that writing and work with it more fully.

46. Make a list of really "tacky" things, like yard art: fat wooden ladies bending in gardens, motel art, plastic Jesus, Christmas toilet seat covers on which Santa Claus closes his eyes while the lid is up. After you make your list, write!

47. List sayings common in your family, then write.

48. Choose two pictures of faces from newspapers or books. (Try to avoid faces you know.) Write alternating paragraphs or verses about the two people, or write in their voices.

49. Write about "that narrow line that separates flesh and spirit." (Tony Hillerman)

50. Write about something gentle: a sweet night, or someone who forgives, or a safe place.

Afterword

When all is said and done, writing is a primitive act. Before we wrote on tablets of stone, we wrote on the air—our stories spilling out of us, our chants and songs ringing off the walls of caves.

My own grandmother, the daughter of an American Indian man and a woman of unknown heritage, could not write her own name. Until the day she died, she signed her name with an "X." How vast is her silence in the ears of her granddaughter!

I have a snapshot of a quilt she pieced, gone to a faded remnant before I found it on the porch rail outside her daughter's trailer house on a gravel road in the Ozarks. Her daughter, my aunt, was dying of alcoholism and emphysema. I met her just in time to catch a few stories of my grandmother, and to take a snapshot of that frayed quilt.

We treasure the voices of our ancestors; we warm ourselves with the worn fragments that we have of the stories of their lives.

We ourselves will be ancestors one day.

This book is a celebration of the written word. It is an invitation to you, no matter who you are or what your experience with writing has been, to draw onto the blank page your letters, words, poems, stories— your wild beasts, the visions that you alone see by the light of the fire in the cave of your heart.

No one has seen the night sky from exactly your trajectory. No one has loved exactly the people and places you have loved.

Who will tell that part of the earth's story, if you do not?

List of Exercises

Exercise: Beginning at Your Own Beginning 18
Exercise: Healing the Wounds of Bad Experiences 18
Exercise: Getting Rid of Internal Critics 22
Exercise: Beginning (Again) 32
Exercise: Free Writing... 35
Exercise: "In This One . . ." 36
Exercise: The Well 70
Exercise: Clustering and Mapping... 70
Exercise: Writing a Letter 71
Exercise: List of Nouns 72
Exercise: Other Uses of the List.. 73
Exercise: Drawing What You Can't Write 75
Exercise: Show, Don't Tell 77
Exercise: The Room 80
Exercise: The Town 80
Exercise: Experimenting with Form 80
Exercise: Writing a Dialogue 83
Exercise: Trying Imitation 88
Exercise: Being Brave... 90
Exercise: Using Your Own Original Voice 95
Exercise: Using Your Primary Voice... 96
Exercise: Eavesdropping 102
Exercise: Writing from Different Points of View 103

Exercise: Writing in Several Voices at Once 104

Exercise: Suggesting a Character's Voice without Using It 104

Exercise: A Poem as Trigger 130

Exercise: Using Random Words 131

Exercise: The Scramble 132

Exercise: A Villanelle Made (Relatively) Painless 136

Exercise: Creating an Original Form 137

Exercise: Breaking into Fiction #1 142

Exercise: Breaking into Fiction #2 143

Exercise: Someone in Shadow 147

Exercise: Writing a Short-Short Story 147

Exercise: Writing from Something You Love 149

Exercise: Free Writing in the Classroom 201

Exercises for Writers with Limited Formal Education 275

Exercise: What Matters? 300

Exercise: Choosing from a Group of Objects 302

Exercise: "I Am From . . ." 304

Exercise: Imagining a Place 306

Exercise: The Photograph Collection 308

Exercise: The Fragmentary Quote 309

Exercise: Writing Dialogue (Group Exercise) 312

Exercise: Writing in Response to Music 313

Exercise: Writing about Sex 315

Exercise: Religious Tradition 317

Exercise: Cut and Paste 317

Exercise: Details of Direction 318

Exercise: Making the Unfamiliar Familiar 319

Exercise: Taste 320

Exercise: Ransom Note 321

Exercise: Biography 322

Exercise: Dream Image 323

Exercise: The Sense of Touch 324

Exercise: Writing Directly to Someone 324

Exercise: Daily News 325

Exercise: The Fearful Scene 326

Exercise: Something You Know by Heart 327

Exercise: The Absolute Relative 329

Exercise: Face-to-Face with an Animal 330

Exercise: Magical Realist 331

Exercise: Giving or Receiving Advice 332
Exercise: Writing What You Don't Know about What You Know ... 333
Exercise: Writing about Writing 333
Exercise: Writing a Response to Another Writer 334
Exercise: Writing in the Style of Another Writer 335
Exercise: Writing in Answer to Another Writer 336
Exercise: A Series of Images 338
Exercise: Writing to an Imaginary Relative 338
Exercise: The Uses of the Ordinary 339
Exercise: An Animal Speaks 339
Exercise: Stream of Consciousness 340
Exercise: What's Going On 342
Exercise: Dream House 343
Exercise: Sense of Smell 344
Exercise: Taboo 345
Exercise: The Neighbor 347
Exercise: Freshening a Fragment 348
Exercise: Writing about Illness 349
Exercise: Writing a Ballad 350
Exercise: Father and/or Mother 351
Some Five-Minute Exercises 352
Exercise for a New Workshop: Seven-Minute Autobiography 354
Exercise: A Reflection 355
Briefly Stated: 50 More Exercise Ideas 356

Recommended Resources and Reading List

Resources Available and Forthcoming From Amherst Writers & Artists Press

DVD: *Writing Alone & with Others: A Companion Piece to the Book.* Florentine Films, Diane Garey and Larry Hott, Producers. (A resource for writers and teachers of writing to accompany the book. It contains filmed interviews with Pat Schneider as well as other writers and workshop leaders who use her method. It also contains the film, *Tell Me Something I Can't Forget.*)

Video: *Tell Me Something I Can't Forget: Low-Income Women Write about Their Lives*, Florentine Films, Diane Garey and Larry Hott, Producers. (A 23-minute film about Pat Schneider's original workshop for low-income women. First Prize in the National Educational Film Festival, and First Prize in the Women's Division of C.I.N.E. International Film Festival.)

Benson, Carolyn, and Sara Weinberger, eds. *Voices from Inside: Writing with Women in Prison.*

Bray, Sharon. *Stories of the Journey: Women Writing Together through Breast Cancer.*

Dunn, Kathryn, and Daphne Slocombe, eds. *The Other Side of Silence: The Passion and Practice of Writing Workshops with Special Populations.*

McWha, Susan. *Voices of (dis)Ability.*

Schneider, Pat. *The Clearing: Collected and New Poems.*

————. *Wake Up Laughing: A Spiritual Autobiography.*

————. ed. *In Our Own Voices: Writing by Women in Low-Income Housing.*

Therrien, Robin. *Voices from the 'Hood: How to Start and Sustain a Writing Workshop for Youth at Risk.*

For resources and information, contact Amherst Writers & Artists Press, P.O. Box 1076, Amherst, MA 01004. Website: www.amherstwriters.com. Telephone: 413-253-3307. Email: awa@amherstwriters.com.

Recommended Reading

Anglesey, Zöe, ed. 1999. *Listen Up! Spoken Word Poetry.* New York: One World.

Appelbaum, Judith. 1998. *How to Get Happily Published,* 5th edition. New York: HarperPerennial.

Atwood, Margaret. 2002. *Negotiating with the Dead.* New York: Cambridge University Press.

Augenbraum, Harold, and Margarite Fernández Olmos, eds. 1997. *The Latino Reader: From 1542 to the Present.* Boston: Houghton Mifflin Company.

Bell-Scott, Patricia, ed. 1999. *Flat-Footed Truths: Telling Black Women's Lives.* New York: Owl Books/Henry Holt.

Behn, Robin, and Chase Twichell, eds. 1992. *The Practice of Poetry: Writing Exercises from Poets Who Teach.* New York: HarperPerennial.

Bessler, Ian, ed. 2002. *2003 Song Writer's Market.* Cincinnati: Writer's Digest Books.

The Best American Short Stories. 1978–. Boston: Houghton-Mifflin.

Beyers, Chris. 2001. *A History of Free Verse.* Fayetteville: University of Arkansas Press.

Bly, Carol. 2001. *Beyond the Writers Workshop: New Ways to Write Creative Nonfiction.* New York: Anchor Books.

————. 1996. *Changing the Bully Who Rules the World: Reading and Thinking about Ethics.* Minneapolis: Milkweed Editions.

————. 2000. *My Lord Bag of Rice: New and Selected Stories.* Minneapolis: Milkweed Editions.

————. 1990. *The Passionate, Accurate Story.* Minneapolis: Milkweed Editions.

Boland, Eavan. 1996. *Object Lessons: The Life of the Woman and the Poet in Our Time*. London: Vintage/Random House.

Bolker, Joan, ed. 1997. *The Writer's Home Companion*. New York: Henry Holt and Company.

Bowling, Anne, and Vanessa Lyman, eds. 2002. *2003 Novel and Short Story Writer's Market*. Cincinnati: Writer's Digest Books.

Bradbury, Ray. 1990. *Zen in the Art of Writing*. Santa Barbara: Joshua Odell Editions.

Brande, Dorothea, and John Gardner. 1981. *Becoming a Writer*. New York: J. P. Tarcher/Putnam.

Breen, Nancy, and Vanessa Lyman, eds. 2002. *2003 Poet's Market*. Cincinnati: Writer's Digest Books.

Brogan, Katie Struckel, and Robert Brewer, eds. 2002. *2003 Writer's Market*. Cincinnati: Writer's Digest Books.

Browne, Renni, and Dave King. 1993. *Self-Editing for Fiction Writers*. New York: HarperCollins.

Buber, Martin. 1974. *I and Thou*. New York: Touchstone Books.

Burroway, Janet. 2003. *Imaginative Writing: The Elements of Craft*. New York: Longman.

———. 2002. *Embalming Mom: Essays in Life*. Iowa City: University of Iowa Press.

———. 2000. *Writing Fiction: A Guide to Narrative Craft*, 6th edition. New York: Longman.

———. 1977. *Raw Silk*. Boston: Little, Brown and Company.

Busch, Frederick, ed. 1999. *Letters to a Fiction Writer*. New York: W.W. Norton & Company.

Cameron, Julia. 1992. *The Artist's Way: A Spiritual Path to Higher Creativity*, 10th edition. New York: J. P. Tarcher/Putnam.

———. 1998. *The Right to Write*. New York: J. P. Tarcher/Putnam.

———. 2002. *Walking in This World*. New York: J. P. Tarcher/Putnam.

Cisneros, Sandra. 1994. *The House on Mango Street*. New York: Alfred A. Knopf.

Collett, Jonathan, and Serrano, Basilio. 1992. "Stirring It Up: The Inclusive Classroom." *Teaching for Diversity* 49 (Spring): 35–48.

Cook, Marshall. 1995. *Freeing Your Creativity: A Writer's Guide*. Cincinnati: Writer's Digest Books.

———. 1992. *How to Write with the Skill of a Master and the Genius of a Child*. Cincinnati: Writer's Digest Books.

————. 1995. *Leads and Conclusions: Elements of Article Writing*. Cincinnati: Writer's Digest Books.

Davis, Sheila. 1985. *The Craft of Lyric Writing*. Cincinnati: Writer's Digest Books.

————. 1996. *The Songwriter's Idea Book*. Cincinnati: Writer's Digest Books.

————. 1988. *Successful Lyric Writing: A Step by Step Course and Workbook*. Cincinnati: Writer's Digest Books.

The Directory of Literary Magazines. New York: The Coordinating Council of Literary Magazines.

Edwards, Sharon A., Robert W. Maloy, and Ruth-Ellen Verock-O'Loughlin. 2003. *Ways of Writing with Young Kids*. Boston: Allyn and Bacon.

Elbow, Peter. 2000. *Everyone Can Write: Essays toward a Hopeful Theory of Writing and Teaching Writing*. New York: Oxford University Press.

————. 2002. "Vernacular Englishes in the Writing Classroom: Probing the Culture of Literacy." *ALT DIS: Alternative Discourses and the Academy*. Portsmouth: Boynton/Cook-Heinemann.

————. 1998. *Writing without Teachers*. New York: Oxford University Press.

————. 1998. *Writing with Power*. New York: Oxford University Press.

Engel, Lehman. 1993. *Planning and Producing the Musical Show*. New York: Random House.

————. 1989. *The Musical Theater Workshop (Sound Seminars Series)*. Guilford: Jeffrey Norton Publishers.

————. 1983. *Getting the Show On: The Complete Guidebook for Producing a Musical in Your Theatre*. Lexington: Museum of Our National Heritage.

————. 1977. *The Making of a Musical*. New York: Macmillan Publishers.

————. 1976. *The Critics*. New York: Macmillan Publishers.

————. 1975. *The American Musical Theater*. New York: Macmillan Publishers.

————. 1973. *Getting Started in the Theater*. New York: Macmillan Publishers.

Evans, Glen, ed. 1988. *The Complete Guide to Writing Non-Fiction*. New York: Perennial Library.

Fagin, Larry. 1991. *The List Poem: A Guide to Teaching & Writing Catalog Verse*. New York: Teachers & Writers Collaborative.

Field, Joanna [Marion Blackett Milner]. 1983. *On Not Being Able to Paint.* Boston: J. P. Tarcher.

Finch, Annie, ed. 1994. *A Formal Feeling Comes: Poems in Form by Contemporary Women.* Brownsville: Story Line Press.

Fitzgerald, Sally, ed. 1980. *The Habit of Being: Letters of Flannery O'Connor.* New York: Vintage Books.

Fowler, H. W. 1996. *The New Fowler's Modern English Usage.* New York: Oxford University Press.

Friday, Nancy. 1998. *My Secret Garden.* New York: Pocket Books.

Fulton, Len. 2002. *The International Directory of Little Magazines and Small Presses,* 38th edition. Paradise: Dustbooks.

Gardner, John. 1985. *The Art of Fiction: Notes on Craft for Young Writers.* New York: Vintage Books.

———. 1983. *On Becoming a Novelist.* New York: Harper & Row.

Gardner, John, and Lennis Dunlap. 1962. *The Forms of Fiction.* New York: Random House.

Goldberg, Natalie. 1986. *Writing Down the Bones: Freeing the Writer Within.* Boston: Shambhala.

Goldman, William. 1983. *Adventures in the Screen Trade: A Personal View of Hollywood and Screenwriting.* New York: Warner Books.

Harper, Michael S., and Anthony Walton, eds. 1994. *Every Shut Eye Ain't Asleep: An Anthology of Poetry by African Americans Since 1945.* Boston: Little, Brown and Company.

Heilbrun, Carolyn. 1990. *Hamlet's Mother and Other Women.* New York: Columbia University Press.

———. 1989. *Writing a Woman's Life.* New York: Ballantine Books.

Hemingway, Ernest. 1996. *A Moveable Feast.* New York: Scribner Classics.

Hirsch, Edward. 1999. *How to Read a Poem and Fall in Love with Poetry.* New York: Harcourt Brace & Company.

hooks, bell. 1999. *Remembered Rapture: The Writer at Work.* New York: Henry Holt.

———. 1997. *Wounds of Passion: A Writing Life.* New York: Henry Holt.

King, Steven. 2000. *On Writing: A Memoir of the Craft.* New York: Scribner.

Lamb, Wally. 2003. *Couldn't Keep It to Myself: Wally Lamb and the Women of York Correctional Institution.* New York: HarperCollins.

Lamott, Anne. 1995. *Bird by Bird: Some Instructions on Writing and Life.* New York: Anchor Books.

Levine, Philip. 1981. *Don't Ask.* Ann Arbor: University of Michigan Press.

Lewis, Richard, ed. 1984. *Miracles: Poems by Children of the English-Speaking World*. New York: Simon and Schuster.

Linkon, Sherry Lee, ed. 1999. *Teaching Working Class*. Amherst: University of Massachusetts Press.

Lopate, Phillip, ed. 1994. *The Art of the Personal Essay: An Anthology from the Classical Era to the Present*. New York: Anchor Books.

Lorde, Audre. 1984. *Sister Outsider: Essays and Speeches*. New York: Crossing Press.

Lyon, George Ella. 1999. *Where I'm From, Where Poems Come From*. Spring: Absey & Company, Inc.

Macrorie, Ken. 1985. *Telling Writing*. Upper Montclair: Boynton/Cook Publishers.

Metcalf, Linda Trichter, and Tobin Simon. 2002. *Writing the Mind Alive*. New York: Ballantine Books.

Metzger, Deena. 1992. *Writing for Your Life: A Guide and Companion to the Inner Worlds*. San Francisco: HarperSanFrancisco.

Moffett, James, and Kenneth R. McElheny, eds. 1995. *Points of View: An Anthology of Short Stories*. New York: Mentor.

Morrone, John, ed. 2002. *Grants & Awards Available to American Writers*, 22nd edition. New York: PEN American Center.

Neff, Jack and Glenda. 2000. *Formatting and Submitting Your Manuscript*. Cincinnati: Writer's Digest Books.

Oberhaus, Dorothy Huff. 1995. *Emily Dickinson's Fascicles: Method & Meaning*. University Park: Pennsylvania State University Press.

Olds, Sharon. 1987. *The Gold Cell*. New York: Knopf.

Knowles, Elizabeth, ed. 1999. *The Oxford Dictionary of Quotations*, 5th edition. New York: Oxford University Press.

Paley, Grace. 1998. *Just as I Thought*. New York: Farrar, Straus & Giroux.

Pope, Alice, and Mona Michael, eds. 2002. *2003 Children's Writer's & Illustrator's Market*. Cincinnati: Writer's Digest Books.

Poynter, Dan. 1989. *The Self-Publishing Manual: How to Write, Print and Sell Your Own Book*. Santa Barbara: Para Publishing.

Progoff, Ira. 1975. *At a Journal Workshop: The Basic Text and Guide for Using the Intensive Journal Process*. New York: Dialogue House Library.

Rico, Gabriele Lusser. 1983. *Writing the Natural Way: Using Right-Brain Techniques to Release Your Expressive Powers*. Los Angeles: J. P. Tarcher.

Robison, Margaret. 1992. *Red Creek: A Requiem*. Amherst: Amherst Writers & Artists Press.

Rukeyser, Muriel. 1996. *The Life of Poetry*. Williamsburg: Paris Press.

Savageau, Cheryl. 1995. *Dirt Road Home*. Willimantic: Curbstone Press.

Schneider, Rebecca. 1997. *The Explicit Body in Performance*. New York: Routledge.

Scholder, Amy, and Ira Silverberg, eds. 2002. *High Risk: An Anthology of Forbidden Writings*. New York: New American Library/Penguin.

Seger, Linda. 1992. *The Art of Adaptation: Turning Fact and Fiction into Film*. New York: Henry Holt.

———. 1990. *Creating Unforgettable Characters*. New York: Henry Holt.

———. 1987. *Making a Good Script Great*. New York: Dodd, Mead.

Stafford, William. 1986. *You Must Revise Your Life*. Ann Arbor: University of Michigan Press.

———. 1978. *Writing the Australian Crawl: Views on the Writer's Vocation*. Ann Arbor: University of Michigan Press.

Sternburg, Janet, ed. 1992. *The Writer on Her Work: Vol. I*. New York: W.W. Norton & Company.

———. 1992. *The Writer on Her Work: Vol. II*. New York: W.W. Norton & Company.

Strunk, William Jr., and E. B. White. 2000. *The Elements of Style,* 4th edition. Boston: Allyn & Bacon.

Taylor, Jeremy. 1983. *Dream Work: Techniques for Discovering the Creative Power in Dreams*. New York: Paulist Press.

Ueland, Brenda. 1987. *If You Want to Write*. St. Paul: Graywolf Press.

Williams, Miller. 1986. *Patterns of Poetry: An Encyclopedia of Forms*. Baton Rouge: Louisiana State University Press.

Webb, Jimmy. 1998. *Tunesmith: Inside the Art of Songwriting*. New York: Hyperion.

Woodruff, Jay, ed. 1993. *A Piece of Work: Five Writers Discuss Their Revisions*. Iowa City: University of Iowa Press.

Wylie, Max. 1970. *Writing for Television*. New York: Cowles.

Periodicals

Creative Nonfiction, 5501 Walnut Street, Suite 202, Pittsburgh, PA 15232. Phone: 412-688-0304. Fax: 412-683-9173. Email: information@ creativenonfiction.org.

The Dramatists Guild Newsletter, 234 West 44th Street, New York, NY 10036

Poets & Writers Magazine, 72 Spring Street, New York, NY 10012. Phone: 212-226-3586. Website: www.pw.org/mag.

The Writer's Chronicle, Associated Writing Programs, Tallwood House, Mail Stop IE3, George Mason University, Fairfax, VA 22030.

Websites

The Academy of American Poets: www.poets.org
Amherst Writers & Artists: www.amherstwriters.com
Dramatists Guild: www.dramaguild.com
Funds for Writers: www.fundsforwriters.com
Poetry Society of America: www.poetrysociety.org
Winning Writers: www.winningwriters.com

Musical Theater Training: Contact Information

For training in musical theater, there are no better resources than the books and tapes by Lehman Engel. The Broadcast Music, Inc. workshops are for writers who have already done professional theater. For information about these and other musical theater workshops, write Norma Grossman, Director, B.M.I. Lehman Engel Musical Theater Workshop, 320 West 57th Street, New York, NY 10019.

Credits

Lyon, George Ella. "Where I'm From" from *Where I'm From: Where Poems Come From*. Copyright © 1999 by George Ella Lyon. Reprinted by permission of Absey & Company, Inc. All rights reserved.

Sommers, Nancy. Excerpt from "Between the Drafts" in *College Composition and Communication*. Copyright © 1992 by the National Council of Teachers of English. Reprinted by permission of the National Council of Teachers of English. All rights reserved.

Steinbeck, John. "2/13–14/1962 letter to Robert Wallsten" from *Steinbeck: A Life in Letters*, edited by Elaine A. Steinbeck and Robert Wallsten. Copyright © 1952 by John Steinbeck, © 1969 by the Estate of John Steinbeck, © 1975 by Elaine A. Steinbeck and Robert Wallsten. Reprinted by permission of Viking Penguin, a division of Penguin Putnam Inc. All rights reserved.

The author gratefully acknowledges the publishers of the following periodicals and books in which some of these poems and stories first appeared:

Bufford, Bridget. Excerpt from *Minus One: A Twelve-Step Journey*. Binghamton: Alice Street Editions, 2003.

Dreier, Alexander. "Turquoise Prayer of Spring." *RE:AL, The Journal of Liberal Arts* 27:1&2 (2002).

Fitzpatrick, Evelyn. "Crows." *Peregrine* 17 (1998).

Gleason, Kate. "Fracture." *Making as if to Sing*. Amherst: Amherst Writers & Artists Press, 1989.

Hicks, Alison. Excerpt from *Love, a Story of Images*. Amherst: Amherst Writers & Artists Press (forthcoming).

Johnson, Steve. Untitled prose poem. *Sahara* 1 (Spring/Summer 2000).

Leff, Valerie. "The Way the Wind is Blowing." *Carolina Quarterly* 55.2 (Spring 2003).

Lewis, Patricia Lee. "Two Hundred Wings." *Berkshire Review* 10 (2002).

Pfeifer, Teresa. "For My Son Robert: Novice, Age Five." *In Our Own Voices*. Ed. Pat Schneider. Amherst: Amherst Writers & Artists Press, 1989.

Robison, Margaret. Excerpt from *Red Creek: A Requiem*. Amherst: Amherst Writers & Artists Press, 1992.

Schneider, Pat. "Letting Go" and "Personal Address." *Long Way Home*. Amherst: Amherst Writers & Artists Press, 1993.

—————. "Your Boat, Your Words." Amherst: Amherst Writers & Artists Press, 1987.

Schneider, Peter. "At Seventy." *Peregrine* 20/21 (2001).

Walker, Sue. "You Ain't Jesus, Brother." *Blood Must Bear Your Name*. Amherst: Amherst Writers & Artists Press Book, 2002.

The following pieces appeared in Pat Schneider's book *The Writer as an Artist: Writing Alone & with Others* Los Angeles: Lowell House, 1993:

Barrows, Paul. Untitled.

Chhoun, Sophal. "Waking from Nightmare."

Eagan, Jim. Untitled.

Hastings, Robert. "Weed."

Heggerty, Moya. "Cow Dung."

Kennison, Cynthia. "A Fatal Attraction."

Mercier, Diane. "What Keeps Me Ticking."

Solomont, Sue. "mother mother/buried in father."

Welch, Enid Santiago. "Popping Out Babies While Dragging Your Placenta to the Mailbox."

Zeiger, Gene. "Family."

Index

Abandonment: need for in writing, 5, 11, 16, 17, 59, 195, 234; writing about, 64

Adams, Paula Sheller, xv, "Armistice," 301

Adams, Sue Ann: "Kaleidoscope Vision," 264

Affirmations, five essential, ix–x, 186

Allison, Dorothy, 162, 278

Amherst Writers & Artists (AWA), ix–x, xv, basic affirmations of, 186; basic practices of, 186–87; basic principles of, 194–95; Institute (AWAI), 259–292 (sample workshops, 260–61); Method, 30, 92, 166, 167, 186–87, 191–94 (in classroom, 196–214; training in, 183, 208, 215, 219, 221); origins, 30, 58, 185, 197, 216; Press, 210, 367–68; Workshop, xii, 208, 219–58, 321

Andersen, Hans Christian, 4

Anderson, Carlos, Rev., 154

Anderson, Maxwell: "Lost in the Stars," 64

Anger: writing out of, 37, 90, 112, 158

Anthologies, 108, 109, 110, 129, 151, 161, 170, 190, 254. See also Journals, literary; Publications about writing

Aquinas, Thomas: *Summa,* 4

Art form, writing as, xxi, 30; belonging to all, xx, 186, 212; claiming, xxii, 39, 63; free from constraints, 160, 241; journal keeping and, 33, 64; practicing, 63, 106, 111, 155, 200, 350; *vs.* craft, xxii, 144

Ashton, Jennifer, 312

Atwood, Margaret, 36, 312

Auchincloss, Louis, 6

Auden, W. H., 59, 90, 125

Audience, 33, 35, 99, 103, 144, 200, 205, 314

Autobiography (*see also* Fiction): experimenting with, 80–81, 142–43, 234, 235, 354; fiction and, 37, 92, 138, 161, 165, 187, 194, 195, 203, 227, 239, 241, 280; journal keeping and, 65; self-revelation and, 26, 33, 160, 172, 231, 235 (*see also* Self-revelation)

Barrows, Paul, 36, 353

Beecher Stowe, Harriet, *Uncle Tom's Cabin,* 158

Bell, Marvin, 312

Benard, Julie, 264

Benson, Carolyn, xvi, 268; "Much," 74

Bentley, Dick, 146, 296

Beyers, Chris: *A History of Free Verse,* 124
Bigelow, Donna, 66
Biography, 82; experimenting with, 322
Bishop, Elizabeth: "One Art," 136; "The Art of Losing Things," 136
Black, Maria, 318
Blake, William, 152
Bliss, Corinne Demas, 304
Block, writer's: fear and, 3, 16, 21, 33, 139, 142; exercises to help, 19, 22–23, 142–43, 147; overcoming, xx, 10, 24, 28, 31, 48, 51, 54, 57, 58, 62, 178; sources of, 144, 234, 248, 249, 298
Bly, Carol, 151; *The Passionate, Accurate Story,* 113, 141, 150
Boland, Eavan, 164, 165
Bolker, Joan: *The Writer's Home Companion,* 87, 151
Booth, Carol, xvi, "In Her Eyes," 355
Boyd-Owens, Rebekah, "Lover's Leap," 309
Bradbury, Ray, 99, 312; *Zen in the Art of Writing,* 72
Brand, Ruth Bolton, 299; "Sixty-Sex," 315
Brande, Dorothea, 12, 35, 144, 340; *Becoming a Writer,* xxii, 57, 111, 143, 157, 350
Bray, Sharon, xvi, 34, 266, 349
Brecht, Bertolt, 164
Brown, Eva, 224, 225–26
Browning, Sarah, 30, 334
Bryan, Jennifer, 341
Buber, Martin: *I and Thou,* 54
Buchinsky, Karen, xvi, 268; "The Story of the Child Molester Next Door," 347
Bufford, Bridget: *Minus One: A Twelve-Step Journey,* 316
Burkart, Barbara, 35
Burns, Ken, 168
Burroughs, William, 40
Burroway, Janet: *Raw Silk,* 51, 70; *Writing Fiction: A Guide to Narrative Craft,* 71, 113, 139, 150
Burton, Bob, 69
Burwell, Deb, 30, 262

Busch, Frederick: *Letters to a Fiction Writer,* 151
Byrn-Julson, Phyllis, xx

Cameron, Julia, 35, 144, 193, 340; *The Artist's Way,* 158; *The Right to Write,* 158
Campbell, Joseph, 47, 50
Capote, Truman, 311
Carver, Raymond, 110, 312; "At Night the Salmon Move," 130; "Drinking While Driving," 130, 146, 278; "Photograph of My Father in His Twenty-Second Year," 130
Certification, teaching writing, 183. *See also* Amherst Writers & Artists (AWA)
Chandler, Genevieve, 210
Character(s) (*see also* Dialogue; Voice): believable, 193, 253, 316; describing, 77, 79, 140, 148, 326, 356, 357; developing, 68, 73, 111, 141, 146, 149, 229, 322, 343, 348–49, 353; dialogue and, 82, 84, 150–51, 312–13; real people and, 11, 13, 82, 138, 143, 165; voice and, 93, 97, 100, 103, 104, 145
Chernin, Kim: *The Woman Who Gave Birth to Her Mother,* 351
Chhoun, Sophal: "Waking from a Nightmare," 207
Chicopee Workshop for Low-Income Women (*see also* Low-income writers): documentary film, *Tell Me Something I Can't Forget,* 227, 263, 367; origins, 262, 268; participants, 28, 57, 94, 97, 119, 259, 264, 281, 289, 291, 317
Children and childhood: parents of, 28, 54–59, 260, 262, 264, 285; class and, 167–68; diaries of, 5–6, 64, 75; images of, 20, 32, 77, 224, 301; language or voices of, 31–32, 83, 93, 95–96, 110, 210, 300 (*see also* Voice); memories of, 7–9, 20–21, 90–92, 190, 196, 201, 227, 240, 260, 267, 276; workshops for, 10, 30, 119, 203, 240, 269–70, 280, 285, 351; as writing "capital," 6;

writing in a classroom for, 13–14,
193, 196, 202–4, 212, 214
Cisneros, Sandra: "The House on
Mango Street," 259
Clark, Deene, 222
Clark, Florence, 102
Class (see also Chicopee Workshop for
Low-Income Women; Ethics; Low-
income writers; Politics): challenges
to writing and, 57, 167, 291;
disempowerment and, 181, 271;
language and, 286–90; privacy and,
162; writing about, 167–68
Classroom, writing in a, 196–214 (see
also Leader(s); Teacher(s); Teaching); advice for students, 199–200;
advice for teachers, 200–214;
children, 202–4; college, 208–9;
grading, 211–13 (see also Grading
writing); graduate school, 209–10;
high school, 204–7; and other than
writing courses, 210–11; some basic
practices of, 213–14
Clod, Bente, 356
Coccoluto, Diana, 20, 21
Cohen, Frances, 90
Collaboration, 121, 153, 179
Confidence, 15 (see also Support);
encouraging, 213, 224, 279;
growing in, 203, 210, 212, 273;
undermining, 109, 182, 199
Confidentiality, 166, 187, 195, 203,
235, 285. See also Privacy
Conrad, Joseph, 99, 311
Consciousness. See Unconscious
Cortazar, Julio, 88
Courage, 226, 231, 244, 267;
practicing, 89–90, 92, 106;
teaching and, 198, 231, 235, 272;
writing and need for, 5, 26, 38,
178, 231, 270, 272
Craft, xxii, 76–92; deepening, 116, 18,
295–96; developing, 76–92, 106,
116; in fiction, 141–52 (see also
Fiction); natural 15, 126; practicing, 50, 63, 129, 177 (courage, 89–
92; using concrete, specific
language, 76–79; using details, 79–

80; using dialogue, 82–86; using
form, 80–82; using imitation, 87–
89); revising and, 111–13; studying,
110–11; teaching, 182, 186–87,
199–200, 210, 212, 334
Craig, Pat, 216
Creative genius: in everyone, xxi, 21,
186
Creativity, 10, 24, 45, 47, 64, 68, 115
Critics: academic, 45–47; internal, 15,
22–23, 35, 48, 50, 114; literary, 16,
49, 68, 122, 162, 193
Critiquing writing. See Responding to
writing

Davis, Heather: "Advice," 332
Davis-Cannon, Marcia, 34
DeGeiso, Dee, 326
Dialogue, 95, 117, 177, 309 (see also
Character(s); Language; Voice);
practicing, 23, 32, 81–86, 150–51,
312–13
Dickinson, Emily, xxi, xxiii, xxv, 27,
41, 45, 59, 68, 99, 176, 311, 324
Dillard, Annie: Pilgrim at Tinker Creek,
339
Diop, Birago, 190
Discipline: challenges to, 42–48;
danger of criticism present, 44–45;
external and internal "committees,"
45–48; ghost of criticism past, 43;
other commitments, 42; disciplined
writing life, 40–62 (suggestions for
a, 48–62); fruits of, 41–42
Diversity, 168, 209, 211; workshops
and, 195, 218, 226, 290; ethical
imperative of, 257
Drafts, 242, 247 (see also Editing;
Responding to writing; Revising);
journals and, 65; not revising, 12–
13, 114, 141, 146, 187, 191, 194,
197, 232; privacy and, 12, 91, 235,
285; reading, 191, 200, 235, 279;
revising, 109, 111–13, 128, 214,
252
Dream(s), 54, 56, 65, 67, 82, 138,
144, 146, 323, 343 (see also
Unconscious); "dreaming place"

Dream(s) (*continued*), and, 3, 12, 17, 20, 26, 34, 38, 114, 356; creative genius and, 21, 30; writing the mind's, 28

Drier, Alexander: "Turquoise Prayer of Spring," 123

Dunlap, Lennis, 100; *The Forms of Fiction,* 138

Dunn, Dorothy, 196

Dunn, Kathryn, xvi, 78, 188, 205, 207, 321, 356; "Legacy," 130

Eagan, Jim, 22, 84, 331

Ecstasy: writing and, 101, 158, 190, 191

Edelstein, Carol: "Very First Itemized Expenses," 73, 85

Editing (*see also* Responding to writing; Revising): manuscripts, 235, 247, 248; writing without, 12, 68, 197, 348

Elbow, Peter, ix–xiii, xv, 93, 144, 151, 185, 201, 203, 340; *Everyone Can Write,* 197, 202; "Vernacular Englishes in the Writing Classroom: Probing the Culture of Literacy," 198; *Writing with Power,* 88, 200; *Writing without Teachers,* 35, 215

Eliot, T. S., xx, xxiii, 99, 110, 152, 311, 312, 333

Ellis, Charlene, 84

Empowerment (*see also* Self-esteem; Silenced): teaching, 191, 186–87, 214, 238; writing for, xvii, 39, 259–92

Equality: risk-taking and, 187, 191, 197, 279–80; writing groups and workshops and, xxi

Espada, Martín, 119, 311; *Imagine the Angels of Bread,* 165

Ethics, 157–74 (*see also* Confidentiality; Politics); privacy and, 159–63 (*see also* Privacy); writing as a spiritual practice and, 157–59 (*see also* Spirituality)

Exercises (*see also* Triggers): additional writing, 295–359; guidelines for good, 296–300; list of, 363–65

Fagin, Larry: *The List Poem,* 73

Fahy, Anne, 72

Fairchild, B. H., 36

Fear, xxi, 3–23; apologizing ("apron wringing") and, 237, 238; of fear itself, 16–18; of—or for—someone else, 13–15; scar-tissue fears, 15–16; of success, 15–16; of the truth about ourselves, 3–10, 173; of writing, 34, 42, 66, 146, 163, 165, 189, 191, 196, 200, 208, 210, 211, 230, 269; writing about, 80, 147, 170, 227, 239, 326, 353, 356

Feedback. *See* Editing; Responding to writing; Revising

Feelings and writing. *See* Abandonment; Anger; Courage; Ecstasy; Fear; Fun; Hate; Humor; Joy; Love

Fiction (*see also* Autobiography; Character(s); Form): craft in, 141–45; journals as a source for, 70; long works of, 146–48 (novel(s), 100, 146; short story, 147–49, 150); resources, 87, 111, 117, 150–52; revising, 113–15; treating all workshop writing as, 187; truth and, 4, 10, 203, 227, 274; what is, 138–41

Finch, Annie, 111, 130, 326; *A Formal Feeling Comes: Poems in Form by Contemporary Women,* 110, 129

Fisher, Don, 179; "Ransom Notes," 321

Fiske, Hannah, 133; "Breakfast," 135

Fitzgerald, F. Scott, 77, 86

Fitzpatrick, Evelyn, 289; "The Crows," 290

Forché, Carolyn, 131, 311; "The Colonel," 147, 334; *The Country Between Us,* 147

Form, 116–156; experimenting with, 60, 116, 137, 186, 195, 210, 213, 218–19, 234–35, 296, 350; fiction, 138–52 (*see also* Fiction); the journal, 33, 64; the letter, 34; other, 152–56 (musical theatre, 155; non–fiction, 153; playwriting, 153–54; screenwriting, 156; songwriting, 154–55); poems, 118–37 (*see also* Poetry); "shape of content" and, 17, 80, 116

Foster, Carol: "Eve's Ballad," 350
Fowles, John: *The French Lieutenant's Woman,* 145
Free writing, 35–36; in the classroom, 201–2
Friday, Nancy: *My Secret Garden,* 231
Frost, Robert, 78, 122, 125, 145; "Stopping by Woods on a Snowy Evening," 79, 126, 129, 289
Fun: exercises, 321, 322, 352; teaching and, 201, 266; writing and, 119, 136, 153, 273

Gallagher, Tess, 17; "Each Bird Walking," 11
Garcia, Jerry, 312
Gardner, John, 87, 110, 151, 331; *The Art of Fiction,* 111; *The Forms of Fiction,* 138; *On Becoming a Novelist,* 100, 114, 138
Gates, Donna, 312
Gender (*see also* Low-income writers): discrimination, 162, 168 (*see also* Ethics; Politics); reading about, 110; writing, 13, 102, 161, 170–71, 211; writing groups and, 217, 270
Genre(s). *See* Form
Gillespie, Peggy, 253
Ginsberg, Alan, 74, 311
Gleason, Kate: "Fracture," 137
Goldberg, Natalie, 35, 144, 340
Goodspeed, Lynn (Lyn), xvi, 259, 262, 264, 281, 282; "Again, Again," 283; "Obesity," 284
Grading writing, 199, 211–13
Graduate Theological Union Workshop, Berkeley, California; grading and, 212; participants, 15, 69, 99, 139, 172, 303, 321, 349
Graham, Martha, 60
Growing as a writer, 106–15; finding a good teacher and, 106–8; reading and, 108–10; revising and, 115; studying craft and, 110–11
Gryszan, James, 322

Hacker, Marilyn: "Coming Downtown," 136
Hall, Ali: "Here," 321

Harjo, Joy, 119
Hastings, Robert, 351; "Weed," 352
Hate: one's own writing and, 92
Healing: keloid, 169–70; stories, 272–73; *vs.* therapy, 265–66; wounds of bad experience, xx, 18–21, 91–92; writing and, 54, 139, 180–81, 241, 263–66
Hegerty, Moya: "Cow Dung," 148
Heilbrun, Carolyn, 151; *Hamlet's Mother and Other Women,* 152
Heller, Joseph, 311
Hellman, Lillian, 312
Hemingway, Ernest, 106, 110, 147; *A Moveable Feast,* 38
Hicks, Alison, xvi; *Love: A Story of Images,* 149
Hierarchies in workshops. *See* Equality
Higginson, Thomas Wentworth, 45
Hildegard of Bingen, 64
Hirsch, Edward: *How to Read a Poem and Fall in Love with Poetry,* 130
Hirshfield, Jane, 311, 358
Hitler, Adolph, 190, 193
Hoffman, Alice, 180
Hook, Beth, 346
hooks, bell, 110, 165; remembered rapture, 27, 64, 158, 162
Housing projects. *See* Chicopee Workshop for Low-Income Women; Low-income writers
Hughes, Langston, 350
Hugo, Richard, 17, 334, 358; *The Triggering Town,* 16, 80
Humor: exercises and, 83, 95, 309, 322, 352; teaching and, 216, 278
Hymes, Kate, xvi, 115, 169

Ideas, writing, 31, 111, 116, 192, 293–356 (*see also* Exercises, 293–359, Prompts, Topics)
Images, 189, 295; childhood, 6, 8, 96; concrete, 9, 16, 77–78, 88, 121, 149, 190, 213, 295–96; triggering 16–18, 20–21, 32–35, 70, 111, 139, 140, 145, 230, 296–359
Imagination, 5, 10, 142, 236; truth and, 8, 11, 32, 273; reader's, 80, 104; writing autobiography of the, 11, 138

Imitation, 63, 87, 88
Inability to write, 20–21
Incarcerated, 74, 260–61, 270, 304
Ireland, workshop: origins, 67;
    participants, 67, 136, 148, 166,
    203, 240–41, 299, 307

Jacobs, Loren, 268
James, Ruby, 101
Jarrell, Randall, 74, 110, 122
Johnson, Steve, 192
Jordan, June, 88, 110, 119, 248; "Alla
    Tha's All Right, But," 129;
    "Nobody Mean More to Me Than
    You and the Future Life of Willie
    Jordan," 94
Journal, 20, 28, 33, 34, 63–75; journal
    keeping, 29, 63–66 (bad habits and,
    68; clustering and mapping and,
    70–71); memory and, 68; natural
    speech and, 68; as part of the
    world's story, 60, 69; significance of,
    33, 66–67
Journals, literary, 37, 44, 108, 110,
    154, 171, 220, 230, 233, 255, 256,
    262, 285, 334 (see also Magazines;
    Publications about writing);
    offering work to, 178, 179, 194,
    222, 253, 254, 255
Joy: of workshops, 266, 268–69; of
    writing, 39, 48, 51, 56, 155, 158,
    210
Joyce, James, 87, 152, 255; Portrait of
    the Artist as a Young Man, 255;
    Ulysses, 15

Kafka, Franz, 26, 160
Kapp, Sharleen, xvi, 25, 66, 141, 320,
    356
Kavanagh, Sarah, xvi, 335
Keller, Helen, 2
Kennison, Cynthia, 146, 181, 353; "A
    Fatal Attraction," 329
Kenyon, Jane, 311
Kierkegaard, Søren, 69
King, Stephen, 151; Desperation, 109;
    On Writing, 109
Kissam, Dorothea, 38

L'Engle, Madelaine, 25
Langland, Joseph, 129
Language (see also Silenced): music of,
    118, 123, 206, 210; natural, 31, 96,
    99, 114, 118, 120, 197, 198, 213
    (see also Voice); poetic, 119, 126; of
    power and prestige, 197; unnatural,
    110, 112; using concrete, specific,
    74, 190, 209 (see also Craft)
Laurence, Larry, 312
Leader(s), 154, 178, 182–83, 187,
    189–91 (see also Teacher(s);
    Teaching; Workshop(s)); becoming
    your own workshop or writing
    group, 183, 215–58; goals of, 264;
    responsibilities of, 178, 193, 194,
    217, 222, 232, 238, 253 (creating a
    safe environment and maintaining
    boundaries, 192, 227, 240–41,
    256–57, 279–80, 285, 324;
    honesty, 272, 280; preparation,
    271, 297; responding to manu-
    scripts, 247, 280–85; teaching craft,
    210, 278, 334; using appropriate
    language, 286–90; of writing groups
    vs. workshops, 215–17)
Leff, Valerie, 254–55; "The Way the
    Wind Is Blowing," 342
LeGuin, Ursula, 29, 151
Lessing, Doris, 311
Letters: uses of, 33–34; writing in
    journals and, 71–72
Levertov, Denise, 67, 68, 311
Levine, Philip, 124, 125; Don't Ask,
    130; "Gin," 129; "The Simple
    Truth," 124
Lewis, Patricia Lee, xvi, 358; "Two
    Hundred Wings," 318
Leydon, Angie, 190, 332
Lichtenstein, Ali, 208, 212
Lists, 72–75; of nouns, 72–73; uses of,
    73–75
Lorde, Audre, 99, 110, 165; Sister
    Outsider, 170
Love: as a block to writing, 48;
    discipline of writing and, xviii, 45,
    51, 52, 60, 62; as a muse for
    writing, 29; writing about 23, 31,
    32, 84, 149, 357–58

Lowell, James Russell, 122
Lowell, Robert, xxii, 162
Low-income writers, 97, 185, 271, 279–80, 299 (*see also* Chicopee Workshop for Low-Income Women; Class; Silenced); anthology by, 161, 367; empowerment of, 164, 260, 263–64; financial considerations for, 257, 261; sensitive issues and, 10, 162, 263, 270, 274, 276, 281; who should work with, 266–69; why work with, 290–92
Lyon, George Ella, 269, 306, 311; "Where I'm From," 305

Ma, Yo-Yo: "Hush Little Baby," 105
Mackley, Mary, 196
MacMaster, Claire, 49
Macrorie, Ken: *Telling Writing,* 83
Magazines, 151, 153, 171, 180, 194, 222, 254. *See also* Journals, literary; Publications about writing
Magritte, René, 308
Mailer, Norman, 312
Marsalis, Wynton, 168, 169
Marshall, Paule, 99
Martin, Valerie, 143
Martula, Tanyss Rhea: "Burger King," 102; "Anniversary," 313
McCoy, Marjorie Casebier, 6
McCullers, Carson: *The Heart is a Lonely Hunter,* 171
McElhen, Kenneth R.: *Points of View,* 151
McFerrin, Bobbie: "Hush Little Baby," 105
McNeely, Gina, 305; "Waking Up Found," 306
McNeill, Heather, 203
McPhee, John, 33, 144
Meccouri, Linda, xvi, 211
Memories, 11, 275–76, 344 (*see also* Dream(s); Unconscious); child-hood, 9, 18, 95; painful, 21, 92, 189, 266, 270; as source of important information, 6, 8, 36, 100, 296
Men. *See* Gender

Mercier, Diane, xvi, 21, 97, 98, 99, 271, 272, 274, 278, 286, 288; "What Keeps Me Ticking," 97
Metaphor, 5, 9, 287, 289; and the unconscious, 13, 21, 78, 142, 145 (*see also* Unconscious); as writing trigger, 8–9, 11, 138, 317
Method. *See* Amherst Writers & Artists
Meyers, Jack, 317
Michelangelo, 4, 189
Miller, Henry, 255
Milton, John, 74
Moby Dick, 324
Moffett, James: *Points of View,* 151
Moore, Judith, 66; "Save Your Life: Notes on the Value of Keeping a Diary," 67
Morago, Cherrie: *The Last Generation,* 162
Moran, Kathleen: "A Collection of Classic Apron Wrings," 238
Moshiri, Shahrzad, 71
Mother tongue, xxiii, 93–94, 96, 125, 197, 198. *See also* Language, Voice
Murphy, Kate: "A Writing Workshop In Northern Ireland," 166
Musical Theatre (*see also* Form): resources, 155

Nabokov, Vladimir, 9, 79, 301
Neruda, Pablo, 336
Neugenboren, Jay, 254
Newman, Barnett, 245
Nin, Anaïs, 255
Nolley, Justine V.: "Black Doll," 37
Non-fiction (*see also* Form): creative non-fiction, 153; personal essay, 153; resources, 153
Novel(s). *See* Fiction

O'Callahan, Jay, 95, 104
O'Connor, Elizabeth, 12
O'Connor, Flannery, 6, 21, 75, 99, 123, 151, 302
O'Donohoe, Máire, xvi, 67, 299
Oberhaus, Dorothy Huff, 27; *Emily Dickinson's Fascicles: Method & Meaning,* 41
O'Keefe, Georgia, 77

Olds, Sharon, 140, 278, 311; "I Go Back to May, 1937," 274; *The Gold Cell,* 90; "The Takers," 129
Olsen, Tillie: "I Stand Here Ironing," xx
Outlines, writing, 115, 141

Paganini, Nicolo, 25
Paley, Grace, 88, 96, 99, 278: "A Man Told Me the Story of His Life," 31, 164, 334; *Later the Same Day,* 31
Parker, Dorothy: "The Waltz," 104
Pascal, 311
Patterns: of speech, 95, 96; of thought, 132, 332; of writing, 25, 26, 28, 50, 58, 74, 122, 131, 140, 332; respecting your own, 25–26
Peggy Gillespie, 322
Pelletier, Carolyn, xvi, 123, 147
Peregrine, 58, 99, 256, 284, 285
Perlman, Itzhak, 63
Peters, David, 172; "Dear Bishop," 173–74
Pfeifer, Teresa, xvi, 43, 262; "For My Son Robert: Novice, Age Five," 317
Phillips, Elizabeth Earl, 131; "Windswept," 132
Piercy, Marge, 51, 179, 256
Plath, Sylvia, 130
Playwriting, 153–54, 232 (*see also* Form); dialogue and, 81, 84, 101–102; resources, 154
Poetry, 17, 118–37 (*see also* Form); experimenting with form (creating original, 137; the list, 73–75; random words, 131–32; the scramble, 132–36; the trigger, 130; the villanelle, 136–37); political, 163–65, 334; prose, 147; resources, 88, 110–11, 113, 129–30, 350; rhymed, 122, 125–28; ten steps to writing, 120–21; unrhymed, 122–25; what makes, 118–20
Point of view, 77, 103, 141, 147, 228, 318
Politics, 97, 158, 242, 255, 303; some basic assumptions and, 163–67; writing and, 163–74, 342, 345 (*see also* Ethics)
Pond, Deb: "Rumi, My Love," 335

Poor. *See* Class; Chicopee Workshop for Low-Income Women; Low-income writers
Pound, Ezra, 122, 163
Powell, Mary Clare, 47
Practice, writing, xxi, xxv, 101, 106, 111, 113, 123, 129, 144, 152 (*see also* Journal; Craft); discipline and, 45, 48, 52, 54; genius and, 27, 63; journal writing and, 68, 70
Practices, five essential, x, 186–87
Presley, Elvis, 192, 193, 338
Principles, twelve basic workshop, 194–95
Privacy, 159–63 (*see also* Confidentiality; Ethics; Retreats, writing); claiming, 28, 30, 42, 51; conference, 187, 244, 279, 280, 333; need of, 19, 24–25, 28; in workshops, 27, 187, 194, 225, 265, 280; about others, 10–12, 160–63; the personal question, 160
Progoff, Ira, 32, 70, 84, 330; *The Intensive Journal,* 65
Prompts, writing. *See* Exercises; Triggers
Prose, Francine, 171
Publications about writing (*see also* Journals, literary; Magazines): Directory of Literary Magazines, 222; *Poets & Writers Magazine,* 151, 180, 222, 254; *The American Poetry Review,* 222; *The Chronicle,* 222, 254
Publishing, 215–16, 231; help in, 30, 59, 178, 229, 253–56; relation to art, 154, 186

Race, 168–70. *See also* Ethics; Politics
Ransom, John Crowe, 163
Reading: aloud in workshops, 186, 191–92, 198, 237–39; public, 58, 129, 162, 213, 229, 254; as a writer, 108–10
Reber, Peggy, 42, 339; "I Dream, Therefore I Am," 340
Respect, 59, 268; as essential to writing, 13, 197, 226, 236, 257; of secrets, 162, 235, 260; of writers as

artists, 186–87, 200, 263, 272; your own patterns, 25–26, 62, 140
Responding to writing, 71, 199, 245 (*see also* Assumptions, five essential; Practices, five essential); and first drafts, 187, 191, 194, 197, 225, 232 (*see also* Drafts); in groups, 191, 193, 197, 222, 223, 225, 231, 250–53, 279, 280; and manuscripts, 187, 194, 195, 197, 242–53; negative, 15, 107, 230, 279, 288; and revising, 111–15 (*see also* Editing; Revising); supportive, 106, 107, 178, 187, 197, 213–14, 229, 266 (*see also* Support); and work read aloud, 239–41
Retreats, writing, 51, 55–57, 85, 95, 183, 215, 219, 318
Revard, Carter, 311
Revising (*see also* Editing; Responding to writing): letting go of, 59; need for, 111–15, 178; for publication 194; risks of, 109, 112, 120, 124; truth-telling and, 13, 113, 120–21; writing without, 13, 146, 192, 239
Rich, Adrienne, 163, 164, 165, 312
Rico, Gabriele Lusser: *Writing the Natural Way,* 70
Rilke, Rainer Maria, 27, 311
Risk(s): intentional, 299; support in taking, 129, 144, 178, 187, 197–98, 214, 231, 239, 279 (*see also* Support); vulnerability and, 15, 68, 280; writing and, ix–xii, xxi, xxiv, 15, 230
Robertson, AnnieMae, 146
Robison, Margaret, xvi, 30, 108, 113, 118, 197; *Red Creek: A Requiem,* 301
Roethke, Theodore: "The Waking," 136
Rohrer, Jane, 311, 313
Roosevelt, Eleanor, 45
Rukeyser, Muriel: *The Life of Poetry,* 356
Rumble, Walker, 58
Rutledge, Ella, 201, 208

Safety (*see also* Confidentiality; Fear; Privacy; Respect): creating environ-ment of, x–xxi, 3, 194, 225, 227, 237, 256, 354; journals and, 65–66; writing practice and, 91, 186–87, 191–92, 200, 279–80, 324
Safire, William, 163
Saint Augustine, 64
Saint Patrick, 64
Santiago Welch, Enid, 10, 30, 203, 262, 269, 351; "Popping Out Babies While Dragging Your Placenta to the Mailbox," 119
Sapphire: *PUSH,* 294
Savageau, Cheryl, 119, 312; "Crazy Ol' Baker," 278, 347; *Dirt Road Home,* 347
Schneeloch, Jane, 53, 204
Schneemann, Carolee: *More Than Meat Joy,* 89
Schneider, Bethany, xv
Schneider, Laurel, 65
Schneider, Pat, 136, 204, 220, 223, 281, 358; *Berries Red,* 84, 101; "Letting Go," 128; "Nursery Rhyme," 127; "Personal Address," 325; *After the Appplebox,* 165; *Long Way Home,* 310, 335; *Olive Street Transfer,* 310; *The Poor Don't Talk about the Sphinx,* 165; *The Writer as an Artist,* 160; *Wake Up Laughing: A Spiritual Autobiography,* 5, 33, 70, 128, 161
Schneider, Paul, xv, 52
Schneider, Peter: "At Seventy," 78
Schneider, Rebecca, xv
Schneiders, Jay, 312
Schott, Penelope Scambly, 311, 312
Screenwriting (*see also* Form): re-sources, 156
Secrets: difficult, 21, 26; need to tap into, 8, 18, 56, 91, 241, 356; respecting, 162, 235, 260; writer's block and, 139; writing and, 3, 6, 104, 241
Self-esteem, 18, 185–86, 250, 264, 266, 288. *See also* Empowerment
Self-revelation, 11, 13, 26, 160, 235, 266, 332. *See also* Autobiography
Sexuality, 171–74. *See also* Ethics, Politics

Sexton, Anne, xxii
Shahn, Ben, 116; *The Shape Of Content,* 17
Shakespeare, William, xxi, 87, 350
Sharleen Kapp, 25, 320, 356
Shoenblum, Susan, 311
Short Story. *See* Fiction
Silence, 189, 260, 358; need for, 19, 27, 55–56, 300 (*see also* Solitude); oppressive, 14, 16, 21, 64, 162, 176, 270, 286 (*see also* Silenced); political, 164, 172
Silenced, 259–92 (*see also* Class; Chicopee Workshop for Low-Income Women; Low-income writers); educational level and, 186, 218, 271, 288; stories that heal, 272–73; workshops for (exercises for participants with a limited education in, 275–79; finding participants and, 269–70; first meeting and, 273–75; goal and purpose of, 263–65; healing *vs.* therapy in, xxii, 265–66; language in (the danger of, 286–89; the opportunity of, 289–90); teaching practices in, 270–72; writing to empower in, 260, 263–64, 276 (*see also* Empowerment; Self-Esteem)
Silkin, Jon, 190
Simic, Charles, 119, 132, 332
Simon, Tobin: *Writing the Mind Alive,* 35
Slocombe, Daphne, xvi, 117, 158; "Now," 159
Smithline, Diane, 21
Softky, Deborah Campbell, 303
Solitude (*see also* Privacy; Retreats, writing; Silence); need for, 26–31, 42, 56, 57, 177, 300
Solomont, Sue, 44
Sommers, Nancy: "Between the Drafts," 46
Sonchez, Sonia, 110
Songwriting, 154–55 (*see* Form); resources, 155
South, Myra, 76
Spann, Chip, 180

Spirituality: writing and, 26–27, 30, 38, 40, 54–55, 157–59
Stafford, William, xxv, 5, 59, 130, 311; "Witness," 129; *Writing the Australian Crawl,* 113; *You Must Revise Your Life,* 113, 114
Starting to write, 24–39, 121, 340
Steinbeck, John, 59; "Letter to Robert Wallsten," 144; *The Grapes of Wrath,* 88, 205
Stepleton, Susan, 5
Sternburg, Janet: *The Writer on Her Work,* 151
Stevens, Wallace: "13 Ways of Looking at a Blackbird," 88
Stix, Nicholas, 311
Straus, Hedy, 348
Sugiura, C. Misa, 91, 92
Sullivan, Brooke, 330
Sundiata, Sekou, 169
Support (*see also* Assumptions, five essential; Practices, five essential; Responding to writing; Risk(s)): consequences of lack of, 156, 187–88; ways of offering, 30, 43, 144, 186–87, 251–54
Swanson, Catherine, 307; "Night Feeding," 308
Swartz, Sue, 327;"Writing About the Taboo," 345
Swenson, May, 312

Taboos, writing, 119, 170, 172, 178, 241, 299, 345–46
Tan, Amy: "Mother Tongue," 94
Tate, James, 119, 132, 332
Taylor, Jeremy: *Dream Work,* 65
Teacher(s) (*see also* Classroom, writing in a; Leader(s); Teaching): finding good, 106–8, 182, 196, 199–200; learning from students, 200–1, 226, 228, 233, 257, 279, 291; tasks as, xxiv, 113, 198, 200–1, 248, 257, 289; ten qualities of good, 107; writers as, 108–10, 151, 186
Teaching, xxiv, 185 (*see also* Classroom, writing in a; Leader(s); Teacher(s)); bad, 14–15, 35, 49, 75, 180, 187–

88, 193, 196; craft 186 (*see also* Craft); good, 193, 197–98, 274, 278; oneself to write, 87, 112, 215; practices for the classroom, 213–14

Tennyson, Alfred Lord xxiii, 122

Therapy: *vs.* writing group, 189, 239, 241, 263, 265–66; writing as, xxii, 65, 70, 74

Therrien, Robin, xvi, 28, 227, 262, 288; *Voices From the 'Hood*, 260, 367

Thurber, James, 66

Topics, 200, 202, 204, 208, 211 (*see also* Ideas, writing; dangerous and difficult, 211, 275, 345–7 (*see also* Taboos, writing)

Trichter Metcalf, Linda: *Writing the Mind Alive*, 35

Triggers, writing, 190–91, 271, 300 (*see also* Exercises); images as, 16–17; list of music as, 313, 363–66; pictures and objects as, 140, 308, 332; poems as, 130–31, 278, 309–10; quotations as, 309–10; surprise and, 295–97, 309

Trilling, Lionell, 163

Trust, ix, 5, 17–18, 57, 285, 298; instinct and intuition and, 107, 144, 178, 183, 226; mutual, 187, 245, 268, 288; voice and, 31–32, 44, 50, 93–94, 100, 113

Truth, 230, 267 (*see also* Autobiography; benefits of, 39, 59, 67, 126, 170, 249; fear of, 3–10, 138–39, 172 (*see also* Fear); fiction and, 11, 138–39, 161, 227 (*see also* Fiction); need in writing for, 13, 32, 90, 113, 121 273, 301; risks of, 10, 160, 249 (*see also* Risk(s))

Turner, Elise, xvi; "Evocations on Reading Neruda's Oda Al Diccionario," 336

Twain, Mark, 255

Tyler, Anne: *The Best American Short Stories 1983*, 12, 229

Ueland, Brenda, 35

Unconscious, 26, 58, 68, 138, 198, 246 (*see also* Dream(s)); accessing, 13, 31, 32, 57, 78, 289; creative genius and, 9, 17, 54, 55, 129, 142, 145; "magic apron" and, 4–5, 6, 10, 34; as reservoir of fears, memories, and truths, 3, 4, 6, 8, 18, 139, 213 (*see also* Fear; Memories; Truth)

Vidal, Gore, 162

Viereck, Peter, 350

Voice, 49, 93–105, 110, 190–91 (*see also* Character(s); Dialogue; Language); distractions to, 55, 58, 114, 249; finding your own, 28, 34, 93–100, 107, 200, 226 (*see also* Trust); original, 95–96, 186, 200, 213; other or acquired, 100–105; practicing, 23, 31–32, 38, 44, 84 (different points of view, 71, 103–4, 339, 359; eavesdropping, 102–3; several at once, 104; suggesting, 104–5); primary, 96–100 (*see also* Children and Childhood; Mother Tongue); strengthening, 129, 172, 185, 252, 263, 272–72 (*see also* Silenced)

Wade, Antoinette: "After an Ancient Irish Curse," 136

Walker, Alice, 311

Walker, Sue, xvi; "Hammering Virgins: The Dream of Female Signs in James Dickey's (Un)Broken Hungering," 335; "You Ain't Jesus, Brother," 338; *Blood Must Bear Your Name*, 335, 338

Watson, Ellen Doré, 190, 311, 332

Weaver, Gordon, 50

Welch, Enid Santiago, xvi, 10, 30, 119, 203, 262, 269, 351

Welty, Eudora, vi, xvi, 138, 333

Wesley, John, 64

Whitman, Ruth: "Climbing Jacob's Ladder," 87

Whitman, Walt, 66, 74, 255

Wilbur, Richard, 88, 122

Williams, Miller, 350; *Forms of Poetry*, 110; *Patterns of Poetry*, 88, 129, 136

Women. *See* Chicopee Workshop for Low-Income Women; Gender; Low-income writers

Wood, Jean, 189
Wood, Joan Marie, xvi; "Rose Cologne," 344; *Her Voice Is Blackberries,* 344
Woolf, Virginia, xxii, 82, 88, 99, 138, 152, 255, 335; *A Room of One's Own,* 28; *To the Lighthouse,* 171, 335
Woolman, John, 64
Wordsworth, William, xxiii, 17, 122; *Two-Part Prelude,* 149
Workshop(s), 177–292 (*see also* Affirmations, five essential; Amherst Writers & Artists (AWA); Chicopee Workshop for Low-Income Women; Graduate Theological Union Workshop, Berkeley, California; Ireland, workshop; Practices, five essential; Principles, basic, 194–95); creating your own, 215–58 (*see also* Leader(s); Teacher(s); Teaching); and ethics in group setting, 256–58; and helping participants publish, 253–56; and practical matters, 219–23; and responding to manuscripts, 244–53; and sample workshop, 224–35; and the workshop meeting, 236–44; and deciding what kind, 217–19; *vs.* writing groups, 215–17
Writer alone, xix, 1–174; and developing craft, 76–92; and the disciplined

writing life, 40–62; and ethical questions, 157–74; exercises for, 293–359; and feeling and facing fear, 3–23; and the form your writing takes, 116–156; and getting started (again), 24–39; and growing as a writer, 106–15; and the journal, 63–75; and voice, 93–105
Writer(s): tasks as, xxiv–xxv
Writing groups, 182–83, 215–17. *See also* Workshops
Writing Practices: five essential, x, 186–87; for teachers, 213–14
Writing Process Movement, 144, 151, 185, 202, 295
Writing with others, xvii, 175–292; and how it can help you, 177–81; and options for (community-based writing group or workshop, 182–83; creative writing classes, 182; finding a writing companion, 181; starting your own writing group or workshop, 183)
Wyman, Midge, 104; "Dance Hall," 105

Yeston, Maury, 60

Zeiger, Gene: "Family," 343
Zucker, Rob and Andrea, 266